Kilellan Farm

Kilellan Farm, Ardnave, Islay

Excavations of a Prehistoric to Early Medieval Site by Colin Burgess and others 1954–76

Edited by
ANNA RITCHIE

With contributions by
Sheila Boardman, Ann Clarke, Rosemary Cowie, John G Evans,
Fraser Hunter, Anna Ritchie, Alan Saville, Dale Serjeantson,
Stephen Speak and Paul Wilthew

Principal illustrations by
Alan R Braby

Edinburgh 2005
SOCIETY OF ANTIQUARIES OF SCOTLAND

Published in 2005 by the Society of Antiquaries of Scotland

Society of Antiquaries of Scotland
Royal Museum of Scotland
Chambers Street
Edinburgh EH1 1JF

Tel: 0131 247 4115
Fax: 0131 247 4163

Email: administration@socantscot.org
Website: www.socantscot.org

British Library Cataloguing-in-Publication Data
A catalogue record for this book is available from the British Library

ISBN 0 903903 35 0

Copyright © Society of Antiquaries of Scotland and individual authors, 2005

All rights reserved. No part of this publication may be reproduced, stored in or introduced into a retrieval system, or transmitted, in any form, or by any means (electronic, mechanical, photocopying, recording or otherwise) without the prior written permission of the publisher. Any person who does any unauthorised act in relation to this publication may be liable to criminal prosecution and civil claims for damages.

The Society gratefully acknowledges grant-aid towards the publication of this volume from

Typeset by Waverley Typesetters, Galashiels
Design and production by Lawrie Law and Alison Rae
Manufactured in Great Britain by The Bath Press, Bath

Contents

List of illustrations — vii
List of tables — xi
List of main contributors — xiii
Acknowledgements — xv
Summary — xvii

1. Introduction — 1
   Anna Ritchie

2. The excavations — 7
   Anna Ritchie
   - Summary of site stratigraphy — 7
   - Raised beach and peat deposit *by* Stephen Speak — 11
   - Phase 1 The Mesolithic horizon — 13
   - Phase 2 The Early Bronze Age midden — 17
   - Phase 3 The Late Bronze Age/Early Iron Age occupation — 30
   - Phase 4 The Middle Iron Age settlement — 39
   - Phase 5 Early Historic activity — 47
   - Phase 6 Later activities — 48

3. The pottery — 49
   Rosemary Cowie

4. Struck lithic artefacts — 97
   Alan Saville

5. Coarse stone artefacts — 133
   Ann Clarke

6. Metal, bone, glass, clay and fine stone artefacts — 143
   Anna Ritchie

7. Animal husbandry and the environmental context — 151
   Dale Serjeantson, V Smithson and T Waldron

8. The charcoal — 169
   Sheila Boardman

9.	Marine mollusca *John G Evans*	171
10.	Discussion *Anna Ritchie*	175

Appendix 1	History of excavations at Kilellan Farm, Islay *by* Stephen Speak	181
Appendix 2	Analysis of unusual bone pins from Kilellan Farm, Islay, and MacArthur Cave, Oban *by* Fraser Hunter	183
Appendix 3	Analysis of a silver and garnet pin from Kilellan Farm, Islay *by* Paul Wilthew	185
Appendix 4	Plant remains from the peat deposit on the raised beach at Kilellan Farm, Islay *by* Robert Lord, Elaine Matheson and Nicola Williams	187

References 189
Index 195

List of illustrations

Front cover: Excavations at Kilellan in 1976.

1.	Maps showing the location of a. Islay, b. Ardnave Point, c. Kilellan.	xviii
2.	From Kilellan looking east across Loch Gruinart.	1
3.	The open bunker at Kilellan in 1960, with Kilellan Farm in the background.	2
4.	Excavation of the face of the bunker in trench F2 in 1960.	2
5.	Excavations at Kilellan in 1973.	4
6.	Colin Burgess discussing the excavation with Steve Palmer in 1976.	4
7.	Contour plan showing the location of trenches in 1973 and 1976.	8
8.	The south-west corner of trench G1 shows a typical section through the Burgess sequence.	9
9.	North section of trench H1 across the raised beach.	12
10.	The surface of the raised beach coated with peaty deposit in trench H1.	13
11.	Plan showing the trenches containing Mesolithic artefacts.	14
12.	A patch of close-set flat stones in trench B3 represents Mesolithic activity.	15
13.	In trench B2 an arc of small stones on the right lay within the Mesolithic silver sand.	15
14.	A patch of small rounded cobbles within the Mesolithic silver sand in trench A2.	15
15.	Plan of the Mesolithic structures in trench G2.	16
16.	A patch of small rounded cobbles (132A) within the Mesolithic silver sand in trench G2.	17
17.	Plan showing the extent of the Early Bronze Age midden.	18
18.	Plan of the main area of the Early Bronze Age midden published by Colin Burgess (1976, fig 10.3).	19
19.	The natural sand bank ran from top left to bottom right across trenches A1 and F1.	20
20.	Plan of the Early Bronze Age structures revealed by excavations between 1954 and 1973.	21
21.	Plan of palisade slots and locations of sections in trench G2.	22
22.	Section P–Q–B across the palisade slots in trench G2.	23
23.	The 'drain' and palisade slot in 1961 trench I.	24
24.	Sections A–B–C–D–J, C1–D1, I1–J2 and X–Y across the palisade slots in trench G2.	24
25.	Section Q–R–T across palisade slot 108 and the hollow in trench G2.	25
26.	Trench G2 at a final stage in its excavation.	26
27.	One of the subrectangular stone settings of Phase 2.3 in 1961 trench I.	27
28.	The south section of trench F1.	27
29.	Trench F1: the natural sand bank crosses the trench in the foreground.	28
30.	Plan of clay floor 100 in trench G4 and location of section B–BB.	28
31.	Section B–BB across pit 101 and the clay floor 100 in trench G4.	29
32.	Trench G4 from the north.	29
33.	Section A across trench L2 at the level of the occupation floor 10.	30
34.	Trench L2 under excavation.	30
35.	Plan of stone-built structures and contemporary late features in trench L2.	31
36.	Plan of all features in trench L2 at the level of the sand (11) below occupation layer 10.	32
37.	Section B–B across the stone-lined pit 126, pit 127 and the souterrain 118 in trench L2.	33
38.	Section C1–C1 across the stone-lined pit 126, hearth 114 and underlying pit 183, and pit 165 in trench L2.	33
39.	Sections across pits 119 and 117 in trench L2.	34
40.	Section across pit 128 in trench L2.	34

41.	Stone-lined pit 126 with lintels in place, and the section B–B.	34
42.	Stone-lined pit 126 with fallen lintels and lintels in place.	35
43.	Stone-lined pit 126 emptied of its filling but with lintels in place.	36
44.	Stone-lined pit 126 entirely excavated.	36
45.	Hearth 114 showing the upper filling of greasy black sand.	37
46.	The top of layer 10 in trench L2 showing ardmarks, spade-dug furrows and spade-marks.	38
47.	Plan of souterrain and possible house in areas J and K.	40
48.	Trenches K2 and K3: on the left the house wall 102 and top right the stone pile 108.	41
49.	Section A–B in trench K3.	41
50.	Dark spade-marks appeared in trench L2 in the sand below the occupation layer 10.	42
51.	Sections D–C and E–F across the souterrain 110 in trench J2.	42
52.	The boulder wall of souterrain 110 in trench J2 where fully excavated.	43
53.	Souterrain 110 in trench J2.	43
54.	It is possible that the souterrain in trench J2 extends southwestwards into trench K3.	44
55.	Large boulders lay along the line of the souterrain in J2.	45
56.	Small cobbles were laid across the souterrain in trenches J1–2.	46
57.	Possible bedding-trenches were dug into sterile sand upslope from the house wall in trench K2.	46
58.	The possible bedding-trenches in trenches K1–2.	47
59.	Pottery rim classifications.	50
60.	Pottery nos 1–10.	53
61.	Pottery nos 11–16.	54
62.	Pottery nos 17–27.	56
63.	Pottery nos 28–9.	59
64.	Pottery nos 30–5.	60
65.	Pottery nos 36–45.	61
66.	Pottery nos 46–8.	62
67.	Pottery nos 49–51, 53–4.	63
68.	Pottery nos 56–62.	64
69.	Pottery nos 63–70.	68
70.	Pottery nos 71–2.	69
71.	Pottery no 73.	70
72.	Pottery nos 74–7, 79–81, 83–6.	72
73.	Pottery no 88.	73
74.	Pottery nos 89–90.	75
75.	Pottery nos 91–4, 96–7, 99–101, 103–6, 108–12, 122, 142–4.	80
76.	Pottery no 98.	83
77.	Pottery nos 150–1, 153–4, 156–60.	84
78.	Cores.	101
79.	Cores, hammerstone, unretouched blades and truncated flake.	106
80.	Serrated flake and scrapers.	109
81.	Scrapers, edge-trimmed flakes and knives.	111
82.	Microliths, microburins and related pieces.	114
83.	Knives and piercers.	116
84.	Arrowheads and miscellaneous retouched pieces.	118
85.	Refitting pieces.	120
86.	Refitting pieces.	121
87.	Coarse stone artefacts: 1, no 22; 2, no 84; 3, no 26; 4, no 77.	134
88.	Coarse stone artefacts: 1, no 68; 2, no 35.	135
89.	Pebble hammer no 84.	136
90.	Silver pin no 1.	143
91.	Iron, copper alloy artefacts nos 2–5.	145
92.	Bone, glass and clay artefacts, nos 2–12 and 14–15.	146
93.	Serpentine artefacts (no 18), 1–7.	147

94. Serpentine artefacts (no 18), 8–11, and bevelled polisher (no 19), 12.	148
95. Environs of the site at Kilellan.	151
96. Age at death of cattle and sheep (upper and lower midden combined).	156
97. Iron Age cattle and sheep (upper and lower midden combined), per cent survival of parts of the body.	162
98. Coracoid of a medium-sized gadfly petrel.	164
99. The Bronze Age house at Ardnave 1, Islay.	177
100. Back scattered electron image of the surface of the silver pin no 1.	185

List of tables

1.	Correlation of trench stratigraphies.	10
2.	Radiocarbon dates.	20
3.	Total quantities of pottery and daub from all seasons.	49
4.	Breakdown of pottery by form.	51
5.	Rim forms.	52
6.	Combinations of decorative techniques.	57
7.	Relative frequency of impressed decorative techniques.	57
8.	Relationship of motif to form and rim type.	58
9.	Comparison by trenches of quantities of decorated and plain pottery.	71
10.	Total sherds from site L2.	78
11.	Total sherds from sites J and K.	81
12.	Total flint assemblage from the 1959–76 fieldwork (including one surface find from 1977).	97
13.	Stratigraphic contexts of microliths and arrowheads.	98
14.	Unmodified pebbles: maximum dimension data (n=85).	99
15.	Unmodified pebbles: weight data (n=85).	99
16.	Trench 76/G2: flint artefact colours by context.	100
17.	Cores: basic classification.	102
18.	Cores: maximum dimension data.	102
19.	Cores: maximum dimension ranges.	103
20.	Cores: weight data.	103
21.	Cores: maximum surviving negative flake scar lengths.	104
22.	Cores: all stratified cores assignable to common cross-site horizons.	104
23.	Cores: colours by type.	104
24.	Unretouched flakes from silver sand contexts in trenches 73/E1 and 73/E2: total sample.	105
25.	Unretouched flakes from silver sand contexts in trenches 73/E1 and 73/E2: flake categories represented among the complete flakes.	107
26.	Unretouched flakes from silver sand contexts in trenches 73/E1 and 73/E2: length range data for all complete flakes.	107
27.	Unretouched flakes from silver sand contexts in trenches 73/E1 and 73/E2: complete flakes over 20mm in length or breadth.	108
28.	Unretouched flakes from silver sand contexts in trenches 73/E1 and 73/E2: length/breadth index values of complete secondary and tertiary flakes over 20mm in length or breadth.	108
29.	Distribution of scrapers, edge-trimmed flakes, knives, piercers and serrated flake.	112
30.	Typology and distribution of microliths, and distribution of microburins and truncated blade.	115
31.	Typology and distribution of arrowheads (n=7).	117
32.	Distribution of burnt pieces (only contexts with five or more burnt pieces are included).	119
33.	Comparison between the total assemblages from the silver sand and the midden.	123
34.	Flint totals by trench and year.	126
35.	Catalogue of illustrated flints.	127
36.	Coarse stone artefacts by period.	133
37.	Kilellan: animal bones from the Mesolithic, Early Bronze Age and Middle Iron Age deposits.	152
38.	Stages of eruption and wear of cattle and sheep teeth.	152

39.	Early Bronze Age: species present and number of identified fragments.	153
40.	Early Bronze Age: sheep, cattle and red deer: number of identified fragments and minimum number of bone elements.	154
41.	Early Bronze Age: eruption and wear of cattle and sheep teeth, after Grant (1982).	155
42.	Measurements of red deer, after Driesch (1976).	157
43.	Hebridean assemblages of the second millennium BC: cattle, sheep, pig and red deer.	157
44.	Middle Iron Age: lower and upper middens: species present and number of identified fragments.	158
45.	Middle Iron Age: bones with evidence of carnivore gnawing, butchery and burning.	159
46.	Middle Iron Age: cattle: number of identified fragments and minimum number of elements.	160
47.	Middle Iron Age: sheep: number of identified fragments and minimum number of elements.	161
48.	Middle Iron Age: pig: number of identified fragments and minimum number of elements.	162
49.	Middle Iron Age: eruption and wear of teeth of cattle and sheep, according to Grant (1982).	163
50.	Middle Iron Age: red deer: number of identified fragments and minimum number of bone elements.	165
51.	Percentages of cattle, sheep, pig and red deer on Hebridean Iron Age sites.	165
52.	Marine mollusca.	172

List of main contributors

SHEILA BOARDMAN
School of Conservation Sciences, Archaeology and the Environment, University of Bournemouth BH12 5BB

ALAN R BRABY
9 Adelphi Place, Portobello, Edinburgh EH15 1BG

ANN CLARKE
Rockville Lodge, by Kingston, North Berwick, East Lothian EH39 5JN

ROSEMARY COWIE
Dundreich, Old Edinburgh Road, Eddleston, Peebles EH45 8QP

JOHN G EVANS
15 Fairleigh Road, Cardiff CF11 9JT

FRASER HUNTER
Department of Archaeology, National Museums of Scotland, Chambers Street, Edinburgh EH1 1JF

ALAN SAVILLE
Department of Archaeology, National Museums of Scotland, Chambers Street, Edinburgh EH1 1JF

DALE SERJEANTSON
Archaeology Division, School of Humanities, University of Southampton SO17 1BJ

STEPHEN SPEAK
Archaeology Department, Tyne and Wear Museums, East Lodge, Jesmond Old Cemetery Gates, Jesmond Road, Newcastle upon Tyne NE2 1NL

ANNA RITCHIE
50 Spylaw Road, Edinburgh EH10 5BL

PAUL WILTHEW
Department of Conservation and Analytical Research, National Museums of Scotland, Chambers Street, Edinburgh EH1 1JF

Acknowledgements

Colin Burgess is grateful to the late Francis Celoria, who first inveigled him into taking on the Kilellan site as part of the Islay Archaeological Survey; to Islay Estates Ltd, through their factor, David Boyd, and to successive tenants, the late A 'Sandy' Maclellan and T Epps, for permission to carry out the work; to Roy Ritchie, Patrick Ashmore and David Breeze of the Department of the Environment (now Historic Scotland) for facilitating the work in 1973 and 1976; to the late Robert B K Stevenson and to Joanna Close-Brooks and Trevor Cowie of the National Museum of Antiquities of Scotland (now the National Museums of Scotland) for all their help; to all those Islay residents who contributed so much, including H Cockburn of the Bowmore Distillery, T Crawford of Bowmore High School, the Reverend Munroe of Bowmore, Mr Woodroe, Contractor, of Bowmore, and especially the late Gordon Booth of the Islay Museums Trust.

The work was financed by the Islay Archaeological Survey Group, by the Northumberland Archaeological Group (which was brought into existence by the need to raise funds for the project), by the Society of Antiquaries of Scotland, by the Department of the Environment and by the University of Newcastle, to all of whom CB is very grateful.

Of the many people who participated in the fieldwork over the years, special thanks must go to those who undertook specific responsibilities such as site-supervision, cataloguing and survey: James and Mona Atkinson, John and Kathy Barrett, Norma Burgess, David and Barbara Esslemont, Stratford Halliday, Frank Harland, Peter Hill, Alex Hunter, C M Johns, Gordon Moir, Stephen Palmer, Stephen Speak, Peter Topping, Margaret Walton (now Cutts), Adam Welfare and Caroline Wickham-Jones. Ron Moss deserves special thanks for his work as site photographer in 1973 and 1976; Bob Lord, Nicola Williams and Elaine Matheson for their work on the plant remains; Clive Bonsall for his work on the Mesolithic flintwork; George Hodgson for his work on the animal bones from the 1961 season; and Lucy Rickards for catering so splendidly. Alas, space does not permit mention of all the volunteers who participated in the various excavation campaigns, and CB begs their forgiveness for not acknowledging individually their sterling work.

A great debt is owed to Peter Topping for preliminary work on the flint and stonework, Alex Gibson for preliminary work on the pottery, Zillah Pettit (now Richards) and Angie Townshend for the illustrations used in Burgess 1976 and many unpublished drawings, and especially Steve Speak, who did so much to unscramble the history of the site and to relate the work of the 1950s and 1960s with that of 1973 and 1976. Finally CB owes a vast debt to Anna Ritchie for taking off his hands the problem of Kilellan, which he took on so reluctantly so many years ago. Inevitably in a project that has stretched over such a timespan, some people will not have been mentioned here who should have been thanked, and to these he offers his sincere apologies.

Anna Ritchie is very grateful to Colin Burgess for all his help and patience and to all those who kindly read and commented upon the draft version of the excavation report in 1993: Colin Burgess, Alan Saville, Stephen Speak, Peter Hill and Stratford Halliday. She is doubly grateful to Colin Burgess, Alan Saville and Stephen Speak for reading the final report in 2004. She wishes to acknowledge the huge value of the post-excavation work carried out by the Newcastle team, particularly by Stephen Speak and Peter Topping, and hopes that they will understand why, a decade on in Edinburgh, it was necessary for a team not involved in the original excavations to begin again. She would like to record her thanks to David V Clarke, Keeper of Archaeology, National Museums of Scotland, for providing a home in his Department for the work on Kilellan to be carried out over such a long period. She is very grateful to Alan Braby for his patience and skilful draughtsmanship. She is also grateful for advice on geology to Brian Jackson of NMS Department of Geology and to Colin Chapman and Robert Reekie formerly of that Department, on Anglo-Saxon dress-pins to Seamus Ross, on pedlars and chapmen to Dorothy Kidd of the Scottish Life History section of NMS Department of Social and Technological History and Roger Leitch, on the radiocarbon dates to Gordon Cook and Patrick Ashmore, and for help in weighing the stone artefacts to Matthew Ritchie. She is grateful to Graham Ritchie for sharing his knowledge of Islay and the Ardnave peninsula, for reading both the draft and final report and for much practical support.

Rosemary Cowie wishes to thank Alan Saville and Alison Sheridan for much useful advice and information while working on the pottery in the congenial surroundings of the Artefact Research Unit of the Department of Archaeology, Alan Braby for preparing the illustrations and Trevor Cowie for help in a variety of ways but particularly for his assistance with the final stages of completion of the report.

Dale Serjeantson, V Smithson and T Waldron wish to thank the following people who contributed to the recording of the animal bones and the environmental study: Alan Cohen, John Archer, Mark Bracegirdle, Jan Butler, Bernice Cohen, Marion Goring, Val Sellins and Gillian Waldron. This research was carried out between 1983 and 1988 at Birkbeck College, London University. The authors would like to thank A J Legge for use of the zooarchaeology facilities there and acknowledge the following students at the Centre for Extra-Mural studies who contributed to the recording of the bones and the environmental study: John Archer, Mark Bracegirdle, Jean Butler, Alan Cohen, Bernice Cohen, Val Sellins and Gillian Waldron.

The finds from the excavation at Kilellan have been assigned to the National Museums of Scotland, Chambers Street, Edinburgh, and the paper archive to the National Monuments Record for Scotland, Royal Commission on the Ancient and Historical Monuments of Scotland, John Sinclair House, Bernard Terrace, Edinburgh.

This project could not have taken place without the support of Historic Scotland and its predecessor institutions, through the interest and help of Patrick Ashmore and Rod McCullagh, to all of whom grateful thanks are offered. The fieldwork in 1973 and 1976 received funding from the Department of the Environment, and the various stages of post-excavation work were funded by the Ancient Monuments Branch of the Scottish Development Department (1982), by Historic Buildings and Monuments (1991) and by Historic Scotland (1999 and 2003). Historic Scotland also provided funding for radiocarbon dating analyses and towards publication.

Summary

This prehistoric to early medieval site lies just to the north of Kilellan Farm on the Ardnave peninsula, which forms the west side of Loch Gruinart, a sea loch on the north coast of the island of Islay in the Inner Hebrides (NGR NR 286721). It was excavated over a number of seasons from 1954 to 1976, principally by Colin Burgess.

Traces of Mesolithic activity (Phase 1) were found in a layer of acidic sand upslope from a freshwater marsh that had formed over the raised beach of the Main Postglacial Shoreline. Small patches of pebbles and of flat stones, a shallow pit and a concentration of flints suggested that the site may have acted as a temporary stopping-place on hunting expeditions. The flint assemblage fits in with the general pattern on Later Mesolithic sites in Scotland, and the technology includes anvil-knapping as well as platform cores. A refitting exercise undertaken on the assemblage demonstrated that much of it had been produced on the site. The character of the flint-working suggests that Mesolithic activity took place within the period 7000–5500 BC.

The freshwater marsh was still in existence in Early Bronze Age times, when domestic refuse was dumped immediately inland from it (Phase 2). Interleaved deposits of sand and midden accumulated to a maximum depth of 1m over a culturally homogeneous period indicated by radiocarbon dating to have been within the bracket 2130 to 1748 cal BC. The midden began to accumulate (Phase 2.1) on top of an old turf-line that represented the ground surface sealing the Mesolithic horizon. Two palisade slots, pits, post-holes and a large hollow were dug into the surface of the midden (Phase 2.2), and a series of stone structures, pits and post-holes replaced one of the palisades (Phase 2.3). Midden began to accumulate over these abandoned structures (Phase 2.4), and a house or working floor was established upslope from the main midden (Phase 2.5). Finally, midden was deposited on top of the floor and adjacent midden (Phase 2.6). This sequence suggests that there was a settlement in the immediate vicinity of the excavated midden, and that the surface of the midden was used for a variety of activities. The refuse in the midden included pottery, animal bones, marine mollusca and carbonized barley, but fish bones were almost entirely lacking. The sherds of pottery recovered represent more than a hundred vessels, many of which were richly decorated, and the assemblage is important to Early Bronze Age pottery studies in validating the relationship between vases, vase urns and encrusted urns.

A millennium later, a domestic site was established upslope from the earlier midden (Phase 3). The character of this site was difficult to identify, despite a heavy concentration of structural traces, and finds were few and culturally undiagnostic. A stone-lined souterrain and a stone-lined and roofed pit appear to indicate a need for cool storage, and radiocarbon dates from one of the many other pits and from a floor deposit indicate that activity took place during the period 828–412 cal BC.

To the south of the last site, a stone-walled round house was built towards the end of the first millennium BC (Phase 4.1), which may have been contemporary with traces of cultivation by ard and spade that overlay the Phase 3 site. The house was partially dismantled in order to construct a stone-lined and stone-roofed souterrain (Phase 4.2). The midden contemporary with the souterrain (Phase 4.3) was dated by radiocarbon analysis to the period between 183 cal BC and cal AD 224 and contained animal bones, marine mollusca and plain pottery.

Artefacts of early medieval date from Kilellan may represent activity on the site during a period (Phase 5) in which two early ecclesiastical foundations were established in the area: Kilnave and Nave Island with their 8th-century high crosses. One of these artefacts is a rare and costly silver pin set with garnets, which may have been a stray loss but which might equally suggest the presence in the vicinity of a high status settlement.

A relatively recent phase (6) of activity was represented by a grid of U-shaped slots, which may have been associated with wooden racks for drying fish in the 19th century.

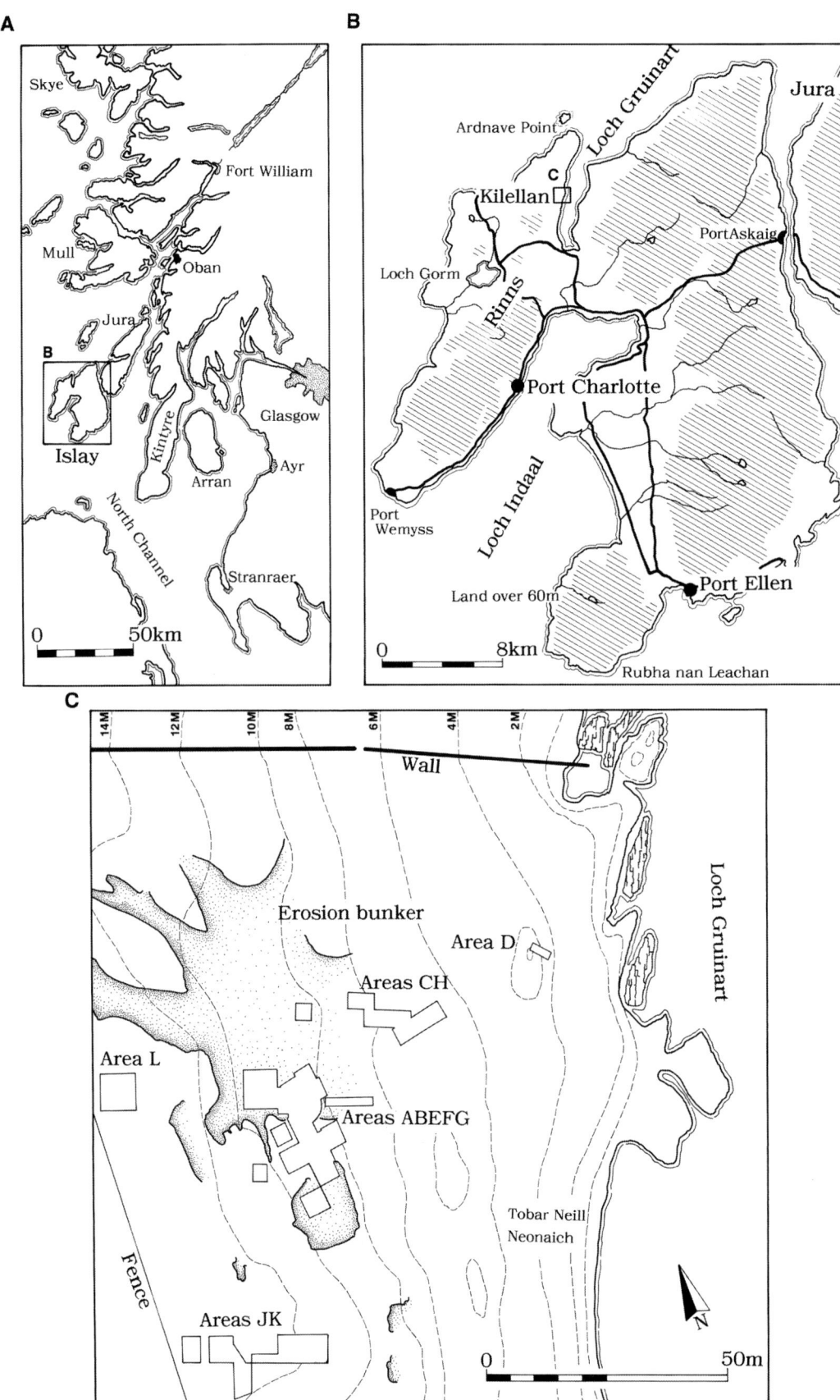

1 Maps showing the location of a. Islay, b. Ardnave Point, c. Kilellan.

Chapter 1

Introduction

ANNA RITCHIE

The archaeological site lies just to the north of Kilellan Farm on the Ardnave peninsula, which forms the west side of Loch Gruinart, a sea loch on the north coast of the island of Islay (NGR NR 286721) (illus 1–2). The site itself lies on machair, which has formed on top of and behind a raised beach at 8m OD, and in recent times grazing by cattle and sheep and the burrowing activities of rabbits have led to sand blow erosion, creating open bunkers and exposing the archaeological deposits. The choice of this particular spot for settlement is likely to have been related to its immediate topography: a sheltered landing-place for boats at Port na Feannaige and a reliable freshwater supply from the spring known as Tobar Neill Neonaich (the well of Neill the Curious), as well as the many springs and streams of the peninsula. Loch Gruinart is a large sandy intertidal zone and today has inflow-outflow channels along its eastern and western shores. The configuration of Loch Gruinart has, however, changed since 1848, when Stephen McDougall's map shows a single central channel, and no doubt there have been many changes since prehistoric times. Until as late as the first millennium BC, Islay was divided into two islands by a tidal strait

2   From Kilellan looking east across Loch Gruinart.

3   The open bunker at Kilellan in 1960, with Kilellan Farm in the background and trench L23 in the foreground. (Ranging pole in feet.)

4   Excavation of the face of the bunker in trench F2 in 1960. The band of white windblown sand seals the Early Bronze Age midden, and the variation in humic content in the midden is visible in the pale to dark lenses. (Ranging pole in feet.)

along the geological fault line represented today by Lochs Gruinart and Indaal (Dawson & Dawson 2000). The site at Kilellan lies on the north-east coast of the western island, which comprises the area now known as the Rinns of Islay. The Ardnave peninsula with its high sand dunes and machair grasslands is designated a Site of Special Scientific Interest. The Coastal Zone Assessment Survey of Islay confirms that erosion along the Kilellan stretch of the coast is relatively stable (Moore & Wilson 2003, map 22). The underlying geology is predominantly slatey rocks with thin bands of grits and schistose greywackes, and the site lies on drift behind the rocky platform of the foreshore. A detailed survey of the modern environment of Kilellan is provided in Chapter 7.

Two other sites of prehistoric occupation have been excavated farther north on the Ardnave peninsula: Ardnave 1 (see below) and Ardnave 2 (Ritchie & Welfare 1983), both of which testify to use of the area in Bronze Age and Iron Age times. Traces of a possible dun were identified by RCAHMS at NGR NR 285743 (1984, no 177). Both inhumation and cremation burials have been recorded nearby (Ritchie & Welfare 1983, 361–2), and in 1992 a collapsed long cist was observed by the writer in the eroding face of a very high sand dune at NGR NR 294748 on Ardnave Point. The crannog in Ardnave Loch is likely to be of prehistoric or Early Historic date (RCAHMS 1984, no 303). A rosette pin and bow brooch of the 3rd or 4th centuries AD were found close to a slab-built hearth at NGR NR 289745 (Ritchie & Welfare 1983, 302, 313, 341–3, figs 3 & 18), and stray finds in the area include a ring-headed pin and a disc-headed pin of the 9th or 10th centuries AD (ibid, 341–3, fig 18). Early Christian activity in the area is well attested by the place-name and 8th-century cross at Kilnave (RCAHMS 1984, no 374) and by the remains on Nave Island, off Ardnave Point (RCAHMS 1984, no 383).

Attention was drawn to the archaeological deposits at Kilellan in the 1950s when an amateur archaeologist, James Whittaker, added to the surface collections already made by the farmer, Sandy Maclellan, and discovered stone structures in the eroding sand bunkers (Appendix 1). In two visits in 1954 and 1956 Whittaker found a stone-lined hearth close to the area where later a souterrain was found (1976, trenches J and K), and a U-shaped setting of stones close to the main area of Early Bronze Age activity (1961 trench I and 1973 trench A1) (illus 20). He recorded the stratigraphy of the face of the bunker and excavated a trench at the foot of the face down to the natural subsoil. Funding was provided by the Society of Antiquaries of Scotland. In 1954 and 1956, Whittaker also excavated outside the cave at Kilchoman, some 11km to the south-west of Kilellan (NGR NR 220633; RCAHMS 1983, 18–19).

In 1959 systematic surface collection of artefacts and excavation began under Francis Celoria and Susannah Pearce with the Islay Archaeological Survey Group (IASG 1960, (1) 21). A grid of 10ft squares was laid out by plane-tabling and the surface soil from the face and floor of the bunker was sieved. One trench, F1, was excavated from the bunker face into the undisturbed Early Bronze Age deposits. Trench F2 was excavated alongside in 1960, and trench L23 was excavated on the northern edge of the bunker (illus 3–4). The Islay Archaeological Survey Group's work continued in 1961 under the direction of Colin Burgess, and three trenches were excavated (I–III) on the same grid and in the central area of Early Bronze Age activity (Burgess 1976), again not penetrating into the underlying Mesolithic level (illus 18 & 20).

The first major season of excavation took place in 1973 under Colin Burgess and the Northumberland Archaeological Group (illus 5), with material assistance from the Department of Adult Education, University of Newcastle upon Tyne (Burgess 1976). Using a different grid, 12 trenches were excavated (A–F), mostly in the eroding bunker area but including one trench on the raised beach (C1) and one on an oval mound close to the shore (D1) (illus 1 & 7). Despite a local tradition that the mound covered a Viking ship burial, it proved to be a fossil sand dune. One trench (B1) was related to the 1960 grid in order to examine a small undisturbed area of midden between the 1960 trenches I and III before erosion of the bunker face destroyed it. The Mesolithic date of the sand layer sealed by an old turf line beneath the Early Bronze Age midden was recognized and the layer examined. Three small test-pits, Z1–3, were dug on the bluff to the south in an area that was subsequently excavated in 1976.

In response to the threat of accelerating erosion, a final season of excavation was directed by Colin Burgess for the Northumberland Archaeological Group in 1976 (illus 6), with material assistance again from the University of Newcastle and additional funding from the Department of the Environment (Property Services Agency) and the Society of Antiquaries of Scotland (RCAHMS 1983, no 270). Fourteen trenches were excavated (G–M) on a new north–south grid (approximating to the grid used in 1959–61) except for trench G1 which was inserted into the gap between 1973 trenches A2, E2, B3 and B2, and therefore conformed to the 1973 grid (illus 7). By this time, the central Early Bronze Age area had been excavated on no fewer than five occasions,

5   Excavations at Kilellan in 1973.

6   Colin Burgess (on the right) discussing the excavation with Steve Palmer in 1976.

with the result that trench G2 was a patchwork of disturbed and undisturbed areas, complicated further by the farmer's use of the ground for burying dead stock (illus 22). Trench G4 and most of trench L2 were excavated by a small team after the end of the main season, extending into November that year, under the direction of Stratford Halliday and Peter Hill respectively.

An entirely separate site, a hut-circle found in the sand-dunes north-east of Ardnave Loch and some 880m north of Kilellan (NGR NR 287730), was excavated in 1976 as trench N by Peter Topping. It was published in the Royal Commission *Inventory* (RCAHMS 1983, no 241) as Ardnave 1 (illus 98). Finds included sherds of undiagnostic pottery and a perforated bone pin, and the house is therefore undatable (although the lack of bone artefacts from Kilellan and Ardnave 2 may suggest that Ardnave 1 was later in date).

Post-excavation work on the results of the 1973 and 1976 seasons began under the supervision of Colin Burgess in Newcastle, using both Job Creation Schemes and funding from the Scottish Development Department (Ancient Monuments). Stephen Speak was the principal researcher, and the work finished in 1983. With the full co-operation of Colin Burgess, Historic Scotland, through the offices of Patrick Ashmore, agreed to transfer the project in 1991 to the former Artefact Research Unit (ARU) at the National Museums of Scotland, Edinburgh. Alan Saville, Head of the ARU, acted as the project administrator. The main funding was provided by Historic Scotland, supplemented by resourcing from the National Museums of Scotland. Completion of the restarted Kilellan Project, originally scheduled for 1995, was delayed by the closure of the ARU when the National Museums embarked on work towards the new Museum of Scotland. The specialist reports for the Project were completed between 1992 and 2004.

Note on sections and plans

A minimalist approach has been adopted to the numbering and visual presentation of layers in section, in order to draw attention to critical layers mentioned in the text. Occasionally on both sections and plans features such as pits and post-holes lack numbers, either because the context sheet has not survived or because the feature was recognized only in section.

Chapter 2

The excavations

ANNA RITCHIE

The archaeological deposits at Kilellan have been shown to extend intermittently over an area of about 5000 sq m (illus 1c, 7). The trenches that were dug on higher ground to the west (L2) and south (J and K) of the main erosion bunker revealed structures and deposits which are unrelated to those elsewhere on the site and which will be treated separately, although it is possible to link them in to the overall site stratigraphy. Burgess noted that erosion of the bunker during the 12 years between the 1961 and 1973 seasons had resulted in the loss of half of the main Early Bronze Age settlement area (1976, 186), and a site visit by the writer in February 1992 confirmed that the machair bluff had receded beyond that area but that regeneration of the turf cover had stabilized the surface of the bunker itself. The basal Mesolithic level is thus protected. Both the surface collection of artefacts and the excavations were carried out using grid systems, ultimately involving, as described in Chapter 1, three different but related grids. Records of individual contexts were not kept prior to 1973.

SUMMARY OF SITE STRATIGRAPHY

Colin Burgess published an overall stratigraphic sequence for the excavations up to 1973, consisting of nine layers (1976, 186–7), and the descriptive sequence of the layers involved held good for the 1976 season of excavation in the main bunker area (G2):

Layer 1   fine turf and dark sandy topsoil

Layer 2   brown sand streaked with up to eight old turf-lines

Layer 3   black sand representing a major turf-line

Layer 4   pale yellow-brown sand

Layer 5   very pale yellow sand, a fine wind-blown deposit covering the prehistoric occupation, up to 0.6m thick

Layer 6   dark mottled brown sand, interleaved with patchy bands of black shelly midden, Early Bronze Age occupation, on average 0.5m–1.0m thick

Layer 6a   thin black band of sand representing an old turf-line

Layer 7   fine silver sand, acidic in character rather than calcareous, containing Mesolithic activity

Layer 8   black peat deposit overlying the raised beach.

Illustration 8 shows a typical section through this stratigraphy. In the case of trenches located in open erosion bunkers, the upper layers had been truncated. Modern pottery was found in layer 3 and a gun cartridge case in layer 4, and it was clear that layers 1–4 were of relatively modern origin. Layer 5 was effectively a 'marker' layer that sealed the undisturbed prehistoric levels across the lower part of the site. It was not present on the higher ground in trenches L2, K or J2–3 and was present in J1 only in that part of the trench that was below the current 14.5m contour. The Mesolithic layer of silver sand had formed on top of undisturbed natural subsoil varying from orange sand on the upper slope of the site to a dark chocolate-brown soil with pebbles. The natural subsoil was not reached in a number of trenches (B2, F2, G1, G2, G3, G4, J1, J2, K3, L1, L2), nor in the pre-1973 excavations with the exception of the trench dug in 1956. In trench L2 the Mesolithic silver sand (12) was separated by a thin old turf-line (13) from natural ginger sand (14), while in K1 and K2 at a similar distance upslope from the raised beach the silver sand (8) lay upon a mottled yellow/orange/cream/black sand (9) on which the old turf-line may have been disturbed by wind erosion. Downslope in trench L1 a sterile silver sand (7) again overlay a mottled orange/black sand on which iron pan had formed and presumably affected the colour of the sand beneath (8). In A3 and F1, a natural bank of hard compact sand curved round a shallow hollow on its south-west side (illus 19). North and east of this bank the natural subsoil was orange sand, but within

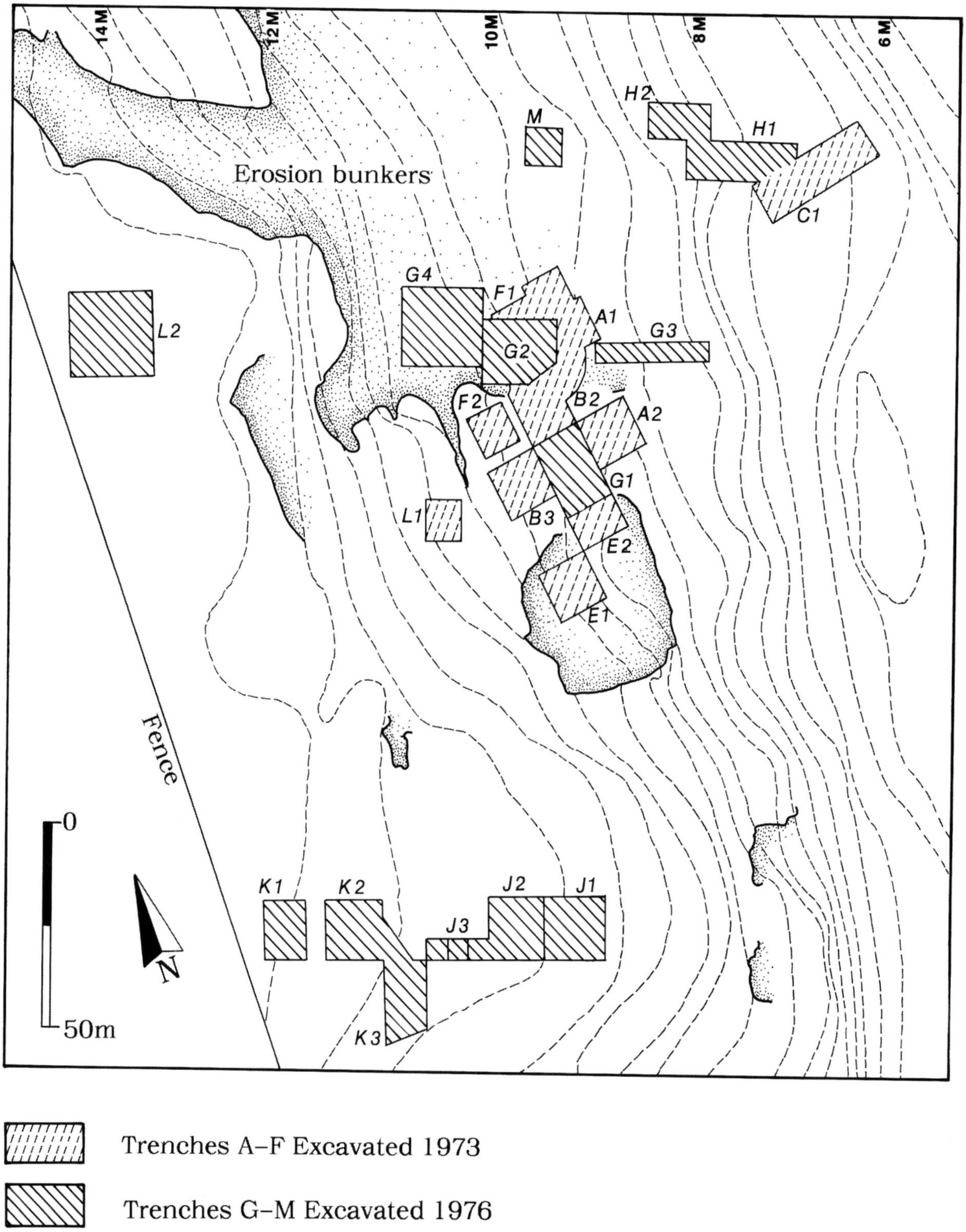

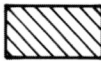

	Trenches A–F Excavated 1973
	Trenches G–M Excavated 1976

7 Contour plan showing the location of trenches in 1973 and 1976.

THE EXCAVATIONS

8 The south-west corner of trench G1 shows a typical section through the Burgess sequence: recent layers 1–4 and the marker layer 5 of pale yellow sand sealing the midden layer 6. The fine black line at the base of the section represents an old turfline layer 6a, and beneath is the Mesolithic silver sand layer 7. The shallow hollow in the surface of layer 7 is the base of a pit (feature G103) dug from a high level in the Early Bronze Age midden. (Ranging pole in 10cm sections.)

the hollow lay a dark chocolate-brown silt with pebbles embedded into it (A2 7; B1 and B3 8; E1 5; E2 8). A little further east in the narrow trench dug in 1956, beneath 'fine sand' that is likely to represent the Mesolithic sand layer, there was carbonized material which may have been either an old turf-line or the peat deposit found in the 1970s' trenches C and H.

The upper layers of recent origin (1–4) were present in the trenches on higher ground to the west and south of the bunker, but, as explained already,

TABLE 1
Correlation of trench stratigraphies.

	A1	A2	A3	A4	B1–3	E1	E2	F1–2
topsoil	1	1	1	1	1	1	1	1
grey brown sand	–	2	–	–	2	–	2	2
old turf line	–	3	–	–	3	–	3	3
light brown sand	–	4	–	–	4	–	4	4
white sand	–	4a	–	5	5	2	5	5
midden	2	5	2	6	6	3	6	6
old turf line	2b	5a	–	–	6a	3a	6a	–
silver sand	7	6	–	–	7	4	7	–
natural subsoil	–	7	–	–	8	5	8	7

	G1–2	G3	G4	I–III	1951 F1	1960 F2
topsoil	1	1	1	1	I	I
grey brown sand	2	–	–	2	–	II
old turf line	3	2	–	3	II	III
light brown sand	4	–	–	4	–	–
white sand	5	–	2	5	III	IV
midden	6	3/4	3	6	IV/V	V/VI
old turf line	7	5	–	–	VI	VIa
silver sand	8	7	–	–	–	–

	C		H1–2
topsoil	1	topsoil	1
grey brown sand	2	light brown sand	2
old turf line	3	old turf line	3
light brown sand	4	light brown sand	4
white sand	5	white sand	5
stained white sand	6	yellow brown sand	6
peat deposit	7	silver sand	7
raised beach	8	peat deposit	8
		raised beach	9

THE EXCAVATIONS

	J1	J2	K3	K1–2
topsoil	1	15	1	1
yellow brown sand	2	16	2	2
white sand	3	17	–	–
grey yellow sand	4	18	–	–
midden	5–13	19/30/32	5	–
yellow sand	14	–	–	–
midden	20–8	–	–	–
yellow sand	29	29	6	–
old turf line	–	–	7	7
silver sand	–	–	8	8

	L2	
topsoil	1	
yellow brown sand	2	
old turf line	3	
yellow brown sand	4	
old turf line	5	
pale brown sand	6	
grey brown sand	7	
yellow brown sand	8/9	
yellow black sand	10	= occupation horizon
ginger sand	11	
silver sand	12	
old turf line	13	
ginger sand	14	

layer 5 was present only in the eastern part of J1 and otherwise the lower stratigraphy was internal to the two areas of L and J/K. Table 1 provides a correlation of layer numbers across the site with Burgess' ideal sequence, based on analysis carried out by Stephen Speak.

A separate prehistoric occupation site was excavated in trench L2 (illus 34–46), belonging to the first millennium BC. Its stratigraphy was largely internal and consisted of a black occupation horizon (layer 10) sealed below cultivated soils of medieval or later date (layers 2–6), which probably correlate with layer 2 in trenches K1–3. Within and below this occupation horizon was a series of well-preserved structural features, including a stone-built souterrain, a stone-lined and lintelled pit, hearths, pits and postholes, all penetrating into the sand beneath (layers 11–14).

To the south of the earlier sites, a Middle Iron Age settlement was found in the final season of excavations in trenches J and K (illus 47–55). This consisted of midden deposits that had accumulated, or been redeposited, on top of another stone-built souterrain, which appeared to have been cut through an earlier house in K2–3. The decision was made at the end of the excavation season in 1976 to leave the underlying deposits in this area undisturbed.

RAISED BEACH AND PEAT DEPOSIT

Stephen Speak

Two adjoining areas of a raised beach deposit were examined in 1973 and 1976, totalling an area of 73 sq m. Initially the area was tested to examine the nature of a low sinuous ridge on the seaward side of the main

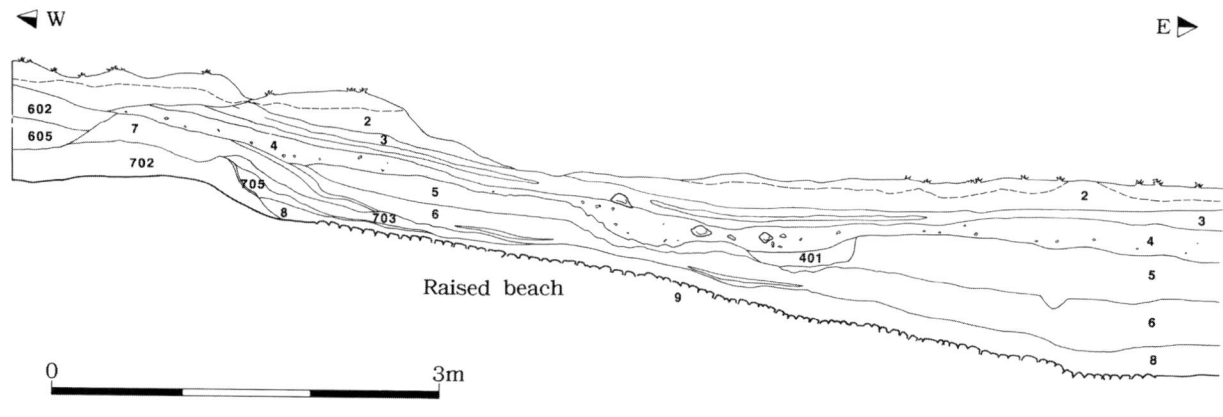

9   North section of trench H1 across the raised beach.

prehistoric activity. The 1973 trench C cut a strip 1.5m by 11.3m at right angles to the general course of this ridge. The complex stratigraphy suggests that the ridge is a dune line built up against a slightly raised area of bedrock towards the loch shore. The western end of this trench consisted of numerous sand-blows against this dune line, with occasional stable periods indicated by the presence of thin old turf-lines. Below this sequence lay the 'marker' layer (5) of white sand, which was at its thickest (c 1.0m) immediately to the west of the bedrock, where it heaped up to form the 'backbone' of the dune-ridge. Below this white sand lay a fossilized raised beach overlain by a peat deposit. The raised beach dropped gently towards the modern shore (dropping 1.0m in a distance of 10.5m) and consisted of well-rounded cobbles and boulders, tightly packed, up to 0.40m in size.

This raised beach also occurs in trench E, c 45m to the south-west, but with no attendant peat deposits. Here its presence some way inland must indicate the presence of a former inlet, which may have attracted Mesolithic fisher-gatherer groups. The raised beach lies c 7m (22 feet) above sea-level and can be equated with the traditional 25ft raised beach.

The preliminary examination of the preserved organic material in the trench C peat deposits warranted the search for further material. Trenches H1 and H2 were cut in 1976, slightly to the inland side of the dune-ridge on the assumption that the peat was derived from a stream or pond backing on to the dune-ridge itself and with the raised beach as its base. The north section of H1 (illus 9) shows two layers of sand (2 and 4) separated at the western end of the trench by a thick turf-line (3), which rose towards the west and was truncated by the open bunker. Layer 5 is the 'marker' windblown white sand, with damp yellow-brown sand below (6), both backing up against the Mesolithic silver sand of layer 7. The stratigraphy at the west end of the trench was complicated by colour changes within layer 6, which ranged from a reddish-brown sand (601), orange-brown sand (602), grey sand streaked with black (603) to a wet grey sand (604). The latter, confined to the south side of the trench, rested not on layer 7 but directly on top of layer 8 and the raised beach, beyond the point at which the silver sand of layer 7 petered out. Layer 7 also consisted of lenses of differently coloured sand, paler at the top end of the raised beach and mottled orange to brown as it came into contact with layer 8 downslope. Layer 8 was the peat deposit lying on top of the cobbles of the raised beach, a compact black sand 0.25m–0.5m in thickness containing vegetable matter and insects, and this deposit was sampled extensively for its plant remains (Appendix 4) (illus 10). Most of the species are indicators of freshwater or fen conditions, and they suggest that there was formerly a marshy pond on the inland side of the dune-ridge. The discovery of an abraded sherd of pottery with applied decoration (Chapter 3, no 68) at the base of layer 604 indicates that this pond was in existence in Early Bronze Age times.

The presence of a natural sand bank running across trenches A1 and F1 seems to have caused the development of a pond-like feature to its immediate south: beneath the silver sand in the south-west part of A1 (7) and in A2 (7), B1 (8), B3 (8), E1 (5) and E2 (8) was a dark chocolate brown silt with pebbles embedded into it.

PHASE 1
THE MESOLITHIC HORIZON

The silver sand in which Mesolithic flintwork was found was a fine acidic sand, lacking the shell content of later sand-blows, and it is likely to represent a leached version of the sterile discoloured sand beneath it, an altered 'soil' that had formed on acidic rocks (layer 7 in trenches A1, B1–3, E2, layer 6 in trench A2, layer 4 in trench E1, layer 7 in trenches G3 and H1–2, layer 8 in trenches G1–2 and K1–2, and layer 12 in trench L2). This silver sand layer was an average 0.2–0.3m thick and had formed on top of sterile subsoil. Excavation had ceased before this layer was reached in all pre-1973 trenches with the exception of Whittaker's 1956 slit trench, and in trenches A4, G4, J1–3 and K3, and the layer was only sampled in L2. Prior to 1973 this basal sand was assumed to be sterile. Mesolithic flintwork was widely distributed over the site (illus 11), but the main concentration of flintwork was in a strip behind the raised beach in trenches E1, E2, B2, G1 and G2. In the 1976 season, the silver sand was regularly gridded into 1m squares in order to record the horizontal distribution of the flints (these data were recorded in relation to individual flints in G2). Flints were found throughout the vertical dimension of the layer, but the concentration in trench E1 was found mostly in the upper part of the sand.

The absence of any Neolithic layer between the Mesolithic sand and the Early Bronze Age midden suggests that there had been severe erosion of the area in Neolithic times, before the sand was stabilized by vegetation that resulted in the layer 6a old turf-line. Support for this interpretation is provided by the discovery of a leaf-shaped arrowhead in the silver sand (Chapter 4, illus 84, no 4036) and a barbed-and-tanged arrowhead in the old turf-line (Chapter 4, illus 84, no 264).

Several structural elements belonging to the Early Bronze Age midden were dug through the old turf-line into the Mesolithic silver sand, most notably the two

10 The surface of the raised beach coated with peaty deposit in trench H1.

palisades. This may well have led to displacement of Mesolithic flints into the midden above but is unlikely to have caused the reverse displacement of later material without discolouring the sand.

Apart from the deposition of flints, there were structural traces of Mesolithic activity in the form of patches of apparently deliberately laid stones and cobbles and at least one shallow pit, mostly at or close to the base of the silver sand. A patch of small and close-set flat stones about 1.4m across was found lying

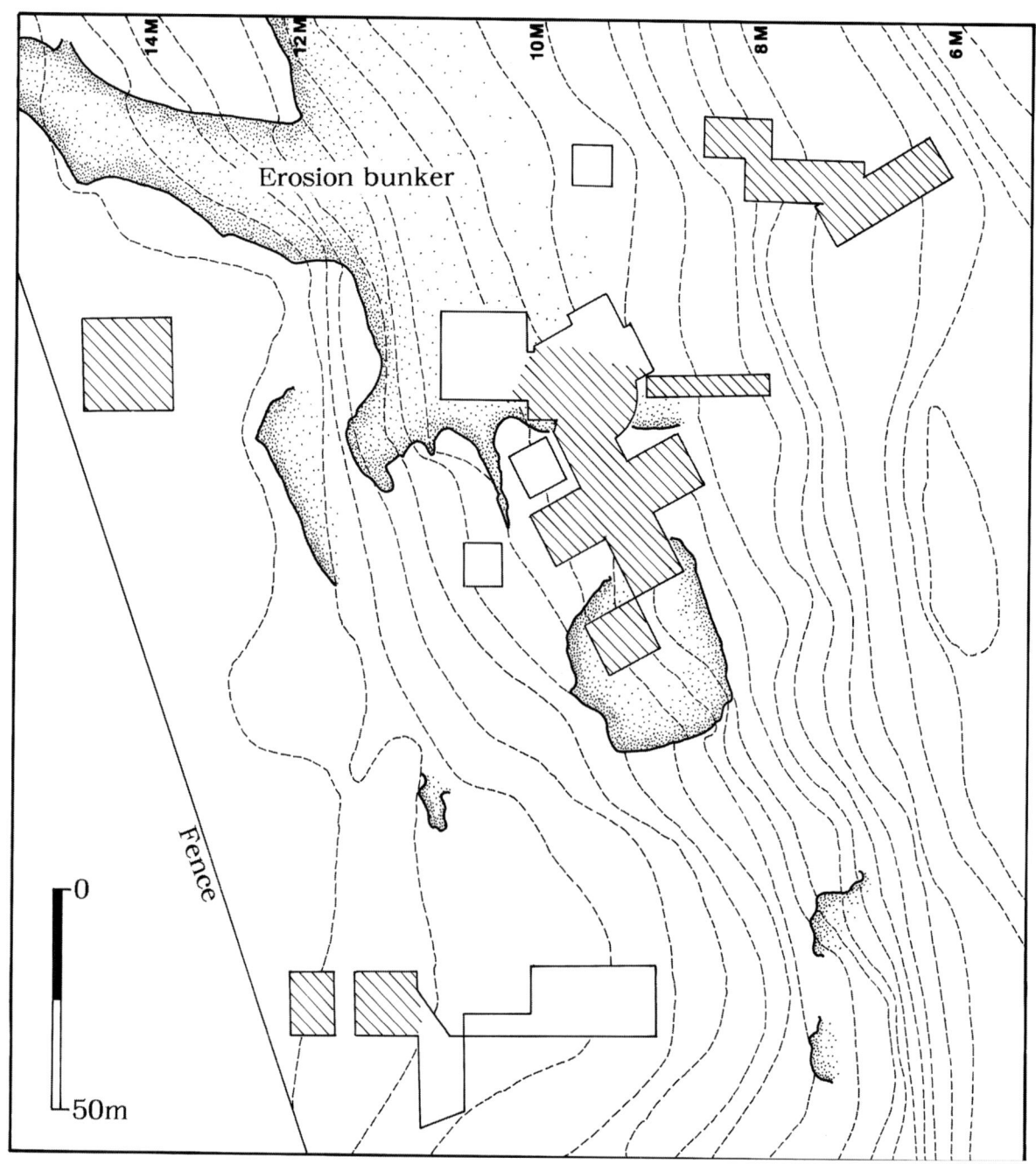

11 Plan showing the trenches containing Mesolithic artefacts.

near the base of the Mesolithic sand in trench B3 (illus 12), and a rough arc of stones in trench B2 (illus 13). Patches of rounded cobbles were recorded in 1973 trench A2 and 1976 trench G2: the former was oval and about 2.0m long (illus 14), while the latter (G2 feature 132A) was oval and just over 0.1m across (illus 15 & 16). A concentration of flints, feature 131, lay about a metre from the cobble patch in G2 (illus 15). All these features were lying within the basal part of the sand, and pit 132 was a shallow oval scoop about 0.2m deep, the fill of which included 89 flints, one of which was a scalene triangle microlith (Chapter 4, illus 82, no 1170), and an unmodified pebble. The flint scatter 131 yielded 288 flints: a core (no 882), a microlith,

THE EXCAVATIONS

12 Patch of close-set flat stones in trench B3 represents Mesolithic activity.

13 In trench B2 an arc of small stones on the right lay within the Mesolithic silver sand (the larger stones were at a higher level at the base of the later midden).

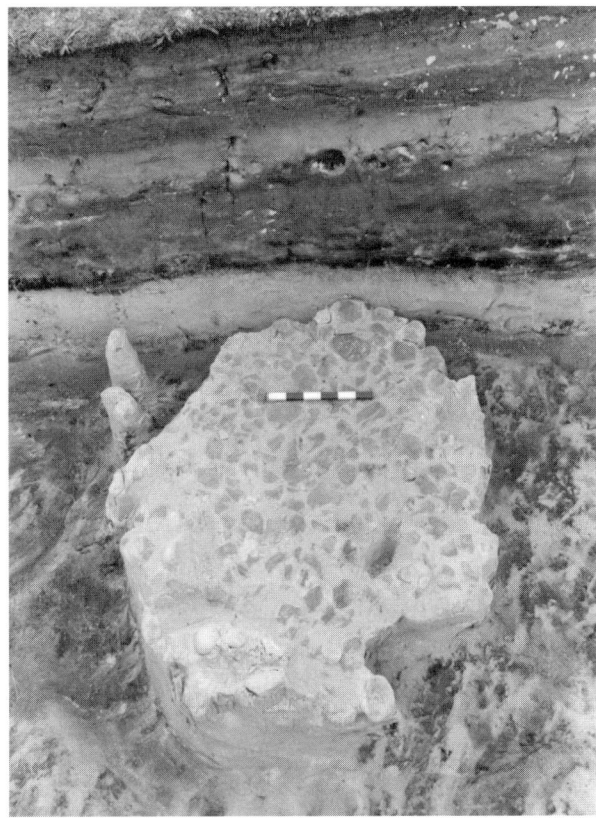

14 A patch of small rounded cobbles within the Mesolithic silver sand in trench A2.

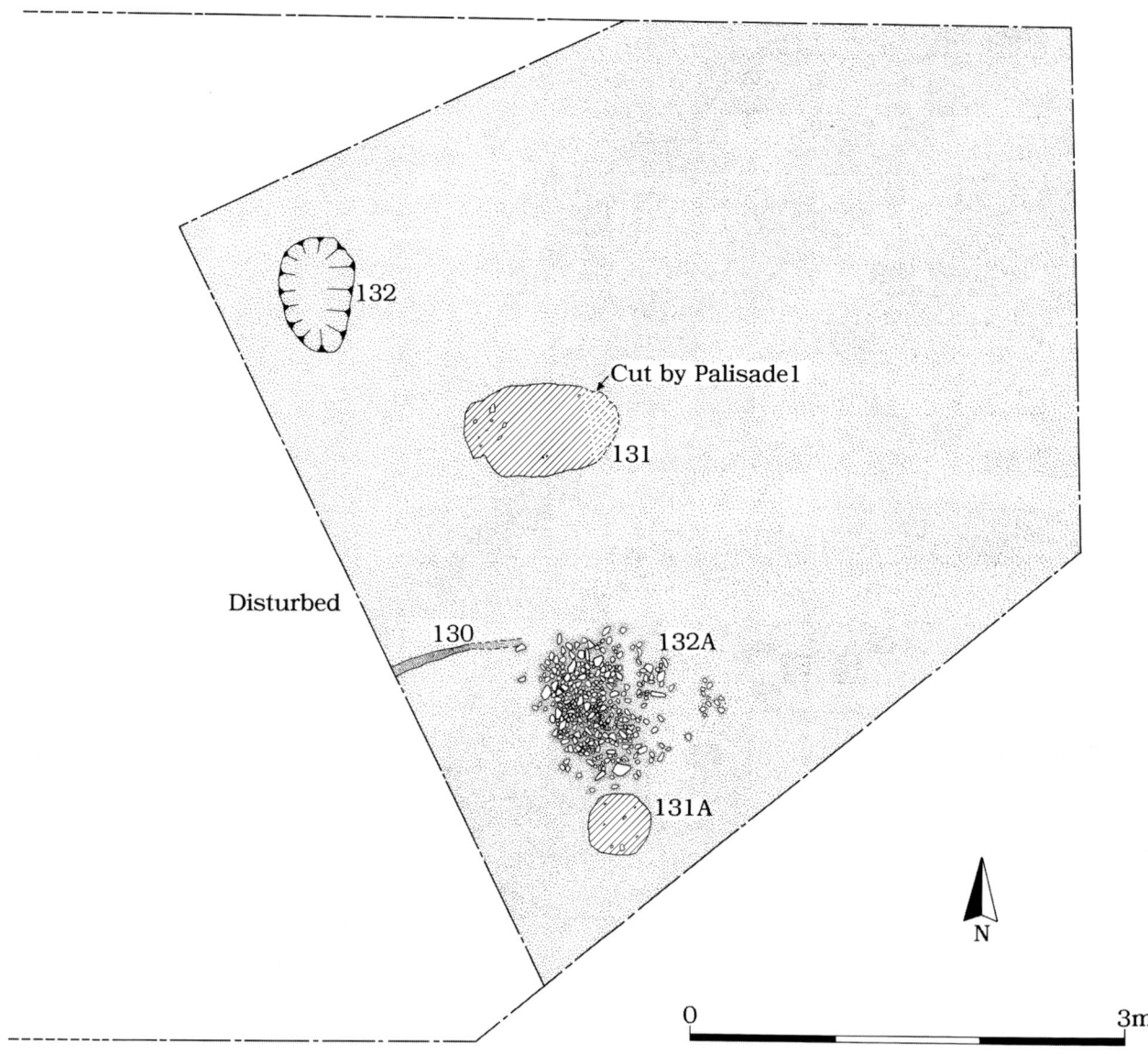

15 Plan of the Mesolithic structures in trench G2.

a microburin, and 283 unretouched flakes including refitting flakes (Chapter 4, illus 86, refitting group 27). Feature 130 was a ginger strip forming a small gully and contained no flints.

The main area of Mesolithic activity was contained to the north and east within the low natural bank described above. There were post-holes along the crest and on either side of the bank (illus 19 & 20), most of which were truncated and which were 0.06m to 0.26m in depth. Colin Burgess suggested that this bank had been modified by Mesolithic people, perhaps even to the extent of timber screening along its length (1976, 187, 190), although the stratigraphical relationship of

most of the post-holes was uncertain. The exception was a post-hole in F1, which was sealed by a pile of winkles early in the Early Bronze Age midden. These post-holes will be discussed again in connection with the Early Bronze Age activity with which they seem best related.

Mesolithic flints were found in the peat deposit above the raised beach and on the raised beach itself in trenches C1 (layers 7, 8) and H1 (layers 8, 9; illus 9). Cobble tools with simple wear traces were also found in the Mesolithic sand, including a facially pecked cobble (no 41) and plain hammerstones (nos 47, 48, 62, 64) (Chapter 5).

THE EXCAVATIONS

The silver sand was sealed by a thin but unmistakeable black sandy humic band representing an old turf-line. It was only 10–20mm thick, suggesting a relatively short period during which the sand-dunes stabilized and acquired a turf cover, before the midden began to accumulate. It was consistently present in the main area beneath the Early Bronze Age midden (E1 3a; E2 6a; B1–3 6a; A1 2b; A2 5a; G1–2 7), except where it had been removed by the erosion that created a hollow (see below, Phase 2.2, feature 609a) and where it survived only in patches (G3 5). A small number of pottery sherds of Early Bronze Age date was retrieved from the immediately underlying silver sand, which may have been the result of patchy turf-cover or local disturbance of the turf, but it could also imply that the turf-line itself dates to the Early Bronze Age.

This turf-line was also found upslope to the south-west in K1–3 (7), again sealing the silver sand (8), but excavation in J1–3 did not penetrate deeply enough to record its presence. The natural sequence was somewhat different in L2, where silver sand (12) was covered by a layer of ginger sand (11) and separated below by a turf-line (13) from ginger sand (14); here the ginger sand (14) must be the unleached equivalent of the silver sand elsewhere, and the silver sand (12) was presumably redeposited by wind action from the eroding lower slope.

PHASE 2
THE EARLY BRONZE AGE MIDDEN

On top of the old turf-line, deposits of domestic midden began to accumulate, the excavated extent of which, some 650 sq m, is shown in illustration 17. The midden varied both in colour and in texture from a mid-brown sandy matrix, which could exist in a sterile form on the perimeter of the midden or be mottled with humus-rich patches in the midden proper, to the patches of dense black shelly midden, the overall extent of which was plotted by Burgess (1976, fig 10.3; illus 18). Prior to the 1976 season the variations

16 A patch of small rounded cobbles (132A) within the Mesolithic silver sand in trench G2.

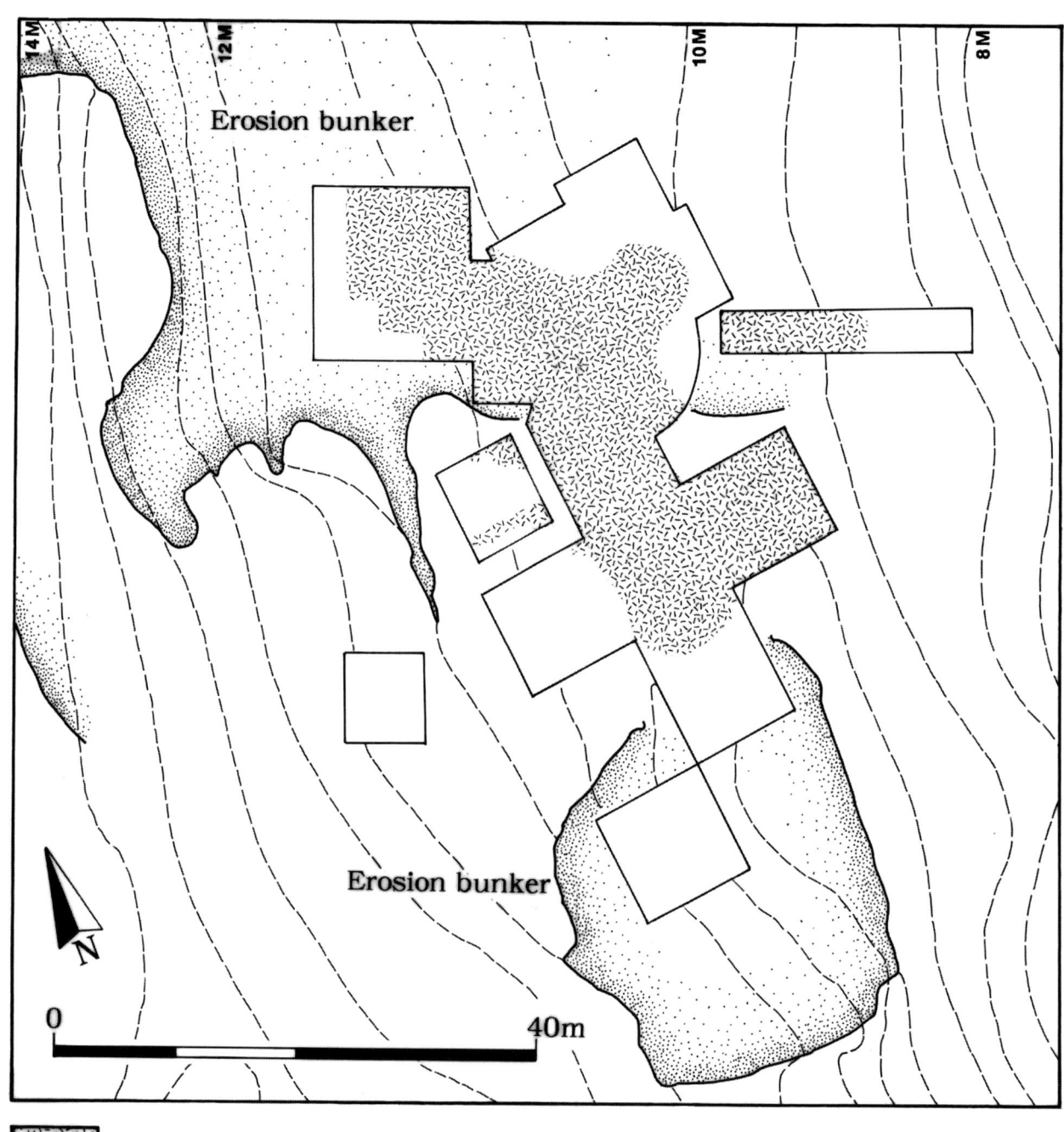

17 Plan showing the extent of the Early Bronze Age midden.

in the midden were not separately numbered, for it was recognized that, although the midden could be up to a metre thick, the artefacts within it indicated a relatively short-lived cultural homogeneity. In 1976 the opportunity was taken to re-excavate the central area of the midden in order to excavate an L-shaped baulk left intact between previous trenches (illus 18, shown by cross-hatching) and in order to extend westwards into the open bunker. This exercise was not only difficult but also very unpleasant, owing to recent

THE EXCAVATIONS

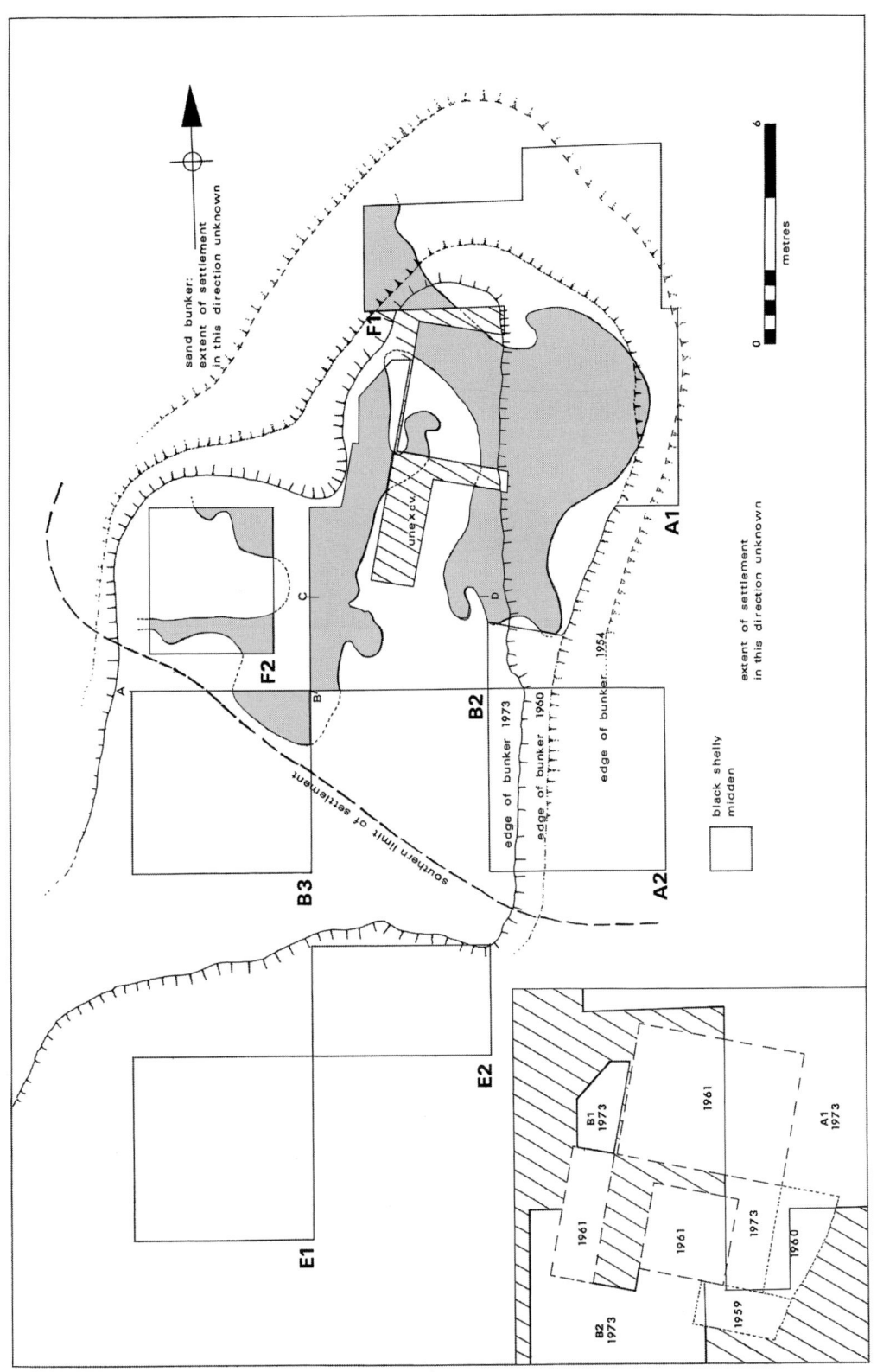

18 Plan of the main area of the Early Bronze Age midden published by Colin Burgess (1976, fig 10.3). It shows the extent of the black shelly midden and the rate at which the bunker eroded between 1954 and 1973.

TABLE 2
Radiocarbon dates.

The following five samples of material collected in 1976 were kindly dated in 1992 by Gordon Cook of the Scottish Universities Research & Reactor Centre. The calibrated dates are those given in Ashmore 1997.

Lab code	Description	Calibrated date @ 95.4% probability	Lab age BP	d13C‰
GU–3517	Charcoal from upper midden G2 layers 607, 631, 655, 100 (birch, alder, oak, hazel, willow, Pomoideae)	2130–1748 cal BC	3590±60	–26.5‰
GU–3518	Charcoal from L2 pit 117, filling layers 02 & 03 (birch, hazel, willow, oak)	808–517 cal BC	2550±50	–26.0‰
GU–3519	Charcoal from occupation floor L2 layer 10 (alder, birch, hazel, oak, Pomoideae)	828–412 cal BC	2560±70	–26.2‰
GU–3516	Cattle bone from midden J1 layer 22	183 cal BC-cal AD 116	2030±60	–23.8‰
GU–3515	Cattle bone from midden J2 layer 30/39	115 cal BC-cal AD 224	1970±7	–26.2‰

19   The natural sand bank ran from top left to bottom right across trenches A1 and F1.

THE EXCAVATIONS

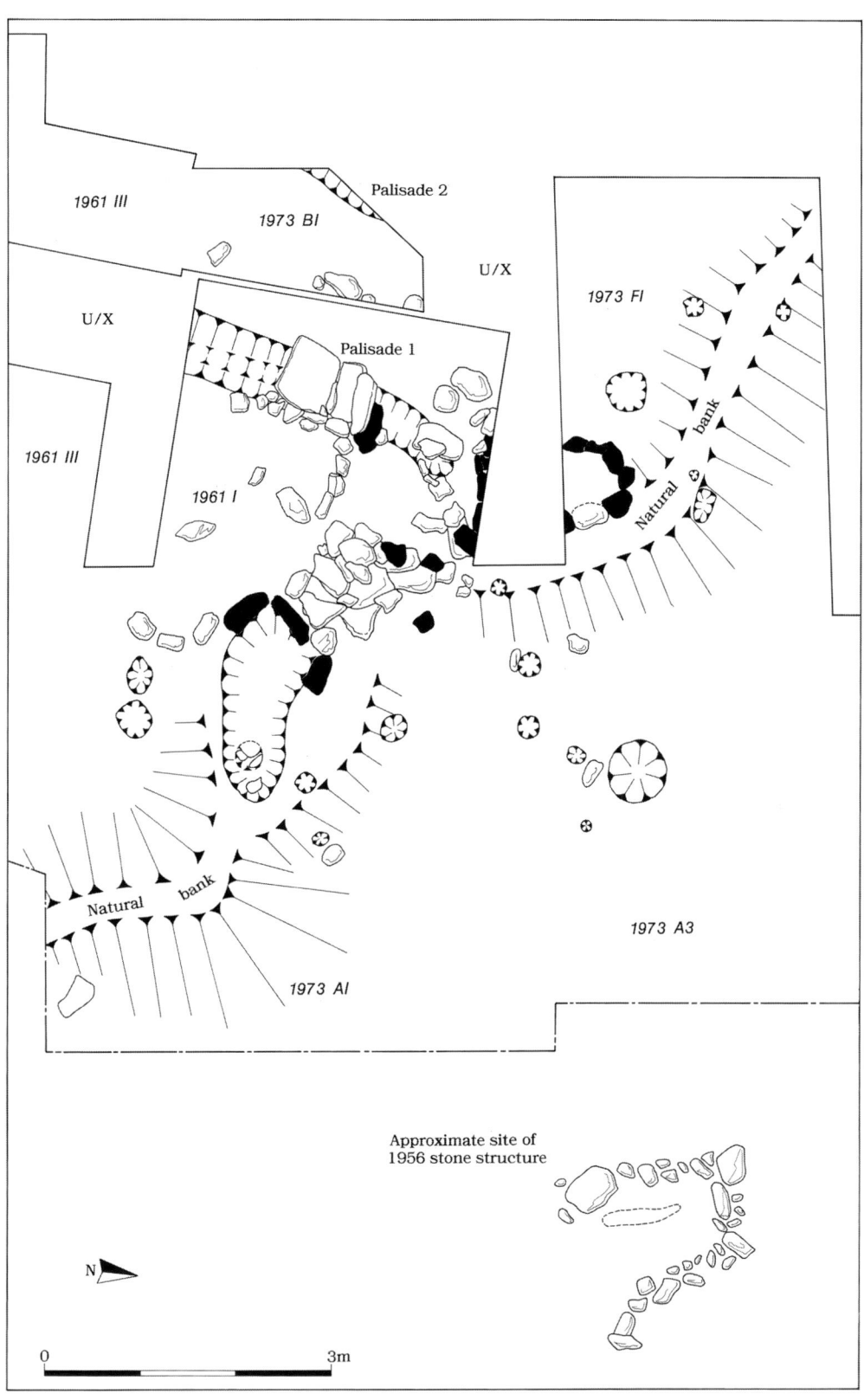

20 Plan of the Early Bronze Age structures revealed by excavations between 1954 and 1973 (based on Burgess 1976, fig 10.4).

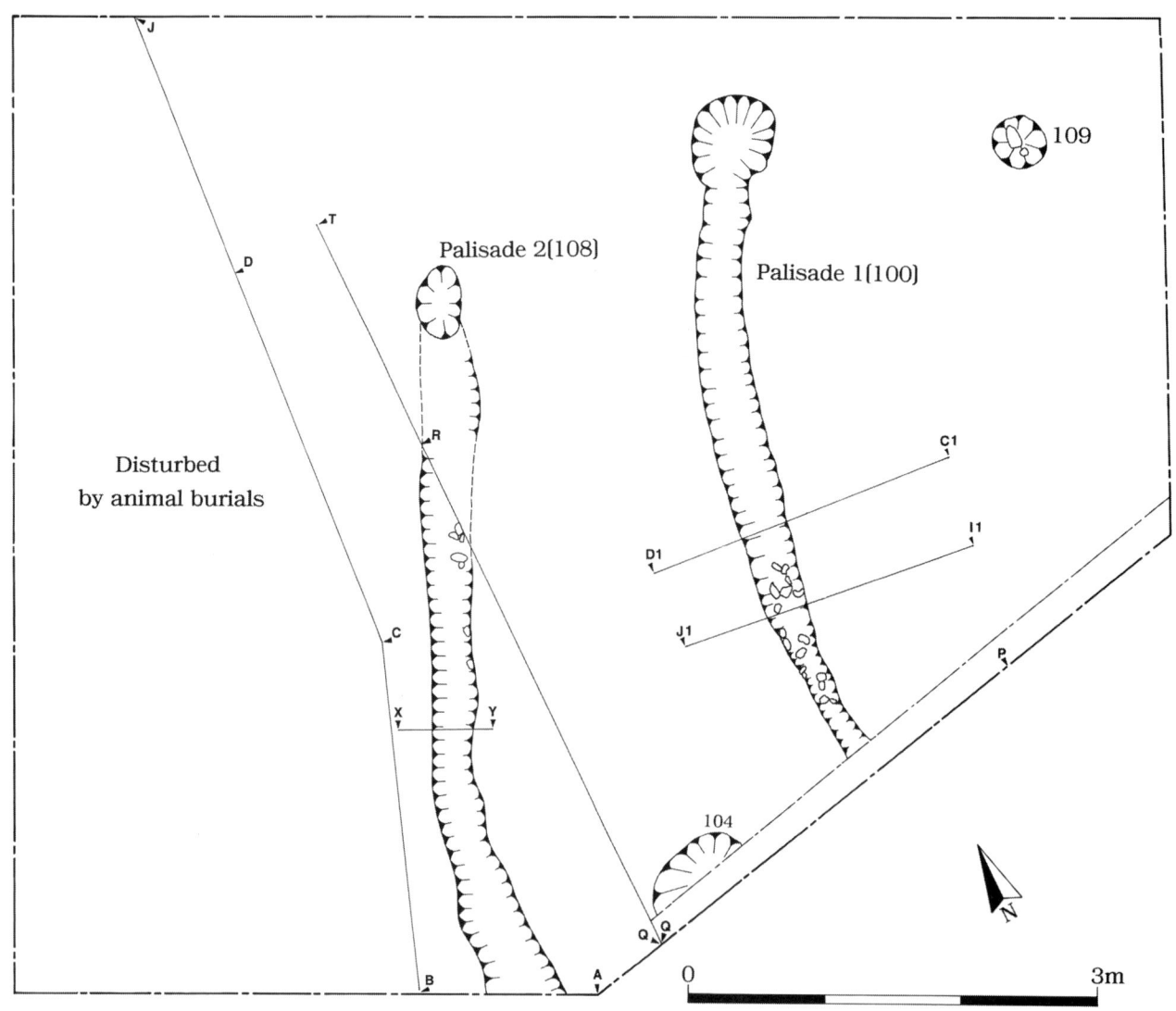

21 Plan of palisade slots and locations of sections in trench G2.

burials of dead livestock in the backfilled old trenches. The L-shaped baulk proved nonetheless to be crucial to an understanding of the 'drain' found in 1961. The midden in this area was both thick and complicated in its structure, and an attempt was made to identify and to excavate separately the individual lenses or deposits within it. This very difficult task was only partially successful, for some lenses merged imperceptibly with others or could only be recognized in section and not in their horizontal dimension. In 1973, samples of midden were dry-sieved, and in 1976 samples were wet-sieved.

Erosion of the bunker to north and east of the main Early Bronze Age midden had truncated the stratigraphy in those areas, with the result that the natural bank running north-west/south-east across trenches A1 and F1 appears misleadingly to bound the Early Bronze Age occupation (illus 19). In reality both Mesolithic and Early Bronze Age layers existed to the east of the bank and were intact when Whittaker worked on the site in 1954 and 1956. He drew a schematic profile of the bunker wall, which lay approximately along the line of the east side of the 1973 trench A1, and the layering of turf-lines, sand-blows and midden reflects very accurately the stratigraphy of the main midden excavated by Burgess.

In 1959 the midden excavated in trench F1 was numbered layer IV and the dark shelly lens within IV was numbered V, but pottery and flints were also

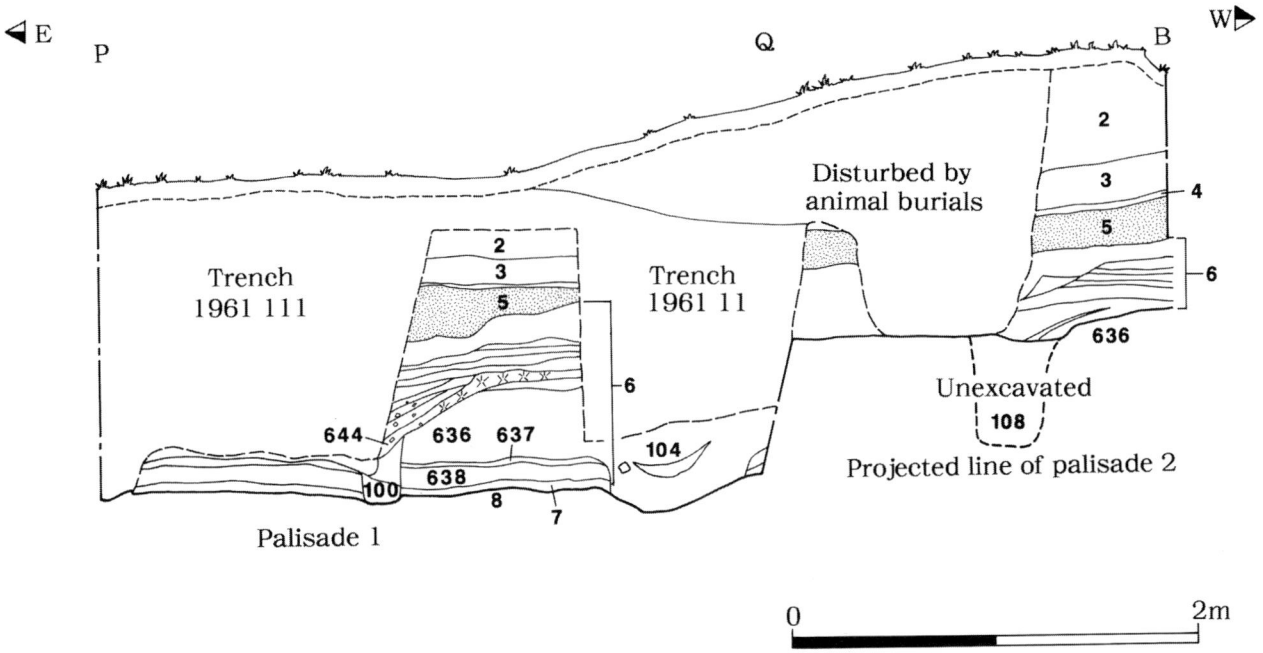

22 Section P–Q–B across the palisade slots in trench G2. Owing to the unstable nature of the trench sides, palisade slot 108 was not excavated as far as the section.

collected from the surface of the bunker where midden was exposed in E1, F1–6 and G3–5. In 1960 the midden excavated in trench F2 (illus 4) was numbered V and the dark shelly lens within it VI. In 1961 and 1973, the midden was consistently numbered layer 6 in trenches I–III and trenches A4, B1, B2 and F1, but layer 2 in trenches A1 and A2 and layer 5 in trench A2. In 1976 the midden was numbered layer 6 in trench G1 (illus 8) and subdivided into five artificial spits each 50mm thick (0601–0605), and the trench was divided horizontally into areas a–d. It was also numbered layer 6 in trench G2 and numbered internally according to the individual lenses into 0601, 0602 and so on, and the trench itself was divided horizontally into areas a–d. In trench G4 the midden became layer 3 and the lenses again numbered 0301 upwards.

Early Bronze Age pottery was found in the midden in 1959 trench F1, 1960 trench F2, 1961 trenches 1, 2 and 3, and in the main excavations in trenches A1–4, B1–3, F1–2, G1–4 and H1–2, and the assemblage represents more than 100 vessels, many of them decorated (Chapter 3). The horizontal and vertical distribution of conjoining sherds of pottery has useful implications for the internal stratigraphy of the midden, for sherds from the same pots were scattered over a wide area and at varying depths in the midden. This suggests either that midden material was moved about by human agency or that refuse and/or broken pots went through more than one process of deposition. Pits were dug into the midden at various stages of its accumulation (see below, Phase 2.2), and this will have contributed to the effects of redeposition.

The presence within the midden of structural elements implies an internal phasing which is only partially understood from the results of the excavation. The fact that the main midden area was excavated piecemeal over such a long period, together with the inversion effects of shifting sand, erosion and disturbance from rabbits and animal burials, means that the detailed processes by which the midden accumulated are irrevocably obscured. Nevertheless, there is evidence to support an outline sequence for the internal stratigraphy of the Early Bronze Age midden in the area covered by 1961 trench I and trenches B1, F1, G2 and G4:

1. midden deposits began to accumulate on top of an old turf-line;
2. two palisade slots, pits, post-holes and a large hollow were dug into the midden;
3. a series of stone structures, pits and post-holes replaced at least one of the palisade trenches;

KILELLAN FARM, ARDNAVE, ISLAY

23 The 'drain' and palisade slot in 1961 trench I. The south section was somewhat forward of that re-excavated in 1976 and drawn as section C1–D1. The stones post-date both slot and pit. (Ranging pole in feet.)

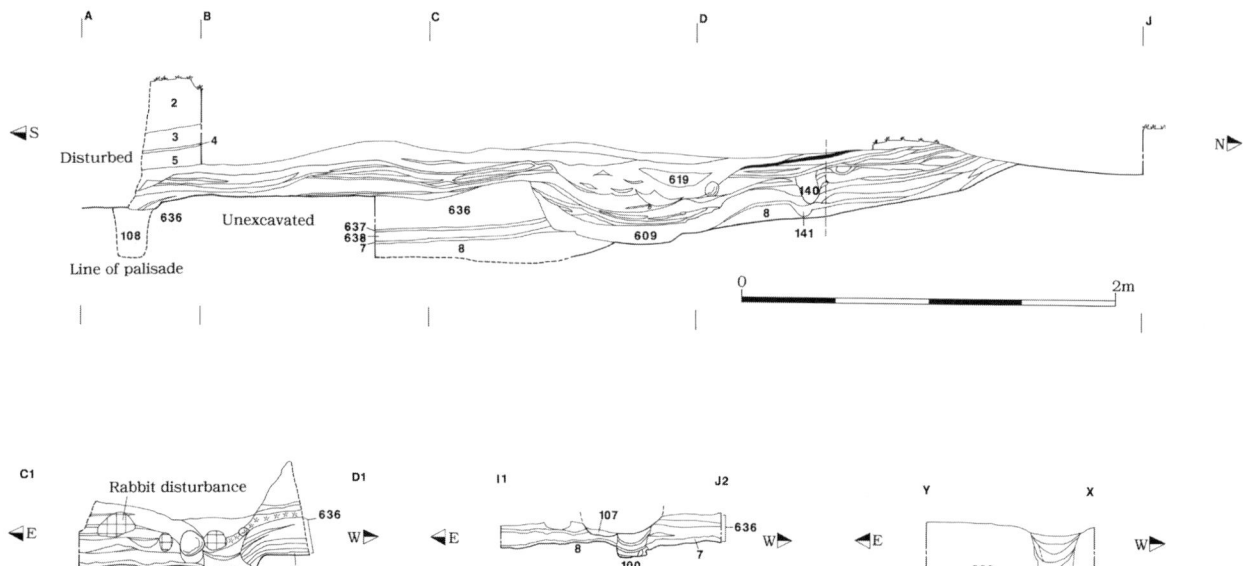

24 Sections A–B–C–D–J, C1–D1, I1–J2 and X–Y across the palisade slots in trench G2.

THE EXCAVATIONS

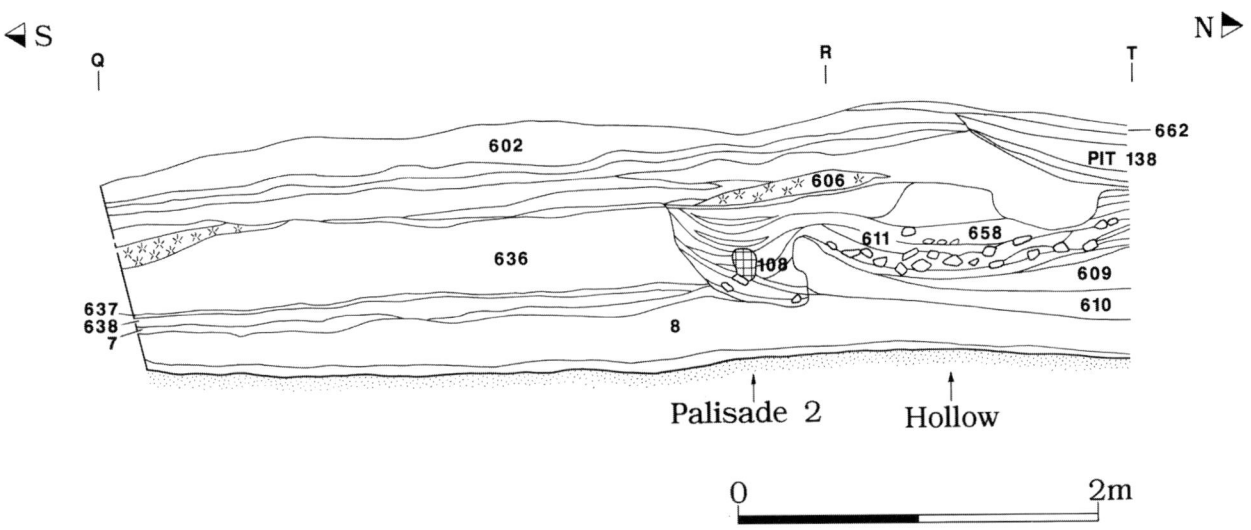

25 Section Q–R–T across palisade slot 108 and the hollow in trench G2.

4. midden began to build up again, filling the hollow and sealing the abandoned structures;
5. a house or working floor was established upslope from the main midden;
6. midden built up on top of the floor and adjacent earlier midden.

The second stage in this sequence (Phase 2.2) is associated with a radiocarbon date derived from charcoal which gives a timespan at two sigma of 2140 to 1740 cal BC (GU–3517) (table 2). This is the only scientific date for the midden, but the cultural homogeneity of the whole midden suggests that the four-hundred year span provided by that single date probably covers the entire history of the Early Bronze Age activity as revealed by excavation.

PHASE 2.1 THE PRIMARY MIDDEN

Intermittent dumping of midden material on top of the old turf-line led to the initial build-up of the Early Bronze Age midden. Initially labelled layer 6a in trenches B1–3 and E2, 5a in A2, 3a in E1 and 2b in A1, the turf-line was subsequently numbered 7 in G1–2 and K1–3 and 13 in L2. The midden was labelled 6 in trenches I–III, B1–3, E2, F1–2 and G1–2, but in A2 was numbered 5, in E1 numbered 3, in A1 and A3 numbered 2, and in G3–4 numbered 3. The primary midden consisted of pale to dark brown sand with interleaving bands of domestic refuse including marine shells, animal bones, flint and stone tools and pottery, and it was up to 0.6m in depth. There is no means of judging how long a period was involved in the accumulation of this primary midden, but it appears to have built up without any significant break. Pits were occasionally dug within it, for example the shallow pits 103 in trench G1 and 104 in trench G2, both of which extended into the silver sand layer 8 (illus 21). No major structures were associated with the midden, and the focus of settlement was presumably outside the area excavated, perhaps farther to the north on the edge of the fen or on higher ground to the west.

PHASE 2.2 TIMBER STRUCTURES WITHIN THE EARLY BRONZE AGE MIDDEN

The first significant episode within the midden was marked by the construction of a number of timber features at the point marked by the top of layer 636 in trench G2 (illus 21). This was presumably a period at which dumping had ceased temporarily in this area of the midden and its surface was being used for other activities.

Palisade slots

Illustration 20 is a revised version of the plan published previously (Burgess 1976, fig 10.4), and

26 Trench G2 at a final stage in its excavation. The section in the background is P–Q–B, and that running across the trench beside the ranging poles is Q–R–T.

(feature 108) appears to have been straightforward, consisting of a narrow slot 0.3m–0.5m wide at the top and 0.38m deep, terminating in an oval pit of the same depth which was dug into the fill of the Mesolithic pit below (feature 132). Palisade 1 (feature 100) was more difficult to understand, partly because it was excavated in two seasons 15 years apart and partly because more than one phase of use was involved. It appeared in 1961 as a slot 0.1m wide and 0.1m deep in the bottom of a linear feature interpreted as a 'drain', which was 0.4m to 0.6m wide at the top and 0.23m deep (illus 20). When this area was re-excavated and extended through the L-shaped baulk in 1976, the slot was not found beyond the south side of the earlier trench B1 (illus 24, sections C1–D1 and I1–J2). Instead the re-excavated feature appeared as a continuous palisade slot varying in width from 0.2m to 0.4m, which terminated to the north in a shallow pit (illus 21). The differences between the plans of this feature in illus 20 and 21 are simply the result of two episodes of excavation and the inevitable erosion between them.

Both palisade slots became filled with midden, and the northern part of palisade 1 was subsequently overlain by three large stone slabs and smaller stones (illus 20 & 23), which belonged to Phase 2.3.

The two palisade slots were both dug from the same point in the midden stratigraphy (layer 636) and were probably broadly contemporary (illus 22 & 24). The distance between them varied from 1.6m at the north to 2.6m towards the south. There was no trace of post-pipes and only a few possible packing stones, including a large grinder (Chapter 5, no 65), and their interpretation as palisades must remain tentative. Their northern points of termination appear to be related to the location of the natural bank, and they were not picked up at all beyond the southern side of trench G2, presumably because they had been destroyed by later activity in the area of trenches B2, B3 and F2.

A primary phase of the midden was thus succeeded by a phase in which the surface of the midden to

it shows at least two structural phases which can only partially be separated: palisade 1 (feature 100) was clearly earlier than the stones laid on top of it, but the relative dates of the other features, both pits and stone structures, are uncertain. One post-hole set into the west side of the sand bank was sealed beneath a large winkle pile in F1. Palisade 1 first emerged in 1961 as a slot in the base of a 'drain' (illus 20; Burgess 1976, 190) and was subsequently identified as a palisade after a second palisade was discovered in 1976.

In 1973, trench B1 clipped the side of another slot some 1.6m upslope to the west of the first (illus 20). The existence of this second slot (108) was confirmed in 1976 in trench G2 and found to run roughly parallel with the first at a distance of about 1.6m to 2.6m (illus 21 & 24). At the same time the northern part of palisade 1 (100) was re-excavated and it was traced farther southwards through the previously unexcavated L-shaped baulk. Palisade 2

THE EXCAVATIONS

27 One of the subrectangular stone settings of Phase 2.3 in 1961 trench I. The flat slabs in the background cover the 'drain'. (Ranging pole in feet.)

south and west of the natural bank was used for activities involving the construction of two possible palisades (it is impossible to judge how many of the other features shown on illus 20 were in use at the same time).

Pits

In addition to the pits shown in illustration 20, which varied in depth from 0.07m to 0.45m, pits of varying sizes and depths were found in other trenches in the main midden area, but it was rarely possible to assign them to a particular phase of the midden. Pits 103–6 and 108 in G1 were truncated and visible in plan only where they cut through layer 6 and into the underlying silver sand of layer 8, but there were traces in section that showed that they had been dug from within the midden layer 6 and were probably either contemporary with the palisades, or, in the case of pit 104, earlier than the palisades (illus 24).

Hollow

A large hollow (feature 609a) was cut by wind erosion into the pre-palisade midden at the same level as the palisades and to the west of palisade 2. It was not visible horizontally, but it appears on sections A–J (illus 24) and Q–R–T (illus 25 & 26), as well as on other sections, implying that it was some 2.0m or more across. The hollow was about 0.6m deep on its steeply cut south side, and it sloped up northwards with the natural rise of the subsoil. Its primary fill was sand, which was deposited prior to the clipping of its south-east edge by palisade 2 (illus 25, layer 609).

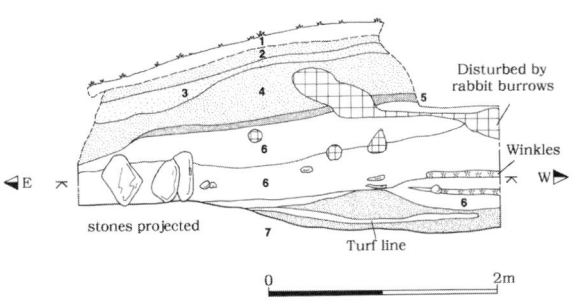

28 The south section of trench F1, showing the upright stones that probably lined a pit cut into the lower midden 6.

29 Trench F1: the natural sand bank crosses the trench in the foreground, the winkle pile is to the right and the upright stones are in the left background close to the south side of the trench. (Ranging pole in feet.)

fire-cracked stones. This was only a few metres to the east of the natural sand bank and may have been part of the same phase of activity represented by the stone settings found in the later excavations.

PHASE 2.4 LATER MIDDEN

After the abandonment and removal of the two palisades, deposition of midden deposits continued above the level of layer 636 in G2 to a maximum depth of 0.4m. These included a very distinctive series of deposits of dense black shell-rich midden, the extent of which was recorded on Burgess 1976, fig 10.3, here reproduced as illus 18. Although lenses of rich midden were interleaved with lenses of paler sand with little organic content, there were no sterile layers and the paler lenses probably represent trampled sandy surfaces as the midden accumulated. Carbonized grain was recovered from G2 midden layers 603d, 606a and 6246 and from G1 102, all of which was identified as naked barley,

PHASE 2.3 STONE SETTINGS IN THE EARLY BRONZE AGE MIDDEN

After the 'drain' had filled in with sand and midden, three large stone slabs were laid on top, perhaps to provide a stable surface. A series of small oval and subrectangular settings of stones were laid out nearby, using both horizontal and upright stones (illus 20, 23 & 27). Colin Burgess suggested that these might have some link with a large pile of winkles in adjacent trench F1 (illus 28 & 29) and that they had perhaps been used for seafood preparation (1976, 192). An arc of upright stones in F1 appeared to line a pit dug through the lower midden (illus 19 & 20) and may belong to a later phase of activity than that represented by the subrectangular settings in trench I.

Stones were otherwise a rare component of the midden. In the main bunker area in 1956 Whittaker found a U-shaped setting of horizontal boulders (illus 20), measuring internally 3.02m by 1.07m, within which was a narrow gully, about 1.2m long and 0.1m deep, which contained carbonized material and

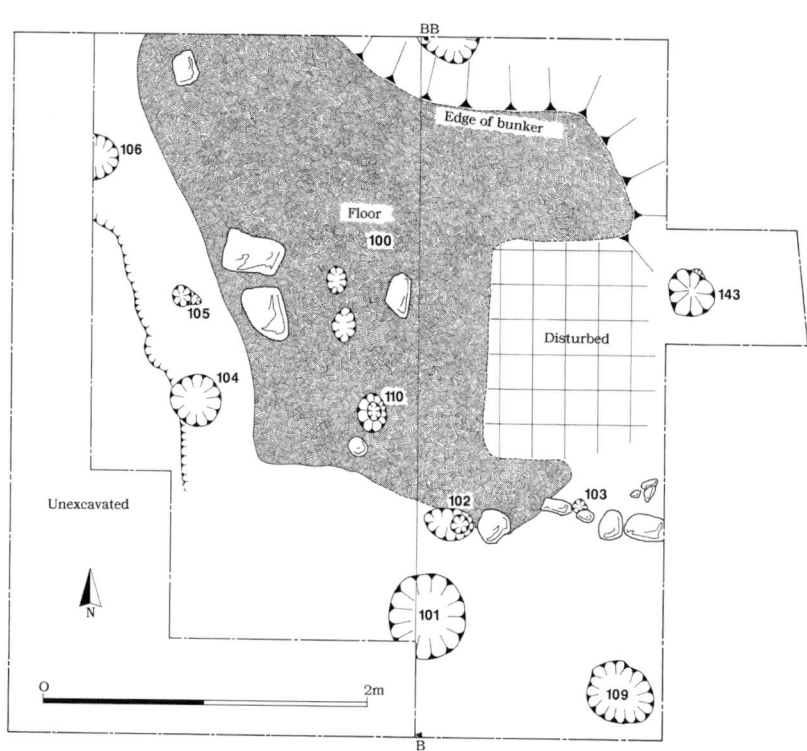

30 Plan of clay floor 100 in trench G4 and location of section B–BB.

THE EXCAVATIONS

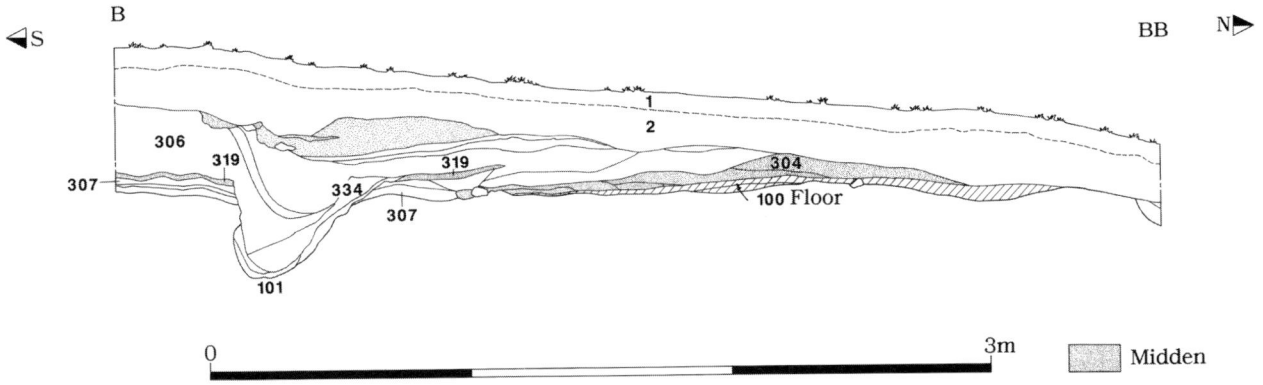

31 Section B–BB across pit 101 and the clay floor 100 in trench G4.

Hordeum vulgare var *nudum*. Conjoining sherds were found in layer 611 in the upper fill of the hollow 609a and in layer 317 in trench G4 abutting the clay floor on the south-east, confirming the contemporaneity of the later midden in G2 with the midden deposits in G4 (Chapter 3, nos 28 & 29). A sample of charcoal identified as birch, alder, willow, hazel, oak and Pomoideae from G2 upper midden layers 607, 631, 655 and the filling of palisade 100 yielded a radiocarbon date with a span of 2130–1748 cal BC (GU–3517; Table 2).

PHASE 2.5   CLAY FLOOR IN TRENCH G4

Trench G4 was laid out in November 1976 by Stratford Halliday in the open bunker immediately west of G2, in order to explore what appeared to be the floor of a house (illus 30 & 31). It was not unfortunately possible to relate the floor precisely to the stratigraphy recorded in G2, but it was clearly relatively late in the overall sequence. The floor consisted of a brown clayey layer (feature 100), the thickness of which varied from a few millimetres to patches of composite floor deposits up to 100mm thick (illus 31), and only its laminated clay content made it recognizable. The floor lay on sand upslope from the main Early Bronze Age midden. The sand beneath it was not excavated but was mottled grey/ grey and silver sand, which is likely to have been the equivalent of the grey and silver layer 8 beneath the hollow at the north end of section A–J (illus 22). The south-western perimeter of the floor followed at a distance of 0.5m the line of a shallow cut in the sand, which represented a deliberate levelling of the house-site (illus 30 & 32). Pits 106, 104 and 102 were well situated to have been post-holes for a house wall, but only 104 was of a suitable depth at 0.35m (106 and 102 were only 0.16m and 0.15m deep respectively). None of the pits shown on illustration

32 Trench G4 from the north, showing the clay floor and, in the right background, the cut in the sand that allowed a level floor.

29

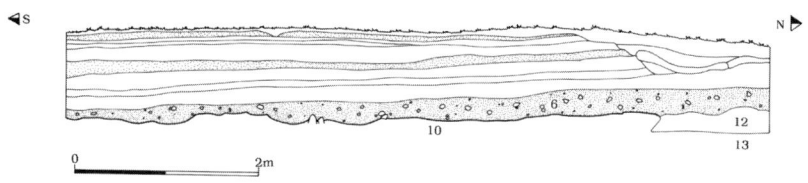

33 Section A across trench L2 at the level of the occupation floor 10.

overlying the midden and petering out against the rise of the slope, which indicates that its duration spanned the Middle Iron Age. A blue glass bead dating to the 7th–10th centuries AD (Chapter 6, no 14) was found in the upper part of layer 5, which provides a *terminus ante quem* for the formation of the layer.

30 was truncated and all, apart from 104, were too shallow to have held load-bearing posts (pits 101 and 109 were at a lower level than and unrelated to the floor). It is therefore impossible to estimate the size of the structure to which the floor (100) belonged, or even whether the floor was associated with a roofed building, for it may have been an open-air working area. A few large slabs lay on the western part of the floor (illus 30 & 32).

PHASE 2.6 FINAL MIDDEN

Above the clay floor in trench G4 were layers of midden deposits (layer 3, subdivided into 301–5), which were noticeably less shell-rich than Phase 2.4 of the main midden apart from a dump of shells in the south-west corner of G4 (illus 31). Owing to the fact that trench G4 was excavated after the completion of the excavation of G2, it was not possible to correlate their respective stratigraphies on the ground, which would only have overlapped slightly because the level of the underlying silver sand (8) was rising towards the north. Nonetheless, conjoining sherds of pottery were found in the midden in G4 and in G2, thereby demonstrating the continuing processes of midden redeposition already noted.

The Early Bronze Age midden was sealed by a layer of windblown sand, the 'marker' layer 5 in the overall site sequence (numbered as 1959 F1 III; 1960 F2 IV; 1961 5; 1973 E1 2, E2 5, F1–2 5, A2 4a, B1–3 5, C 5; 1976 G1–2 5, G4 2, H1–2 5). There is no evidence to date either the start of this sand blow or its duration, but the excavators identified its presence in the eastern part of trench J1,

PHASE 3
THE LATE BRONZE AGE/ EARLY IRON AGE OCCUPATION

In 1976 a trench 3.5m square was opened on the machair plateau to the west of the main bunker in order to discover whether there was any trace there of the Early Bronze Age midden (illus 7). The work was begun under the direction of Colin Burgess but was carried out mostly under Peter Hill after the end of the main season of excavation. A possible house floor was found and the trench was subsequently extended to form a final trench L2, 7.6m square. Layers 1–5 represented relatively recent sand-blows and turf-lines, layers 6–9 were pale yellow brown cultivated soils and layer 10 was a dark brown black sand, the

34 Trench L2 under excavation. The central dark patch is the remains of layer 10 as it was being stripped off to reveal the stone-built structures and pits. The souterrain 118 is in the foreground and the stone-lined pit 126 in the centre.

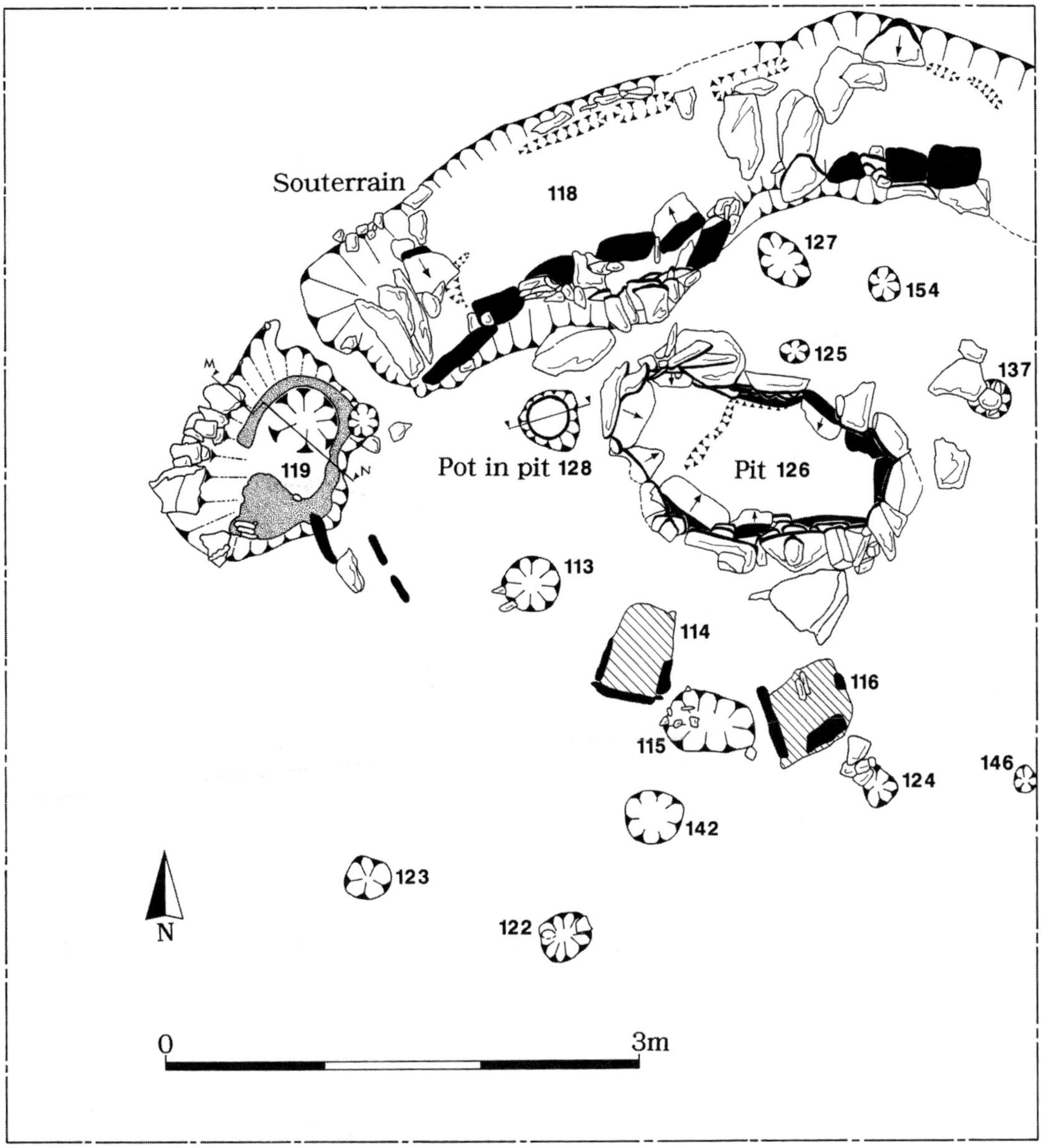

THE EXCAVATIONS

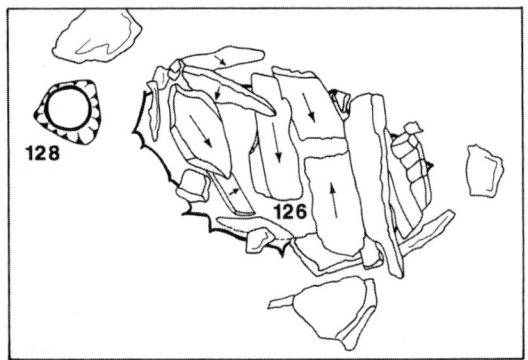

35 Plan of stone-built structures and contemporary late features in trench L2, and, below, plan of the roofing lintels over pit 126.

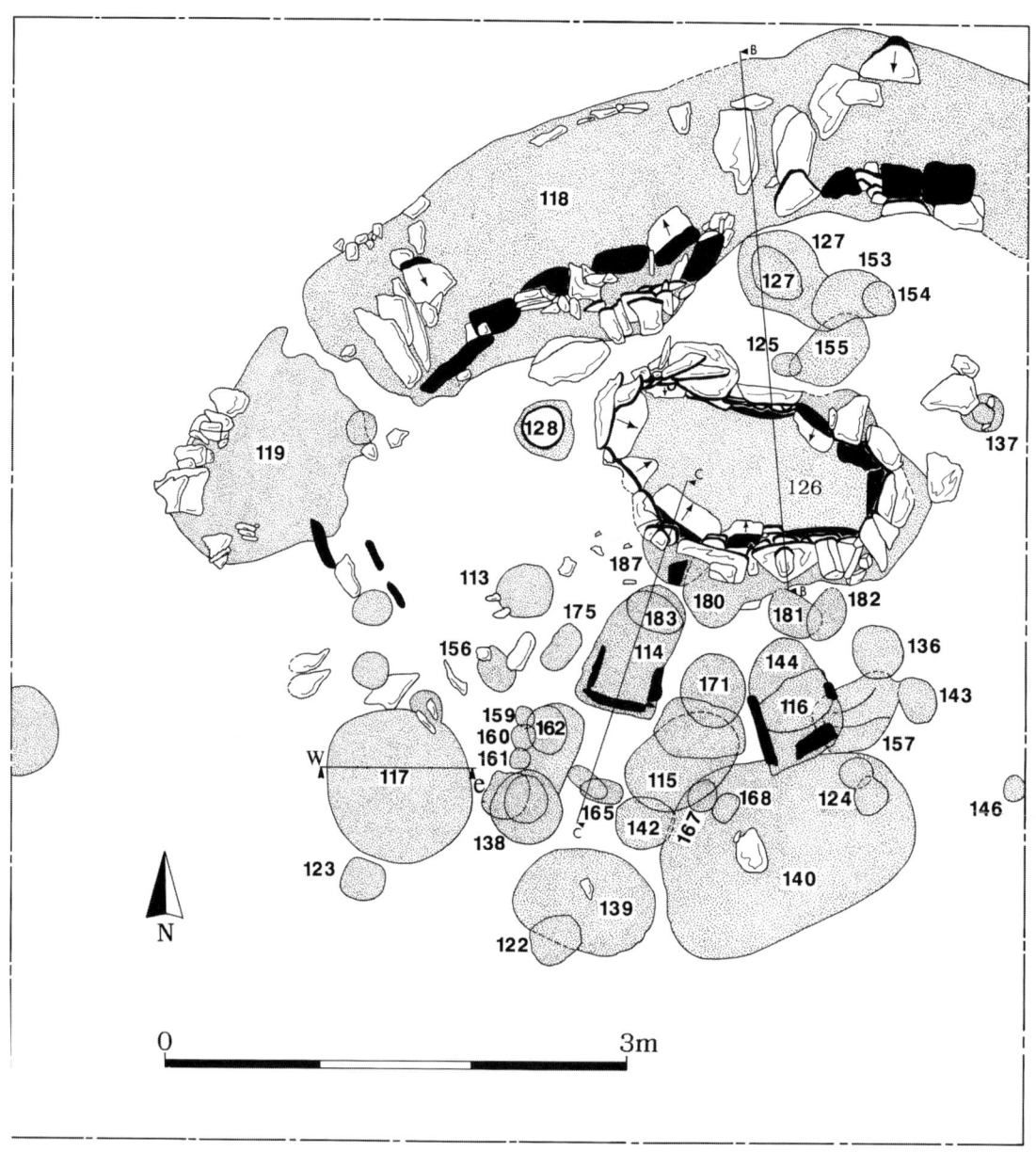

36 Plan of all features in trench L2 at the level of the sand (11) below occupation layer 10.

possible house floor (illus 33). Beneath layer 10 and its associated pits and other features was an iron-rich ginger sand (layer 11), and beneath that a silver sand (layer 12), apparently redeposited by wind erosion from downslope on top of a turf-line (layer 13) that sealed an unleached ginger sand (layer 14).

PHASE 3.1

Within and beneath layer 10 were numerous postholes, pits, hearths and other features, some seen only in section and not in plan, but all sectioned and recorded in detail (greater detail than is presented here will be found in the archive). They were clearly visible in the sand beneath layer 10, but, either the dense black nature of the latter obscured the points from which they had been dug within it, or they were clearly earlier than layer 10, which represented a late phase of activity on the site (illus 34). Most of the sections through individual features were necessarily drawn after the removal of layer 10. Thus, despite the

THE EXCAVATIONS

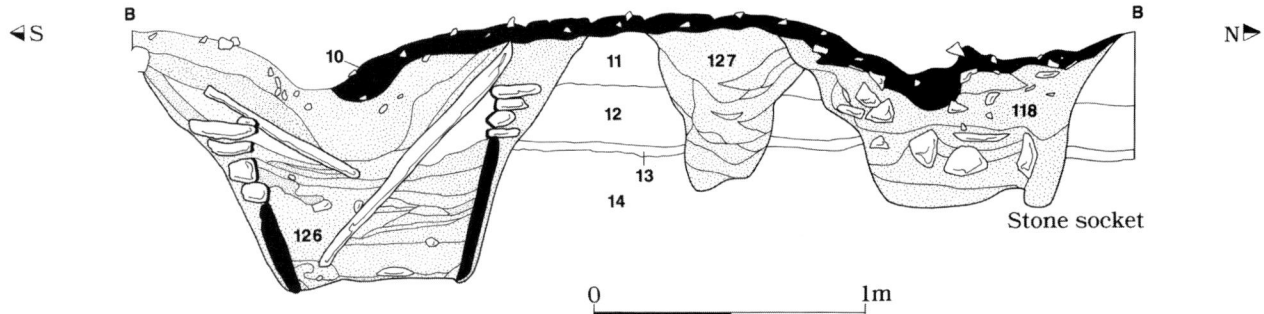

37 Section B–B across the stone-lined pit 126, pit 127 and the souterrain 118 in trench L2.

detailed recording, the overall relative stratigraphy is unclear, and illustrations 35 and 36 represent between them an amalgam of at least five structural phases, which were the result of intense activity over a single continuous and probably short-lived period of time.

The major structural elements comprise a stone-built souterrain (feature 118), a large stone-lined pit (feature 126) and two stone-lined hearths or boxes (features 114, 116), together with a large number of pits and post-holes showing several phases of construction and individual complexities. The stone-built features appear to have been broadly contemporary and to have become gradually engulfed by sand before the accumulation of layer 10. Some pits and post-holes may have been contemporary with the stone structures, but others were certainly earlier. For example, pit 140 was cut by hearth 116 and pit 139 by pit 122 (illus 36), pit 127 was cut by the souterrain 118 (illus 37) and pit 183 was overlain by hearth 114 (illus 38). Pit 117 was about 1.6m in diameter and 1.4m deep, and its filling suggested that it had been used, latterly at least, as a dump for the burnt debris from hearths, including 29g of charcoal (Chapter 8) (illus 39, 2). The lower of the main layers consisted of grey-black sand (11703), the middle of greasy black sand with charcoal (11702), and the top of brown/black sand and charcoal (11701). Pit 117 also contained an unusual quantity of pottery (Chapter 3, no 143). Many of these pits had been dug through not only the redeposited silver sand layer 12 but also the old

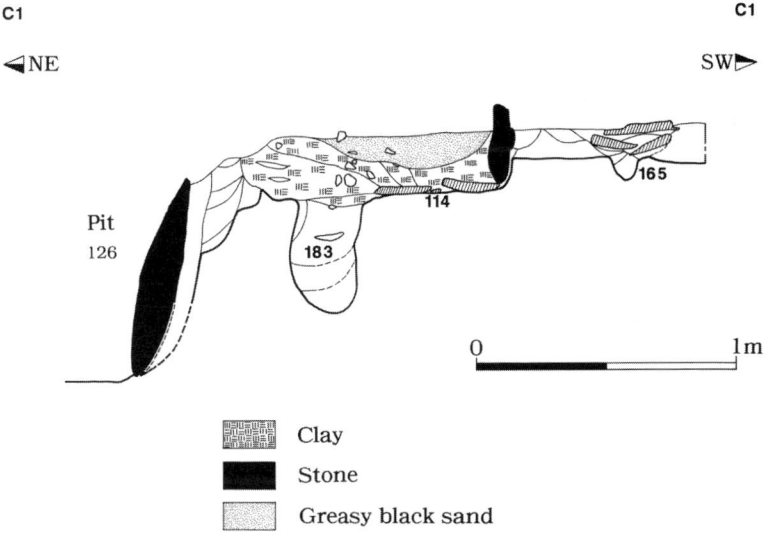

38 Section C1–C1 across the stone-lined pit 126, hearth 114 and underlying pit 183, and pit 165 in trench L2.

KILELLAN FARM, ARDNAVE, ISLAY

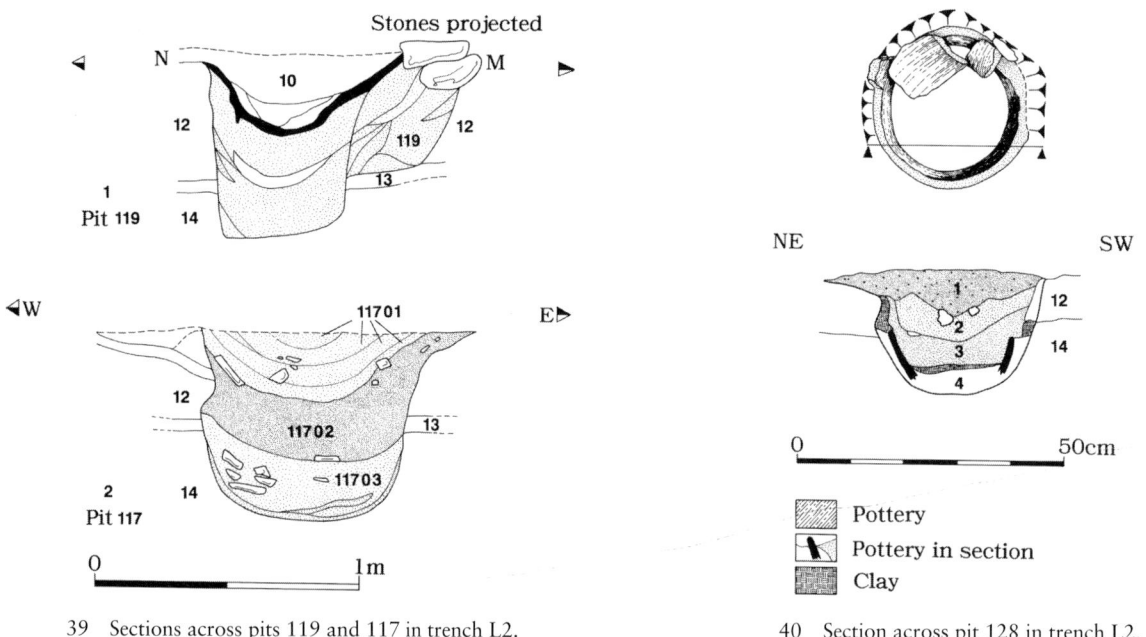

39 Sections across pits 119 and 117 in trench L2.

40 Section across pit 128 in trench L2.

41 Stone-lined pit 126 with lintels in place, and the section B–B.

THE EXCAVATIONS

42 Stone-lined pit 126 with fallen lintels and lintels in place.

the site, including 64.6g of charcoal (Chapter 8). If it had been roofed with stone lintels, none survived either in its fill or elsewhere in the trench. There was evidence in the form of a double thickness of orthostats of major repairs to the stonework along the south side. The floor was not paved. The souterrain and the stone-lined pit 126 had been dug from the same level and, assuming that the souterrain had originally been roofed, their roofs would have been at the same level (illus 37). Despite the lack of evidence for a roof, there can be little doubt of the nature of 118 as a souterrain, for its dimensions and building technique are suitable, although its function is uncertain. Access was presumably from the east on the downslope beyond the edge of the trench.

The stone-lined pit 126 survived almost intact, its roof lintels partially slumped into the interior (illus 40 & 41). Like the souterrain, the method of construction had been to dig out a pit from the natural sand and line it with orthostats and horizontal walling. The oval pit measured 2.1m by 1.45m and 0.75m deep, with sloping sides (illus 42 & 43). Lined with stone the internal dimensions were 1.35m by 0.85m at the top and 0.93m by 0.57m at the flat bottom, which was not paved. At the east end, three roofing lintels were still in position, but the rest had slumped into the pit at a time when it was still virtually empty of fill (illus 37). Collapse of the roof led to partial infilling of the pit by layers of sand, presumably derived from gaps in the walling and roof. Two conjoining slots across the floor of the pit had originally held two upright slabs, which suggested that, in an earlier phase, it was smaller in size with a length of about 1.0m. This interpretation is supported by the contrast in building technique shown by the two ends of the pit: east of the slots the pit wall was lined with orthostats, whereas to the west it was lined with horizontal stones. Access to this pit must always have been by removing one or more roof lintels, but there was no evidence to suggest its function.

'Hearth' 114 consisted of base slabs and three upright side-slabs forming an open-ended box 0.35m by 0.45m, and it had been built in a pit dug through into the natural sand (illus 38 & 45). The east side-slab was a re-used possible saddle quern (Chapter 5, no 72). 'Hearth' 116 had undergone modification but began as an open-ended stone box of similar dimensions. In both cases, the fill as it survived consisted of a basal sandy clay, with greasy black sand above, and the inside faces of their side-slabs and base-slabs were not burnt, and thus their interpretation as hearths must remain tentative.

turf-line beneath the silver sand (layer 13) and into the ginger sand below (layer 14).

The souterrain 118 survived incompletely but its original construction was clear: a trench averaging 1.1m wide and 1.0m deep with battered sides was dug into the natural sand and the sides were lined with orthostats to create an internal space 0.6m–1.0m wide. Where most complete along the south side, there were horizontal slabs on top of the orthostats to make up the height to that required for the roof. The trench came to a rounded end within trench L2 and extended in a gentle curve for 4.5m to the east side of L2, and its total length is therefore unknown, for it clearly extended beyond the excavated area. The souterrain had begun to fill with sand by the time that the orthostats along the north side of the souterrain had been removed, leaving empty slots in the floor. Subsequently it was deliberately infilled with material from elsewhere on

35

43 Stone-lined pit 126 emptied of its filling but with lintels in place.

The pits varied considerably in diameter and depth, but their filling consistently showed a banding of sandy layers of pale to dark colour, implying that they had been left open to infill gradually and naturally. The complex history of pit 119 was typical (illus 39, 1): a pit some 0.8m deep had filled with lenses of clean and dirty sand before being cut by a deeper pit, about 1.2m deep and 1.16m in diameter, which itself became filled with sand. There was evidence of intense burning in some features, for example in the upper fill of pit 119 (illus 39, 1), but there was no direct evidence to indicate metalworking and the cause of the burning is likely to have been secondary use of these features as hearths. The short arc of walling to the north-west of pit 119 could be interpreted as a windbreak for this secondary hearth, though it could also relate to the floor represented by layer 10 (see below).

Pit 128, immediately west of the stone-lined pit 126, contained the basal part of a large and heavy pot, fitting the pit tightly as if the latter had been

44 Stone-lined pit 126 entirely excavated, with the souterrain 118 in the right background and pit 128 with its clay and pottery lining.

THE EXCAVATIONS

dug for that purpose (illus 35 & 43). As it survived, the maximum internal diameter of the vessel was 0.25m. The base was missing and had been replaced by a layer of brown clay, and the same clay adhered to the walls of the pit above the pottery lining. The purpose of the pot and clay was presumably to make the pit watertight, and heavy sooting on the internal surface of the pot suggests that this was a fire-pit. Unfortunately, only two sherds of this pot have survived (Chapter 3, no 145).

It is difficult in this necessarily simplified account to convey the extraordinary complexity of the site in L2. Despite the apparent brevity of its occupation, the density of intercutting pits suggests intense activity perhaps of an industrial nature, which may have included bronze-working. Minute quantities of metalworking debris were recovered, which R F Tylecote, who visited the site in September 1976, identified as connected with the working of a high-lead copper-alloy (*in litt*). There were 1.6kg of small pieces of fired clay or daub, but their function is unclear.

PHASE 3.2

All the pits and stone-built features of Phase 3.1, apart from the two putative hearths (114 & 116), had become filled with layers of sandy material before being sealed by the development of the black floor layer 10. The horizontal extent of layer 10 is shown in illustration 46 and, while the northern edge is likely to reflect a true edge, elsewhere in the trench the irregular edge had resulted from depredation from later agricultural activities. Layer 10 varied in thickness from about 30mm to 150mm, and its surface was scored by plough-marks and spade-dug furrows (see below, Phase 6). The furrows had exposed the tops of upright stones belonging to features 114 and 116 which would otherwise have been covered over by layer 10. These two 'hearths'

45   Hearth 114 showing the upper filling of greasy black sand.

may have belonged to an early phase of the activity represented by layer 10.

The most significant aspect of the occupation layer 10 is the correlation between the north-west edge of the layer and the curve of the northern side of the souterrain, which can hardly be fortuitous despite the chronological gap between them and which suggests not only a relationship between the two but also a genuine edge to the 'floor'. The chronological gap indicated on stratigraphical evidence need not, however, have been of significant duration. The short arc of boulder walling to the north-west of pit 119

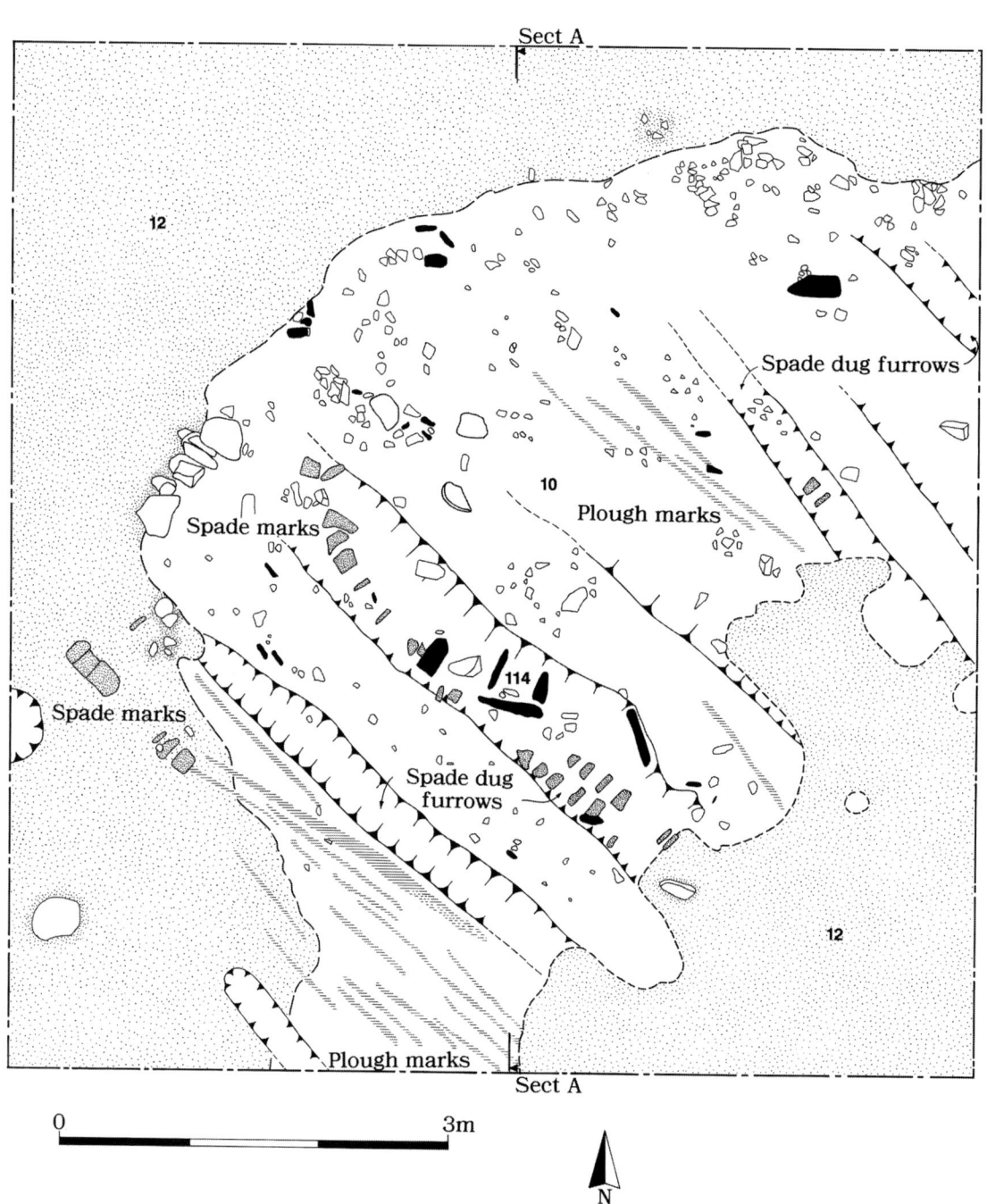

46 The top of layer 10 in trench L2 showing ardmarks, spade-dug furrows and spade-marks.

might then represent the remnant of a stone revetment against the sand, the inner face of a house wall, the rest of which has been removed by later agricultural activities. Such a house, if circular, would have been about 10m in internal diameter, and the post-holes recognized as late features (122, 123, 124, 125, 137) could have held internal roof supports, although as they survived they were on average no more than 0.10m deep. Two pits containing burnt material (113, 115) had been dug through layer 10 and may have belonged to this phase or may have been considerably later in date. Layer 10 continued to accumulate after virtually all associated structural features had gone out of use, perhaps implying that the area continued in use as unroofed working space.

DATING AND ARTEFACTS FROM TRENCH L2

Two radiocarbon dates were obtained from the features in trench L2 (Table 2). Charcoal identified as birch, hazel, willow and oak from the upper and middle fill of pit 117 gave a dating span of 808–517 cal BC (GU–3518), while charcoal of alder, birch, hazel, oak and Pomoideae from the occupation layer 10 gave a span of 828–412 cal BC (GU–3519), thereby suggesting that there can have been no significant chronological gap between the infilling of the pit and the accumulation of layer 10. The entire site is thus likely to belong to the Late Bronze/Early Iron Age period. In most cases, the various features in trench L2 were barren of finds, but there was pottery from several early pits (144,146,152,178–9), from the souterrain 118, from the upper filling of pits 119 and 126 which derived mostly from layer 10, itself containing scattered sherds, and from a late post-hole 123 (Chapter 3, nos 142–9). Layer 10, the souterrain 118 and pits 119 and 126 also yielded 79 flints (Chapter 4). Overall, the range and quantity of artefacts supports the interpretation of the complex as relatively short-lived. The wall-construction of the souterrain was unlike that of the souterrain in trench J2, which, at least in the small part that was excavated, was built with boulders, but the problems of revetting sand can be met in several ways that carry no chronological implications.

PHASE 4
THE MIDDLE IRON AGE SETTLEMENT

Excavation in trenches J and K on the plateau to the south end of the site revealed midden deposits and stone structures, including a round house and a later souterrain, belonging to the Middle Iron Age. At the time of the excavation and the discovery of the early medieval silver pin (Chapter 6, no 1) in 1976, it seemed possible that this area of the site might be part of a major early medieval settlement, and Colin Burgess decided as a matter of policy that the excavation should not be completed in order to leave its further exploration in the future to a specialist in the period (Colin Burgess pers comm).

PHASE 4.1 THE ROUND HOUSE

The earliest structural phase in area K represented the remains of a stone-built round house. Natural mottled yellow/orange sand (layer 9) was sealed by the dark sand of an old turf-line (layer 7), on which the basal course of a house wall survived in trench K2 (illus 47, 102; illus 48). The band of stones was almost 2.0m wide and was situated on a slight slope, with traces of levelling into the slope to take the outer edge of the wall, and a curving inner wall-face. A single stone possibly representing the continuation of the wall-face was clipped by the north-east corner of trench K3, and the arc thus formed suggests a circular building some 10.0m in internal diameter. A short arc of stones about 1.5m south of the wall-face may indicate that the house was later modified with a contracted internal area (the line of this inner arc has been projected on to section A–B in illus 49), or, in view of the drop in ground level to the south, it may be the remains of an internal bench. The fact that no stonework was found in trench J3 or in the north-east part of K3 (apart from the single stone in the very corner of the latter) suggests that the circular building was dismantled when the souterrain of Phase 4.2 was built, and the stones perhaps used then as building material. Contemporary with the round house wall was a floor deposit represented by layer 502, which was associated with Hearth 112, an irregular shallow pit about 0.7m across, filled with burnt material.

In L2, in a layer of pale brown sand (6) sandwiched between the Late Bronze/Early Iron Age occupation described above (layer 10) and relatively recent sand-blows and turf-lines (layers 1–5), were traces both of ploughing and of spade-dug furrows, though the two were not necessarily contemporary. The traces of ploughing were in the form of ard-marks, mostly preserved in section at the base of layer 6 and as shallow grooves in the surface of the earlier occupation level (illus 46 & 50), but they were also visible in the sand on which the latter had built up.

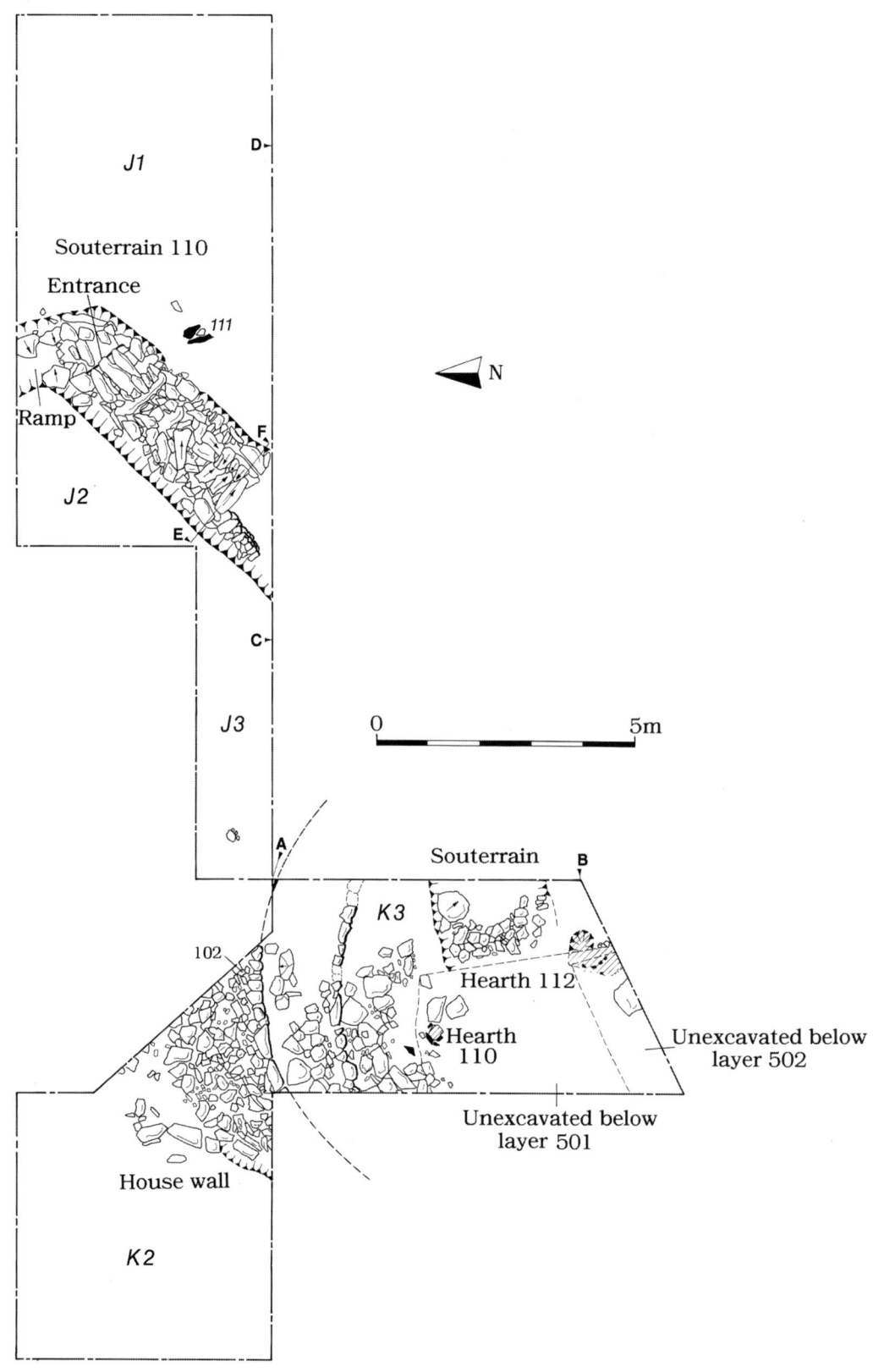

47 Plan of souterrain and possible house in areas J and K.

THE EXCAVATIONS

48 Trenches K2 and K3: on the left the house wall 102 and top right the stone pile 108. Two slabs lining hearth 110 are visible bottom right.

The spade-marks were only visible in the sand, those beneath the occupation layer matching up with the hollow troughs in the surface of the layer but invisible in the dense black material of the occupation layer itself. There was considerable variation in the widths of the spade-dug furrows, from about 0.25m to about 0.6m, and it is likely that this variation reflects more than a single season of cultivation. The ridges were

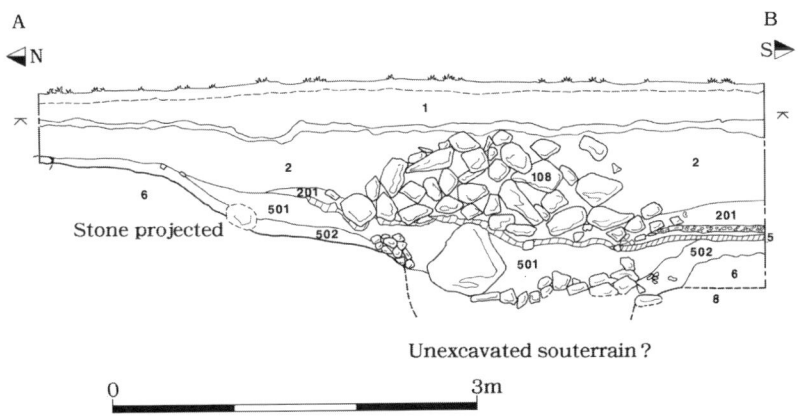

49 Section A–B in trench K3, showing the edge of the house wall at the north end, stone pile 108 and the possible top of the souterrain.

41

KILELLAN FARM, ARDNAVE, ISLAY

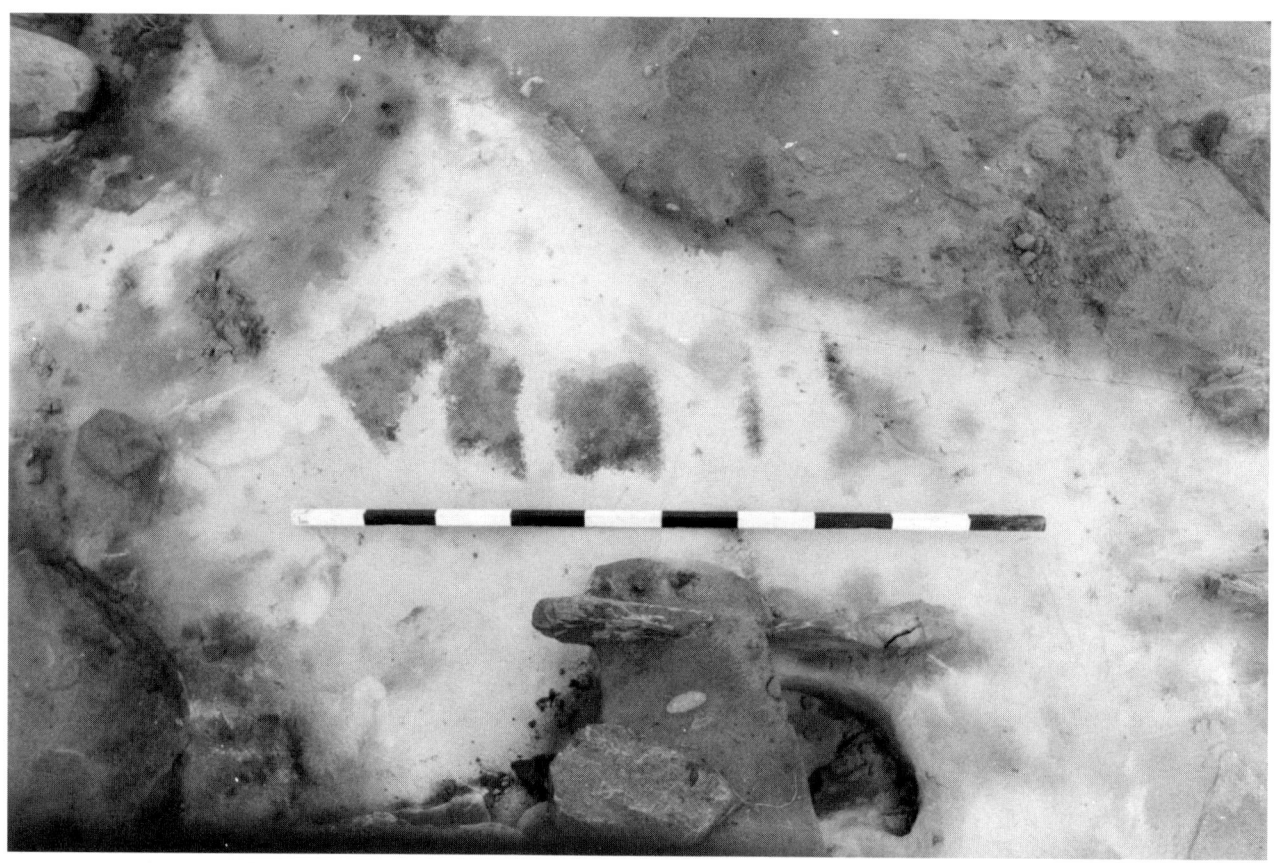

50 Dark square to triangular spade-marks appeared in trench L2 in the sand below the occupation layer 10.

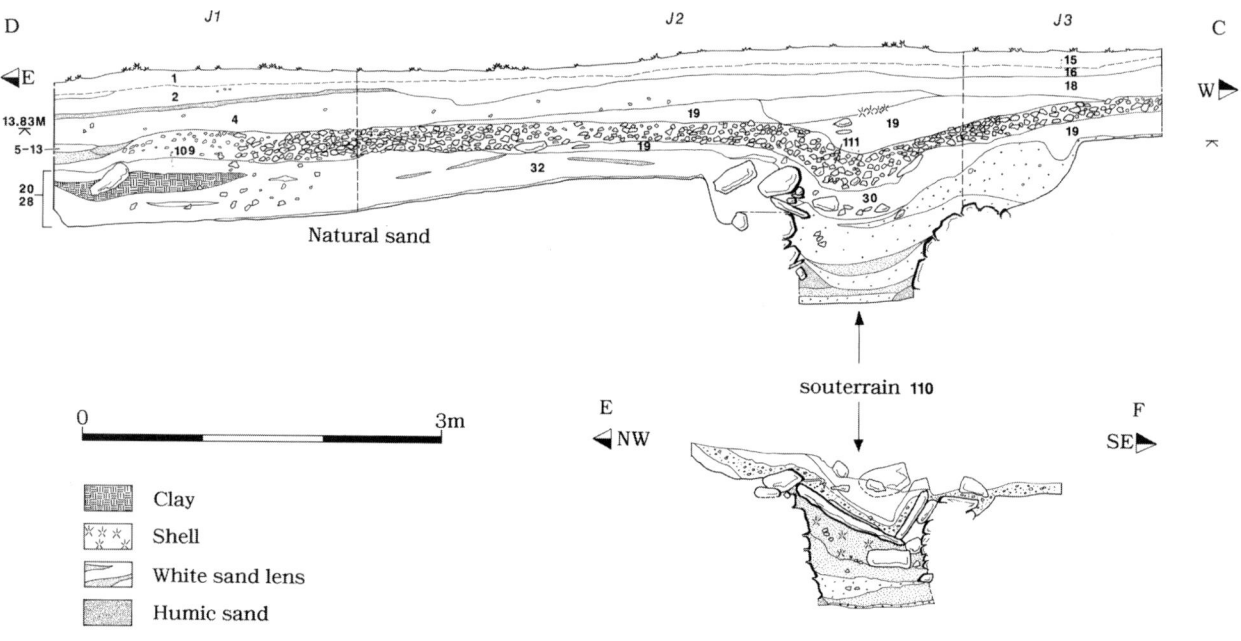

51 Sections D–C and E–F across the souterrain 110 in trench J2.

THE EXCAVATIONS

52 The boulder wall of souterrain 110 in trench J2 where fully excavated close to the south side of the trench.

and internally the souterrain was 0.9m deep from the underside of its roofing lintels (illus 51, section E–F). The floor was not paved in the small collapsed sector of the souterrain that was excavated between the section line E–F and the south side of the trench (illus 53). North of section line E–F the interior of the souterrain was left unexcavated. There appeared to be an entrance at the north end of the stretch exposed in trench J2, marked by three large slabs laid on top of and at right angles to the final roofing lintel and served by a sloping ramp giving access to the interior of the souterrain (illus 53). Both the ramp and the entrance were partially obscured by tumbled stones, but the hollow ramp was traced at an oblique angle from the entrance to the north side of J2 (illus 47). Where excavated, the roof was missing and the

53 Souterrain 110 in trench J2: in the foreground the entrance ramp curves round to the lintelled entrance to the souterrain, and beyond can be seen the collapsed roofing lintels.

c 1.5m to 2.0m apart from crest to crest. To judge by the average width of the spade-marks, the blade of the spade was about 200mm wide (8 inches) (illus 50). There was no dating evidence either for the ard-marks or the spade cultivation, but they are unlikely to be markedly later than the activity below them, and it seems possible that they may belong to the stone round house of Phase 4.1.

PHASE 4.2 THE SOUTERRAIN

In trenches J1–2 a construction trench (feature 113) for a souterrain (110) was dug into natural yellow sand (29). The trench was 2.0m wide and 0.8m deep (illus 47 & 51), and the sides were revetted with large boulders to form a passage 1.0m wide internally (illus 52). Large flat slabs were used to span the width as lintels, with smaller slabs on top,

43

54 It is possible that the souterrain in trench J2 extends south-westwards into trench K3, reappearing beneath the stone pile against the east section A–B.

souterrain itself had partially filled with layers of sand, presumably derived from seepage between the boulders of its walls. The removal of this part of the roof must have taken place before the midden (layer 30) was deposited on top. The souterrain was not dismantled and should still exist.

The souterrain was exposed for almost 6.0m in trenches J1–2, from its entrance to the point where it ran into the south side of the trench. The top of a feature of similar width appeared in the east side of trench K3 (illus 47 & 49, 113), again dug through a dark humus-rich sand (layer 502, the round house floor deposit) into natural yellow sand (layer 6, the equivalent of layer 29 in trench J2) and covered by stones. In the south-east corner of K3 where the natural subsoil sloped downwards, the feature was also cut into the Mesolithic silver sand (layer 8). The excavation of K3 was not however completed and it is not known whether this putative extension of the souterrain extends across the width of the trench. If it can be assumed that the two structures in trenches J1–2 and K3 are part of one souterrain, its length is at least 15.0m (illus 54).

The 'souterrain' in K3 was sealed by a layer of grey brown sand and one of black midden containing animal bones, marine shells and pottery (illus 49, section A–B, layers 501 and 5). This black midden is likely to have been the equivalent of the midden sealing the souterrain in J1–2 (layer 5/32/30/19), especially as it contained discrete piles of winkle shells in both areas (K3 109, J2 103). An iron sickle (Chapter 6, illus 91, no 3) was associated with the winkles in K3.

It is impossible to establish without further excavation whether there was a structure at ground level to which the souterrain belonged. In K3, the roof of the putative extension of the souterrain was sealed by a layer of grey brown sand (501), in which a hearth lay, which may belong to the period of use of the souterrain. Hearth 110 was only 0.28m square, built of stone with upright stone slabs forming a kerb round three sides of a basal slab, and two large horizontal slabs nearby to the east may have been used as pot rests. The hearth was filled with sand mixed with carbonized material, mostly willow charcoal (Chapter 8), which spread out round the two

THE EXCAVATIONS

55 Large boulders lay along the line of the souterrain in J2.

PHASE 4.3 THE MIDDEN

The souterrain in J was sealed by a substantial layer of domestic midden deposits (layer 32/30/19), which accumulated (or was deliberately redeposited) around and over the boulders on its roof. In K3, a thin layer of midden (layer 5) was deposited over the stones interpreted as the roof of the souterrain, and a pile of boulders placed on top (feature 108, illus 49 & 54). It is difficult not to see these stones as equivalent to the band of boulders along the souterrain in J, here perhaps marking one end of the souterrain.

The midden in the eastern part of trench J1 was divided into two horizontally by a thin layer of sand (14), the upper midden consisting of layers J1 5–7, 10, 11, 14 and the lower of layers J1 21, 23, 25–8. The extent of the midden is uncertain, but it appears to have been a localized patch. Overall the midden was up to 0.5m thick and contained substantial numbers of bones of cattle, sheep, pigs and red deer (Chapter 7), many shells of limpets, winkles and cockles (Chapter 9) and many sherds of plain pottery (Chapter 3, nos 150–69). Bone artefacts include a perforated bone mount (Chapter 6, illus 92, no 12), but there were very few flints (Chapter 4). Dating evidence is provided by two radiocarbon dates derived from cattle bone, both of which indicate that the midden accumulated during the period 183 cal BC to cal AD 224 (Table 2, GU–3516 and GU–3515). These dates also offer a *terminus ante quem* for the souterrain, providing that the midden accumulated *in situ* and had not been redeposited.

PHASE 4.4 COBBLED SURFACE

A cobbled surface 0.2m thick, perhaps a path, was laid down over the midden and across the line of the souterrain (illus 51, section D–C, layer 109; illus 56). Both midden and cobbles slumped into the top of the souterrain where the roof of the latter had collapsed or been removed (illus 51, section D–C).

adjacent horizontal slabs. The fact that the entrance ramp for the souterrain in trench J2 leads to the northwest might suggest the former existence of a house in that area, since souterrains were often entered from within above-ground structures, but no trace of any building remained. Over the roof of the souterrain in area J were piled large boulders, as if the intention were to ensure that the line of the souterrain was obvious at ground level (illus 55 & 56), and this may suggest that it was an entirely free-standing structure rather than partially within a house.

56　Small cobbles were laid across the souterrain in trenches J1–2.

57　Possible bedding-trenches were dug into sterile sand upslope from the house wall in trench K2. The main bedding-trench crosses from bottom left to middle right, and another bedding-trench approaches from the right at right angles to the first.

THE EXCAVATIONS

58   The possible bedding-trenches in trenches K1–2: in the farther trench K1 two bedding-trenches lie parallel to the one in trench K2, and all three meet the main bedding-trench crossing trench K2 from bottom right to middle left.

PHASE 5
EARLY HISTORIC ACTIVITY

A silver pin set with garnets (Chapter 6, illus 90, no 1) was found at the base of layer 201 in trench K3 and cannot be associated clearly with any major structural phase of the site, although a hearth (110) lay nearby (illus 47). It is likely to date from the 7th or 8th centuries AD, and other finds of this period from K3 layers 2 and 201 include an iron knife, bone pins and a bone playing piece (illus 91–2, nos 2, 7, 8 and 9). Another artefact of Early Historic date recovered from Kilellan is the bent shank of a bronze loop-headed dress-pin (illus 91, no 5), which was found in a disturbed context in 1961 trench I (layer 4a of yellow brown sand, which also contained a spent cartridge case, above the 'marker' layer 5 of white sand). Both pins indicate activity in the area in the 6th to 8th centuries AD. A small blue glass bead from G2 layer 5a (illus 92, no 15) was also a stray loss.

It is possible that a hearth found by Whittaker (Hearth A) in an open bunker between the later trenches E and J belonged to this period or later, because the stratigraphy described by Whittaker was closer to that of trenches J than to that of trenches E. Its location in an open bunker means, however, that it could equally well date from relatively recent times. The hearth was oval, 0.36m long internally, and kerbed with nine large upright slabs, with a gap at one end where there were two horizontal stones, and it was full of ash, identified at the time as derived mostly from oak. On a flat slab about 0.4m to one side of the hearth were eleven pieces of green serpentine and one of green ozocerite (Chapter 6, illus 93–4, no 18), and from the hearth came a piece of copper-rich ferruginous quartz or chalcedony (no 17). Robert B K Stevenson suggested in a letter to James Whittaker that the serpentine pieces were industrial polishers. The wear patterns on them indicate that they were cut by hand, probably with a metal wheel and hard sand. Among the NMS accessions attributed to Hearth A is a triangular bevelled smoother of metamorphic mica schist (no 19), but it was not mentioned by Whittaker or Stevenson in their correspondence, nor was it included in Whittaker's photograph of the finds from Hearth A. In many ways it would be more at home with the finds from outside the cave at Kilchoman, which Whittaker excavated in the same seasons as his work at Kilellan. None of these artefacts is diagnostic of date, and they may all relate to the presence of tinkers or packmen, who were certainly active in Argyll from the late 16th century onwards (Roger Leitch pers comm).

PHASE 6
LATER ACTIVITIES

Within the relatively recent upper levels of sand and old turf-lines on the higher ground in trenches K1–2 were traces of activities for which there is no direct dating evidence and which are presumed to be of relatively recent date. Above the midden and cobbling were accumulated layers of windblown sand (J1–3 4/18, J1–3 3/17, J1–3 2/16; K1–3 2). In K1 and the north-west part of K2, where layer 2 was separated from sterile basal sand only by an old turf-line, there were the remains of possible bedding-trenches in the form of U-shaped slots averaging 0.4m wide and 0.3–0.4m deep. They appeared to form part of a grid with its side running along the edge of the plateau and extending inland, and they had been dug from an old turf-line below the yellow brown sand of layer 2 into sterile orange yellow sand (layer 6) (illus 57 & 58). They were filled with mottled orange and brown sand. Drainage would have been unnecessary on this sandy soil, and interpretation in terms of a standing structure seems the most likely.

Chapter 3

The pottery

ROSEMARY COWIE

The ceramic material from all phases of the site totals 8398 pieces weighing 60kg, to which may be added 409 pieces of daub and clay weighing 3kg. Table 3 gives a breakdown of the pottery from the site as a whole.

Owing to the rarity of contemporary domestic assemblages, it was felt that the Early Bronze Age pottery from Kilellan merited treatment in some detail. In particular, it was hoped that despite the variable quality of the recording in the early seasons of the excavations, information might be gleaned regarding the patterns of deposition of the pottery and that light might be shed on activities carried out at the site. In attempting to set the assemblage in its wider context, specific consideration was given to the possible relationship between the pottery from Kilellan and the nearby site of Ardnave (Ritchie & Welfare 1983).

The later phases of occupation at Kilellan (sites L2 and J/K) produced a far smaller quantity of pottery than the Bronze Age midden. It was hoped that analysis of the plainware would help to elucidate the nature and date of the later occupation phases on the site.

The assemblage was analysed following the methodology outlined in PCRG 1992. As a result of post-excavation work carried out prior to 1982, a large proportion of the pottery had been sorted and joined but no comprehensive catalogue had been made. The entire collection was therefore initially catalogued by the writer, together with any available contextual information. No fabric analysis was carried out, and the fabric groups must be regarded as provisional. Copies of the archive catalogue and a full discussion of the pottery are lodged with the site archives.

THE EARLY BRONZE AGE MIDDENS

Approximately 101 to 120 pots appear to be represented, the uncertainty being due to the fact that some vessels are represented only by tiny fragments while others, identified as separate vessels on the basis of decorative scheme, may in fact derive from vessels with contrasting decoration (see below). It has not been practicable to attempt an estimate of the maximum number of vessels represented owing to the difficulty of accounting for the large quantities of plain wall sherds. The midden produced very little daub and, where provenanced, it accounts for less than 1% of the Bronze Age assemblage by weight.

The Early Bronze Age midden covered an area of some 650 sq m and in places the deposits were up

TABLE 3
Total quantities of pottery and daub from all seasons.

	No of pieces	% pieces	Weight gms	% weight
Bronze Age trenches, all seasons	6914	82	55285	91
Trenches H & C, 1973 & 1976	11	1	217	1
Trench L2, 1976	344	4	1357	2
Trenches J & K, 1976	1129	13	3835	6
Totals	8398	100	60694	100

to 1m thick. Trenches producing Early Bronze Age pottery (catalogue numbers 1–138) were as follows: KN 59 F1; KN 60 F2; KN 61 1, 2, 3; KN 73 A1, A2, A3, A4, B1, B2, B3, F1, F2; KN 76 G1, G2, G3, G4, H1, H2.

Prior to 1976 no contextual distinction was made between the midden deposits and the fill of pits and post-holes incorporated within it. In 1976 an attempt was made to unravel the stratigraphy of the midden but this met with only partial success. Furthermore, Burgess commented that in the 12 years between the 1961 and 1973 seasons of excavation 'the machair bluff covering the main settlement area had lost half its area to wind erosion' (1976, 186). Despite such extensive erosion, only four contexts were contaminated by modern pottery, namely: KN 76 G2 4, KN 76 H1 2, KN 76 H2 1 and KN 76 H2 602.

The quality of the sherds is in general very good. Even sherds from surface collections are relatively unabraded, but there is some obvious abrasion on sherds from within the midden deposits (6% by sherd count, 4% by weight).

Fabric

All the pottery was stone-tempered. A provisional series of ten fabric divisions was made macroscopically, on the basis of the predominant rock type present. A full description of the fabric types identified is included with the site archive.

Fabric groups 1–3, which are dominated by varying proportions of white-black speckled, subangular inclusions, account for 68% of catalogued vessels and are also in the majority among the uncatalogued, plain wall sherds. Fabric groups 4–10 account for only 17% of catalogued vessels. An eleventh category comprises miscellaneous vessels which could not be assigned to a particular fabric group (15% of catalogued vessels), either because inclusions were indistinct or sherd size too small to permit identification. All fabrics are coarse but show a range of variation from fairly 'finely' crushed inclusions from 1–4mm in size up to very coarsely crushed mixes with grits up to 15mm in size.

The fabric divisions should be viewed more as a working guide to the distinctions between individual pots and pot groups. They do not relate to differences in the clay sources utilized (although, distinctions in clay type were occasionally noted between pots with similar lithic temper), nor do they relate to any technological differences implied by the choice of a particular fabric 'recipe'. It should be noted, however, that at the level of the individual vessel, almost every pot is distinguishable in terms of feel, colour, firing and inclusions. The only exceptions to this are the sherds from vases with all-over-herringbone decoration (nos 26–31) and those from jars with ridged internal bevels (nos 60–7), which are generally so similar in all respects that it is only on the basis of slight differences in rim diameter and decoration that they have been separated into individual vessels.

Form

In order to facilitate description of the assemblage, vessels were assigned to one of four categories, primarily on the basis of capacity and rim diameter,

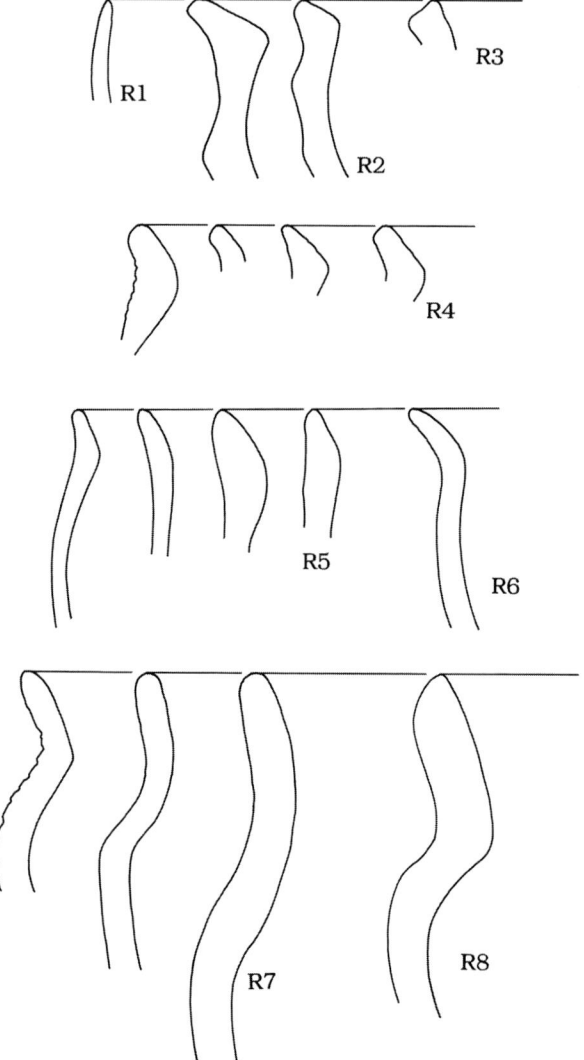

59 Pottery rim classifications.

TABLE 4
Breakdown of pottery by form.

Type	Form	Rim forms	Rim diameter	Wall thickness	Estimate of height	No of vessels min	No of vessels max
A	Cup	R1; R2; R4	60–100	4–7	>42	4 (5%)	4 (3%)
B	Bowl	R2	170	11–13	130	1 (1%)	2 (2%)
C1	Small vase	R2; R3; R4; R5; R6; R7	120–200	6–12	>155	30 (41%)	43 (34%)
C2	Large vase	R2; R4; R5; R7; R8	200–300	7–14	>200	16 (22%)	25 (20%)
D1	Medium jar	R7; R8	200–280	13–19	?	15 (20%)	33 (26%)
D2	Large jar	R7; R8	300–400	13–19	>380	8 (11%)	21 (16%)
Totals						74 (100%)	128 (100%)

but also on criteria such as wall thickness and fabric when further refinement was thought to be merited (illus 59). Table 4 gives the percentages of the different forms represented in the assemblage, but must be interpreted with caution: in the first place, the creation of a terminological framework is inevitably a somewhat artificial construct and every framework will have its disadvantages. Moreover, not only has an unknown proportion of the site been lost to erosion, but selective biases may well have been in operation in the deposition/dumping of material (a point discussed further below).

The term 'cup' describes the smallest vessels with rim diameters of less than 100mm; the term 'bowl' has been retained, following established Food Vessel terminology, to describe the vessel already published by Burgess as an example of an 'Irish-Scottish Tripartite Bowl' (1976, 200). The third category comprises a range of taller vessels, for the most part decorated, but occasionally plain, which have been subdivided into two groups: small vases (with rim diameters between 120mm and 200mm) and large vases (with rim diameters between 200mm and 300mm). The vase group incorporates some vessels formerly included by Burgess under the umbrella heading 'shouldered jars' (1976, 196). However, in 1976, no substantial reconstructions of decorated 'shouldered jars' were available; indeed some decorated vessels then assumed to have been exceptionally tall are now known to have been or more modest proportions (for example, Burgess 1976, 198 figs 10.7:4 & 5).

Burgess's term 'shouldered jars' has, instead, been reserved to describe the fourth category of vessels, comprising both plain and decorated pots with rim diameters between 200mm and 400mm. Such vessels comprise perhaps the largest, and certainly the heaviest, component of the assemblage and would, in a funerary context, have been labelled 'urns', but in a domestic context they may more appropriately be described as 'jars', particularly in view of their presumed function (see below). Inevitably, there is some overlap between the larger vases and the smaller end of the jar range, particularly with regard to rim diameter and wall thickness. In the absence of evidence for height, in many cases, a distinction between the two groups may, nevertheless, be made on the basis of fabric: in general, grit sizes are larger in the latter category and the clay used consistently fires to an orange-brown colour over a blue-grey core, as compared to the rather darker colours of the vases. In only one instance does a 'vase' appear identical in fabric to a so-called 'jar' (compare the small rimless vase no 74 and the large decorated jar no 96).

While differences in capacity, wall thickness and fabric are factors of function (cf Rice 1987, 207–43), the significance of subtle differences in vessel morphology, such as variations in rim and shoulder form, is more open to doubt. For recording purposes, rims were subdivided as set out in table 5. The slightly everted or upright rim form (R7) is the most common type, while rims with a concave internal bevel (R8) are an infrequent variation on this theme. The expanded rim (R2) comes a rather distant second in frequency to the upright rims. Both R7/8 and R2 forms occur on vessels with angular shoulders. Rim groups R4–6 are intermediate between the expanded form and the upright form. No pot with an R4 type rim has a shoulder surviving and, represented only by small rim sherds, the vessels may not form a coherent group. Both the R5 and R6 rims appear on vessels with slack or rounded shoulders; in the case of no 29, which has an R5-type rim, the shoulder is non-existent. As rim groups, R1 and R3, are represented by only one or two vessels each, it is uncertain what emphasis should be placed on these groups. One rim form, R9, is represented by a single small flat-topped rim sherd from a surface collection; the sherd is unlike any of the excavated material, and is not considered further.

The few surviving bases at Kilellan are flat and, occasionally, slightly concave. Type B1 has a wall angle varying from upright to gently flaring. Type B2 has a footed appearance due to the presence of finger indentations made during the forming of the base. In the few cases where basal diameter can be estimated, sizes range from 86mm to a maximum of 160mm diameter, while the thickness of surviving basal sherds varies from as little as 10mm to over 40mm. The fragmentary basal angle sherd (no 8), published as a survival of a round-based Late Neolithic bowl (Burgess 1976, fig 10.8:11) may more easily be interpreted as deriving from a portion of wall, curving outwards from the flat base of an expanded rim-type vase (compare the profile of no 10). A similarly decorated, expanded rim sherd (no 8), in the same

TABLE 5
Rim forms.

Rim type	Form	Internal bevel	Shoulder	Min no of pots (estimated)
R1	simple, pointed, inturned	none	none	1 (2%)
R2	expanded, with/without external bevel	narrow (14mm) to broad (30mm)	angular	11(18%)
R3	broad, external bevel	none	no firm evidence	1 (2%)
R4	expanded and everted, with/without external bevel, varied shapes	steeply sloping	no evidence	7 (11%)
R5	slightly expanded and everted, variable/fluid in shape	ill-defined, narrow (15–23mm)	rounded/slack/none	5 (8%)
R6	simple, pointed, outcurved	shallow (15mm), smooth curve between internal bevel and wall	rounded/slack	3 (5%)
R7	simple, pointed, upright or slightly everted	deep (30–60mm), marked angular profile of bevel to body	angular, occasionally rounded	30 (49%)
R8	simple, pointed, slightly everted, intermediate between R2 and R7	deep (c 53mm), concave	angular	2 (3%)
R9	flattened, concave top; moulding below rim interior. NB unstrat	none	no evidence	1 (2%)
Totals				61 (100%)

THE POTTERY

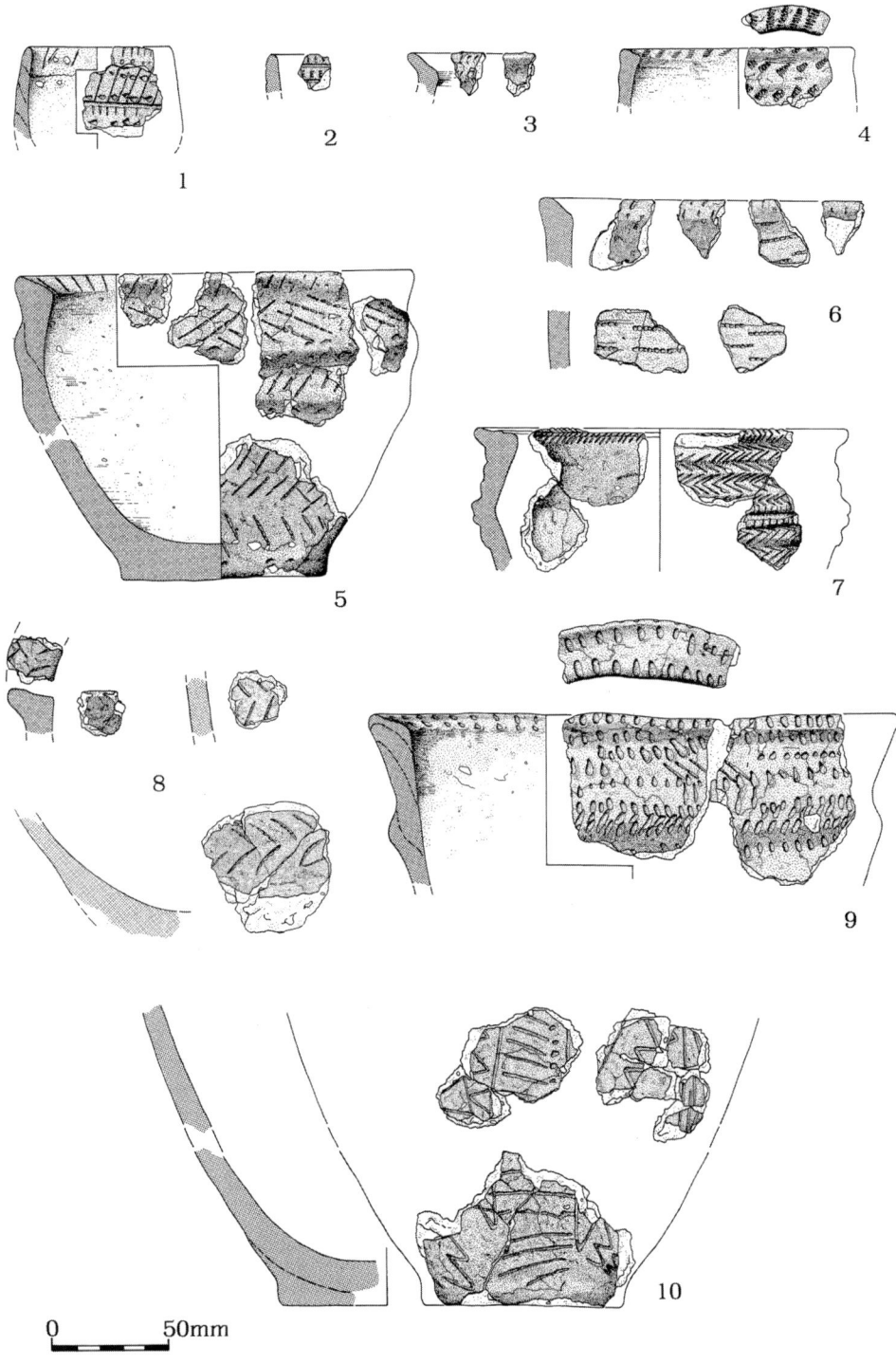

60 Pottery nos 1–10.

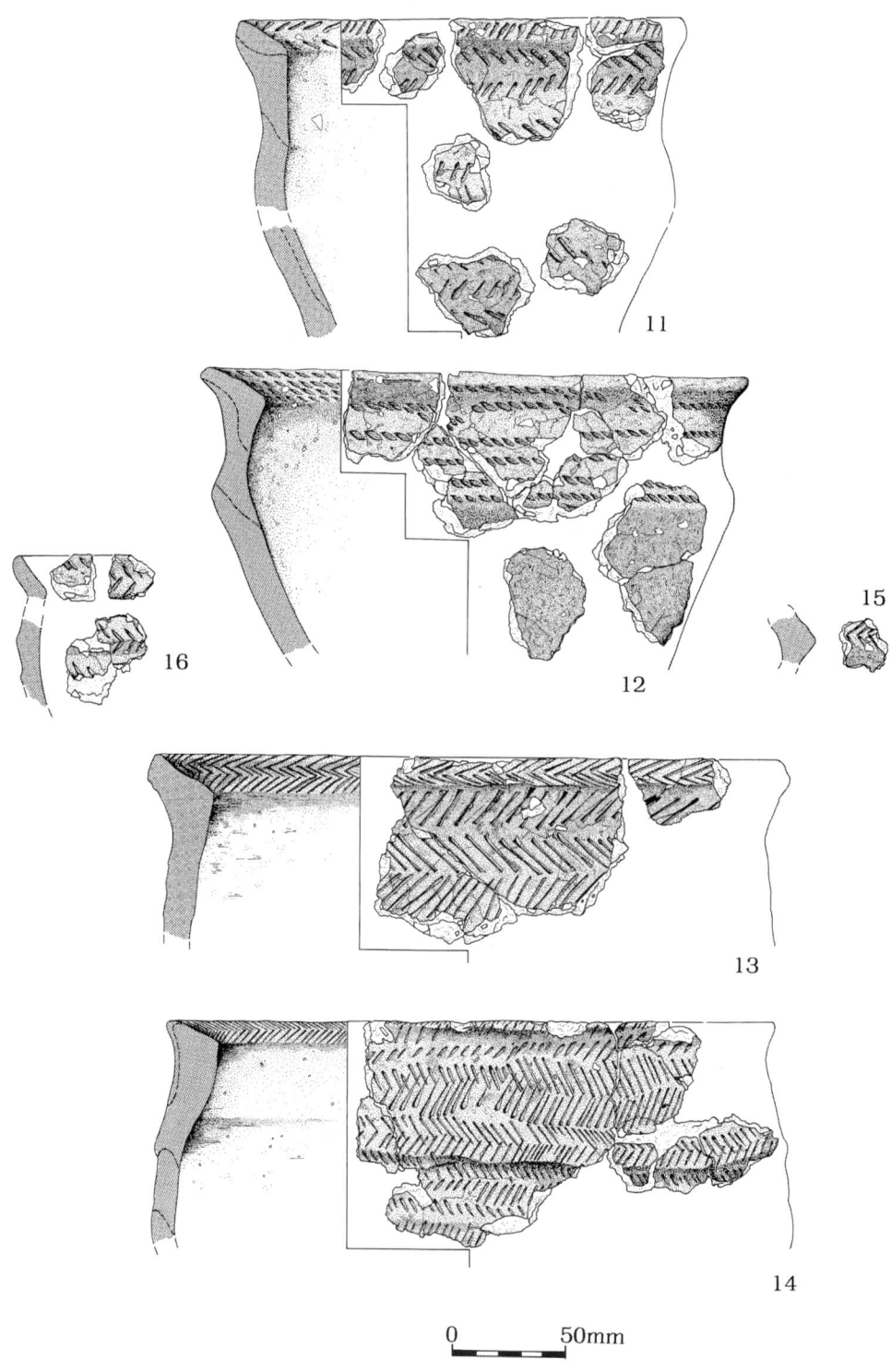

61 Pottery nos 11–16.

distinctive fabric (F8), is assumed to derive from the same vessel.

Burgess (1976 and *in litt*) has suggested that certain vessels in the assemblage may have had round bases, partly in view of the absence of much evidence for flat bases and partly because this would have been a practical solution for pottery vessels intended to be grounded in sand. While this suggestion cannot be excluded entirely, the present writer is inclined to see the pottery as primarily flat-based. Flat bases may be few in number but they are present, whereas there is no unequivocal evidence of round-based pottery. Burgess may well be correct in suggesting that vessels may have been driven into sand to keep them upright, but one upshot of this might then have been the physical separation of the component portions of vessels following breakage, leading to under-representation of the lower bodies and bases. If the sandy environment of the settlement had been a significant factor governing the form of the pottery, then a similar response might have been expected from potters at the nearby settlement of Ardnave (Ritchie & Welfare 1983), whereas the vessels there are indisputably flat-based.

CAPACITY

Given the marked lack of pots with complete profiles, it has only been possible to calculate the approximate capacity in a few cases (ie nos 1, 5, 26, 33, 35, 43, 88). This shows a range from 112cc (no 1) to approximately 23,372cc (no 88).

MANUFACTURE

The assemblage shows abundant evidence of ring construction, not only in the cross-sections of sherds, but also in the undulations, produced by finger-indentations, which are frequently found running horizontally around the interior surface of a vessel just above the ring junctions (eg no 29). Examples of vessels without obvious signs of construction technique are rare (eg nos 5 & 33). In the majority of cases, the construction join is obliquely scarfed. Many sherds have broken along such joins, indicating that the upper edge of each coil dried out slightly before the next ring was applied, resulting in poor bonding of the rings (cf Rice 1987, 125–8). Oblique construction joins are at their most obvious in the restored vessels, no 29 and no 35, the latter showing clearly that the construction join becomes longer and more pronounced, the closer the position of the ring is to the base of the vessel. Ring construction was used both for making very small vessels, such as the cup (no 1) whose total height was little more than 42mm and for the construction of large jars, such as no 88, with a height of over 380mm. Generally speaking, the more massive the vessel, the greater the thickness of the individual rings.

In a few instances, vessels show the use of the tongue-and-groove construction technique (eg nos 71 & 89), while some reveal use of both tongue-and-groove and obliquely scarfed construction joins in the same vessel (eg nos 14 & 90). The most elongated example of a tongue-and-groove join is shown by the large jar (no 89), where the join attaching the neck to the lower body measures 95mm in overall height. This vessel, which was found *in situ*, is also noteworthy for displaying, not only a marked disparity in thickness between upper and lower wall sherds (with the neck sherds appearing top-heavy), but also pronounced textural differences; these suggest that the lower body was coil- or ring-built in contrast to the upper body apparently formed from a single slab of clay (cf Stevenson 1953; Rye 1981; Rice 1987).

Rims and shoulders frequently reveal the use of a number of different construction strategies, varying even between rims of similar outward form (nos 9, 11–14, 43 & 46). Evidence for base construction is scanty given their poor survival rate. The base of the large jar (no 75) was probably modelled in one piece with the lower wall, while the remainder of the body was added by coil construction.

SURFACE TREATMENT

All the pots are well smoothed, although rims and necks generally show a higher degree of finishing than lower body sherds. Grits have largely been removed from the exterior surfaces, but invariably protrude on the interior surfaces. Wipe marks are sometimes very clear (cf nos 31, 56 & 90) and are especially common on both large plain jars and jars with ridged internal bevels. The jar (no 90) must have been wiped after the clay had partially dried out giving rise to distinctive drag marks on the lower body. The fine 'brush' marks on the exterior surface of no 62 and just below the applied horseshoe of no 71, must have been produced while the clay was still wet and plastic. The interior surface of the neck of no 30 shows evidence of thinning of the clay using some type of knife. Vertical trimming marks are visible above the base of no 69.

The colour of the plain pottery is generally an orange-brown over a grey or blue-grey core. A few pots are blackened, perhaps deliberately (eg nos 47–9 and see also below). The colour of decorated pots varies between pinkish brown, orange-brown and in some cases a yellowish brown.

DECORATION

The decoration of the Early Bronze Age assemblage is rich and varied. Decorated vessels account for 23% of the assemblage by sherd count and 35% by weight. However, the majority of the plain vessels were thicker-walled and of larger capacity than the decorated vessels and may thus be over-represented in the sherd count. If the figures are adjusted to take account of the large numbers of plain sherds made in the same fabrics as the decorated jars and which may,

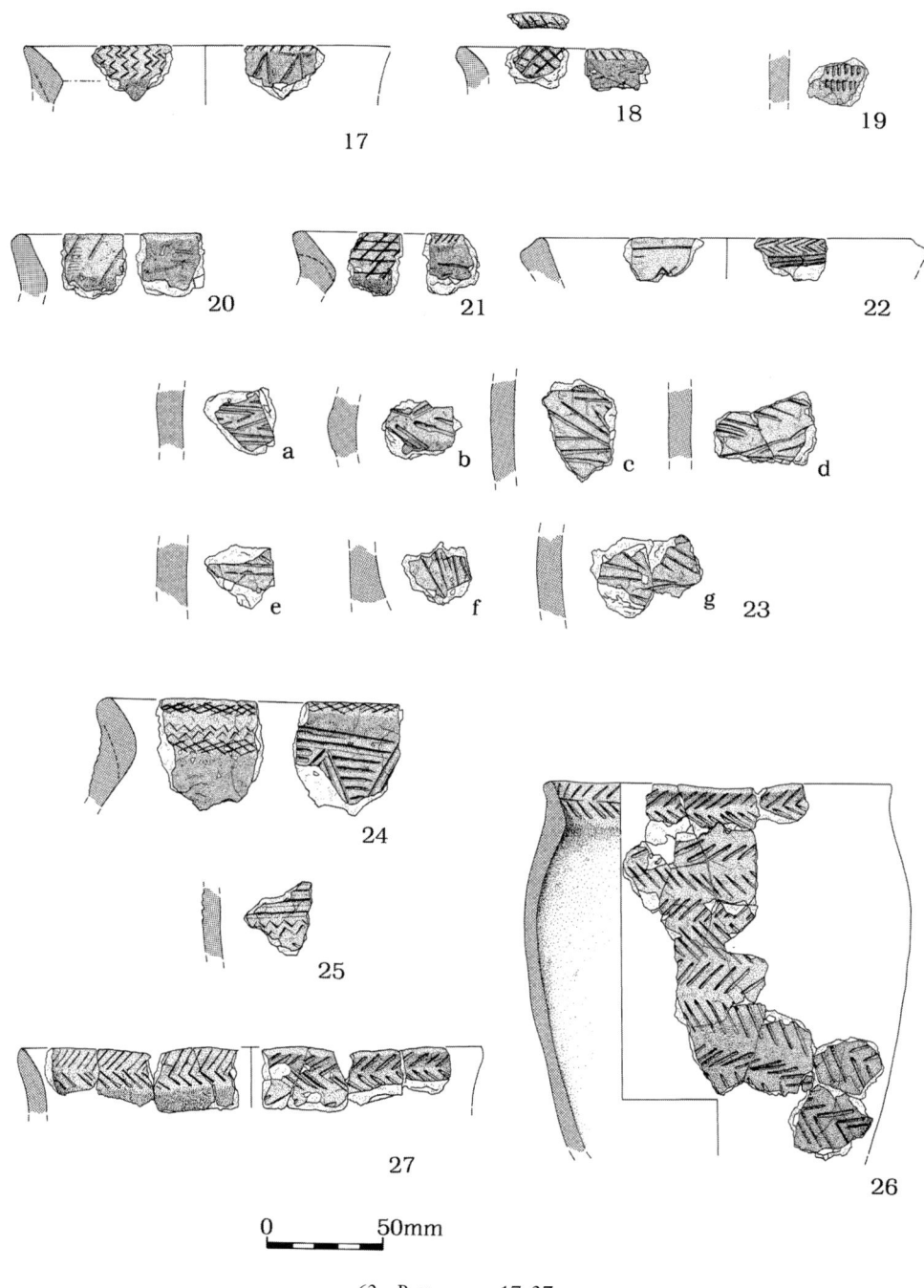

62 Pottery nos 17–27.

TABLE 6
Combinations of decorative techniques.

	Impressed	Incised	Grooved	Applied	Cordoned	Infilled
Infilled						
Cordoned						
Applied						
Grooved				X		
Incised			X	X	X	X
Impressed		X	X	X		X

therefore, derive from decorated jars with plain lower bodies, then the figure for decorated pottery may be as high as 38% by sherd count and 48% by weight. It should be stressed that the high ratio of decorated to plain vessels in the itemized catalogue (a minimum of 78 (77%) decorated vessels to only 23 (23%) plain vessels) simply reflects the difficulty of trying to distinguish individual vessels on the basis of plain sherds.

Decoration was generally carried out while the clay was still wet (cf Rye 1981, 66). Impression is the commonest decorative technique (69 vessels), followed by incision (34 vessels), grooving (19 vessels), applied (11 vessels), cordoned (2–4 vessels), infilled decoration (max 3 vessels) and false relief (1 true false-relief and 1 pseudo false-relief). These decorative techniques are not exclusive of each other (table 6).

Impressed decoration (table 7) involved the utilization of a wide variety of both man-made tools and unaltered organic materials. Shells used included *cardium edule* (eg no 35) and *mytilus edulis* (eg no 34). A chisel-type tool was used to form the crisp, wedge-shaped impressions on no 74, while a blunt-ended tool created the tadpole-shaped stab and drag impressions seen on no 14. The twisted cord decoration is always

TABLE 7
Relative frequency of impressed decorative techniques.

Tooled	16
Shell	14
Spatula	8
Twisted cord	7
Point	7
Whipped cord	3
Comb	2
Fingernail	1

TABLE 8
Relationship of motif to form and rim type.

FORM	RIM	A	B	C	D	E	F	G	H	I	J	K	L	M	N	O	P	Q	R (Ridged)
A	R1	X	X	X										?					
A	R2			X															
B	R2			X	X	X													
C1	R2	X	X	X	X														
C2	R2			X		X													
C1	R3		X		X														
C2	R3		X																
A	R4				X														
C1	R4		X	X	X		X		X		X								
C2	R4		X				X				X	X							
C1	R5	?	?		X														
C2	R5		X	X	X		X												
C1	R6	X	X	X															
C1	R7	X	X	X	X			X						X	X				
C2	R7		X	X	X	X	X	X							X				
D1	R7	X		X	X		X	X	X									X	X
D2	R7	X	X	?			X	X				?						X	X
C2	R8			X															
D1	R8							X											X
D2	R8			X	X														

formed by a cord with a 'z-twist' (eg no 33), while the few whipped cord impressions derive from cords composed of very fine fibres (eg no 40). The comb used on no 5 is rectangular, while the punctulation on no 97 may have been made with a pointed comb. There is only one clear example of fingernail impression (no 51), although the fine incisions on no 7 and no 17 may also have been produced by sharp nails. Many of the impressed techniques are used in combination with each other. With the exception of spatulate impressions, however, all these techniques, may be employed as the sole means of decoration on a particular vessel.

Incision was carried out using either a sharp-edged tool (eg nos 17 & 24) or a blunt tool (eg no 23), techniques sometimes described as narrow incision and broad incision (cf O'Riordain & Waddell 1993, 3). Where incision occurs alongside impression, pots tend to be elaborately decorated (eg nos 24/25, 39, 42, 45, 71 & 104).

Grooved decoration leaves broader and more controlled impressions than does incised decoration and, on occasion, has been carried out using a plant stem pressed horizontally into the clay (eg nos 41–3). Grooving always appears in combination with other decorative techniques and is common only on vases with upright rims (nos 35–43), where it is used both to delimit horizontal zones and as an integral part of a design resembling basketry (see below). Grooving also appears on pots with distinctive decoration (nos 1, 7 & 24/25) and on two shoulder sherds from large jars (nos 104 & 105).

Infill, involving the apparent use of an unidentified white inlay, is a very rare technique and appears only on vessels which possess other distinctive features (cf nos 1, 7 and possibly 16).

Applied decoration is well represented on both large and medium jars. It takes two forms: namely strips of clay applied to the internal bevels of jars (nos 60–5), creating a series of either pronounced ridges and grooves, or flattish undulations (no 67); alternatively, strips of clay may be applied externally in the form of ribs (no 67) or horseshoes (nos 66 & 71).

The removal of clay to create a ridged or corrugated effect is very rare, since with the exception of no 98,

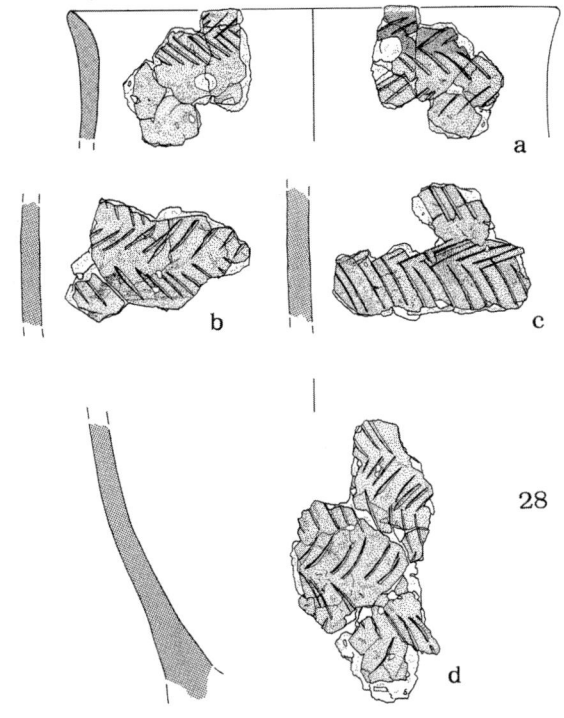

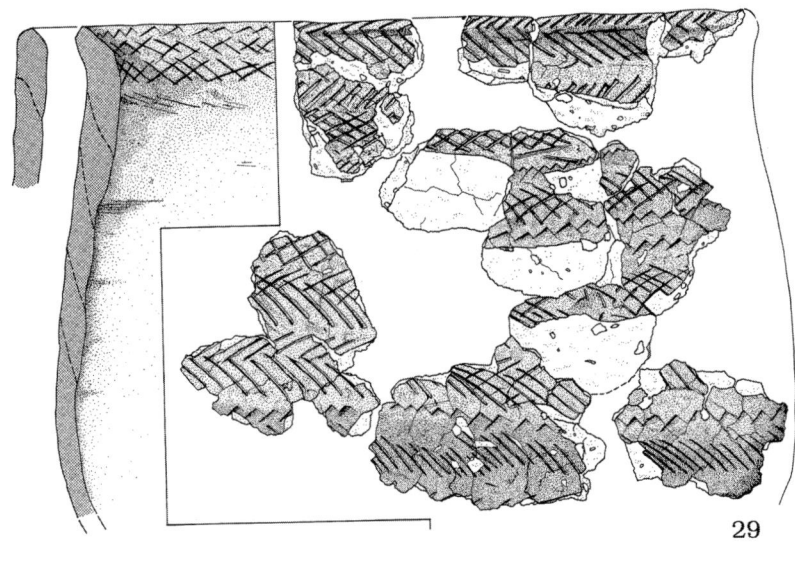

63 Pottery nos 28–9.

While the exterior of no 98 appears to be cordoned or ridged above the shoulder, the start of the internal bevel shows an applied ring of clay, suggesting that the internal bevel may have been decorated in the same manner as those of other internally-ridged vases (cf nos 60–5).

Decorative motifs are summarized in table 8. Simple, straight-line motifs are favoured, in particular, rows of oblique impressions singly or opposed to form horizontal herringbone patterns. There is no clear case of any design based on curving lines; on no 33, a folded length of twisted cord has been used to produce pairs of vertical cord impressions linked by a cord arc, but the arcs are barely visible and the emphasis is on the vertical element of the design.

In general, decorative schemes are zonal, particularly in the case of a group of vases with upright rims, where the decoration of the upper body relies heavily on the use of horizontal panels, delimited by grooving and infilled with herringbone or oblique impression (eg no 43). By contrast, decoration on the lower bodies of these vases, may involve the use of one or more reserved zones in conjunction with grooved panels (eg nos 35 & 40) or, alternatively, free decoration may replace the panels (eg nos 41 & 43). Two further vessels, nos 96 and 111, also make use of continuous horizontal panels, infilled with an oblique and/or herringbone design. However, as their rims are missing, their general affinities are unknown. The use of vertical panels is known in only one instance – on the lower body of a vessel, also missing a rim (no 10). A possible skeuomorphic design is evident in a number of upright-rim vases, where the use of closely spaced, intersecting, vertical and horizontal lines in two different mediums, such as vertical shell-edge (or whipped cord) and horizontal grooving, has created an effect reminiscent of 'basketry' (eg nos 35–8, 40).

the only sherds treated in this manner are either small (no 99) or so abraded as to make their inclusion in this category open to doubt (nos 100 & 101).

Generally speaking, the shape of an individual vessel provides a number of naturally occurring zones which appear to dictate the siting of decoration. The internal bevel of both expanded rim and upright rim pots provides the most obvious example of a decorative zone, there being only one instance, among decorated vessels, of a plain, albeit weak, internal bevel (no 51). Furthermore, the deep bevels of upright rim vases often carried quite complicated designs, while the neck, in many cases, was unadorned (eg nos 35, 36, 39, 43, 46, 72), suggesting that the decoration on the internal bevel was intended to catch the eye. An outstanding example of a decorated internal bevel on a vessel with a plain neck is provided by no

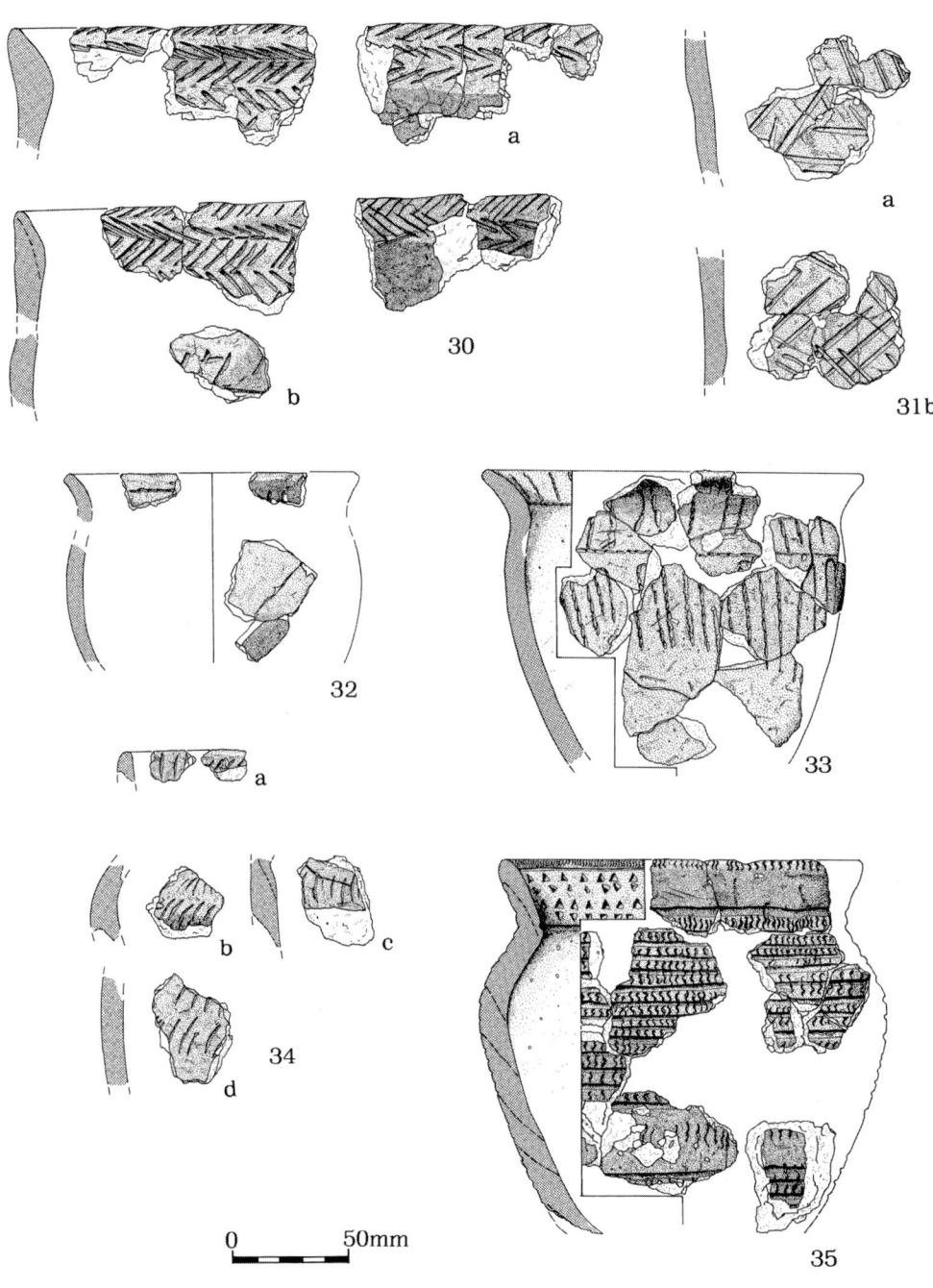

64 Pottery nos 30–5.

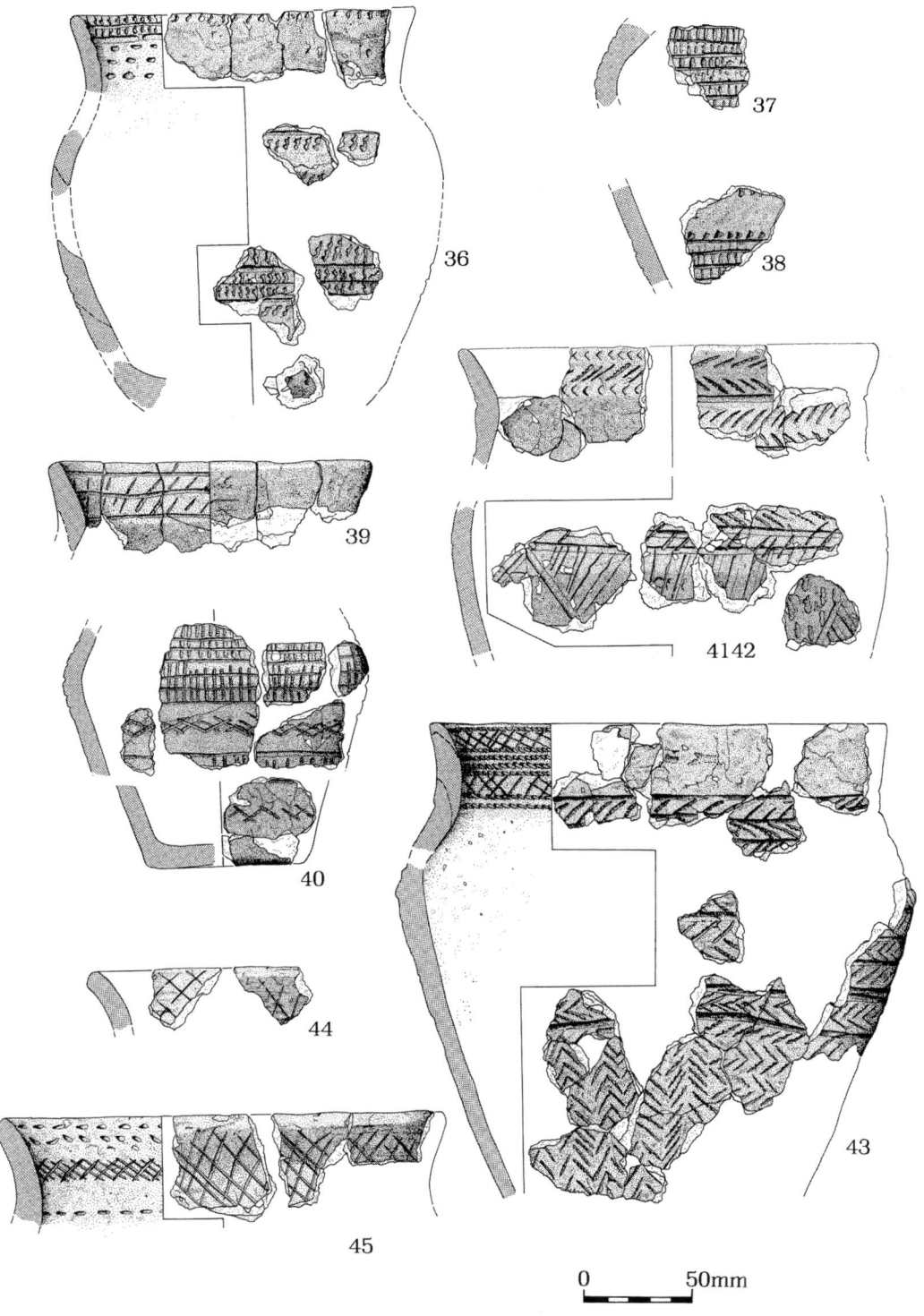

65 Pottery nos 36–45.

43, which has multiple horizontal rows of twisted cord, in place of the more usual grooves, separating two panels infilled with a unique criss-cross design executed in shell-edge.

External bevels, which commonly occur both on vessels with expanded rims and on those with upright rims, are often utilized for decoration, although there are many instances of vessels with undecorated external bevels (ie nos 12, 20, 32, 34, 44, 45, 49 & 65). Where external bevels are decorated, the remainder of the upper neck may be left blank (eg nos 18, 21, 35, 36, 46, 47, 60, 62, 65).

Decoration on and above the shoulder appears to be more common than decoration on the lower body but this impression stems from the fact that more upper than lower wall sherds have survived. In only a few cases, is there any certainty that the shoulder marked the lower limit of decoration (cf nos 12, 49, 72, 73 & possibly 74). In addition, there are only two examples of vessels whose decoration is known to have been limited to the internal rim bevel and exterior surface of the neck (nos 46 & 50).

Evidence for all-over decoration is relatively common, particularly among the slack-shouldered group of vases (eg nos 26, 28 & 29) and upright rim vases (eg nos 35 & 43). Shoulders of vessels in the latter group, are often utilized to mark a decorative boundary between contrasting designs on the upper and lower body (eg nos 38, 41/42 & 98). This does not apply in every case, however, for a contrast in decorative design may occasionally be introduced only on the lower third or so of a vessel, despite there being no change in wall profile at this point (eg nos 35 & 43); indeed, in rare instances, decoration of the lower body may cease some distance above the base (eg nos 33, 48, 62 & 96). There is no evidence of decoration on the few basal sherds that have survived.

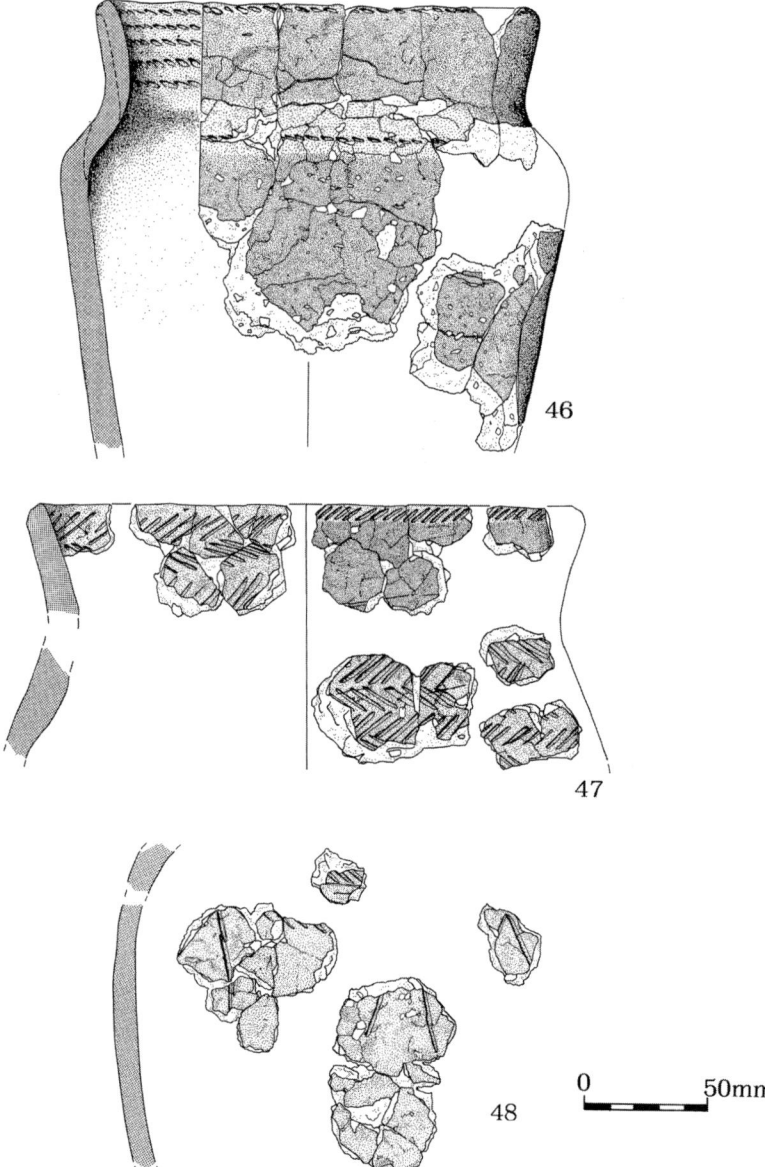

66   Pottery nos 46–8.

VESSEL SUMMARY

When fabric, form and decoration are considered in relationship to one another, it is apparent that none of the four form categories identified earlier – cups, bowls, vases and jars – form a truly coherent group. The cups comprise just four vessels (nos 1–4), each of varying form and quite dissimilar with regard to decoration. As these cups were represented only by tiny sherds, it was not possible to identify their fabric type, but their general feel accords well with the bulk of the assemblage. The bowl category has only one clear example (no 5) assigned to it and a few comb-ornamented sherds which may also derive from a bowl (no 6). It is of interest, however, that these are the only two vessels in the assemblage decorated with rectangular-toothed comb impressions.

The majority of the assemblage, therefore, falls into the vase and jar categories. It is within the vase category that certain recurrent morphological and decorative features may be identified, enabling tentative sub-groupings of vessels. For instance, shouldered vases with expanded R2-type rims (nos 7–9, 11–15) embrace a variety of fabric types, but appear to form a coherent group in terms of decoration, typified by repetitive themes, based on a limited range of motifs, principally herringbone. A much greater variety of decorative motif, including true false relief, is shown by vases with R4-type expanded rims (nos 16–21, 24/25), but, as has been mentioned above, these vases are known only from a few sherds, too small to permit proper analysis. The addition of micaceous rock temper to the fabric recipe (Fab 8) of certain vases makes for a small but distinctive sub-group among vessels with expanded rims, notwithstanding the varied range of decorative techniques and motifs exhibited by these vases (nos 8–9, 18–19). This decorative range is extended by a rimless vase (no 10) in the same fabric, which has the distinction of being the only vessel in the assemblage to display vertically panelled decoration. A further small, but distinctive group of vases comprises the herringbone-decorated, slack-shouldered vases with R5-type rims (nos 26–31). The marked similarity of the fabric of these vases, with their white-black speckled inclusions (Fab 1) and clay, firing to a glossy sheen (not apparently due to burnishing) – makes it difficult to estimate the minimum number of vessels in this group.

As there are only three vases (nos 32–4) with R6-type rims, little can be said about this group, other than to highlight their somewhat atypical decoration, in particular the use of vertical cord on no 33. The most common type of vase in the assemblage is that with an angular shoulder and upright R7-type rim. Such vases are generally similar

in fabric type, with most fabrics containing varying proportions of white-black speckled grits; vases nos 35–48 are ornamented, while nos 53–9, appear to be undecorated. Vases within the former group exhibit

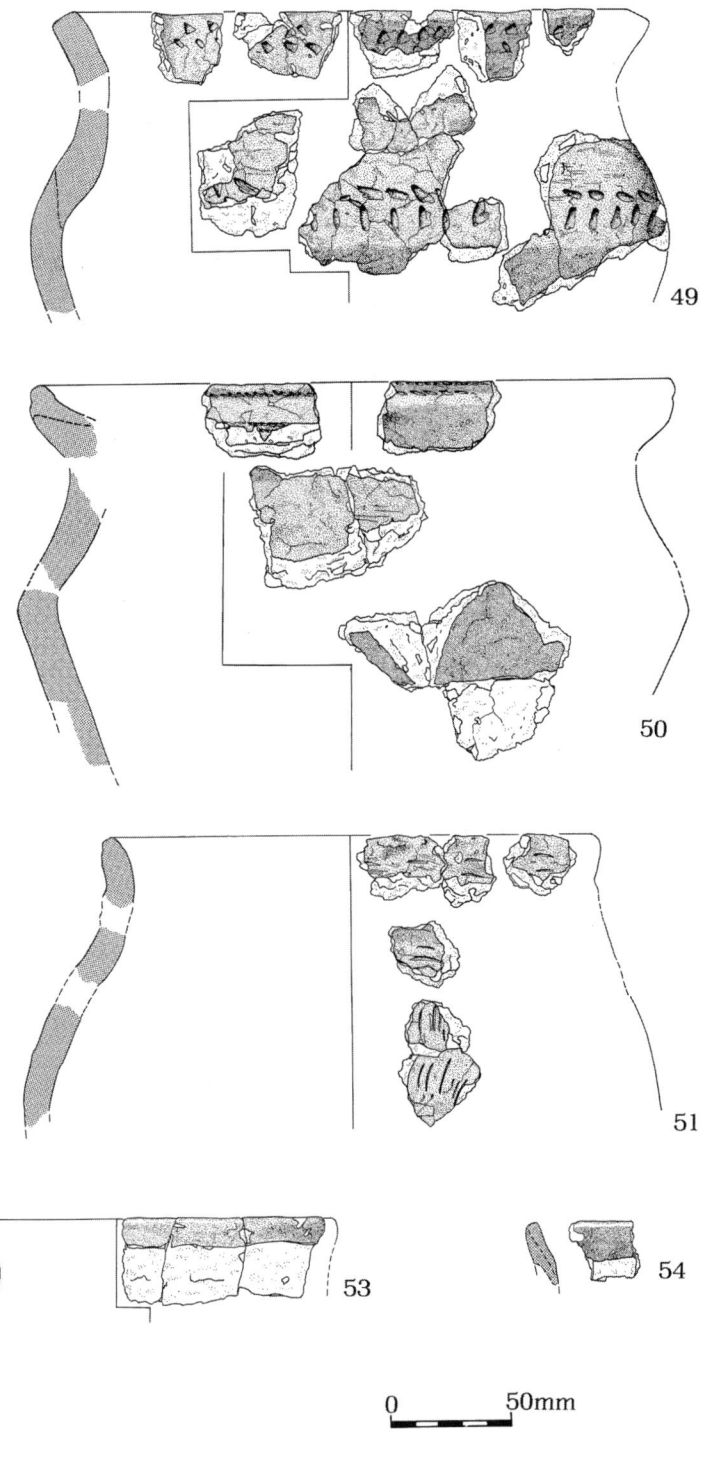

67   Pottery nos 49–51, 53–4.

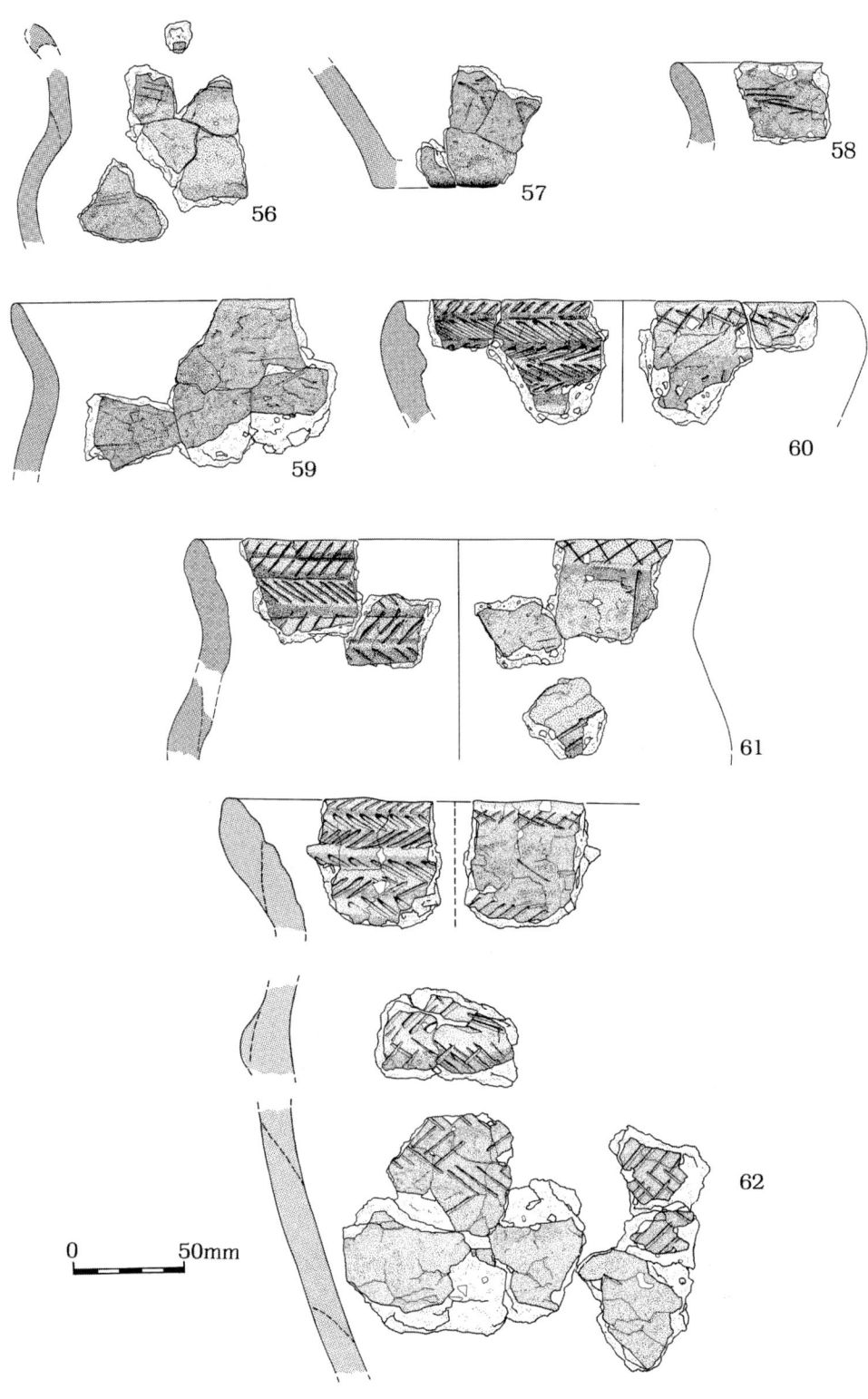

68 Pottery nos 56–62.

a wide variety of decorative themes, ranging from a severely restricted use of ornamentation (no 46) to all-over decoration (eg no 35). The most striking unit within the upright rim group is provided by those vessels employing the so-called 'basketry' motif, in combination with horizontal panels delimited by grooving (nos 35–8, 39/40). These vessels are of similar fabric type (Fab 1), with the exception of nos 39/40, which possess a distinctive fabric (Fab 5), only paralleled in one other instance (no 150 from Site K1). It should be noted that a small rim sherd (no 2) assigned to the cup category also appears to display the start of a 'basketry' design.

Turning now to an overview of the vase category, it is apparent that as all vases can be broadly assigned to one of two major rim types (expanded rims, R2–R5, on the one hand, and upright rims, R6–R7, on the other) it might be expected that other features will also point to the existence of two mutually distinct groups of vases. Closer examination, however, reveals substantial areas of overlap between the two groups: the ratio of rim diameter to aperture is closely comparable for both expanded rim and upright rim vases, indicating a possible common function. In addition, both groups share the same decorative techniques with only two exceptions: pointed, or punched, impressions and wedge-shaped impressions are absent from the upright rim group. Many decorative motifs are also common to both groups, in particular the ubiquitous herringbone motif and rows of obliquely-set impressions. The chief difference in motif, however, is the occurrence, among certain upright rim vases, of the 'basketry' motif and horizontal panels, delimited by grooving, designs which are not paralleled in the expanded rim group. To a certain extent, fabric types reveal a common element, fabrics 1, 2, 3, and 6, being common to both groups of vases, but there is, however, a seemingly greater diversity of fabric type in use among vessels with expanded rims. In five instances, vases appear distinct, with respect to fabric, both from each other and from the rest of the assemblage (nos 7, 13, 15–17).

There are only half as many catalogued jars (no 60–95) as vases (see table 4), a phenomenon which relates in part to a greatly reduced use of decoration in this category, making it difficult to assign sherds to individual vessels. The majority of both plain and decorated jars have simple, upright rims, indicating a strong link with upright rim vases. The repertoire of decorative techniques displayed by such jars overlaps with that of vases (with the exception of the basketry motif), but additionally includes the use of both externally and/or internally applied decoration (eg nos 60–8, 71, 98). Motifs, too, overlap, although jars in general show a heavier emphasis on herringbone motif and cross-hatch, than do upright rim vases.

Jars with applied decoration form a distinct group both decoratively, and with regard to their fabric (Fab 1), with its conspicuous white-black speckled inclusions. The one jar with applied decoration, not conforming to this pattern (no 71), differs in terms of fabric and decorative motif. Jars with ridged, herringbone-decorated internal bevels (nos 60–6, and possibly 67), may be said to mirror, albeit on a larger scale, the similarly tempered, small, slack-shouldered, herringbone-decorated vases (nos 26–8). The rims of some of the internally ridged jars are everted rather than upright (nos 60, 63–5), perhaps to facilitate the application of the series of rings of clay to the internal bevel.

Finally, mention must be made of the two distinctive large jars, nos 74 and 98. The former has an R8-type everted rim, with a concave internal bevel which, taken with its strikingly sharp, wedge-and-tail herringbone decoration, invites close comparison with the similarly decorated no 13, a vase with a classic expanded rim; no 74, however, is similar in fabric (Fab 2) to many of the large plain jars. The other jar (no 98) is missing its rim, though there is a hint of an internally ridged bevel, and is noteworthy for its cordoned upper body, contrasting with an all-over incised lower body.

FIRING

The assemblage exhibits evidence of poor firing control, typical of bonfire firing. Apart from evidence of irregular firing, the most common firing pattern is that of oxidized exterior and interior surfaces over an unoxidized core. This 'sandwich' pattern is particularly common among sherds from jars. Localized fire-clouding is relatively common over the exterior of vessels, especially undecorated vessels, indicating that the pot came into contact with fuel during open firing (Orton et al 1993, 223, quoting Shepard 1956, 92). Heavy sooting is present on the rim exteriors, particularly of large jars, and is often present on the lip of the internal bevel (eg nos 66 & 72). Sooting of rims may indicate that the vessel was placed upside down during firing. It is possible, in a couple of instances, to identify groups of vessels, which may have been the product of a single firing: vases with all-over-herringbone decoration (nos 26–8, 30–1) and jars with ridged internal bevels (nos 60–7), are so closely comparable in all respects, that they can only be separated into individual vessels on the basis of minor differences in rim diameter and decoration. One pot, no 29, provides the only evidence in the assemblage for a waster, being crumbly in the extreme, with poorly bonded ring junctions and an unevenly fired rim.

FUNCTION

Information about function was deduced from indirect evidence, in the form of variables such as vessel form, capacity, mouth aperture, wall thickness and fabric (cf Rice 1987, 207–43). The presence of organic residues was noted in the course of recording the assemblage and offers considerable scope for analysis, perhaps most profitably as part of a research programme examining a range of ceramic assemblages from the region to investigate variations between sites and through time.

The wide range in capacity, displayed by the assemblage, indicates that vessels were designed for a variety of domestic purposes. The small capacity of the cups may imply that their use was the same as that of our modern cups, or that they may have held precious substances used in small quantities (eg medicines?). Both bowls and small vases may have served as containers for individual portions of solid food, perhaps to be eaten with fingers, as their interior surfaces do not show signs of abrasion from scraping with an implement; alternatively, they may have held drink (it has been suggested that the purpose of the broad rim expansion on food vessels may have been to trap the lees of beverages; Sheridan, 1993, 71, quoting Hawkes 1981, 255). Large vases may have been used for serving drink or food, such as gruels or stews, to groups of people – the exceptional, eye-catching internal bevel of no 43, described above, may imply that this vase fulfilled an important communal function, perhaps as a container for beverages, supped using a ladle or scoop. Jars, on the other hand, with their thick walls, heavy bases and large capacity, may well have been used for dry storage; top heavy jars such as no 89 may have been stood in sand to render them stable.

The large quantity of decorated sherds recovered from the midden may suggest that decorated vessels were in daily use alongside the plain ware. On the other hand, in the absence of any definite house structure, and given the proportion of midden lost to erosion, it is impossible to ascertain whether the excavated midden deposits are representative of the site as a whole. The general scarcity of evidence for cooking vessels further illustrates this point and yet such vessels, by their very nature, presumably suffered high breakage rates. The recognition of cooking vessels depends not just on the presence of organic deposits on sherds, but on attributes such as coarseness of fabric (to reduce thermal shock), unevenness of surfaces (to create a larger area for heat absorption) and wall thickness (cf Rice 1987, 237–40; Orton et al 1993, 220). These features, however, are all typical of the majority of Scottish prehistoric pottery. On the question of thermal-shock resistance, initially raised by Rye (1981), there is no real evidence to indicate that prehistoric potters were even aware of the problem (cf Gibson & Woods 1990, 33–6). Relatively few pots show signs of organic encrustation, although some, such as nos 30, 47/48, 49 and 51, possess soot-blackened and/or crazed surfaces, indicative of use over a fire. Decoration on these pots is cruder than average and, indeed, no 51 is unique in having a plain interior bevel, and a very roughly formed rim. An additional vase (no 12), which may be considered here as a possible cooking vessel, has a crazed surface with heavy organic encrustation on the interior below the shoulder (the exterior of the lower body, however, is not sooted). Very few bases have survived, which is unfortunate, as bases can be one of the most informative parts of a pot (cf Rice 1987, 235). In view of the scarcity of evidence, it must be supposed that cooking vessels were disposed of on another part of the site, or that cooking may have been carried out without the use of pottery vessels, for example by means of 'earth ovens' (Gibson & Woods 1990, 35) or by boiling in troughs.

The suitability of any of the Kilellan pots for water storage is questionable. As fresh water was readily available from a spring at the site (Tobar Niall Neonaich), evaporation from porous vessels may not have been a serious disadvantage; alternatively, skins may have been used as water containers. Ethnographic evidence shows that the porosity of pot surfaces can be diminished by means of impregnation with resins, vegetable matter, juices or by means of sooting or burnishing (Rice 1987, 163, 231; Orton et al 1993, 126, 221, quoting Schiffer 1990), but there is no evidence as to whether any of the above techniques were used at Kilellan.

The presence of abrasion on sherds may be informative, but it is frequently difficult to determine whether its origin is use-related or due to weathering. The most interesting pattern of abrasion is that apparent on the internal bevels of a number of vases possessing expanded, R4-type rims, or upright, R7-type rims. While the exterior surface of the neck is frequently well-preserved, the internal bevel, is often abraded (eg nos 3, 36, 39, 41, 45, 46, 59). The abrasion on the bevels of vases, nos 20 and 21, is so severe that the design is almost obliterated; abrasion is also exceptionally heavy on the bevels of the apparently plain vases, nos 53, 54 and 55. A roughened surface, or surface deliberately left unsmoothed, can be an aid to handling a pot, and this may have been true of no 46, but the majority of these vases are not particularly large or heavy. Although this pattern of abrasion suggests a common origin, its cause is uncertain.

It is of interest that there is no evidence of old repairs among the Kilellan assemblage, perhaps indicating that broken vessels were easily replaced. Although the pattern of handling what may have been ceremonial vessels may have been different from those destined for everyday use, Tomalin has highlighted the general absence of old abrasions and repairs on Irish Bowls and Food Vessels, suggesting by way of explanation that vessels were carefully bound and suspended when not in use (Tomalin 1983, 29).

Studies of usage are further complicated by the recognition that the function of a pot may have changed through life. A discussion of the continuing use of vessels and/or sherds after their original function had ended is given by Rice (1987, 209, 224). Needham and Stig-Sørensen (1988, 124) also explore the possibility that pottery may have passed through many different stages of use before deposition on a midden. Further confusion may arise due to post-depositional changes occuring in sherds (cf Orton *et al* 1993, 214). There are numerous examples of sooting of sherd edges occurring post-breakage (eg nos 9, 14, 41, 43, 51, 109, 110), and some reconstructed vessels include the occasional sherd burnt after breakage (eg nos 26, 35, 41, 43, 45, 98), indicating that sherds from broken vessels were added to the midden in different stages, some becoming incorporated in hearth material, prior to final disposal on the midden.

DISTRIBUTION AND PHASING

Information regarding distribution and phasing is limited, because prior to the 1976 season, no distinction was made between the midden layers and the fill of features incorporated within it; furthermore, the trench was the main unit in all seasons for the horizontal recording of finds, and as such is too insensitive to permit detailed analysis of the spatial distribution of sherds. In an effort to shed more light on this aspect, the find numbers marked on the sherds were assessed, where these were available, to determine if these might be used as a rough guide to the associations of particular pots, there being numerous instances where single find numbers were allocated to entire groups of sherds; on occasion, such groups comprise as many as a hundred or even two hundred sherds.

The full results of this analysis, which met with only partial success, have been deposited in the site archive, along with a discussion of the possible distribution patterns of the various vessel forms. In addition, an attempt was made to study the vertical distribution of sherds from contexts in trenches KN 76 G2 and G4, which could be assigned to a particular phase. The chief limitation of this exercise (which is presented in full in the site archive) lies in the fact that only 22% by weight of the total pottery from the midden can be attributed to a phased context and, of this total, as much as ninety per cent of the sherds (weight *c* 11kg) derives from phase 4.

To summarize, however, the results of both analyses fully supported Colin Burgess's remarks in the interim report: 'While the pottery is very diverse, it is thoroughly mixed up, and no changes are observable right through layer 6. Sherds from one vessel can be scattered not only from top to bottom in layer 6, but also horizontally in different parts of the site.' (Burgess 1976, 194.) The reconstructed vase no 35, provides an excellent example of this phenomenon, being derived from at least a dozen separate contexts. It is clear, therefore, that the midden had a complex history, the implications of which are discussed below.

While the interpretation of sherd groups based on find numbers has to be treated with caution, there are five clear instances of individual, but incomplete pots, being dumped *in situ* (nos 46, 72, 88, 89 & 90). Given that all the above vessels are either entirely plain or have plain lower bodies, the possibility cannot be discounted that further sherds from these pots may have been distributed more widely over the midden. The 4.8kg weight of the heaviest of the above pots (no 89), highlights the fact that the total of 16.8kg of unassigned plain sherds from the midden, is insufficient to account for the missing bodies of an estimated minimum number of 16 jars and 4–6 plain vases, indicated by surviving rim sherds. It is also suggested that the unassigned plain sherds may represent the thorough mixing of large numbers of different vessels, as can clearly be demonstrated in the case of the decorated pottery (see below).

Table 9 shows that decorated pottery was widely distributed over the entire midden (although it was poorly represented in trenches KN 61 3 and KN 76

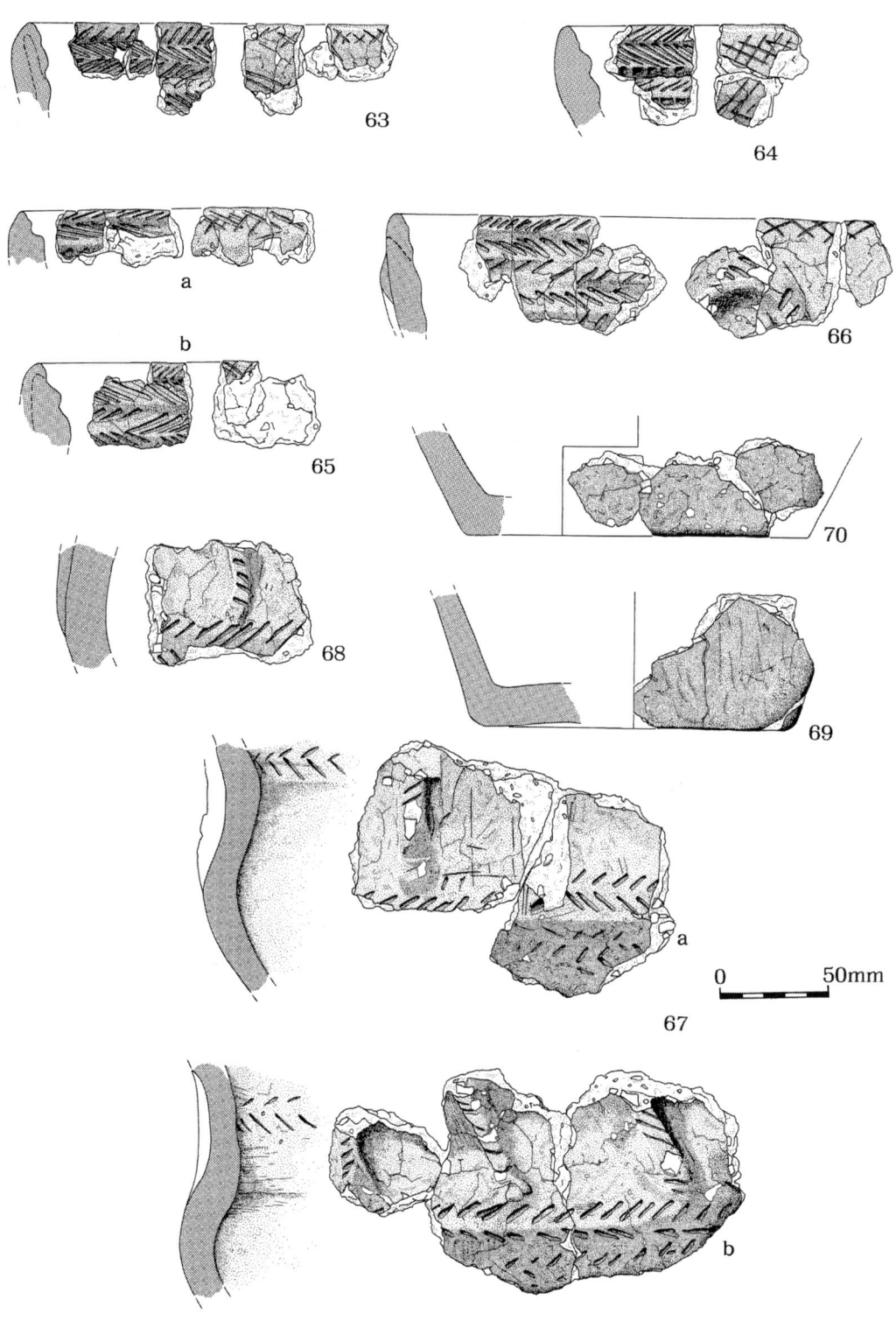

69 Pottery nos 63–70.

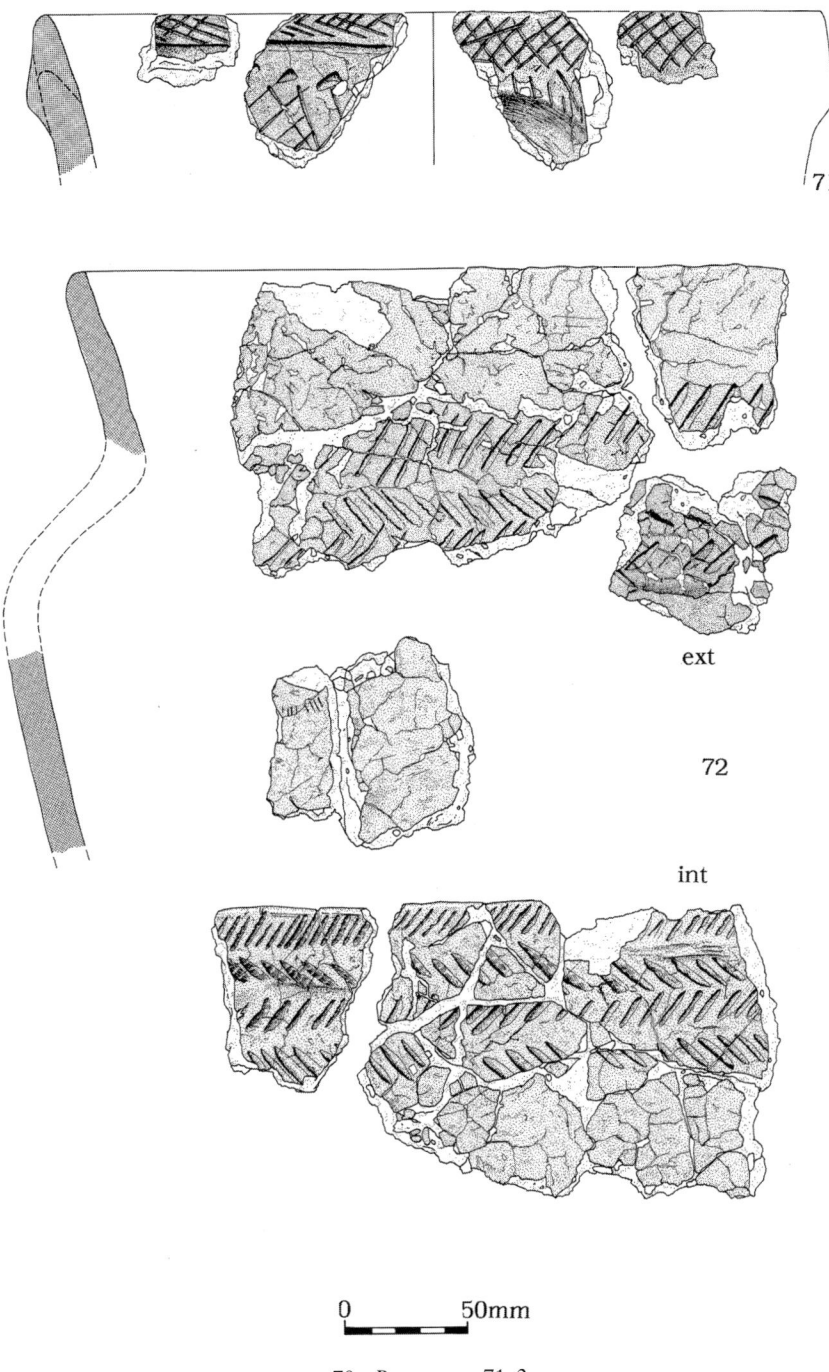

70 Pottery nos 71–2.

G3), yet, in all trenches, the total weight of decorated sherds was surpassed by the quantity of plain pottery present. However, analysis of the decorated pottery reveals that a disproportionately large number of vessels may be represented by very small quantities of sherds, a feature which is well illustrated by the finds from KN 76 G1; although only just clipping the edge of the midden, this trench yielded portions of as many as 12 different vessels from only 125g of decorated sherds.

The main conclusion to be drawn from a study of the decorated pottery, is that there appears to be a

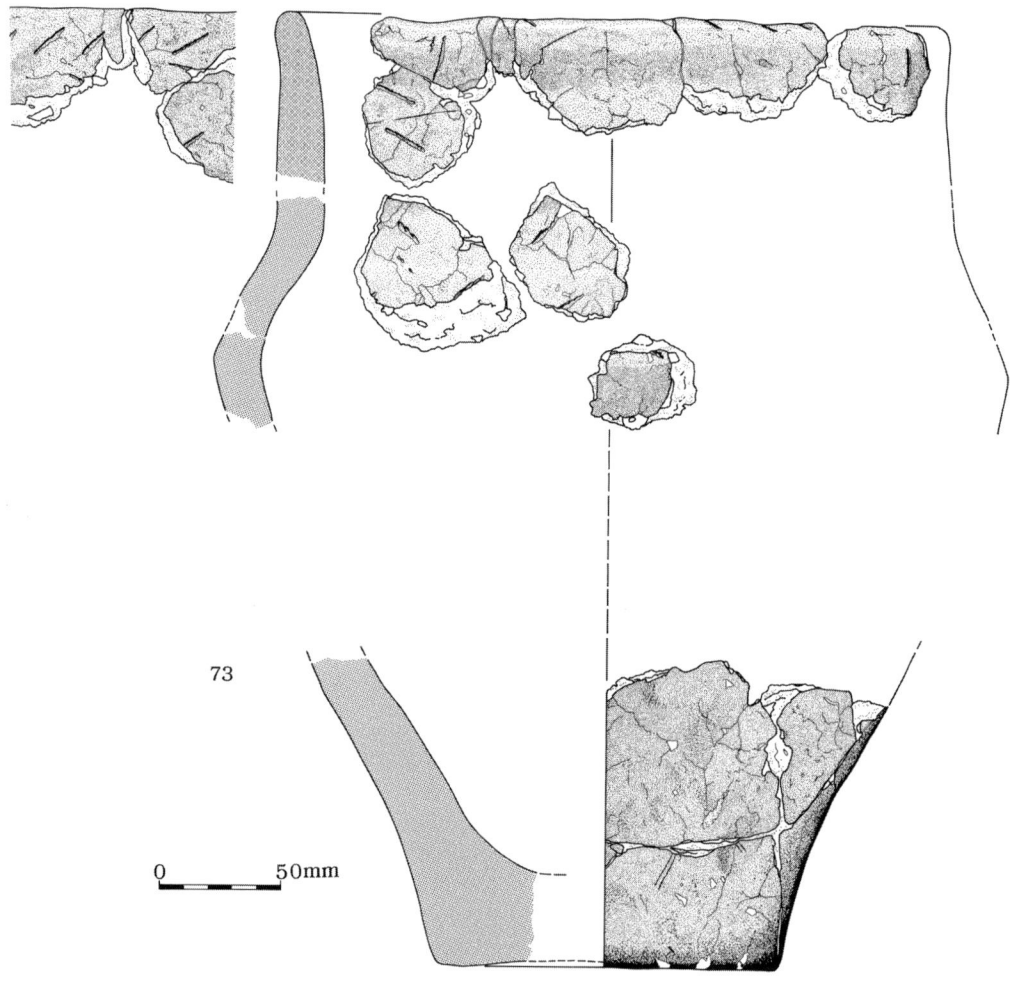

71 Pottery no 73.

distinction between the distribution pattern of vessel forms in KN 76 G4, in comparison with that of other trenches. In particular it may be noted that the pottery from G4 layer 3 belongs to Phase 2.6, the final phase of the midden. Although G4 contains the second largest quantity, by weight (ie 3kg), of decorated pottery from any trench, this total is composed largely of sherds from decorated jars, plus parts of two slack-shouldered vases (nos 28 & 29); expanded rim type vases are not represented in this trench and there are only two examples of upright rim vases, even though both types of vases have a widespread distribution in other trenches. A possible explanation for this distribution pattern may lie in the functional differences between vessel forms which may, in turn, have a bearing on the location of occupation and/or activity areas.

DISCUSSION OF THE EARLY BRONZE AGE ASSEMBLAGE

The importance of Kilellan lies in the fact that it is a domestic site dating to a period whose ceramics are largely known from funerary contexts. Indeed, many of the Kilellan pot types would not be out of place associated with burials (eg nos 1, 7–25, 66–8 & 71). Yet, at Kilellan, the prime functions of these pots were presumably in food service and/or storage. They appear alongside a large number of shouldered vases and jars with thinned rims, either plain or intricately decorated, none of which is represented in funerary contexts in Scotland.

Following Burgess (1976, 196), it would seem that no great timespan was involved in the accumulation of the midden. Almost all the pottery, which can

TABLE 9
Comparison by trenches of quantities of decorated and plain pottery.

Location	Decorated Pieces	Weight	Est min no of vessels	Plain Pieces	Weight	Totals Pieces	Weight	% dec by weight	% plain by weight
61 1	73	1651	22	321	6914	394	8565	19	81
76 G4	171	2097	12	441	6053	612	8150	26	74
76 G2	388	3243	40	932	4372	1320	7615	43	57
73 F2	13	139	7	532	5308	545	5447	3	97
73 B2	48	132	15	958	4305	1006	4437	3	97
73 F1	69	510	22	253	2605	322	3115	16	84
73 A1	106	1063	21	347	1710	453	2773	38	62
73 B1	32	176	19	218	1303	250	1479	12	88
73 A2	21	581	11	40	347	61	928	63	37
60 F2	39	245	20	82	458	121	703	35	65
61 2	8	57	7	39	261	47	318	18	82
61 3	1	7	1	31	292	32	299	2	98
76 G1	16	125	12	81	160	97	285	44	56
73 B3	20	166	4	22	62	42	228	73	27
73 A4	5	74	6	24	125	29	199	37	63
59 F1	4	53	4	21	97	25	150	35	65
76 G3	2	3	2	35	123	37	126	2	98
73 A3	7	20	6	60	74	67	94	21	79
Totals	1023	10342	N/A	4437	34569	5460	44911	N/A	N/A

be allocated to a phase, derives from Phase 2.4 and represents a wide cross-section of the forms present in the assemblage. It seems reasonable, therefore, to suggest that the various pot forms were in use contemporaneously. It may be supposed that the entire range of vessels recovered, had been deliberately discarded. The discarding of pottery in prehistory, however, may have been far removed from the modern concept of waste disposal. A detailed consideration of the processes/mechanics of midden accumulation has been given in the report on the Late Bronze Age midden deposits at Runnymede (Needham & Stig-Sørensen 1988; see also Needham & Spence 1996). No similar study has yet been published for coastal midden deposits. The density of the Runnymede midden was vastly greater than that at Kilellan: a single 13m² area alone produced 72kg of pottery (and 19kg of burnt clay) from a deposit just 30–50cm thick (Needham & Stig-Sørensen 1988, 117). The 56kg of pot and daub from Kilellan, on the other hand, was recovered from a 650 sq m area of midden, up to 1m in thickness. The huge contrast in the total weight of pottery recovered probably relates to differences in the size of population at both sites as well as to differences in the volume of pottery in circulation. It may also relate to variations in the methods of disposal. The thorough mixing of the pottery described by Burgess, may result from the type of refuse management mechanism put forward by Needham and Sørensen, who have suggested that

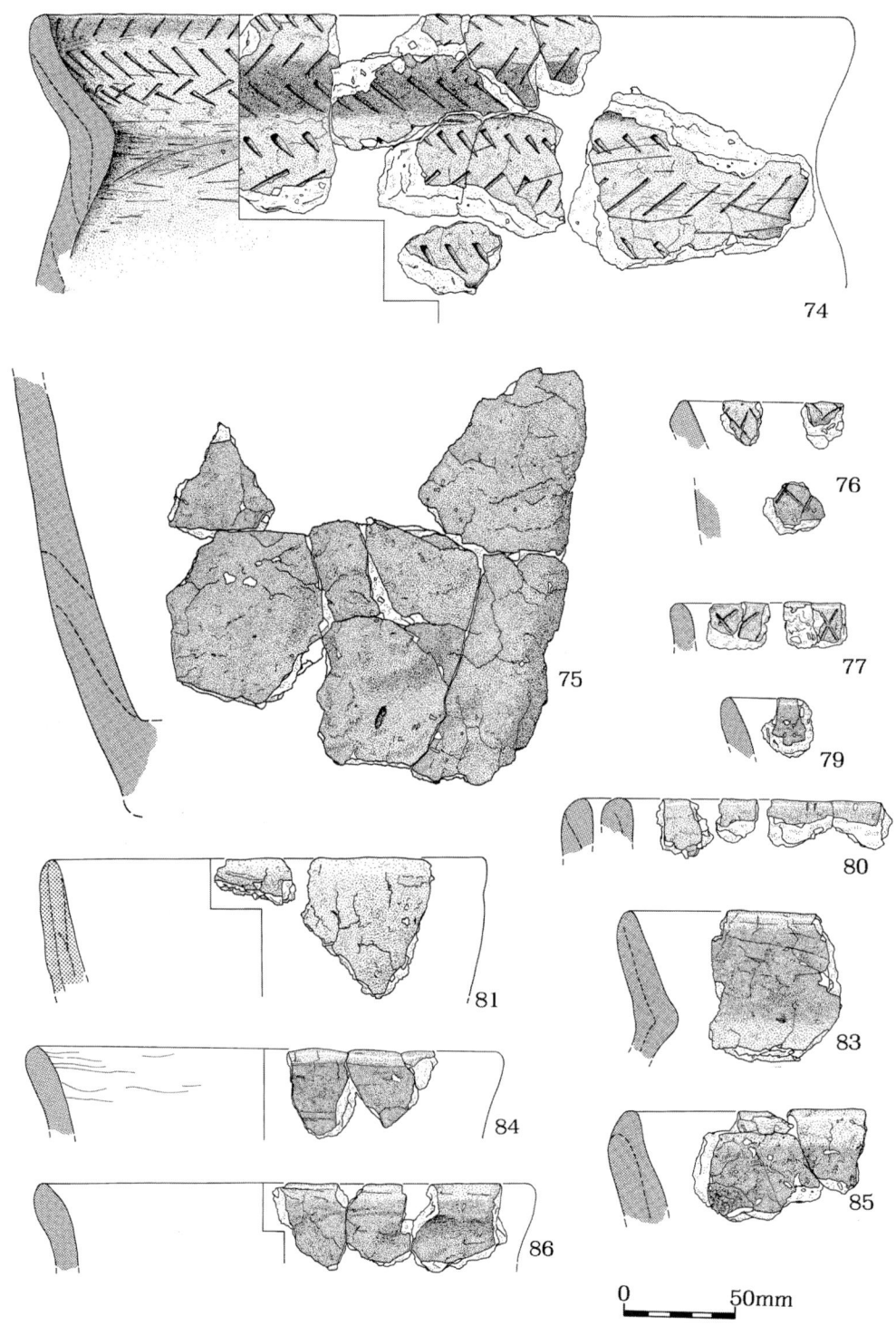

72 Pottery nos 74–7, 79–81, 83–6.

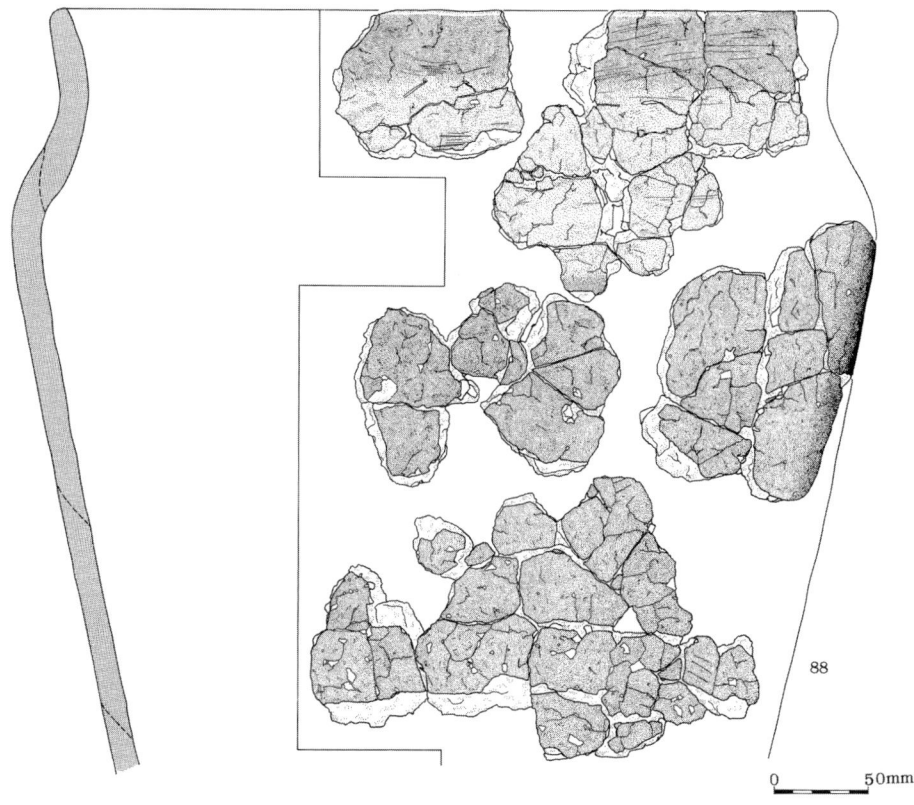

73 Pottery no 88.

'refuse would on occasion have moved through a "chain" of processes' (ibid, 125).

While many of Burgess's remarks in his interim report still hold true, the volume of pottery recovered in the 1976 season of excavations has led to a shift in emphasis. For instance, the statement that 'the bulk of the pottery consists of large plain shouldered jars, with simple thinned rims' (Burgess 1976, 196) needs qualification: plain jars still constitute the bulk of the pottery by weight but, as Orton *et al* have pointed out, 'weight cannot be used to measure proportions in any one assemblage' (1993, 169). Given the unexpectedly large numbers of vessels which may be represented by small groups of decorated sherds, the minimum number of plain vessels in the assemblage cannot be ascertained reliably.

On the other hand, re-examination of the pottery assemblage has also meant that some earlier observations require re-assessment. In the first place, some of the descriptions of Kilellan jars that have appeared in the archaeological literature have proved erroneous. Burgess illustrated two groups of decorated sherds as exceptionally tall jars, and suggested that one 'at least seems to have been round based' (1976, 196, 200; figs 10.7:4 & 5). Subsequently, Gibson and Woods included Kilellan jars in their glossary of ceramic terms describing them as tall and upright, plain or decorated shouldered jars which 'appear to have had rounded bases' (1990, 190). The heights of the decorated jars as illustrated in the interim report have been considerably reduced after reconstruction, while the absence of secure evidence for rounded bases has already been noted above. However, it must be admitted that the reconstruction of the shape and size of the vessels is fraught with difficulty, and, particularly in cases where vessels may be represented by relatively few joining sherds, allowance must be made for potential errors in the estimates of height and diameter.

A second point which requires reassessment is Burgess's proposition that Kilellan may have seen a survival of a round-based Neolithic element (1976, 200). This has no firm evidence to support it: the few surviving bases are flat and the sherd formerly thought to indicate a round-based element (ibid, fig 10.8; 11) is now considered to be part of a flat-based, shell-decorated vase (no 9) of expanded rim type (see above). An extensive search through all the undiagnostic plain sherds and fragments, has revealed no trace of any previously missed, curved base fragment.

Burgess's contention that the Kilellan assemblage included a small Beaker element also requires clarification. The main case for a Beaker element rested on three small wall sherds, thought to come from all-over-corded Beakers, although he did add the caveat that 'the vessels are hardly typical Beakers' (ibid, 200). After the 1976 season, however, new cross-joins showed that the apparent horizontal cord decoration on two of these sherds (ibid, figs 13 & 14) was part of the longitudinal cord decoration on the lower body of an upright rim vase (no 33). The third sherd (ibid, fig 10.8, 12) also has a cross-join (no 109) which, while showing that it does not derive from an all-over-cord Beaker, still leaves its orientation and affinities in doubt. However, in terms of its fabric and wall thickness, this sherd is generally similar to other upright rim vases. Two other pots were mentioned by Burgess in a Beaker connection, while defying easy classification (ibid, figs 10.8, 15 & 16). The former pot (no 40) may now be seen to belong to the Kilellan tradition of upright rim, zonally decorated vases, while Gibson considered that the latter vessel (no 96) was unlikely to be Beaker due to the fact that the decoration commenced well above the base (1982, 176). Although the rim of no 96 is missing, its fabric is very similar to that of some of the Kilellan jars (cf no 74). Gibson included Kilellan in his inventory of 'Beaker Domestic Sites' (1982, 176), on the basis of the three corded sherds, described above, although, elsewhere, he added the proviso that Kilellan was at the tail end of Beaker ceramic survival 'with Beaker influenced pottery, and Beaker decorative traits lingering on some Food Vessels' (ibid, 87). Gibson defined Beaker domestic sites as '... occupation sites which have varying quantities of Beaker pottery associated with at least part of the total lifespan of the site' (ibid, 1). It is now clear that Kilellan does not fulfil even this broad definition of a Beaker domestic site.

Turning next to an examination of the Beaker issue from a broader perspective, it is apparent, as Gibson has pointed out, that decorative themes at Kilellan bear some degree of affinity to those common on Beaker ceramics. This is particularly true of the Kilellan upright rim vases, ornamented with impressed decoration within horizontal panels, demarcated by grooved lines. Given the longevity of the Beaker tradition (cf Kinnes *et al* 1991), it would be futile to seek evidence of zonal decoration at Kilellan having been 'borrowed' from Beaker pottery or equally to argue to the contrary that such decorative themes may have developed in parallel and in isolation. In view of the absence of excavated assemblages, it is unclear whether the zonally decorated vases had a long history, or merely enjoyed a brief and isolated 'floruit' at Kilellan. A single vessel, from the site of Allt Chrisal, Barra, may, however, bear comparison with this class of pottery (Gibson 1995, 114, fig 4.43: 202). Gibson describes this pot as 'a squat vessel with slack bipartite form' and adds that the grooves in the neck and the contrasting geometric decoration on the lower body 'while not out of place in the Food Vessel tradition, do, nevertheless, suggest Beaker affinity'. The evidence from Ardnave, discussed below, throws further light on post-Beaker use of zonal decoration. Nor should it be overlooked that the decoration on Irish tripartite vases usually consists of multiple horizontal zones (O'Riordain & Waddell 1993, 26). If the decorative evidence at Kilellan points to shared traits with Beaker-type pottery, then it does so only to the extent that such designs may have formed part of a common repertoire handed down over generations. The existence of decorative parallels should, therefore, occasion no surprise and may indeed be of minor significance.

The site of Ardnave lies 2.5km from Kilellan and may well have been contemporary, at least for part of its history. The single date from the Kilellan midden has a span of 2140–1740 cal BC (GU–3517; table 2; see Ashmore 1997, 263). At Ardnave, dates derived from material sealed by the period 2 wall have a range of 2274–1884 cal BC (GU–1439) and 2194–1739 cal BC (GU–1371), while charcoal from a hearth beside a secondary occupation level (Period 4), which produced most of the Food Vessel pottery, yielded a date spanning 1749–1212 cal BC (GU–1272) (Ritchie & Welfare 1983, 304; Ashmore 1997, 263, 266). Single radiocarbon dates must be used with caution and, therefore, no conclusion can be reached as to the nature of the chronological relationship between the Food Vessel assemblage at Ardnave and the Kilellan assemblage.

There are, however, a number of strong similarities between both assemblages. It is interesting to note that the characteristic zonal decoration on some of the Kilellan upright rim vases, consisting of grooved horizontal panels, infilled with shell-edge impressions, appears at Ardnave on pots with expanded rims (eg Ardnave SF 2 & 11, although SF 11 lacks a rim).

Catalogue no 43 bears a marked decorative similarity to the Ardnave pots, with zonal decoration on the upper body, contrasting with 'free' decoration on the lower body, consisting of herringbone and chevrons. The Kilellan expanded rim vessels also bear a strong resemblance to the Ardnave vases in form and decoration. Both groups possess well-defined bipartite forms with angular shoulder (ie comparable to bipartite or 'Yorkshire' vases, cf Kitson Clark 1937, 62); both have a large vase with neck moulding (ie no 14 & Ardnave SF7) (cf Burgess's ridge-neck Bipartite Vases, 1980, 87) and both groups possess rounded forms with slackened shoulder (cf Irish bipartite vases 'of gently curving aspect', as described by O'Riordain & Waddell 1994, 27). In addition, a single bowl is present at both sites, although the Ardnave bowl (SF 1) which is decorated in classic Irish-Scottish style, was earlier than the bulk of the Ardnave pottery. It was discovered within a 'tailor-made' pit near the entrance to the Period 2 house (Ritchie & Welfare 1983, 328). The Kilellan bowl (no 5), unlike the general run of Irish-Scottish Tripartite bowls (cf O'Riordain & Waddell 1993, 10), has rather sketchy comb and spatulate decoration and was found scattered through the midden deposits. In decoration, however, the Kilellan bowl, is similar to the biconical vase, Ardnave SF 6.

Other similarities in decoration between the two assemblages include the dragged whipped cord and triangular nicks on no 6 which bear comparison with Ardnave SF 17. The Kilellan shell-decorated food vessels (nos 8 & 11) are paralleled by the shell-decorated vessels at Ardnave (SF 2, 7, 11 & 18a). Twisted cord is known at both sites (cf no 12 and the rim of Ardnave SF 8). The herringbone ornament on certain of the larger vessels (nos 13, 14 & 74) resembles the decoration on the neck of Ardnave SF 8. The technique of false relief is present at both sites (nos 24 & 25; Ardnave SF 22),

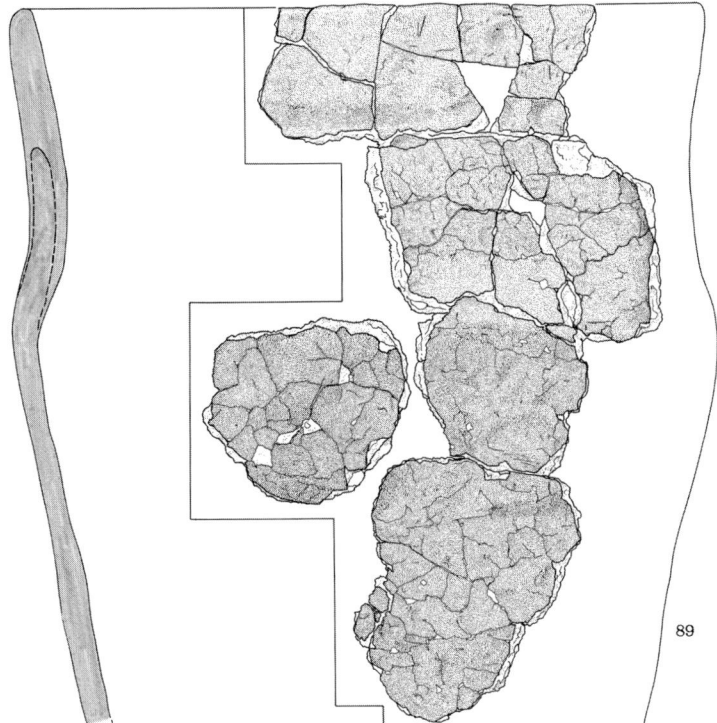
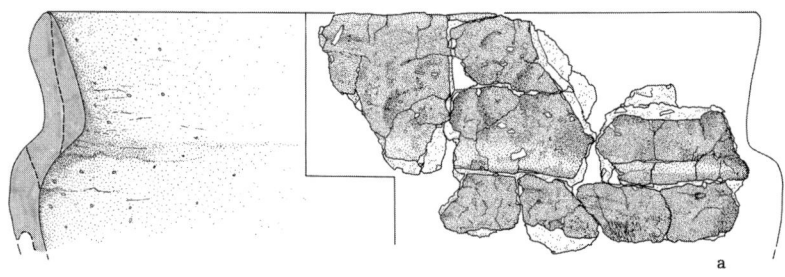
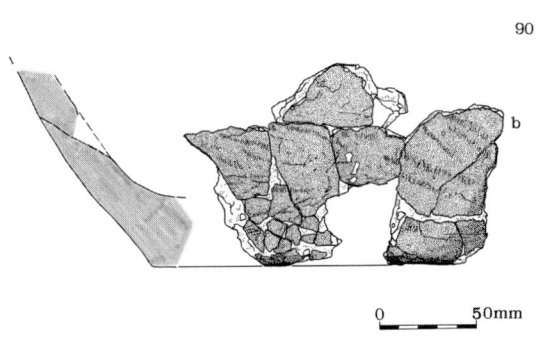

74 Pottery nos 89–90.

as too is broad incision (eg nos 10, 23, 30 & 31; Ardnave SF 4 & 16).

There is, therefore, a close typological similarity between the Ardnave assemblage and a proportion of the Kilellan assemblage. Although the Kilellan assemblage is much larger than the Ardnave assemblage, the size of the expanded rim component at both sites is, coincidentally, almost identical, there being 22–5 vases of rim types R2–R5 at Kilellan and approximately 28 vases from Period 4, Ardnave.

Despite the strength of these similarities, there are nonetheless also marked variations in the complexion of the two assemblages. The most pronounced difference lies in the lack of large plain jars at Ardnave, jars which at Kilellan are assumed to have been appropriate for food storage. Large decorated jars, however, were known at Ardnave, as hinted at by a single rim sherd (SF 14), which closely resembles Kilellan no 73. Cups are absent from Ardnave and so too are the Kilellan upright rim vases with their elaborately decorated internal bevels (lattice decoration is consequently absent from the Ardnave assemblage). The most striking difference between the Kilellan and Ardnave assemblages, however, lies in the fact that Ardnave has yielded a high proportion of base and lower body sherds. Roughly 25% of the Ardnave assemblage has a complete or near complete profile. This factor indicates that substantial differences existed in the methods of disposal prevailing at the two sites. The completeness of so many of the Ardnave pots is no doubt what prompted Ritchie and Welfare's remark that 'decorated pottery at Ardnave appears to be of a higher order, and also more abundant, than at Kilellan' (1983, 319). The overall differences between the two assemblages may be functional rather than chronological or cultural in nature. However, with no evidence for the location of the house-sites associated with the Kilellan and Ardnave Phase 4 middens, it has not been possible to fully evaluate the putative functional differences between the two assemblages.

The links between the Ardnave assemblage and the Irish Vase tradition have already been discussed by T Cowie (1983, 328). These links apply equally to Kilellan, but in addition, the Kilellan upright rim pottery, which was absent from Ardnave, also has affinities with the Irish tripartite vase tradition; similarities of form and motif are shared (eg deep internal bevels and angular shoulders, horizontal zones, herringbone, cross-hatch and lattice motifs), although the Kilellan material has more frequent use of stamped decoration in addition to the incised decoration which is more the norm on Irish tripartite vases (O'Riordain & Waddell 1993, 25). The series of jars at Kilellan with herringbone decoration carried over ridged internal bevels find ready parallels in principle with Irish Encrusted Urns such as those from Knocklishen Beg, Co Carlow; Greenhills, Co Dublin; Castleboy, Tara, Co Meath (Kavanagh 1973, 512–13 and figs 6, 16, 26), but differ in fabric and feel (A Sheridan *pers comm*). In mainland Britain, herringbone decoration is common on the internal bevels of urns (cf Cowie 1978), but a ridged effect, formed by the application of a series of strips of clay to the internal bevel is seemingly known only at Kilellan. The occurrence of a possible version of this technique on a large Beaker vessel from the Beaker I, Northton, Harris should, however, be noted (Simpson 1976, fig 12.3).

Kilellan is the first domestic site to validate the clear relationship that exists between vases, vase urns and encrusted urns (cf Waddell 1990, 10; O'Riordain & Waddell 1993, 25; Tomalin 1983, 15, 16 & 32). Kilellan also furnishes a rare instance of the co-occurrence of a bowl with pottery of the vase tradition. On the basis of the Irish material, O'Riordain and Waddell argue that '... the Vase Tradition, at least in part, superseded the Bowl Tradition' and continue 'it is surely significant that no typical bowl has been found with a typical vase and it seems likely that social or religious factors must have induced this separation in the funerary record' (1993, 37); the authors summarize the Irish evidence for bowl and vase pottery from sites presumed to be domestic, listing five at which bowl sherds have been found and seven possible domestic and/or ritual sites which have produced vase sherds (1993, 5, 25).

The only Irish domestic site to have produced both bowl and vase sherds is that of Dalkey Island, Co Dublin. The stratigraphy at Dalkey Island, however, was poorly understood (Liversage 1968). Both Burgess (1976, 204) and Gibson (1982, 140) have pointed to the similarities existing between some of the Kilellan pottery and certain vessels from Dalkey Island (see Liversage 1968: 116–22; Text figs 3, 15 & 16). A small group of vases from Site V at Dalkey Island are distinguished both by their deep internally decorated rim bevels and by their range in size. For this reason they have a broad similarity to the Kilellan upright rim pottery. There are differences in detail, both decoratively and in the pronounced angularity of form (ibid, p118), but it is interesting to note that lattice decoration was used at both sites (ibid, p117). Gibson differs from Liversage in his reconstruction of the large 'urn' sized pot (Gibson 1982, fig D1.3: 15; Liversage 1968, Text fig 3). Regardless of which reconstruction is the more accurate, however, this large vessel and a sherd (Liversage 1968, p120), both bear a typological resemblance to the Kilellan decorated jars.

Burgess asserts that 'plain shouldered jars may have a wider distribution in the Islands and Irish Sea province' (1976, 204) and pointed to the rim sherd from such a vessel found at Rosinish, Benbecula (Shepherd 1976, fig 11.3:2). Ritchie has also remarked on the discovery of shouldered jars from sites on Coll and their resemblance to the Kilellan vessels (Ritchie & Crawford 1978, 97, fig 3, no 2, & fig 10, no 4). Field work carried out at Cruach Mhor, Islay, in 1959, produced sherds from 'large coarse jars', assumed to be Late Neolithic in date, while a subsequent season of field work in 1977 yielded comb-decorated sherds presumed to date from the Late Neolithic or Early Bronze Age (Alcock & Alcock 1978, 66–7) and it has been suggested that this material may derive from a Kilellan type assemblage. Neither plain nor decorated shouldered jars have been recovered among the large surface collections made at sites in the south and east of Scotland, such as Tentsmuir, Fife (Longworth 1967), which appear to span the entire Bronze Age, an absence which may indicate that the shouldered jars with upright rims were indeed a feature of the Irish Sea region. The only point of similarity with the Tentsmuir pottery, as illustrated, with that from Kilellan are the fine wedge-and-tail impressions on sherds 54a and b (Longworth 1967, fig 12) which come from large shouldered vases of expanded rim type (cf Kilellan no 74).

Among Enlarged Food Vessels or Vase Urns from the Scottish mainland sites are a number of examples with deep internal bevels, reminiscent of the deep bevels at Kilellan. In particular, mention may be made of an urn from Hill of Foulzie, Aberdeenshire (Cowie 1978, ABN 6C), while examples, with more upright rims, and convex internal mouldings, include vessels from Aberlemno (ibid, AGS 1), Dunbeath (FIF 5) and Leuchar Brae (ABN 7). As a result of the application of the new bio-apatite technique of radiocarbon dating cremated bone, a growing number of dates are now available for Scottish Vase Urns (including Leuchar Brae). Overall the dates range from c 2150 to 1500 cal BC at one sigma, but there are now enough dates to support the idea that urn-sized vessels were in use around or just before 2000 BC (Sheridan 2003, 203–6).

Considerable attention has been paid by Tomalin (1983, 32–4, 40–1) to the impact of Kilellan on then-current 'food vessel thought'. Tomalin favoured the view that the geographical location of Kilellan provided 'a specialized environment in which an atypical community might retain an archaic ceramic style far removed from mainland norms'. This southern-centred view appears to ignore the fact that Kilellan has close links with the Irish Vase Tradition: it is the wider Irish Sea Province which provides the key to understanding Kilellan. Tomalin cites the presence of the 'pygmy cup' (sic) (no 1) as evidence of external contact, but the cup from Kilellan is atypical, and in the context of a domestic assemblage it is doubtful if valid comparisons can be made with what may be specialized accessory cups in funerary contexts.

The large volume of pots from Kilellan with evidence of manufacturing technique provide a rich source of information regarding the construction techniques used on Bronze Age pottery and may well repay further study. The evidence from Kilellan refutes Wardle's contention that 'forward oblique' (sic) junctions were a technique reserved for exceptionally large vessels in the 'middle of the Bronze Age' (Wardle 1992, 60–1). Kilellan also provides clear evidence for the occasional employment of a combination of tongue-and-groove and obliquely scarfed joins in the same vessel.

In summing up, it is apparent that quite apart from the intrinsic value of such a varied ceramic assemblage, Kilellan is important as an object lesson in the pitfalls inherent in constructing arguments on the basis of unreconstructed sherds. Above all, the case of the three supposedly all-over-corded sherds, which sparked off the debate about the existence of a Beaker element at Kilellan, highlights the dangers of assigning a few atypical sherds to a particular typological category and then compounding this by pegging a label to the entire site on the strength of those few sherds. Such labels have their place, primarily as a convenient shorthand for facilitating inter-site comparisons between assemblages, but must be based both on reconstructed forms and on the total range of forms present. Even then, they must be deployed with caution: the biases inherent in inventing typological labels have been set out by Barrett, who argues that 'neither cultural nor processual archaeology confront the fundamental issue of human agency' (1991, 202). On these grounds, it would be perhaps equally misleading to label the Kilellan assemblage simply on the basis of the 'Food Vessel' component.

Due to the scarcity of evidence for Early Bronze Age domestic sites, Kilellan currently appears 'unique' in its range of pot types and decoration. In reality, the Kilellan potters have been 'constrained' in the way in which they created their pots (ibid, 202). The basic shape of any vessel at Kilellan is bipartite;

even the cup (no 1) has a bipartite division marked by a centrally placed horizontal groove. Functional considerations may have determined the size of the pots, the thickness of the walls and the type of fabric used. Decoration is less standardized than is form but, even so, is largely dictated by the shape of the vessel, and motifs, although executed using a wide range of materials, are drawn from a limited repertoire.

Despite the problems encountered in unravelling the complex stratigraphy of the midden, the volume of pottery excavated at Kilellan, taken in consideration with the range of form and decorative technique displayed and the absence of any comparable published body of material from a domestic site, will ensure the Kilellan assemblage a place in studies of Scottish Early Bronze Age ceramics for a considerable time to come.

THE POTTERY FROM THE RAISED BEACH DEPOSITS

Three small trenches were cut into the raised beach deposits, trench KN 73 C1 and, alongside it, trenches KN 76 H1 and H2 (illus 7). Eleven sherds of prehistoric pottery were recovered weighing 217gm (nos 68, 139–41), and two pieces of daub weighing 8gm. The largest of these sherds no 68, weighing 120gm, comes from KN 76 H1 6/4, apparently just above the pebbles of the raised beach. This sherd is very abraded but has applied decoration and could possibly be from the same vessel as other sherds from the Bronze Age midden (cf nos 66 & 67), and on those grounds has been catalogued with the Bronze Age pottery. An abraded sherd of possible Early Bronze Age date was recovered from KN 76 H1 7/1 and an undiagnostic bodysherd was recovered from KN 76 H1 2. The upper layers of KN 76 H1 and H2 were contaminated by modern pottery.

Trench KN 76 C1 produced an undecorated rim sherd from layer 8 and seven small wall sherds from layers 7 and 6, all apparently from the same pot (no 141). This pottery differs in form and fabric from the rest of the Kilellan assemblage. The fabric (Fab 12) is laminated and contains small pores; the clay matrix is brown to greyish in colour and inclusions consist of fine rock fragments. The rim sherd is flat-topped and is from a bucket-shaped vessel, and on typological grounds it is more in keeping with the ceramic traditions of the later second millennium or early first millennium BC. Given that sherds from this pot came from layers 6, 7 and 8, it is possible that a feature such as a pit or post-hole has been missed during excavation. A small crumb of pottery in a different fabric was also recovered from C1 8.

THE POTTERY FROM TRENCH L2

Pottery from Site L (nos 142–9) is undecorated and comprises 344 pieces, weighing 1.36 kg and representing a minimum of 5–7 pots (table 10). In addition, there are 225 pieces of fired clay/daub, weighing 1.6kg. The majority of sherds are small, featureless and heavily burnt, and colours, therefore, range from yellowish ochre, through pink to orange brown. Unlike the Early Bronze Age pottery, the majority of Site L pottery contains organic temper.

FABRICS

Much of the assemblage from Site L has been burnt, making fabric identification difficult and distorting the colour of the vessels. Three fabrics were distinguished (Fabs 13–15) and a full description has been included with the site archive. The bulk of the assemblage was

TABLE 10
Total of sherds from site L2.

Pieces			Weight (gm)			Totals		
Sherds	Frags	Crumbs	Sherds	Frags	Crumbs	Pieces	Weight	Average Weight
103	158	83	1017	298	42	344	1357	4

assigned to Fab 13 (81% by pieces, 85% by weight), which is characterized by large-grained subangular grits, up to 11mm in size and numerous small spherical voids from the inclusion of organic material. Fab 14, which contained similar grits to those of Fab 13, but not more than 6mm in size, comprised 9% of the assemblage by pieces and 5% by weight. Fab 15, which could not readily be distinguished from Fab 13 comprised 3% by pieces and 8% by weight. Small sherds and fragments, which it was not possible to assign to a fabric type, account for 7% by pieces and 2% by weight.

FORM

The assemblage from Site L is too fragmentary to allow any pot to be reconstructed. The only definite rim sherd present is a tiny fragment of simple, rounded form (no 142). A bevelled sherd (no 143) has also been recovered but it is uncertain whether this is a fragment from a rim. Of the two basal angle sherds from the site, one (part of no 143) has a flaring basal angle, while the other (no 144) is more upright, with finger pinching at the foot of the wall; the underside of the base is ridged and bears a possible finger impression.

MANUFACTURE, SURFACE TREATMENT, FIRING AND RESIDUES

None of the sherds from L shows clear evidence of manufacturing technique. The majority of sherds are heavily scorched and some are fully oxidized. Wall thicknesses range from 10–17mm, although the lower figure is unreliable. Evidence of surface treatments is largely lacking due to fire damage. The burning has emphasized the protrusion of the grits on both exterior and interior surfaces. No 144, however, has a smoothed exterior and finger-smeared interior. The exteriors of nos 147 and 149 are also smoothed. A few sherds have soot encrustation on their interior surfaces, including no 145, which comprises two large sherds forming part of the lining of a pit.

FUNCTION

With little evidence available as to form and no evidence as to vessel capacity it is impossible to deduce what type of activity may have been carried on at Site L. The total quantity of sherds is small relative to the depth of the deposits. The coarseness of the fabrics, together with the intense burning of much of the material, may indicate that activity at the site was industrial rather than domestic in nature.

Although only two sherds now survive from pit F 128, site notes, plan and section (illus 40) indicate that more than two sherds were found. Clay was used along with part of the lower wall of a pot to line and waterproof a pit, some 400mm in diameter, yet there is no trace of clay remaining on the two surviving sherds. Although the pit was presumably waterproof, the heavy sooting on the interior surfaces of these two sherds indicates contact with fire.

DISTRIBUTION

Much of the pottery comes from layer 10 (35% by sherd count, 22% by weight). Layer 10 consists of an accumulation of midden deposits, or a possible house floor, within and beneath which are numerous post-holes, pits, hearths and other features. The upper levels of layer 10 have been disturbed by later agricultural activity with the result that some sherds have been pulled up into layer 8. There was also some mixing at the base of layer 10 where it rested on the ginger sand, layer 11, dating to the Mesolithic, but this mixing involved only pieces of clay or daub. Layer 10 contains pottery from all three fabric types present on Site L. Other features within or below layer 10 producing pottery comprise F 114, F 117, F 118, F 119, F 123, F 126 and F 128. It is worth noting that the two joining sherds from F 128 constitute the largest single total of pottery by weight from any feature in Site L, amounting to 32% of the total pottery retrieved. Feature 117, a pit within layer 10, also contained more pottery by weight than the whole of layer 10 (34% by sherd count, 26% by weight) although, unlike layer 10, the pottery from this feature was all from one fabric type (Fab 13). Between them, the remaining features within layer 10 account for 20% of the total pottery from L by sherd count, 16% by weight. Both features 123 and 126 contain a high proportion of small fragments of pottery. Unstratified pottery amounts to just 9% of the total by sherd count, and 3% by weight.

DATING

Radiocarbon dates were obtained from charcoal present in layer 10, a presumed occupation deposit, and from the upper and middle fill of a substantial pit 117 sealed by layer 10. The former yielded a date, at 2 sigma calibration, of 830–410 cal BC (GU–3519), while the latter produced a date of 820–410 cal BC (GU–3518) (table 2).

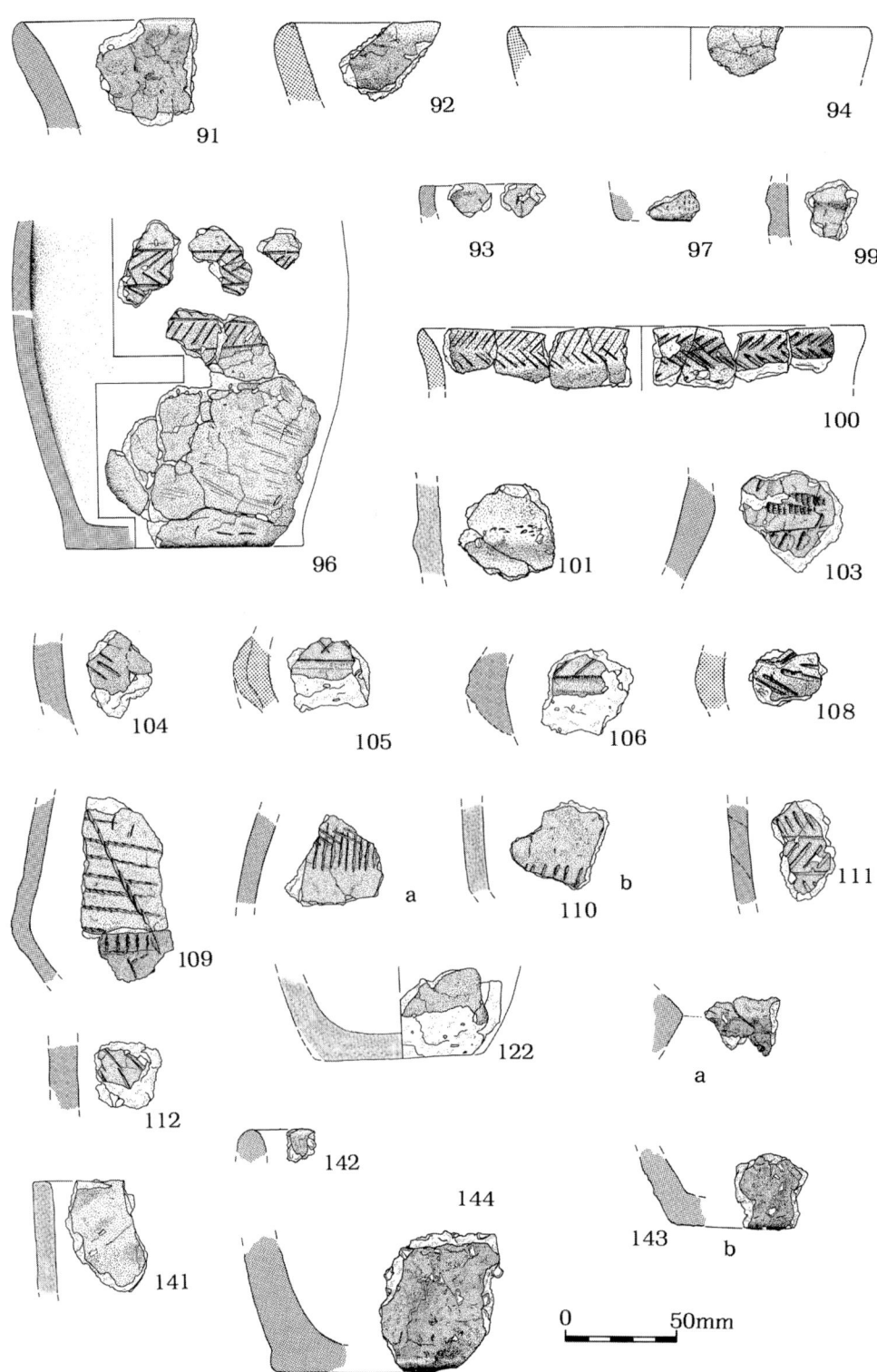

75 Pottery nos 91–4, 96–7, 99–101, 103–6, 108–12, 122, 142–4.

THE POTTERY

DISCUSSION

These dates, together with the meagre pottery evidence, suggest that activity at Site L probably took place over a continuous, but short-lived period of time. The paucity of the assemblage precludes any meaningful assessment of the ceramic evidence, nor is it possible to place the assemblage in a wider setting due to the dearth of ceramic material from the western mainland of Scotland in the early Iron Age (cf Lane & Armit 1990, 126). The site of Balloch Hill, Kintyre, provides the only other excavated example, in the wider region, of a domestic assemblage which, for part of its life, may conceivably have been contemporary with Site L (Peltenburg 1982, 175–83, 203–4). Sherds were associated with deposits containing charcoal, which provided a date with a range of 807–400 cal BC (GU–1105) (Ashmore 1997, 272). The sherds were considered to derive from bucket forms but, as with Site L, the assemblage is too fragmentary to be of value for comparative purposes.

THE POTTERY FROM TRENCHES J AND K

MISCELLANEOUS POTTERY FROM TRENCHES J AND K

The old turf line (layer 7) in KN 76 K1 produced an incised neck sherd from a large vase (no 150). Three abraded body sherds undoubtedly belong to this pot, two from the same layer (layer 7), and the third from layer 203. The fabric (Fab 5) of this vessel appears visually identical to the fabric of an upright rim vase from the Early Bronze Age midden (no 39/40). The form of no 150, together with its decoration, however, distinguish it from any other pot from the Early Bronze Age midden. On the other hand, this decorated sherd does bear a striking resemblance to an enlarged food vessel discovered nearby in a cist at Kiells (Ritchie & Welfare 1983, 362). Both the simple treble zigzag motif and the black fabric with the exterior surface oxidized to a light red/orange are features common to the Kilellan sherd and the Kiells vessel.

Two anomalous abraded bodysherds come from KN 76 K3 5 and from the surface collections made at Kilellan in the 1950s (no 152). Their fabric contains rounded pebbles and does not resemble any other sherds in the Kilellan assemblage.

A tiny burnt rim sherd from KN 76 J2 32 has two parallel grooves possibly on its interior rather than exterior surface (no 151). Although a very tentative parallel may be made with grooved ware ceramics, it seems more plausible to suggest that this may be a 'false rim', consistent with the grass-marked pottery discussed below.

A basal angle fragment with a diameter of about 100mm and three abraded sherds come from KN 76 J2 107, KN 76 K3 5 and 501 (no 167). These sherds differ in fabric from the rest of the J/K pottery and from any other material from Kilellan. The basal sherd has a slightly soapy feel, is laminated and contains finely crushed white grits. They may predate the majority of the J/K material or they may indicate contemporaneous use of a finer class of pottery, alongside the J/K coarse wares.

TABLE 11
Total of sherds from sites J & K.

Site	Pieces			Weight (gm)			Totals				Average weight
	Sherds	Frags	Crumbs	Sherds	Frags	Crumbs	Pieces	% pieces	Weight	% weight	
J1	157	464	347	1993	962	148	968	85	3103	80	3
J2	57	29	49	528	36	6	135	12	571	15	4
J3	2	1	0	21	3	0	3	1	28	1	8
K1	5	0	0	71	0	0	5	1	71	2	14
K3	6	12	0	48	17	0	18	2	65	2	4
Totals	227	506	396	2661	1018	154	1129	100	3838	100	3

It is possible, therefore, that these miscellaneous sherds hint at otherwise undocumented phases of occupation or more transient activity at Kilellan.

THE LATER POTTERY FROM TRENCHES J AND K

The pottery from J and K comprises 1129 pieces (almost 80% of which are fragments and crumbs), weighing 3.8kg (table 11) and representing about a minimum of 11 pots. The maximum number of pots cannot be ascertained. There are also 54 pieces of daub, weighing 334gm. The pottery from J1 and J2 is derived from midden deposits, which had accumulated on top of a stone-built souterrain.

In marked contrast to the Early Bronze Age pottery the sherds from J and K are generally small, powdery and grubby, as if trampled, and frequently have only one external surface remaining. An exception to this is the reconstructed portion of a pot (no 153) whose sherds are in good condition due to their burial in windblown sand (layer 14). In some cases, sherds are heavily burnt (no 162) or coated with ash (no 161).

FABRICS

The fabrics from J/K have been divided into four groups, the full description of which has been deposited with the site archive. All fabrics are chunky in appearance, with inclusions up to 15 mm in size. Fab 16 (24% by pieces, 27% by weight) has sub-angular grey inclusions. Sherds assigned to Fab 17 (9% by pieces, 19% by weight) are so heavily burnt that this may not constitute a fabric group in its own right; the inclusions are blue-black in colour and of a granular, friable texture; in addition, there are numerous spherical voids through the fabric which most likely derive from burnt-out organic material (PCRG 1992, 28). Fab 18 (47% by pieces, 41% by weight) contains inclusions, which are predominately granular and white-black in colour, plus some scarce traces of organic material, which sometimes leaves spherical voids in the fabric. Fab 19 is represented by a single sherd, containing large stone inclusions and possessing a corky texture due to the high proportion of burnt-out organic material. Sherds which have not been assigned to a fabric group, account for 20% by pieces and 9% by weight of the J/K total.

FORM

None of the pottery from J/K has a complete profile. The two largest surviving vessels suggest an open bowl form with gently flaring walls, which angle inwards slightly at the rim (eg no 153). The rim of no 162 appears to be only slightly inturned but, as this pot is powdery, its rim may be quite abraded. The few surviving basal sherds in the assemblage are very fragmentary but are suggestive of flat bases. The majority of the J/K sherds, however, are undiagnostic.

MANUFACTURE, SURFACE TREATMENT AND FIRING

The clearest evidence of construction is provided by no 153, which clearly shows tongue and groove ring junctions. No 157, and possibly no 162, also show tongue-and-groove construction. The base of no 159 shows an obliquely scarfed ring junction.

The most distinctive feature of the J/K pottery is its pimply appearance due to the protrusion of large grits covered by a thin skin of clay, giving the appearance of a slip. No 153, which is the least abraded of the J pottery, has roughly smoothed surfaces, with wipe marks visible on both interior and exterior surfaces, although no attempt was made to conceal the ring junctions on the interior. Accidental fingernail impressions are present on the rim and there is one clear fingerprint. In addition, a small comb impression is visible on the exterior surface, about 2cm below the rim. Wipe marks are common on other sherds (eg nos 154, 158, 169), while finger impressions are present on the interior surfaces (eg no 160).

The surface treatment of nos 157, 158, 160 and 162 is very distinctive, in that the pots appear to have been bound by grass fibres during the drying stage. These have left horizontal grooves in the pot surface, which are randomly spaced and sometimes converge or cross each other. All the grass-marked sherds have been heavily burnt causing the fabric to become very powdery. Even so, wipe marks (or possibly brush marks) are visible on the upper portion of no 162. It is uncertain how many vessels are represented by the grass-marked sherds, perhaps a minimum of two, since some of the small, grass-marked sherds appear to be thinner walled (eg no 157) than no 162, although this may result from a pattern of breakage along construction joins. Despite the burning, grits are not exposed on the exterior surfaces, which are nevertheless very uneven; the grits are, however, prominently exposed on the interior surfaces.

Firing control was poor, indicative of bonfire firing; the majority of the pottery has oxidized surfaces with an unoxidized core. Colours are generally an orange brown, with grey cores, except where distorted by burning.

THE POTTERY

FUNCTION AND USE

Given the fragmentary condition of the assemblage, there is very little evidence of function. There is no evidence for a range in vessel size. The only rim diameters available show that large bowls were in use: no 153 has a rim diameter of 350mm and no 162 a diameter of approximately 300mm. The pimply nature of the J/K fabrics may indicate that these pots were designed for a specific purpose, for which well-finished and smoothed surfaces were superfluous to requirements. Both fabrics 18 and 19 contain organic temper, the presence of which increases porosity, and large chunks of crushed rock, which add strength to the fabric (Rice 1987, 14.1). These features may give a clue to the function for which these rather coarse pots were intended, but they may equally well have been unintentional.

Sooting of surfaces was fairly common; much of the pottery had been burnt, post-usage (cf nos 158 & 162) and some sherds were very powdery and had a whitish ash deposit adhering to their surfaces, as if they had become incorporated in hearth material (eg no 161). A large number of contexts from trenches J1, J2 and K3 produced pottery in a fragmentary condition, but apparently very similar in fabric – all had large grits protruding under the skin of the exterior surface, the interior surface was generally missing and much of this pottery is very grubby, either because the powdery surfaces attracted dirt, or because the sherds may have been trampled (cf no 165).

DISTRIBUTION AND PHASING

No cross-context joins have been found, as the condition of the pottery does not lend itself to a search for joins. The fact that Trench J1 produced by far the greatest quantity of pottery – 80% by weight of the combined J/K total (table 11) – indicates that there was a marked concentration of pottery on the east side of the 'souterrain'. Layer 19 in J2, which relates to midden deposits on the west side of the souterrain produced only 28gm of pottery (<1% by weight), a disproportionately small amount, even allowing for the fact that the area excavated on the west side of the souterrain is far smaller than that excavated on the east. Trench J3, a narrow trench also on the west side of the souterrain, produced only 25gm (<1% by weight) of pottery. Trench K3 which encompasses a possible circular building and, putatively, the westerly continuation of the souterrain, produced only 65gm (2% by weight) of pottery. Most of the sherds from K3 resemble those from J1, but three sherds are anomalous and are discussed separately (nos 152 & 167).

There is no pottery at all from K2 which lies to the NW of the 'house'. Trench K1, which is 2m further west of K2, produced 71gm of pottery, none of which bears any resemblance to the rest of the J and K pottery and has been noted separately (see no 150 in discussion of miscellaneous pottery from J and K, above).

The upper midden in J1 yielded only 4% by weight of the total pottery from J1. The windblown sand, layer 14, produced 35% by weight of the pottery from J1, all, apparently, deriving from one vessel. The heaviest concentration of pottery, however, was recovered from the lower of the two 5cm deep sweeps across J1 (quadrants 25–8), which yielded 53% by weight of the total pottery from the trench. In general, the pottery from spits 20–8 comprised larger sherds and fragments than were found in the

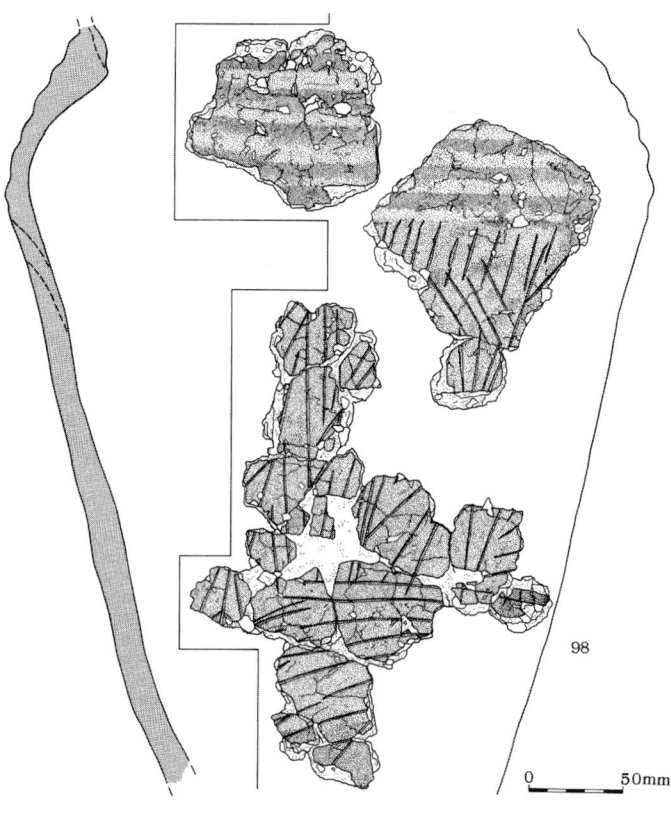

76 Pottery no 98.

overlying spits 6–13. Yet, in form and fabric, the pottery from the upper and lower midden deposits in J1 is essentially the same; the only distinctive sherds from the lower midden are no 160, which incorporates a large quantity of organic temper, and, secondly, no 151, which may represent a false rim and has been discussed separately (see miscellaneous pottery from J and K, above).

Vessel no 153 from layer 14 is the least damaged of the J/K pottery, no doubt thanks to the protection afforded by the sandblow. The pattern of abrasion, revealed by the partial reconstruction of this bowl, may indicate that the pot was originally buried in an inverted position with its lower body exposed long enough to result in some abrasion, before it was covered by further midden deposits.

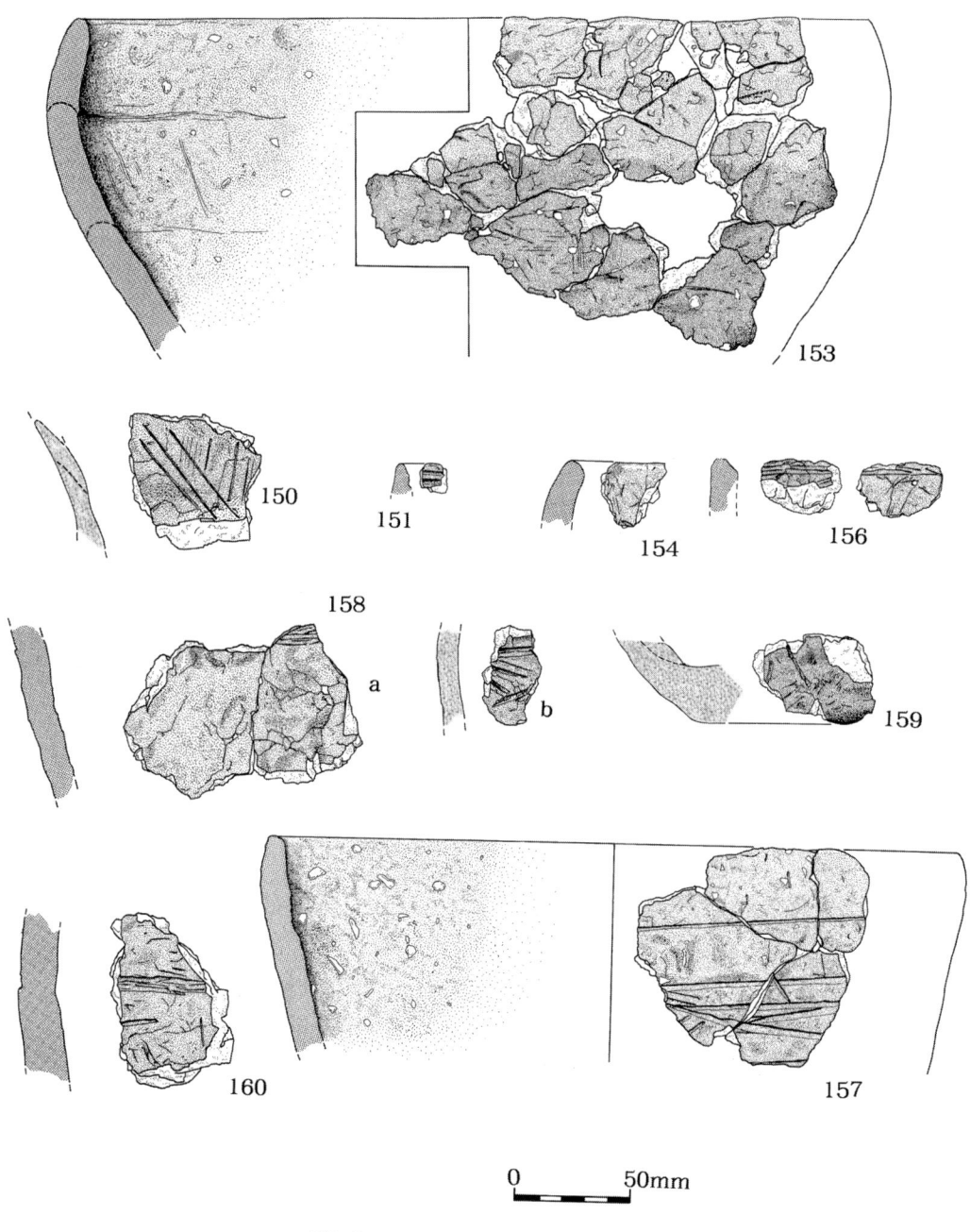

77 Pottery nos 150–1, 153–4, 156–60.

The midden in J2 was some 200–300mm thick but yielded only 15% by weight of the total pottery from J/K. Within J2, layer 19 on the west of the souterrain produced 5% by weight of the total J2 pottery, layer 30 produced 4% by weight and layer 32 yielded 79% by weight of the J2 total. The other features in J2 produced just 11% by weight of the total pottery.

DATING

Two dates were obtained from samples of bone taken from deposits associated with the pottery: layer 22 in the lower midden in J1 produced a date with a span of 200 cal BC–cal AD 120 (GU–3516), while layer 30 in the upper midden in J2 yielded a date with a range of 170 cal BC–cal AD 220 (GU–3515).

DISCUSSION

Lane has highlighted the absence of any clear evidence for a major ceramic tradition in the southern Hebrides after the Bronze Age (1990, 126), in contrast to the situation north of the Firth of Lorn, where assemblages are characterized by the presence of large quantities of high-quality, decorated, Hebridean ceramics (eg Dun Mor Vaul, Tiree: MacKie 1974; Dun Cul Bhuirg, Iona: Ritchie & Lane 1980). The J/K assemblage does little to fill the ceramic void, being comprised of too few sherds to permit meaningful comparisons. The fragmentary nature and general crudity of construction of the vessels add to the difficulty of placing the assemblage in any wider setting. Burgess (*in litt*) has noted the resemblance of some of the pottery from Sites J & K to Grooved Ware. Although the coarse, rather pimply surface of the pottery and the grooves on some of the sherds do bear some comparison to some Orcadian Grooved Ware, this would seem to require special pleading.

Instead, parallels among later prehistoric pottery, while not as compelling as one might wish, offer a better frame of reference for the Kilellan material, more in keeping with the available absolute dates. One of the very few sites in the region to have produced dated, domestic pottery of this general period, is that of Balloch Hill, Kintyre (Peltenburg 1982). The most dependable group of dates for the Phase 3 (Iron Age) occupation, at this site, has a range spanning 767 cal BC–cal AD 72 (GU–1033; HAR–2043) (ibid, 203–4; Ashmore 1997, 273, 275). However, only one group of Iron Age sherds was directly associated with a dated context: the date obtained had a range of 807–400 cal BC (GU–1105) (ibid, 177, 181; Ashmore 1997, 272). The assemblage comprised coarsely-made sherds, some showing ring construction, and which were thought to derive from bucket-shaped vessels (Peltenburg 1982, 175–7).

While the Balloch Hill assemblage is, itself, too limited and fragmentary to permit meaningful comparison with the J/K material, it is, nevertheless, worth drawing attention to a superficial resemblance between the Kilellan grass-marked sherds and a few, small, grass-marked sherds, in a coarse fabric, recovered from Balloch Hill (ibid, 174, fig 13; 175–6). The latter were in turn compared with the very coarse pottery from the vitrified fort of Finavon, Angus, and it was concluded that at least some of the Balloch Hill examples had been deliberately decorated (Peltenburg 1982, 176–7). However, in his original report, Childe considered that the shallow grooves in exterior surfaces of pots had been produced by strands of grass or straw being wrapped round the pot while it was being built up and then burnt away during firing (Childe 1935, 70–1). The haphazard nature of the grass markings on the Kilellan sherds leads the writer to favour Childe's interpretation. The Finavon grass-marked vessels displayed examples of 'false rims', created by the tongue-and-groove construction technique and the main form was described as 'a flat-based pot in which the walls expand slightly from the base upward only to contract again at the mouth' (Childe 1934, 71). While there are clearly resemblances, in form and manufacturing technique, between the grass-marked sherds from both sites, nevertheless, the series of radiocarbon dates from Finavon may be considerably earlier than the J/K dates: the latest determination in the series, associated with the occupation layer of the fort, is 410–190 cal BC (GaK–1223) (MacKie 1969, 16–18, although the uncertainty surrounding the chronology of Finavon has recently been emphasized by Alexander 2002, 54). While the presence of superficially similar, grass-marked sherds at Kilellan, Balloch Hill and Finavon may result from chance, it is just feasible that they derive from a lengthy and widespread tradition, involving the production of coarse vessels for a common purpose.

In the report on the pottery from Balloch Hill, attention was drawn to the links such coarse, bucket-shaped vessels were presumed to share with the coarse wares present on other Scottish Iron Age sites, ranging from MacKie's so-called 'Dunagoil' or 'Abernethy Ware' to Cool's Broxmouth Type I pottery, present on numerous hillfort sites in Lowland Scotland (Peltenburg 1982, 176–7; Cool 1982). For the reasons outlined earlier, it is felt that it would be unwise to attempt to categorize assemblages of very coarse pottery on the basis of vague features, particularly when so little comparative material exists. In any case, the coarseness of the pottery may reflect a response to function, a possibility also raised by Topping in his consideration of 'Dunagoil Ware' (1987, 80), found at Dun Mor Vaul, Tiree and on various mainland hillfort sites, and encompassing a range of plain pottery with thick walls, a general bucket shape and gritty fabric. Furthermore, the presence of four sherds among the J/K assemblage in a finer fabric (see above), raises the possibility of contemporary better quality pottery under-represented among the material recovered from the excavation.

Finally, mention must be made of the Iron Age sherds recovered from the site of Ardnave, Islay, if only to emphasize that these are quite distinct from the Kilellan assemblage. An organically tempered, globular vessel with thin walls and an everted rim was recovered from an old land surface around a hearth. Charcoal taken from the top of the hearth produced a date of 220–390 cal AD (GU–1443). In addition, a deposit of antler within the old ground surface, associated with the same hearth, yielded a date of 420–570 cal AD (GU–1273) and a further sherd of organically tempered pottery was also firmly associated with this deposit (Ritchie & Welfare 1983, 314–15).

POTTERY CATALOGUE

NOTES

1. Format of entries
The aim of the catalogue is to provide a brief description to aid 'reading' of illustrated sherds. Each entry is set out as follows:

Catalogue number
Rim or base form (see text and illus 59 for classifications), rim or base diameter, girth (where no other measurement available), height (where this can be estimated); wall thickness; fabric type (see text)

No of pieces/weight of pieces assigned to vessel
Contexts
Details of illustration in Burgess 1976 (where relevant)

2. Abbreviations
R = Rim Form (illus 59)
RD = Rim Diameter
B = Base Form (illus 59)
BD = Base Diameter
G = Girth
H = Height
W = Wall Thickness
FAB = Fabric
N/A = not available/indeterminate

An asterisk indicates that the sherd(s) is not illustrated.

3. Measurements
All dimensions are given in millimetres; all weights are given in grams.

EARLY BRONZE AGE POTTERY

1–4: cups

1. R1; RD 60; G 70; H >42; W 4–6; FAB N/A
Rim and wall sherd; grooving, shell-edge, fingernail, circular and triangular punctulations; vague diagonal scratch marks on rim interior. Possible traces of decorative white inlay.
3 pieces, 11g
KN 61 I 6; KN 61 II 6; KN 76 G2 100.15
BAR FIG 10.8:9

2. R1; W 6; FAB N/A
Tiny rim sherd; whipped cord, grooving.
1 piece, 1g
KN 73 A1 2

3. R4; RD 60–80; FAB N/A
Tiny rim sherd; incised, fine point; very worn herring-bone pattern.
1 piece, 2g
KN 76 G2 100.15

4. R2; RD 100; W 5–6; FAB N/A
Rim and wall sherd; whipped cord.
2 pieces, 10g
KN 76 G1 102.02

5–25: small bowls and vases

5. R2; RD 170; B2; BD 130; G *c* 175; H *c* 130; W 11–13; FAB 2
Three rim sherds, wall sherds and almost complete base; rectangular-toothed comb, crescentic spatula/fingernail.
16 pieces, 423g
KN 60 F2 6; KN 61 II 6; KN 73 A1/3 2; KN 73 A2 2; KN 73 A4 6; U/S
BAR FIG 10.9:20

6. R2; W *c* 11; FAB 1
Three rim and four wall sherds from bowl or vase; triangular jabs, dragged comb.
7 pieces, 53g
KN 59 F2; KN 59 F4; KN 60 F2 5; KN 73 F1 6; KN 76 G2 108.01; U/S

7. R2; RD 160; G 165; W 8–9; FAB N/A
Rim and wall sherd; grooved, incised; traces of decorative white inlay, especially on rim bevel.
2 pieces, 27g
KN 54 – 'from Hearth Site A, 1954'; KN 59 U/S
BAR FIG 10.9:18

8. R2; B2?; W 7–10; FAB 8
Small rim sherd, wall sherd and large basal angle sherd; shell-edge (or incised?/fingernail?)
4 pieces, 51g
KN 58 U/S; KN 61 I 6; KN 73 A1/3 2; U/S
BAR FIG 10.8:11

9. R2; RD 220–240; W 7–9; FAB 8
Two joining rim sherds and small wall sherds; irregular oval jabbed impressions applied obliquely.
7 pieces, 167g
KN 60 F2 6; KN 61 I 6; KN 73 A1 2.

10. B2; BD 86; W 9–11; FAB 8
Wall and base; incised, oval jabbed impressions.
25 pieces, 270g
KN 59 F1; KN 60 F2 6; KN 61 I 6; KN 73 A1 1; KN 73 A1 2; KN 73 A2 2; KN 73 B1 6; KN 73 F1 6; KN 76 G2 0677e; U/S Surface
BAR FIG 10.10:29 & 30

11. R2; RD 200; W 11; FAB 2
Three rim sherds and wall sherds; shell-edge? (possibly a broken piece of shell as a number of the impressions have a distinctive 'key'-shaped signature).
16 pieces, 271g
U/S (see archive notes); KN 60 F2 6; KN 61 I 6; KN 73 A1 2; KN 73 A1/3 2; KN 73 A2 5; KN 73 B2 6; KN 73 F2 6; KN 76 G1 0603d; KN 76 G2 0603d; KN 76 G2 0634b; KN 76 G2 107.02; U/S
BAR FIG 10.10:25 & 27

12. R2; RD 220; G 230–40; W 11–14; FAB 2
Four rim sherds and wall sherds; twisted cord impressions in loose s-ply; exterior very worn.
98 pieces (of which 64 are frags/crumbs), 537g
KN 61 U/S; KN 61 I 6; KN 73 A1 1; KN 73 A1 2; KN 76 G2 0615d; KN 76 G2 0657d
BAR FIG 10.9:26

13. R2; RD 280; W 13; FAB 10
Three rim and wall sherds; wall thickness reduces noticeably towards lower break-edges; herringbone incised with sharp tool giving wedge-and-tail impressions.
10 pieces, 230g
U/S; KN 61 I 6; KN 73 A1 2; KN 73 A1/3 2

14. R2; RD 260–80; W 9 – max 18; FAB 6
Two large rim and wall sherds; wall, substantially thinner below shoulder; crisp herringbone neatly executed with blunt-ended tool.
13 pieces, 270g
KN 59 surface collection; KN 60 F2 6; KN 73 A2 2; KN 73 A3? 2
BAR FIG 10.9:17 & 19

15. R2; FAB N/A
Small rim fragment; herringbone, blunt tool
1 piece, 6g
KN 76 G2 0631b

16. R4; W 8–9; FAB 9
Small rim fragment and wall sherd from possible vase with at least two horizontal mouldings; fingernail/jabs? giving a feathered/herringbone design; possible traces of decorative white infill or peat ash staining on internal bevel
6 pieces, 22g
'from Hearth site A, 1954'; KN 59 U/S; KN 60 F2 6; KN 73 F1 6

17. R4; RD approx 160; FAB N/A
Small rim sherd; smoothed on surface; exterior very neatly and crisply incised; with traces of chevron design on exterior
1 piece, 9g
KN 73 F1

18. R4; FAB 8
Small rim sherd; incised and cross-hatched
1 piece, 5g
KN 73 A1 2

19. W 9; FAB 8
Small wall sherd; traces of very diffuse impressed decoration – possibly a rolled or very worn cord; perhaps from same pot as 18
1 piece, 5g
KN 76 G1 0601a

20. R4; RD *c* 130, FAB 3
Small rim sherd, heavily abraded; traces of incised decoration on internal bevel
1 piece, 11g
U/S

21. R4; FAB 3
Small rim sherd, heavily abraded; possibly horizontal twisted cord on internal bevel cut by transverse incisions; exterior has incised decoration
1 piece, 9g
KN 73 B1 6

22. R3; RD *c* 160; FAB 3
Small rim sherd, abraded.
1 piece, 7g
Hearth Site A, 1954

23. W 9–10 (13–16 over shoulder); FAB 3
Group of wall sherds with incised decoration, possibly part of 20, 21 or 22; variable wall thickness
26 pieces, 182g
KN 61 I 6; KN 73 A2 3/4; KN 73 A2 5; KN 73 B3 6; KN 73 B3 7; U/S

24. R4; RD *c* 200; W 8; FAB 1
Rim sherd; incised; grooved; false relief
1 piece; 31g
KN 76 G2 0655a

25. W 7; FAB 1
Small bodysherd, grooved; false relief; perhaps from same pot as 24
1 piece; 6g
KN 73 A1 2
BAR FIG 10.10:28

26–34: slack-shouldered or shoulderless vases

26. R5; RD 150; G 160; W 6; FAB 1
Substantial reconstructed section of pot giving complete profile from rim to close to base; incised herringbone; surface lustre
> 37 pieces (not necessarily all same pot), 130g
U/S BUNKER; KN 73 A1 2; KN 73 B1 6; KN 73 B2 6; KN 73 F1 6; KN 76 G1 0603c; KN 76 G2 O2; KN G2 0608; KN 76 G2 0657d; KN 76 G2 0658; KN 76 G2 118; G2 U/S

27. R5; RD *c* 200; W 8; FAB 1
Four small rim sherds; could be same pot as 26 (if rim very variable); surface lustre
5 pieces, 24g
KN 76 G1 0603a; KN 76 G2 0657 a/d; KN 76 U/S

28. R5; W 6–9; FAB 1
Sherds from the rim, wall and start of basal angle, but insufficient to reconstruct profile; incised herringbone; surface lustre
28 pieces, 235g
KN61 III 6; KN 76 G2 0611d; KN 76 G2 0657d; KN 76 G4; KN 76 G4 0317

29. R5; RD *c* 275; G (near base) *c* 300; H >200; W7–13; FAB 1
Substantial portion of a crushed, elaborately decorated vase, although decoration rather uncontrolled; incised, triangular spatulate impressions; firing irregular; ring junctions poorly smoothed; a non-viable pot?
294 pieces, 1200g
KN 76 G2 0611d; KN 76 G2 0657d; KN 76 G2 U/S; KN 76 G4 0301; KN 76 G4 0309; KN 76 G4 0313; KN 76 G4 0317; KN 76 G4 U/S; U/S

30. R5; RD *c* 300; W 8–10; FAB 4
Four rim sherds and wall sherds (profile uncertain), incised herringbone; surface lustre; minimum one, maximum 2 pots
39 pieces, 326g
KN 59 F4; KN 73 F1 6; KN 76 G2 0606a; KN 76 G2 0608; KN 76 G2 0655a; KN 76 G2 O657a; KN 76 G2 0657d; KN 76 G2 0661d; KN 76 G2 100.07a; KN 76 G2 215

31. W 7–10; FAB 4
Numerous bodysherds with random broad incision or impressed design; perhaps from same type of vase as 30; surface lustre; irregularly fired
38 pieces, 200g
KN 73 A1 2; KN 73 A1/3 U/S; KN 73 A2 3/4; KN 73 B1 6; KN 73 B2 6; KN 73 F1 6; KN 76 G2 0650a; KN 76 G2 0655a; KN 76 G2 0657a; KN 76 G2 0657d and e; KN 76 G2 0675e; KN 76 G4; U/S

32. R6; RD 120–30; H >70; W 6–7; FAB 1
Small rim sherd and three joining wall sherds; twisted cord on rim exterior and interior; body plain, if reconstruction correct.
4 pieces, 17g
KN 73 B2 6; KN 76 G4 0301

33. R6; RD 160; G 145; H *c* 130; W 9; FAB 1
Substantial reconstructed portion of small vase giving almost complete profile; twisted cord
26 pieces, 237g
KN 61 I 6; KN 73 A1/3 1; Km 73 A1/F1 1; KN 73 B1 6; KN 73 F1 6; KN 73 U/S; KN 76 G1 U/S; KN 76

G2 0605a; KN 76 G2 O608a; KN 76 G2 0612a; KN 76 G2 0672e
BAR FIG 10.8:13 & 14

34. R6; W 9–10; FAB 1
Small rim sherd and seven wall sherds; shell-edge
8 pieces, 73g
KN 61 II 6; KN 73 B2 6; KN 73 F2 6; KN 76 G2 0602/0604

35–46: shouldered vases

35. R7; RD 155; G 175; H > 155; W 12; FAB 1
Substantial reconstructed portion of vase but lacking base; shell-edge, grooving; triangular stamped impressions.
46 pieces, 520g
U/S; KN 60 u/s; KN 61 I 6; KN 73 A1 2; KN 73 A4 6; KN 73 B1 6; KN 73 F1 6; KN 73 F2 6; KN 76 G2 O2; KN 76 G2 0601c; KN 76 G2 0602a; KN 76 G2 0605a; KN 76 G2 0661d; KN 76 G2 U/S; KN 76 G4 0307
BAR FIG 10.7:4

36. R7; RD 150–60; H < 180; W 9, FAB 1
Four rim sherds and nine wall sherds; shell-edge, grooving, crescentic spatulate impressions
15 pieces, 111g
KN 61 I 6; KN 61 II 6; KN 73 A1, KN 73 BI 6; KN 73 B2 6; KN 73 F1 6; KN 76 G2 0605; KN 76 G2 100.03b; KN 76 G2 U/S; U/S
BAR FIG 10.8:7 & 8

37. W 10–12; FAB 1
Two wall sherds from shoulder of vase decorated in similar way to 35; shell-edge, grooving
2 pieces, 24g
KN 73 B1 6; KN 73 F2 6

38. W 8–9; FAB N/A
Three wall sherds from lower body of vase decorated zonally using shell-edge and grooving but with addition of spatulate impressions
3 pieces, 25g
KN 59 G3; KN 59 G4; KN 60 F2 6

39. R7; RD 135–50; W *c* 8?; FAB 5
Three joining rim sherds and three neck sherds; interior bevel very abraded; perhaps horizontally impressed cord cut by oblique incisions, cf 21; possibly this is the rim of 40

6 pieces, 73g
KN 59 F1 6; KN 60 F2 5; KN 60 F2 6
BAR FIG 10.10:24

40. B1 (concave); BD *c* 70; G *c* 140; W 7; FAB 5
Sherd with basal angle, eleven lower wall sherds and shoulder sherds; zonal decoration, whipped cord, grooving; perhaps body of 39
13 pieces, 126g
KN 59 F1 6; KN 60 F2 6; KN 61 I 6; KN 73 B1 6; KN 73 B2 6
BAR FIG 10.8:15

41. R7; RD 170–95; W7; FAB 1
Small rim and neck section of vase, possibly rim of 42; shell-edge, grooving, spatulate impressions (cf 5); heat-damaged
5 pieces, 49g
KN 61 I 6; KN 73 FI 6; KN 73 A2 1; KN 76 G2 0605
BAR FIG 10.10:22

42. G *c* 200; W 8; FAB 1
Numerous small wall sherds from below shoulder of vase; possibly the body of 41, shell-edge, grooving, incision, surface lustre
23 pieces, 148g
KN 61 I 6; KN 73 A1 1; KN 73 A1 2; KN 73 A1 SONDAGE; U/S
BAR FIG 10.7:5 (lower wall sherd only)

43. R7; RD *c* 210; G *c* 240; H > 210; W 8–12; FAB 1
Substantial portion of pot, restored to give an almost complete profile from rim to lower body; shell-edge and twisted cord on internal bevel, shell-edge and grooving on exterior; surface lustre
34 pieces, 361g
KN 60 F2 6; KN 61 I 6; KN 73 A1 2; KN 73 A1 6; KN 73 A1/3 2; KN 73 A2 2; KN 73 A2 7; KN 73 A3 1; KN 73 B1 6; KN 73 B2 6; KN 73 F1 6; KN 76 G2 0605a; KN 76 G2 0613b; U/S BUNKER
BAR FIG 10.7:5 (rim) and FIG 10.8:10

44. R7; W 8; FAB 1
small rim sherd; incised
1 piece, 8g
KN 73 A4 1

45. R7; RD *c* 200; W 9–11; FAB 1
Three rim sherds; incised, crescentic spatulate impressions

4 pieces, 63g
KN 61 I 6; KN 76 G1 0601c
BAR FIG 10.7:6

46. R7; RD 116–200; G 210; H >210; W 10–11; FAB 6
Substantial joining section of vase giving rim to lower body profile, numerous non-joining wall sherds; rim curvature and profile irregular; twisted cord.
60 pieces, 1052g
KN 61 I 6; KN 73 F2 6; U/S
BAR FIG 10.6:3

47–52: miscellaneous decorated vases

47. R7; RD *c* 220; W 9–12; FAB 2
Two rim sherds and numerous wall sherds from upper body of a shouldered vase; broad incision; thinning marks on interior surface of shoulder sherds; general similarity to 30; possibly the upper body of 48, although wall much thicker over shoulder.
29 pieces, 206g
KN 61 I 6; KN 61 II 6; KN 73 A1 1, KN 73 A1 2; KN 73 A1 U/S; KN 73 A1 6; KN 73 A1/3 1; KN 73 A2 U/S; KN 73 A4 6; KN 73 B1 6; KN 73 F1 6; KN 73 G2 0606a; KN 73 G2 0624; U/S

48. W 8; FAB 2
Lower wall sherds, some plain; broad incision; same fabric colouring as 47 and found together with part of 47, but appears too thin walled to be lower body of 47
32 pieces, 147g
KN 61 I 6; KN 73 A1 2; KN 73 A1 6; KN 73 A1/3 2; KN 73 A4 1

49. R3 (anomalous); RD *c* 240 max; G 250–70; W 11–14; FAB 2
Three fragmentary rim sherds and large reconstructed shoulder section; irregular ovoid impressions, triangular stamped decoration on rim; reconstruction of profile uncertain since there is no join between rim and neck.
20 pieces, 334g
KN 60 F2 6; KN 73 A1 2; KN 73 B2 1; KN 73 B3 6; KN 73 F1 6; KN 76 G2 0602a; KN 76 G2 0603; U/S

50. R8; RD 250–70; W 15–17; FAB 7
Rim, shoulder and lower wall sherds all in distinct fabric and possibly all from same vase; reconstruction uncertain; unusual 'beaded lip' on rim; twisted cord.
14 pieces, 322g

KN 61 I 6; KN 61 II 6; KN 73 B1 6; KN 73 F1 6; U/S
BAR FIG 10.10:23

51. Rim form uncertain (R5 type?) RD 170–80; W 10–12; FAB 2
Five small rim sherds and ten wall sherds from pot of uncertain profile; fingernail-impressed
15 pieces, 79g
KN 73 A3 2; KN 73 B1 6; KN 73 F1 6; KN 76 G2 0658

52.* Rim form uncertain (R7 type?); FAB 1
Tiny rim fragment; incised
1 piece, 1g
U/S

53–9: undecorated vases

53. R7; RD 150; W 8 ; FAB 1?
Three joining rim sherds and two neck sherds
5 pieces, 42g
KN 73 F1 6; KN 76 G2 0605a; KN 76 G2 0612a

54. R7; FAB 1?
Small rim and wall sherd
2 pieces, 11g
KN 61 III 6

55.* R7; W 8; FAB 1?
Small rim sherd
1 piece, 8g
KN 73 F1 6

56. R7; W 8–10; FAB 3
Rim fragment, neck and shoulder sherds, possibly same pot as 57
13 pieces, 101g
KN 61 I 6; KN 61 III 6; KN 73 B1 6; KN 73 F1 6; KN 76 G2 0605a; KN 76 G2 0607a; KN 76 G2 0631b; KN 76 G2 100.14b

57. B1?; W 11; FAB 3
Four joining wall sherds with basal angle; possibly same pot as 56
4 pieces, 37g
KN 73 A2 5; U/S

58. R7; RD 180–200; W 8–9; FAB 6
Rimsherd
1 piece, 23g
U/S

59. R7; RD *c* 200; W 9–12; FAB 1
Conjoining rim, neck and shoulder sherds and numerous non-joining wall sherds
26 pieces, 254g
KN 61 I 6; KN 61 III 6; KN 73 A2 2; KN 73 A4 1; KN 73 F1 6; KN 73 F2 6; KN 76 G2 0602d; KN 76 G2 0605a; KN 76 G2 0632b; U/S

60–5: jars with ridged internal bevels

60. R8; RD 200–20; W 13; FAB 1
Two joining rim sherds; impressed/incised
2 pieces; 62g
KN 61 I 6; KN 76 G2 08
BAR FIG 10.11:33

61. R7; RD min 220, max 260; W 13; FAB 1
Rim, neck and shoulder sherds; incised/impressed
4 pieces, 107g
KN 61 I 6; KN 73 B1 6; KN 76 G2 0631b

62. R7; RD 240–60; W *c* 14; FAB 1
Rim and wall sherds; profile tentatively reconstructed from sherds found together except for shoulder sherd which may be from a different pot; incised; NB a small fragment of applied rib decoration was found with the wall sherds from this pot.
23 pieces, 494g
KN 73 F1 6; KN 76 G2 0605a; KN 76 G2 0616a; KN 76 G4 0303?

63. R8?, W *c* 13; FAB 1
Two small rim sherds and fragments; incised
6 pieces, 50g
KN 73 F1 6; KN 76 G2?

64. R8?; RD 240; W 14; FAB 1
Two rim sherds and three wall sherds, incised, impressed – some impressions have deep rectangular cross-section
5 pieces, 57g
KN 76 G2 0605a; KN 76 G2 0613b; KN 76 G2 08

65. R8; FAB 1
Two joining rim sherds and fragments; incised
4 pieces, 50g
KN 76 G2 0605a; KN 76 G2 0612a/b

66–71: jars with applied external decoration

66. R7; RD 260–80; W 13–14; FAB 1
Three joining rim/neck sherds; incised; applied horseshoe
4 pieces; 93g
KN 60 F2 6; KN 76 G2 0661d

67. W 13–17; FAB 1
Two large reconstructed shoulder sherds; incised; applied ribs, originally part of applied 'horseshoes'?
9 pieces, 937g
Site B 1954; KN 76 G1? 0602; KN 76 G2 0605a; U/S
BAR FIG 10.11:36

68. W 16–18; FAB 1
Shoulder sherd; applied rib; incised; heavily abraded
1 piece, 120g
KN 76 H1 0604c (from above raised beach deposits)

69. B1; BD 150; W 12; FAB 1
Reconstructed base section possibly from any of pots 60–8; undecorated; one sherd found with or near to part of 62
23 pieces, 298g
KN 76 0605a

70. B1; BD 150–60; W 13; FAB 1
Reconstructed base section and non-joining wall sherds, not necessarily same base as 69; possibly from any of pots 60–8; undecorated; parts found with 69 and near to 62
35 pieces, 655g
KN 61 I 6; KN 73 B2 6; KN 76 G2 0605a; KN 76 G2 U/S

71. R7; RD 300–20; W 15; FAB 4
Two rim sherds; incised, grooved, irregular triangular impressions, applied horseshoe
2 pieces, 89g
1956 U/S; KN 73 A4 6

72–7: large decorated jars

72. R7; RD indeterminate; W 13; FAB 1
Numerous rim and wall sherds from crushed jar, but not possible to reconstruct lower body; interior bevel possibly slightly ridged; shell-edge
39 pieces, 878g
KN 76 G2 0671c; KN 73 B1 6 (1 sherd)

73. R7; RD *c* 270; B1; BD 120; W 16–20; FAB 3
Numerous rim, wall and base sherds from large jar, but not possible to reconstruct rim to base profile; shell-edge
66 pieces; 2,991g

KN 60 F2 6; KN 73 A2 2; KN 73 A2 6; KN 76 G2 0605c; U/S
BAR FIG 10.11:32

74. R8; RD 360–80; W 14–21; FAB 1
Rim, neck and start of shoulder from very substantial jar; sharp wedge-and-tail impressions; possibly same pot as 75
14 pieces, 644g
KN 61 I 6; KN 73 A2 3/4; KN 73 B1 6; KN 73 F1 6; KN 73 F2 6; U/S
BAR FIG 10.11:34

75. B1; W 15; FAB 1
Seven joining wall sherds showing start of basal angle; undecorated; possibly base of 74
7 pieces, 708g
KN 76 G4 0301; N 76 G4 0303

76. R8?; FAB 3?
Two small rim fragments and neck fragment possibly from large jar of similar type to 74 (Burgess; unpublished notes); incised
3 pieces, 14g
KN 59 G3; KN 76 G2 0612; U/S

77. R uncertain; FAB 1
Small fragmentary rim sherd; traces of incised decoration on both surfaces
1 piece, 7gm
KN 76 G2 0616a

78–94/95: undecorated jars

78.* R7, RD c160?; FAB 1
Small rim fragment; high surface lustre
2 pieces, 6gm
KN 73 A1 2; U/S

79. R7, FAB 1
Small rim sherd and 6 wall sherds; heavily abraded
8 pieces, 57g
1956 surface

80. R7; W >13?; FAB 6
Four small rim sherds and wall sherd
5 pieces, 34g
KN 59 G4; KN 73 A1/3 1; KN 73 A3 1

81. R7; RD 200–20; W c 15; FAB 6
Rim sherds, reconstructed shoulder sherds and wall sherds
15 pieces, 416g
KN 61 I 6; KN 73 F1 6; KN 76 G2 0605a

82.* R7/R8; RD c 220; W 13; FAB 3
Two rim sherds and two and wall sherds
4 pieces, 55g
KN 73 A1 2; KN 73 F2 6

83. R7; RD 220; W >13; FAB 1
Three rim sherds, representing minimum one pot, maximum 2 pots
3 pieces, 132g
KN 73 F1 6

84. R7; RD c 210–20; W c 13 variable; FAB 1
Fourteen rim sherds from one or more pots
14 pieces, 140g
KN 73 B2 6

85. R8; RD 220–40; W c 19; FAB 1
Large rim sherd and wall sherds
6 pieces, 133g
KN 73 B2 6; KN 76 G4 0301

86. R7; RD c 240; W >11; FAB 1
Nineteen rim sherds from one or more pots
19 pieces, 181g
KN 61 I 6; KN 73 B1 6; KN 73 B2 6; U/S

87.* R7; RD 280–300; W >15; FAB 1
Large rim sherd
1 piece, 80g
KN 73 B1 6

88. R7; RD 320–400; G c 370; H >380; W 13–16; FAB 3
Large jar, broken in situ; almost complete, but lacking base; too damaged to allow full restoration but a representative profile is illustrated here
67 pieces, 3259g
KN 73 F2 6; U/S
BAR FIG 10.6:2

89. R7; RD 320–40; G >320; H >360: W 11–14; FAB 1
Large jar, broken in situ; lacking base; a representative profile illustrated here; note tongue and groove construction of neck
88 pieces, 4,849g
KN 61 I 6
BAR FIG 10.6:1

90. R8; RD 380–400; B1; W 16–19; FAB 1?
Substantial rim and neck sections from large jar; also part of base, but no rim to base profile
64 pieces, 2970g
KN 76 G4 0301, 0303; U/S

91. R7; W *c* 13; FAB 6
Rim sherd
1 piece, 37g
U/S

92. R7/R8; W 13–14; FAB 3
Small rim sherd
1 piece, 18g
KN 73 A3 2

93. R9; FAB N/A
Tiny rim sherd of atypical form
1 piece, 3g
U/S

94/95.* R7; FAB misc
Small rim sherds and rim fragments probably from large jars
21 pieces, 69g

96–122: decorated pots not represented by rims

96. B1; BD 110; W 8; FAB 1
Part of base and wall sherds forming lower body of vase; incised; blank zone 87mm deep above base
6 pieces, 137g
Surface
BAR FIG 10.8:16

97. FAB N/A
Tiny basal angle fragment; and wall fragment; form indeterminate; fine comb or close-set punctulation
2 pieces, 4g
KN73 A1 2; KN 73 B2 6

98. G *c* 330; H >390; W 11–16; FAB 3
Large reconstructed sections of jar, but lacking rim and base; cordoned upper body; incised lower body
42 pieces, 1138g
KN 60 F2 6; KN 61 3 6; KN 73 F1 6; KN 76 G2 0605a; KN 76 G2 0657d; KN 76 G2 0658; KN 76 G4 0301; KN 76 G4 0315, 0317; U/S

99–101. W 7, and 11; FABS 1 and N/A
Cordoned wall sherds and also associated plain sherds; minimum 2, maximum 3 pots
11 pieces, 112g
KN 73 B3 6; KN 7 G1 0601b; KN 76 G1 102.2; U/S

102.* W *c* 16; FAB 1? (underfired)
Fragmentary neck sherds from jar; incised
14 pieces, 328g
KN 76 G4 0303?

103. W >12?; FAB probably 1 (although obscured by polyvinyling)
Neck sherd; shell impressed; incised
1 piece, 30g
KN 76 G4 0301

104. W *c* 11; FAB N/A
Shoulder sherd from vase; incised
1 piece, 13g
KN 76 G2 0631b

105. W – 14?; FAB 1
Shoulder sherd from large vase/jar; grooved; incised
3 pieces, 26g
KN 61 2 6; U/S

106. W 14–17; FAB 1
Shoulder sherd from large vase/jar; grooved; incised
1 piece, 26g
KN 76 G2 0605a

107.* W *c* 11; FAB 2
Small shoulder sherd; impressed
1 piece, 7g
KN 73 B2 6

108. W 11; FAB 4?
Small sherd from rounded shoulder; broad incision
2 pieces, 14g
KN 73 A3 1; U/S

109. W 8; FAB 1
Two joining sherds perhaps from vessel of beaker form, although relatively thick walled; twisted cord
2 pieces, 43g
KN 73 A3 2; KN 73 B2 6
BAR FIG 10.8:12

110. W 9; FAB 1
Five wall sherds, possibly from same pot; one has start of turn to base; shell-edge
5 pieces, 45g
KN 60 F2 6; KN 73 F2 6; Kn 76 G2 U/S; Kn 76 G4 0301; U/S

111. W 9; FAB N/A
Wall sherd, unusual fabric and decoration, impressed, incised; seed impression on interior identified as *Hordeum* sp. (Chapter 8)

1 piece, 13g
KN 76 G2 121

112. W 13; FAB N/A
Small wall sherd from jar; shell-edge
1 piece, 13g
KN 76 G4 0301

113.* W 8; FAB 1
Small wall sherd; incised
1 piece, 9g
Surface

114.* FAB 1?
Possible fragment of lug
1 piece, 1 g
KN 73 B2 U/S

115–22.* Unassigned decorated fragments catalogued in the archive according to type of decoration ie incised, misc impressed, twisted cord, shell edge, comb, cordoned, none of these obviously from any pot previously catalogued, except for fragments from jars with applied decoration, but which cannot be assigned to individual jars.
195 pieces, 289g

123–25: plain bases

123. B1; BD max 80; W 10–11; FAB 1
Base of a vase (plain or decorated?)
4 pieces, 128g
KN 73 A1 2a; KN 73 A4 1; Kn 73 B1 6; U/S

124. FAB N/A
Two basal angle sherds from plain jar?
2 pieces, 84g
KN 76 G3 4 "lower stone pile"

125. FAB N/A
Two basal angle fragments from two different pots
2 pieces, 8g
U/S

126–38: plain undiagnostic bodysherds

126.* FAB 1
Possibly all from one pot
6 pieces, 25g

127.* FAB 1
Possibly all from one pot
6 pieces, 22g

128.* FAB 1?
Possibly all from one pot, relatively thin-walled
12 pieces, 41g

129.* FAB 9
1 piece, 4g

130.* FAB 2
Group of bodysherds, closely resembling 12 but thinner-walled, some joining from lower body of ?vase
30 pieces, 226g

131.* FAB 1
Plain wall sherds from jars
369 pieces, 3354g

132.* FAB 1
72 pieces, 1619g

133.* FAB 1
16 pieces, 181g

134.* FAB 3
68 pieces, 690g

135.* FAB 3
580 pieces, 9763g

136.* FAB 6
73 pieces, 1165g

137.* FAB 7
3 pieces, 90g

138.* Unsorted fragments and crumbs
3714 pieces, 6013g

Trenches H and C

Note: neck sherd with applied decoration (KN 76 H1 604c) is catalogued above as no 68.

139.* W 13; FAB 3
Plain neck sherd
1 piece, 36g
KN 76 H 701c

140.* W 12 FAB 3
Undiagnostic bodysherd
1 piece, 12g
KN 76 H1 2

141. R10; W 9; FAB 12
Plain rim sherd and seven small wall sherds from a bucket-shaped pot
7 pieces, 47g
KN 73 C1 6,7 and 8

141a.* FAB N/A
One fragment (possibly Bronze Age date)
1 piece, 2g
KN 73 C1 8

Trench L

142. FAB 13
Tiny rim fragment, simple rounded form
1 piece, 2g
KN 76 L 10/101

143. W 11–15; FAB 13
Bevelled sherd, uncertain if part of rim; basal angle sherd, interior possibly missing; numerous wall sherds and further basal fragments; heavily burnt and fully oxidized
265 pieces, 698g
KN 76 L 117, 119, 123, 10/101, U/S

144. W 16–17; BD 100–20; FAB 15
Basal angle sherd, with finger pinching at foot of base; underside of base ridged, possible impression
1 piece, 77g
KN 76 L 118 02

145.* W c 14; existing girth c 260; FAB 13
Wall section from large pot, excavated as part of lining of pit, base replaced by clay; (other sherds missing)
2 pieces, 430g
KN 76 L 128 03

146.* W 10–12; FAB 15
Three small wall sherds and four fragments perhaps from same pot as 144
9 pieces, 32g
KN 76 L 10/101, 10

147.* W 10–11; FAB 14
Six small wall sherds from one or more pots
31 pieces, 62g
KN 76 L 10/101; 126

148.* FAB 13
Fragmentary wall sherd, possibly same fabric as 143
11 pieces, 31g
KN 76 L 123

149.* FAB various
Small miscellaneous wall sherds and fragments
24 pieces, 26g
KN 76 L 10/101, 114, 118, 119 05, 126

Trenches J and K

Miscellaneous

150. W c 9; FAB 5
Incised wall sherd and three abraded bodysherds from large vase.
45 pieces, 71g
KN 76 K1 07; K1 0203

151. FAB N/A
Tiny rim sherd with two parallel grooves on interior surface, burnt; possibly earlier than bulk of J/K material
1 piece, 1g
KN 76 J2 32

152.* FAB N/A; W 13–15
Two anomalous bodysherds; fabric contains rounded pebbles
2 pieces, 38g
Surface; KN 76 K3 05

Lower midden

153. R10; RD 350; W 13–15; FAB 16
Substantial reconstructed portion of a large plain bowl, with a possible comb impression on exterior near rim; mouth incurved, base missing; surfaces very pimply due to underlying grits
247 pieces, 977g
J1 14

154. R10; W 11–12; FAB 18
Small rim sherd, possibly from bowl
1 piece, 8g
J1 26

155.* W c 14; FAB 17
Tiny rim sherd, possibly from incurved rim
1 piece, 3g
J1 27

156. W c 12; FAB 18
Unusual sherd with irregular grass-marked grooves on interior bevel; not necessarily a rim at all
1 piece, 9g

157. W *c* 10; FAB 17
Grass-marked (grooved) wall sherds, similar to 162, but some are thinner-walled and have smooth interior surface, perhaps indicating breakage along construction rings; burnt
6 pieces, 24g
J1 26, 27, 28

158. W 10–12; BT 23; FAB 17
Large wall-sherd, grass-marked but not grooved, two base sherds and further small wall sherds, closely resembling 162 on interior surface
32 pieces, 254g
J1 14, 26, 27, 28

159. W 13; BT >22; FAB 18
Chunky basal angle sherd and large quantity of wall sherds, all similar in form to 153; grass impression on one large bodysherd, some sherds heavily scorched, others abraded and possibly trampled
449 pieces, 1394g
J1 14, 20, 21, 22, 23, 25, 26, 27, 28

160. W 15–19; FAB 19
Chunky wall sherd; grass-marked (grooved); containing greater quantity of organic temper than rest of J pottery; burnt
1 piece, 77g
J1 28

161.* FAB various
Miscellaneous bodysherds, fragments and crumbs, some heavily burnt and ash-coated
154 pieces, 217g
J1 25, 27, 28

Lower midden

162.* R11; RD *c* 300; W 11–12; FAB 17
One large rim and wall sherds from heavily burnt, grass-bound bowl, rim abraded but appears slightly incurving; vesicular fabric, powdery; interior surface very uneven, pimply appearance
57 pieces, 433g
J2 19, 32

163.* FAB 17
Basal sherd and wall sherds resembling 162, but no traces of grass-binding impressions
4 pieces, 26g
J2 19, J3 05

164.* W *c* 15; FAB 16
Wall sherds, possibly from bowl(s) of 153 type; burnt
19 pieces, 67g
J1 105; J2 19, 32, 106

165.* FAB 18
Wall sherds possibly from bowl(s) of 153 type, abraded, trampled?
80 pieces, 157g
J1 105, 102, 05, 06, 07, 08, 11, 13; J2 106, 30; K3 109, 0201, 0202, 05

166.* FAB N/A, like daub
Possible basal fragment with finger pinching at foot of base, plus a small clay moulding, both rather daub-like
2 pieces, 4g
J1 07

167.* BD *c* 100; FAB N/A
Basal angle fragment, interior surface missing, and three further sherds possibly in same fabric, all dissimilar in fabric from rest of Kilellan pottery
4 pieces, 34g
J1 13; J2 107; K3 05; 0501

168.* FAB various
Miscellaneous wall sherds, fragments and crumbs
64 pieces, 61g
J1 105, 08, 25; J2 29, 30, 32, 114; K3 0202, 05

169.* R10; W *c* 14; FAB N/A
Small rim sherd, burnt and abraded, from test trench in J/K area; relationship to upper or lower midden unknown.
1 piece, 6g
KN 73 Z1

Chapter 4

Struck lithic artefacts

ALAN SAVILLE

In total during the various seasons of excavation between 1959 and 1976 some 5133 struck lithic artefacts were recovered, of which most (84%) were found in 1973 and 1976. Table 34 lists the gross distribution by trench, showing the concentration of recovered artefacts to be in trench G2 (20% of total), though of course this gross distribution is biased by such factors as the level to which excavation penetrated in each trench. It does, however, make clear that the area to the south (trenches J, K and test-pit Z) was in general unproductive of lithic artefacts.

Recording practices during the various seasons varied, and while some of the flint artefacts were given individual find numbers, others had group numbers and many were simply located to layer and/or trench or were unprovenanced. During analysis for this report every artefact was examined and allocated an entirely new catalogue number (which is also the numeric element of the National Museums of Scotland registration). Where artefacts are referred to individually in the text or illustration it is this catalogue number which is used (the numbers of the illustrated artefacts are in italics in the text). Table 35 provides a catalogue of the illustrated pieces.

The overall typological composition of the whole assemblage is given in table 12. From the diagnostic implement types present (specifically the microliths and arrowheads: see table 13) it would seem that

TABLE 12
Total flint assemblage from the 1959–76 fieldwork (including one surface find from 1977).

Type	Number	Weight in grams
Unretouched flakes	4201	10408.9
Cores	199	3320.9
Core fragments	170	1569.2
Flaked lumps	12	494.4
Scrapers	69	680.5
Edge-trimmed flakes	29	126.6
Microliths	25	4.6
Knives	18	247.0
Piercers	11	109.1
Arrowheads	7	10.4
Microburins	3	1.5
Truncated blade	1	1.7
Serrated flake	1	1.2
Miscellaneous retouched pieces	126	906.7
Unclassified burnt pieces	260	369.5
Hammerstone	1	33.8
Totals	5133	18286.0

TABLE 13
Stratigraphic contexts of microliths and arrowheads.

Layer	Microliths	Leaf-shaped arrowheads	Barbed-and-tanged arrowheads
2	–	1	–
Midden	3	1	–
7	–	–	1
Silver sand	22	1	–
X	–	2	1
Totals	25	5	2

Key: layer 2 = grey brown sand immediately below topsoil; layer 7 = old turf line between midden and silver sand; X = unstratified/layer not recorded.

flint artefact use and deposition occurred at Kilellan during the Mesolithic, Neolithic and Bronze Age periods. However, the complex stratigraphy, the way excavations proceeded over numerous seasons with different recovery and recording systems, and factors such as bioturbation, redeposition and residuality, all militate against the isolation of discrete assemblages with chronological integrity. The exception to this is in theory provided by the so-called 'silver sand' horizon, which relates to the earliest phase of occupation in the Mesolithic period and which appears to have been sealed before any subsequent occupation of the area. This horizon ought, therefore, to provide an uncontaminated sample of Mesolithic artefacts for analysis. To an extent this is the case, although it would appear that some later material has been intruded by disturbance from above. Overall, the number of artefacts recorded from the silver sand is a significant proportion of the numeric total assemblage (25%), although the number of implements present is relatively low (table 33).

The prospect for isolating any chronologically coherent sample from horizons other than the silver sand is compromised by the residuality factor, since artefacts which are almost certainly Mesolithic are present in all parts and layers of the site. Looking at the most diagnostic implement types, the microliths and arrowheads (table 13), it is apparent that most microliths come from the silver sand, with just a few residual in the midden. One of the leaf-shaped arrowheads also comes from the silver sand, however, possibly suggesting that the formation of the old turf line (layer 7) post-dates the early Neolithic, and even one of the barbed-and-tanged arrowheads apparently comes from this turf line rather than from the Early Bronze Age midden. Consideration of what constitutes post-Mesolithic material amongst the non- or less diagnostic artefacts is thus somewhat subjective, hinging on factors of typology, context and condition.

In the absence of any other evidence for Neolithic activity at Kilellan, particularly pottery, the significance of the four leaf-shaped arrowheads is debatable and need not necessarily imply occupation which resulted in the deposition of other lithic artefacts in this period.

Since flint is almost totally resistant to decay and will survive as a residual element in any disturbed layer, it is somewhat surprising that there are some layers and contexts at Kilellan with no flint artefacts recorded at all. There has almost certainly been differential recovery. One indicator of this is the contrast in the nature of the assemblage recovered from the silver sand, where, especially from context 132 in trench G2, total recovery including all chips (albeit without sieving) seems to have been attempted, and other contexts like the midden, where the small fraction is less apparent. Another is the number of scrapers recovered from superficial and unstratified contexts as opposed to other artefact categories. Because scrapers are readily recognizable (and 'attractive') tools, there is often the tendency for

TABLE 14
Unmodified pebbles: maximum dimension data (n = 85).

Range in mm	Number
10–19.9	6
20–29.9	27
30–39.9	26
40–49.9	18
50–59.9	8

TABLE 15
Unmodified pebbles: weight data (n = 85).

Range in grams	Number
00–09.9	24
10–19.9	24
20–29.9	13
30–39.9	8
40–49.9	8
50–59.9	3
60>	5

them to be recovered on a casual basis when other artefacts, such as unretouched flakes, are not.

RAW MATERIAL

The struck lithic artefacts are entirely of flint except for a single core of a cherty material. Variation within the flint being exploited was noted in that some artefacts were of a somewhat coarser type with inclusions, while the majority utilized good quality, clear-structured flint. All the raw material was obtained in pebble form, presumably all beach pebble in origin, though cortex varied from being heavily chatter-marked to smooth. An insight into the availability of flint at Kilellan is gained from the 85 unmodified pebbles included in the excavated assemblages (from the 1973 and 1976 seasons only; these are not included in the overall total of 5133). The unmodified pebbles were measured and weighed and shown to be rather small (tables 14–15). The size range is 15mm to 58mm and the weight range is one to 113g. Only eight have a maximum dimension of 50mm or over, and only two weigh over 100g. The mean maximum dimension is 34mm and the mean weight is 24g.

Considerable information is now available on the flint raw material from Islay and the unmodified pebbles from Kilellan bear close comparison with those in modern samples taken from beaches on the west coast of the Rinns (Marshall 2000a). Marshall's research suggests that the pebble threshold for utility for platform-core knapping is a minimum dimension of 38–40mm and a minimum weight of 180g. The maximum weight of any of the unmodified pebbles at Kilellan is 113g so it is not surprising that none was used for platform cores, but the larger ones could potentially have been exploited by anvil knapping, since many of the core residuals (see below) are far smaller.

CONDITION

The flint artefacts from Kilellan are mostly corticated, which is to say that the exposed knapped surfaces have undergone alteration, with the result that they are discoloured to a lesser or greater extent. Only 118 artefacts (2% of the total collection) were totally uncorticated and retained surfaces which were the colour of the freshly exposed interior of the beach pebbles, normally grey. The discoloured surfaces of the majority ranged from dense cream or white through to grey with a slight bloom of lighter grey or blue. During cataloguing the colour of each artefact was recorded in case this might be a trait with chronological and/or depositional significance. In the case of the 118 totally uncorticated artefacts, 103 could be related to the following recurrent horizons: topsoil and immediately underlying sand (35 = 30%); midden (66 = 56%); and silver sand (2 = 2%). This pattern was echoed by the collection as a whole, with the less discoloured artefacts (basically grey and variants) predominantly coming from midden contexts, and densely discoloured (basically cream and variants) dominating in the silver sand.

To demonstrate this all artefacts from trench G2 were analysed according to layer and colour (table 16). Minor variations and mixed tones were recorded, but in the final analysis only those colours with more than 10 artefacts are listed separately. As a general conclusion from this, all the densely

TABLE 16
Trench 76/G2: flint artefact colours by context.

Layer	Fresh	Grey	Grey-white	White	Grey-cream	Cream	Other	Burnt	Totals
2	–	16	1	–	4	7	–	1	29
6	14	293	20	14	26	70	37	14	488
7	–	–	–	–	1	3	–	2	6
8	1	5	–	–	3	365	–	84	458
X	2	20	–	1	–	17	1	4	45
Totals	17	334	21	15	34	462	38	105	1026

Key: layer 2 = grey brown sand immediately below topsoil; layer 6 = midden (includes contexts 100, 103, 104, 106, 107, 108, 109, 133 and 138); layer 7 = old turf line between midden and silver sand; layer 8 = silver sand (includes contexts 126, 131 and 132); X = unstratified/layer not recorded.

discoloured artefacts from the silver sand appear to have acquired their discolouration in that context and are Mesolithic. Therefore artefacts with a similar discolouration found in more superficial layers are likely to be Mesolithic items derived from the silver sand. It is not necessarily safe to conclude as a corollary of this, however, that all the undiscoloured or less discoloured artefacts are post-Mesolithic. Mesolithic artefacts disturbed from the silver sand at an early date, or located in an atypical microcontext (natural or otherwise) within the silver sand, might not develop strong discolouration.

TECHNOLOGY

1. CORES (ILLUS 78–9, 85–6)

In examining the basic knapping technology at Kilellan the cores are the obvious starting point; 199 cores were judged to be complete or virtually complete, and these were used as the sample for analysis. In terms of typology there was a major distinction between platform cores, mostly single platform in their final form, and anvil-struck cores with acute-angled, usually keeled, bifacial platforms with a tendency to scalar removals. The latter are often referred to as bipolar cores, after the fact that they very frequently have removals from opposed ends of a core, the result both of knapping at one end and spontaneous modification at the other end from contact with the anvil. This term was not thought sufficiently apposite for the Kilellan cores, however, for two reasons. Firstly, there are cores which are unipolar yet clearly anvil struck. Often the unmodified end on these cores is cortical and the anvil contact has not resulted in any macroscopically visible damage. Secondly there are anvil-struck cores which are tri-, quadri- or multi-polar, the core being rotated on the anvil during knapping. For these reasons the term anvil-struck core is used here instead of bipolar. It is appreciated that it is theoretically possible to remove flakes from a platform core while resting it on an anvil, and there are a few cases (356; 467) where this indeed appears to have been the case. Thus the platform- and anvil-knapping strategies at Kilellan should be seen as part of a flexible continuum rather than meaningfully distinct, at least during the Mesolithic period.

Examination of the cores shows that the use of an anvil for knapping can either follow initial exploitation of a pebble by platform reduction, or can be the initial and sole strategy for exploiting a pebble. In at least one case (3203) an anvil-struck bipolar core has subsequently been exploited in its final phase by removals from a platform. There are also cores that are apparently a combination of platform- and anvil-flaking in a complexly inter-related fashion. Classification of cores (table 17) does of course relate essentially to their final phase of modification when abandoned, and does not necessarily describe their full history of exploitation. In some cases it is possible to see from the pattern

STRUCK LITHIC ARTEFACTS

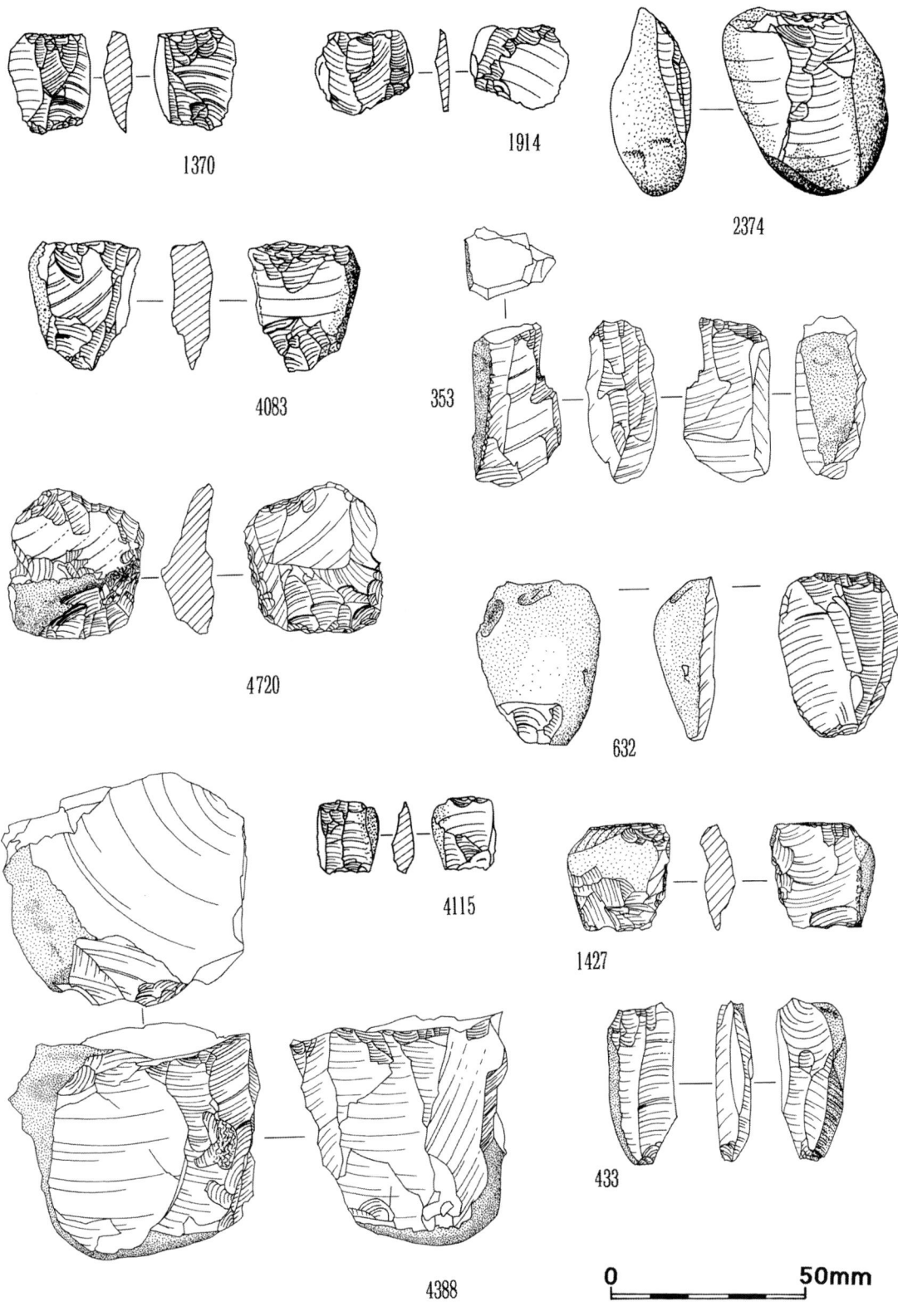

78 Cores (see text and Table 35 for details).

TABLE 17
Cores: basic classification.

	A	B	C/D	Anvil	Totals
Blade	20	5	–	15	40
Blade & flake	17	10	1	46	74
Flake	14	9	4	58	85
Totals	51	24	5	119	199

Key: A = single platform cores; B = two platform cores; C = cores with three or more platforms; D = keeled platform core; Anvil = anvil-struck core.

of remaining flake scars that there has been previous flaking which does not relate to the final platform(s). This was noted for 10 of the class A cores, five of the B/C/D cores, and 17 of the anvil-struck cores. On the other hand, for many of the class A cores it was clear that a pebble had simply been split and that the split surface provided the platform for a single stage of removals (eg illus 79: *3930; 4639*), after which the core was abandoned.

The single platform (A) cores include four A1 types with flaking all around the platform edge. Classic pyramidal bladelet cores are present (352; illus 79: *1586)* but not dominant. Cores with two platforms (B) are predominantly B2 types with non-parallel platforms at irregular angles (illus 79: *4543*), but two B3 types with platforms at right angles (2788; 4717) are present. The four multi-platform (C) cores are all three-platform types (585; 1627; 3294; 3683), and the single keeled (D) core is an oddity (1751) with removals either side of a single platform edge. Anvil-struck cores include examples of the classic thin, bipolar, and bifacial type with scalar-like removals (illus 78–9: *1370; 1427; 1487; 1914; 2265; 4083; 4115*) and of the split pebble unifacial type (illus 78: *632; 2374*), as well as numerous less regular examples.

Platform preparation of any kind is extremely rare and where present seems to relate to the elimination of a particular problem with the platform edge. The only possible knapping tool recovered at Kilellan is a flint pebble-hammer exploiting what was previously a core (illus 79: *3200*). This is a two-platform core of B2 or B3 type, subsequently used as a hammerstone along much, but not all, of the available edge. The character of the crushing and abrasion suggests the function of this hammerstone was probably flint-knapping. The maximum dimension is 36mm and the weight 33.8g. Although this is a surface find, the

TABLE 18
Cores: maximum dimension data.

Maximum dimension in mm	A n=51	B n=24	C/D n=5	Anvil n=119	All cores n=199
Minimum	24	25	27	21	21
Maximum	90	55	44	52	90
Mean	38	38	38	34	35
St. deviation	10.13	8.54	6.57	6.91	8.31

TABLE 19
Cores: maximum dimension ranges.

Range in mm	A	B	C/D	Anvil	All cores
20–29.9	9	6	1	34	50
30–39.9	22	8	1	60	91
40–49.9	18	8	3	22	51
50–59.9	1	2	–	3	6
60>	1	–	–	–	1
Totals	51	24	5	119	199

character and condition of the core indicate that it is a Mesolithic piece. Insofar as can be seen from the cores and flakes themselves, much of the flint-knapping could have been achieved with pebble-hammers like this, though some must also have been undertaken with softer hammers of some kind.

The size and weight ranges of the cores are indicated in tables 18–20 as well as by the illustrated selection. The single platform cores exhibit the widest size range and are generally larger and heavier than the other cores. Why some of the largest examples (illus 78 & 85: *4184*; *4388*) were not exploited further is unclear. Some of the anvil-struck cores are very small indeed, being residual thin slivers with scalar scars all over both faces (3613; 3708; illus 78: *1914*; *4115*). Even so, it is clear that in origin these cores must have utilized pebbles rather larger than most of those unmodified pebbles found on site (tables 14–15).

No attempt was made during analysis to rigorously identify possible core rejuvenation flakes, but some obvious examples were noted (3776; illus 83: *649*) and these confirm the importance of platform flaking and emphasize the fact that larger pebbles were available for exploitation than is immediately apparent from most of the residual cores.

Assessment of the product resulting from core flaking on the basis of the cores themselves is potentially misleading because of the residual and often flawed state in which they are in at abandonment. Nevertheless this was undertaken in order to provide a basis for comparison between the different types of core. Two analyses were undertaken, one was to measure the maximum length of surviving negative flake scar from an existing platform as an indicator of potential (table 21). The other was an assessment from the negative flake scars of the predominant type

TABLE 20
Cores: weight data.

Weight in grams	A n=51	B n=24	C/D n=5	Anvil n=119	All cores n=199
Minimum	3.2	6.0	4.3	2.0	2.0
Maximum	206.1	49.4	53.2	38.6	206.1
Mean	27.2	22.5	23.3	10.7	16.7
St. deviation	29.73	12.26	16.30	8.22	18.61

TABLE 21
Cores: maximum surviving negative flake scar lengths.

Flake scar length in mm	A n=51	B n=24	C/D n=5	Anvil n=119	All cores n=199
Minimum	15	13	12	10	10
Maximum	47	44	30	50	50
Mean	25	26	21	25	25
St. deviation	6.74	7.15	7.09	7.91	7.54

TABLE 22
Cores: all stratified cores assignable to common cross-site horizons.

Horizon	A	B	C/D	Anvil	Totals
Topsoil	1	1	–	14	16
Grey-brown sand	–	–	–	4	4
Old turf line	1	–	–	1	2
Midden	20	8	5	73	106
Old turf line	–	–	–	2	2
Silver sand	25	10	–	10	45
Totals	47	19	5	104	175

(From trenches 1960/FII; 1961/I–III; 1973/A1, A2, A3; B1, B2, B3; E1, E2; F1, F2; 1976/G1, G2, G3, G4, H1, J1, K1.)

TABLE 23
Cores: colours by type.

Core type	Fresh	Grey	Grey-white	Grey-cream	Cream	Other	Chert	Burnt	Totals
A	1	5	2	4	27	11	–	1	51
B	1	6	1	1	14	1	–	–	24
C/D	1	3	–	–	–	1	–	–	5
Anvil	10	52	10	20	11	15	1	–	119
Totals	13	66	13	25	52	28	1	1	199

of product in terms of flakes or blades (table 17). This was on the basis of a blade being a flake with a length two or more times the maximum breadth, but undertaken by visual scanning rather than measurement, so this is an impressionistic overview rather than rigorously objective.

Blade cores predominate among the single-platform cores, which thus contrast markedly with the anvil-struck cores, although there is a surprising number of blade cores produced by this method (illus 78 & 85: *433; 632; 3464*). The surviving maximum flake scar lengths are much the same between the different core types, which have mostly passed the stage of producing flakes or blades which would be useful blanks for tool production or utilization of any kind.

Examination of core type against stratigraphy (table 22) indicates that platform cores are marginally more common in the silver sand, while anvil-struck cores are chiefly from the upper levels, especially the midden. Analysis of the surface discolouration of the cores correlates with this pattern, the platform cores being mainly cream and the anvil-struck cores mainly grey (table 23). There is clearly a chronological dimension to these trends but it is not a simple case of platform cores in the Mesolithic and anvil-struck cores in the Bronze Age. Some of the anvil-struck cores are undoubtedly Mesolithic on the basis of stratigraphy, product and condition (illus 78: *4083; 4115*) but there are relatively few of them. There are no absolutely clear typological or other markers for discriminating between which anvil-struck cores from the upper levels might be Mesolithic and which Bronze Age, though there are many cases where the probability of a core being Mesolithic seems extremely high (eg 1467; 3613; illus 85: *3464*) despite stratigraphy and colour.

Apart from the artefacts classified as cores, a further 170 artefacts were considered cores which are fragmentary to a lesser or greater extent, though in many cases it is difficult to discriminate between the two. This is particularly so with some of the thin anvil-struck cores, which have a tendency to split longitudinally in 'Siret fracture' fashion (Inizan *et al* 1999), after which they could in some cases continue to be knapped. It is also in the nature of anvil-knapping with pebbles that the pebble may often fracture in such a manner that it is difficult to separate which is the core from which is the flake. Flaked lumps are a separate small category to encompass chunky pieces of flint with one or more removals exhibiting no regular pattern, unlike the cores. The few tested pebbles with single removals are included in this category.

2. UNRETOUCHED FLAKES (ILLUS 79)

The cores have already shown that blade production was a significant factor in terms of platform core reduction at Kilellan. Apart from the illustrations of the microliths and some other retouched pieces using blade blanks, four completely unretouched blades are illustrated to show the type and quality of blade being produced (illus 79: *2600; 2884; 3460; 4231*). While in terms of technology and typology each of these appears Mesolithic, only two were stratified in silver sand horizons. Other unretouched flakes and blades are shown in the illustrations of refitting pieces, most of which come from the silver sand. It should perhaps be noted here that the 'curved slivers' of flint referred to by Burgess (1976, 204 & pl 10.III.c) as 'winkle-pickers' are in fact simply unretouched flakes from various contexts and cannot be assigned any more particular classification or function.

TABLE 24
Unretouched flakes from silver sand contexts in trenches 73/E1 and 73/E2: total sample.

	Complete no	Complete weight in grams	Incomplete no	Incomplete weight in grams	Total no	Total weight in grams
E1	194	620.8	140	200.0	334	820.8
E2	53	249.2	46	93.0	99	342.2
Totals	247	870.0	186	293.0	433	1163.0

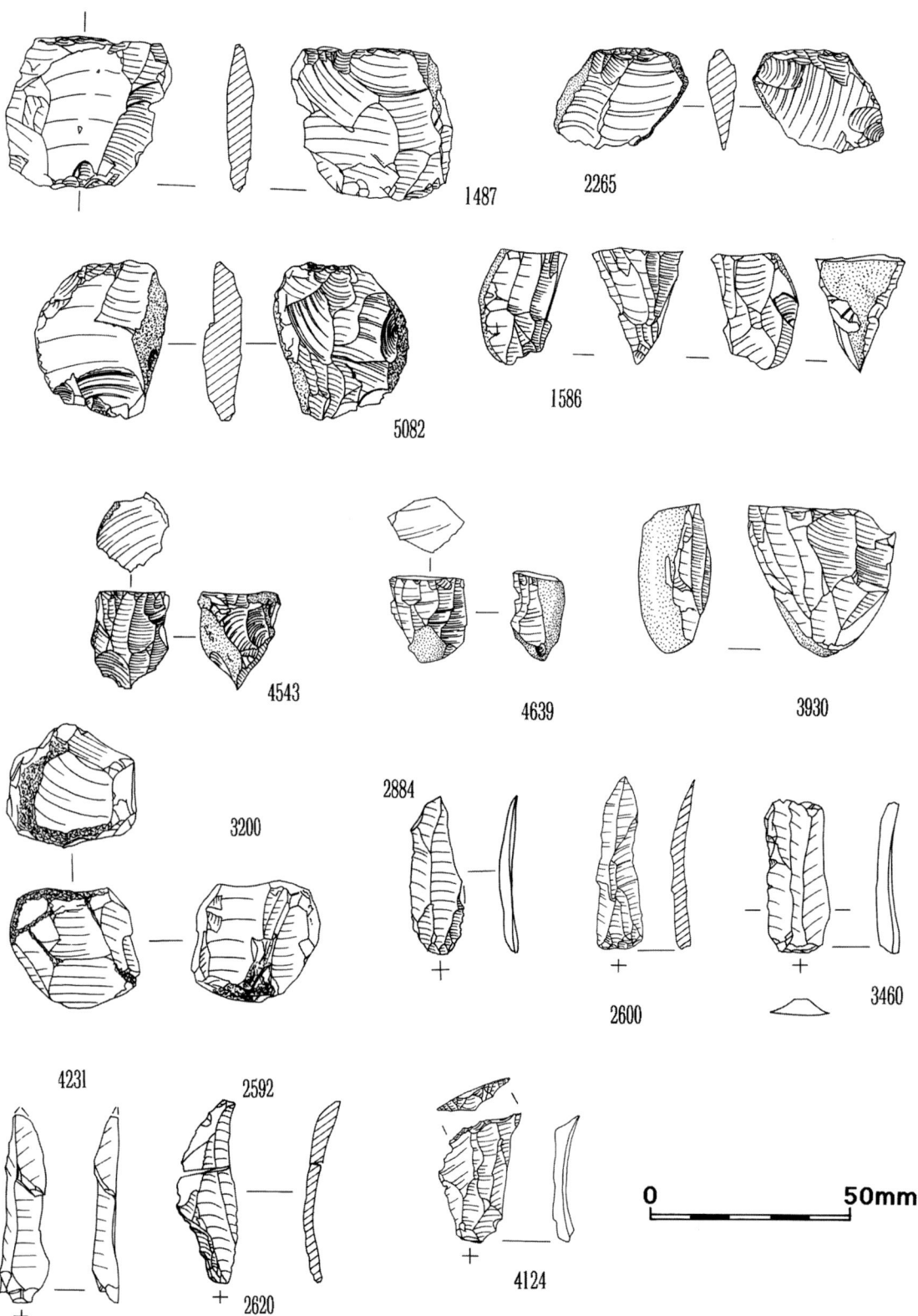

79 Cores, hammerstone, unretouched blades, and truncated flake (see text and Table 35 for details).

TABLE 25
Unretouched flakes from silver sand contexts in trenches 73/E1 and 73/E2: flake categories represented among the complete flakes.

	Primary no	Primary weight in grams	Secondary no	Secondary weight in grams	Tertiary no	Tertiary weight in grams	Total no	Total weight in grams
E1	16	159.6	81	372.7	97	88.5	194	620.8
E2	6	97.8	32	140.7	15	10.7	53	249.2
Totals	22	257.4	113	513.4	112	99.2	247	870.0

Finding a sufficiently large sample of stratified unretouched flakes to be ideal for investigating blade production statistically was not possible. The largest sub-sample available comprised the 283 flakes from trench G2 context 131, but this was dominated by tiny chips and spalls. The next largest sub-samples, from trench E1, layer 4 and trench E2 layer 7, were therefore selected for analysis. In total, 433 unretouched flakes were recovered from these two contiguous silver sand horizons, although only 247 are complete and useful for analyses (table 24). The 247 flakes could be subdivided as in table 25 into the following categories: primary (wholly cortical dorsal surface); secondary (partly cortical dorsal surface); and tertiary (entirely non-cortical). These were all measured for length, breadth and thickness.

The length data (table 26) show that only one flake is longer than 60mm, and that only 6% are longer than 40mm, with 10–30mm the most frequent length (70%). However, as the analyses of the cores have already made clear, the normal cessation of knapping was above a mean length in the 20–30mm range. It was necessary, therefore, to exclude all flakes with either length or breadth less than 20mm from further analyses, since these are much less likely to reflect any intentional product traits.

This left a sample of only 149 flakes (table 27), which is far from ideal for metrical analysis, especially as there are so few tertiary flakes included. Nevertheless, it was felt worthwhile proceeding with a simple analysis of flake shape, to examine any trend towards 'bladedness' (table 28). The primary flakes

TABLE 26
Unretouched flakes from silver sand contexts in trenches 73/E1 and 73/E2: length range data for all complete flakes.

Length range in mm	Primary	Secondary	Tertiary	Totals	%
00–09.9	–	2	13	15	6.1
10–19.9	5	24	61	90	36.4
20–29.9	8	47	28	83	33.6
30–39.9	7	30	7	44	17.8
40–49.9	2	7	2	11	4.5
50–59.9	–	2	1	3	1.2
60–69.9	–	1	–	1	0.4
Totals	22	113	112	247	

TABLE 27
Unretouched flakes from silver sand contexts in trenches 73/E1 and 73/E2: complete flakes over 20mm in length or breadth.

	Primary no	Primary weight in grams	Secondary no	Secondary weight in grams	Tertiary no	Tertiary weight in grams	Total no	Total weight in grams
E1	13	155.9	64	360.2	33	66.6	110	582.7
E2	6	97.8	26	137.6	7	8.8	39	244.2
Totals	19	253.7	90	497.8	40	75.4	149	826.9

were excluded from this analysis since their shape normally relates more to the shape of the nodule being worked than to any intentional product. The results show a significant element of narrow flakes within this sample, with some 15% over twice as long as they were broad. Taking the strict criterion of a blade being a flake the length of which is actually twice or more than the breadth, 22 blades were present, giving a lamellar index of 17%, or a blade to flake ratio of 1:6.

SCRAPERS (ILLUS 80–1)

Scrapers represent the single largest typologically specific group of retouched artefacts at Kilellan. The 69 scrapers comprise 60 which are complete or virtually complete and measurable, and nine fragments. Complete scrapers could be assigned to the following sub-types: 32 end scrapers, of which three have the scraping edge at the proximal end of the blank; 15 extended-end scrapers, where the scraping edge continues down one or both lateral edges of the blank without a pronounced angle; four end-and-side scrapers where the retouch continues down one or both lateral edges with a distinct angle between the lateral edge(s) and the distal scraping edge; and nine side scrapers. All have convex scraping edges except one of the side scrapers (illus 80: *1535*), on which the retouched edge is straight. Only one example (2387) has an overhanging scraping edge.

TABLE 28
Unretouched flakes from silver sand contexts in trenches 73/E1 and 73/E2: length/breadth index values of complete secondary and tertiary flakes over 20mm in length or breadth.

L/B index value	Secondary	Tertiary	Totals	%	General type
0.0–0.5	–	1	1	0.8	Very broad
0.6–1.0	19	4	23	17.7	Broad
1.1–1.5	42	13	55	42.3	Medium/broad
1.6–2.0	18	13	31	23.8	Medium/narrow
2.1–2.5	10	4	14	10.8	Narrow
>2.6	1	5	6	4.6	Very narrow
Totals	90	40	130		

STRUCK LITHIC ARTEFACTS

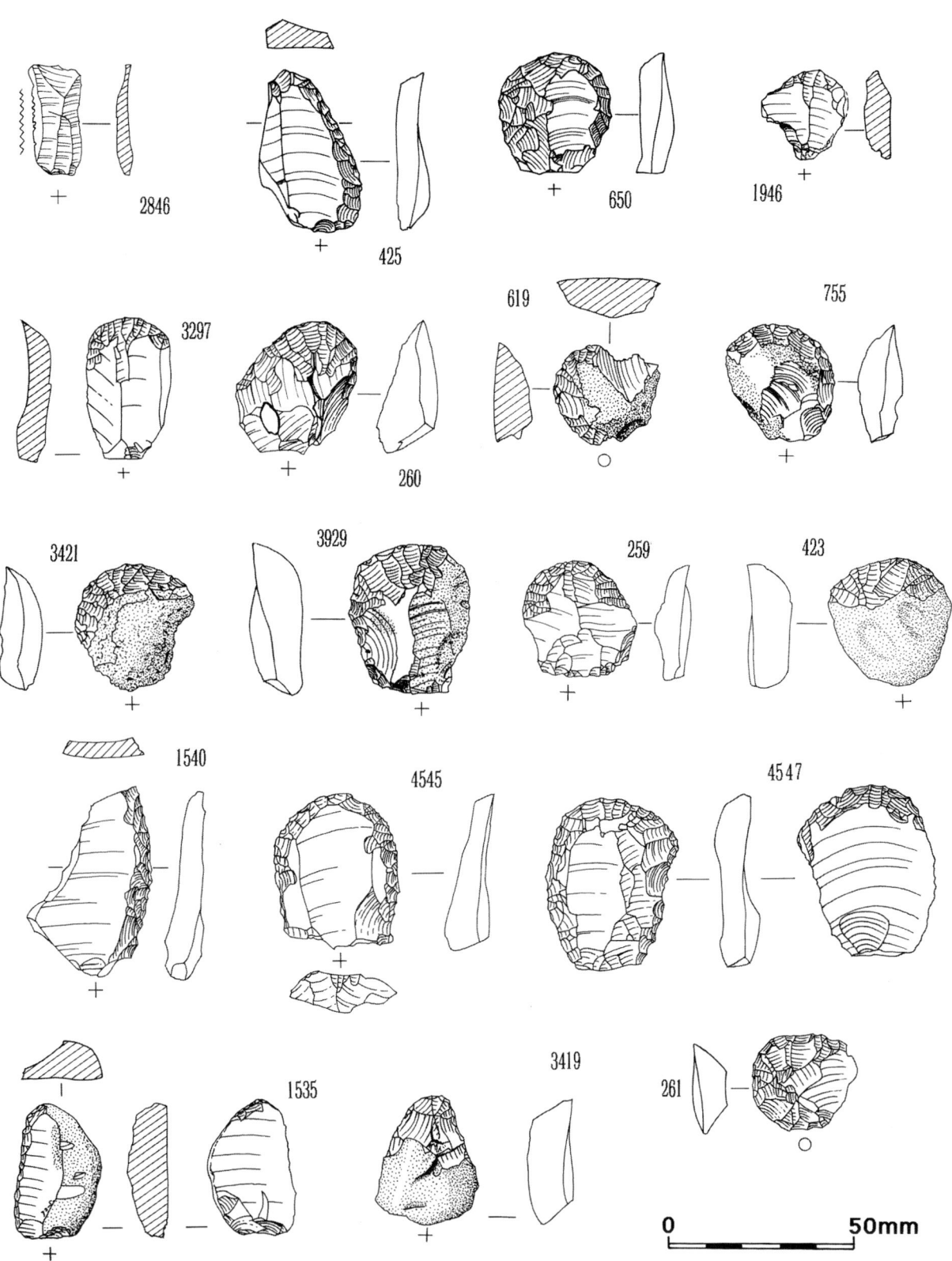

80 Serrated flake and scrapers (see text and Table 35 for details).

Thus the scrapers are dominated by end scraper types. Most of these are of conventional form and include some 'classic' examples, like the end-of-blade scraper (illus 80: *3297*). One of the end scrapers is of the 'nosed' variety (illus 80: *3419*), and on two (3745; illus 81: *4548*) the edge is slightly denticulate in character. Some of the scrapers have elaborate retouch which is quite invasive and 'knife-like' (eg illus 80: *425*; *1540*). During initial analysis a category of knife/scraper was employed to distinguish these examples, and their final classification as either scraper or knife was somewhat subjective. In fact most were classed as knives on the basis of the overall morphology of the blank and the position and extent of the retouch, the character and sharpness of the retouched edge, and the nature of the retouch itself.

In terms of the standard size distinction between long and short scrapers (where the length of a long scraper is 1.5 or more times its breadth), 53 are short and seven long. The length dimensions range from 21mm to 60.5mm, with a mean of 31.9mm; the thickness dimensions range from five to 27mm, with a mean of 10.6mm; and the weights range from 2.6g to 62.8g, with a mean of 10.1g. Forty-three of the 60 retain some cortex, in a few cases exploiting primary split pebble flakes (eg illus 80–1: *423*; *1453*; *3420*), and 35 are on struck flakes retaining plain platforms. Two scrapers are on flakes with faceted platforms (671; illus 80: *4545*), two have platforms which have fragmented during production (619; 2411), and on five the platform has been removed by retouch (eg illus 80: *261*). Approximately 14 scrapers, mainly on the basis of retaining acute-angled linear platforms or polar spalling (eg illus 80–1: *1408*; *1453*; *1535*), seem to have been made on flakes produced by anvil-flaking. In the remaining two cases one scraper has the proximal end of the flake snapped off, while the flake origin of the other is uncertain.

The provenance of the scrapers (table 29) can be summarized as: five from topsoil; six from layers between topsoil and the midden; 40 from midden layers; three from the old turf line below the midden; five from the silver sand, and 10 unstratified. The silver sand scrapers are all from trench E1 and include the illustrated examples *4544*, *4545*, *4547* and *4548* (illus 80, 81, 86). Three of the silver sand scrapers (illus 81 & 86: *4544*, *4548* and *4555*) would readily be accepted as Mesolithic types, while two of the others are surprisingly elaborate (illus 80: *4545*; *4547*) and are perhaps a hint of some Neolithic activity to be linked with the presence of the leaf-shaped arrowheads. A few examples of scrapers which would probably be classified as Mesolithic on the basis of typology (nature and extent of retouch, condition, and character of the blank) came from the midden (3784), the sand between topsoil and midden (3347), from the topsoil (illus 80: *1946*), or were unstratified (2857; illus 81: *2411*). Scrapers with relatively shallow angled, invasive and sometimes 'scalar' retouch, which might typologically be regarded as Early Bronze Age, came from the old turf line between the midden and the silver sand (illus 80: *259*; *260*; *261*) and from the midden (eg illus 80–1: *3297*; *3420*; *3421*; *3929*), while a shallow-angled 'thumbnail' type scraper was a surface find (2551). In general, however, it is problematic to categorize most of the scrapers from the midden or more superficial layers as either Mesolithic or Early Bronze Age purely on the basis of typology.

One of the Mesolithic scrapers (illus 86: *4544*) was the only example with identified refitting flakes (illus 86: *4299*; *4396*; *4566*), also from the silver sand in the same trench (E1). This refit sequence is of technological interest in showing the process of scraper production from initial working of the parent core.

EDGE-TRIMMED FLAKES (ILLUS 81)

This category encompasses all 29 flakes or fragments with macroscopically evident edge modification of a lesser nature than that present on scrapers or knives, but of a regular enough nature to be intentional rather than simply the result of use. In the majority of cases the function of these pieces would appear likely to be as cutting or whittling flakes. None has silica edge-gloss, but this is absent from the entire assemblage and may relate to the obscuring effect of cortication. In six cases slight damage or a more substantial break may mask the fact that the retouched edge or edges originally formed the pointed tip of a piercer, while two blades, one with an intact notch (5062) and another with two notches (illus 81: *4229*) may be related to microlith production.

The modification is on both lateral edges in 10 cases; on the left side only in eight cases; and the right side only in six cases. A transverse distal edge was modified in one case, a distal edge in conjunction with the left side in another, and a distal edge in conjunction with both left and right edges in a third. In two cases the position of the modification on the original blank was uncertain because of its fragmentary nature.

Fifteen of the edge-trimmed flakes are complete or near complete and could be measured, one is probably

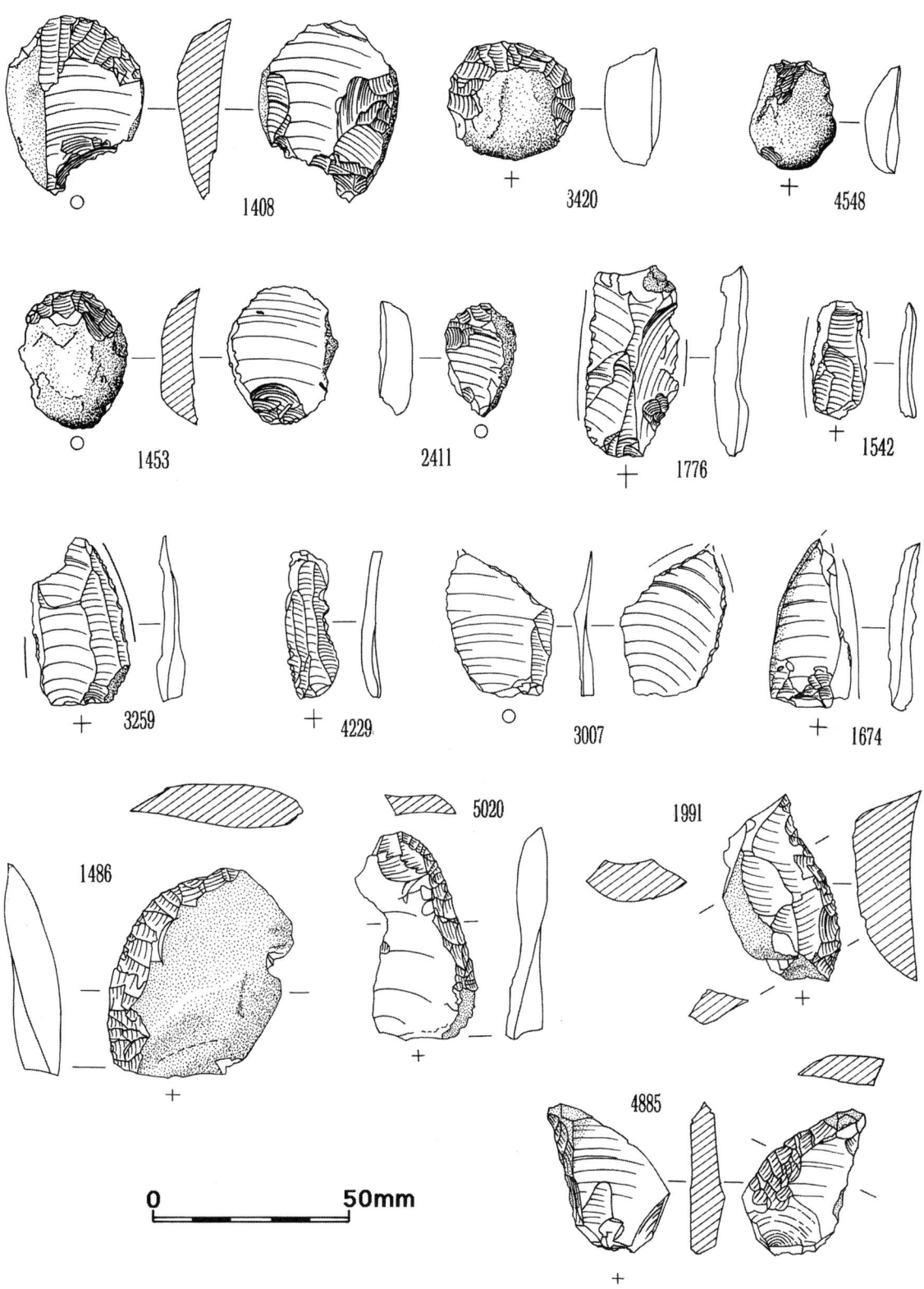

81 Scrapers, edge-trimmed flakes and knives (see text and Table 35 for details).

TABLE 29
Distribution of scrapers, edge-trimmed flakes, knives, piercers and serrated flake.

Year/Trench	Layer or feature	Scraper	Edge-trimmed	Knife	Piercer	Serrated flake	Total
59/C5	Sand	–	1	–	–	–	1
59/F1	5	1	1	–	–	–	2
59/F4	Sand	–	1	–	–	–	1
59	X	3	1	1	1	–	6
60/F2	6	2	–	–	–	–	2
60	X	–	1	–	–	–	1
61/1	4a	1	–	–	–	–	1
61/1	6	5	–	2	–	–	7
61/2	3	1	–	–	–	–	1
61/2	6	1	–	–	–	–	1
61/3	6	–	1	–	–	–	1
73/A1	1	4	1	1	1	–	7
73/A1	2	6	4	1	–	–	11
73/A1	6	–	1	1	–	–	2
73/A1-3	1	–	–	1	–	–	1
73/A1-3	2	2	–	1	–	–	3
73/A2	1	1	–	–	–	–	1
73/A2	3/4	–	–	1	–	–	1
73/A2	4	1	–	–	–	–	1
73/A2	6	–	–	1	1	–	2
73/A3	1	–	–	–	1	–	1
73/A3	2	2	–	–	–	–	2
73/B1	6	2	2	–	–	–	4
73/B2	6	2	2	–	–	–	4
73/B2	7	–	1	–	–	–	1
73/C1	7	–	–	1	–	–	1
73/E1	4	5	1	–	–	–	6
73/F1	6	2	2	3	1	–	8
73/F2	6	1	2	–	–	–	3
73/Z2	6	–	1	–	–	–	1
73	X	6	–	1	–	–	7
76/G1	6	–	–	–	1	–	1
76/G1	7a	2	–	–	–	–	2
76/G1	7b	1	–	–	–	–	1
76/G2	2	1	1	–	–	–	2
76/G2	6	10	1	–	1	–	12
76/G2	138	1	–	–	–	–	1
76/G2	X	–	–	1	–	–	1
76/G3	2	1	–	–	–	–	1
76/G3	4	1	–	–	–	–	1
76/G4	3	2	–	1	–	–	3
76/H1	4	–	–	–	1	–	1
76/H1	7	–	–	–	3	–	3
76/H1	7a	–	1	–	–	–	1
76/K2	106	1	1	–	–	–	2
76/L2	10	–	1	–	–	–	1
76/L2	118	–	1	–	–	1	2
76	X	1	–	–	–	–	1
77	X	–	–	1	–	–	1
	Totals	69	29	18	11	1	128

complete but on a flake with the proximal end removed, and the others are fragmentary. Eighteen are struck from platform cores and have plain platforms, four have acute-angled linear platforms and are anvil-struck, and on the others the platform is either absent or in one case obscure.

Of the measurable examples, the length range is 23.6mm to 46.9mm; the breadth 13.0mm to 38mm; the thickness 3.0mm to 14.2mm; and the weight 1.3g to 24.1g. Seven of the complete examples are on blades.

The provenance of the edge-trimmed flakes (table 29) can be summarized as: one from topsoil; five from layers between topsoil and the midden; 16 from midden layers; two from between midden and silver sand; three from the silver sand; and two unstratified. Of the three from the silver sand, two are Mesolithic blades (4120; illus 81: *4229*), the other is the proximal segment of a Mesolithic blade (2569). Other blanks which are almost certainly Mesolithic come from the topsoil (illus 81: *1542*), the midden (3605; 5102; illus 81: *1776*), or are unstratified (illus 81: *3007*; *3259*). Post-Mesolithic edge-trimmed flakes are more difficult to specify, but this is almost certainly the case with some examples from the midden (3675; 3971; 4891; illus 81: *1674*) and from the old turf line above the midden (2747).

MICROLITHS AND MICROBURINS (ILLUS 82)

The 25 microliths were recovered from silver sand contexts, mostly in the main excavation area but also to the north in trenches H1–2, except for three microliths from midden contexts in trenches A2 and B1 (table 30). Eight of the 25 were unclassifiable fragments, and among the remaining 17 the dominant form is the scalene triangle. It is of interest that four of the scalene triangles exhibit a trait whereby the angle between the retouched edges at the proximal end (the upper end as illustrated) is virtually 90 degrees and the transverse retouched edge is slightly concave (illus 82: *2572*; *2573*; *2593*; *4542*). Two of this type (illus 82: *2572*; *2573*) were found close together in H1/7a, a further example is recorded from H1/7, while the fourth example is from Trench E1. The other 'geometric' microlith type is the single crescent (illus 82: *2023*), blunted on the arc with some slight trimming on the chord.

The three obliquely blunted points (illus 82: *2019*; *3619*; *4556*) are basically simple truncations without additional retouch, though in one case (illus 82: *4556*) there is some slight opposed trimming at the tip. One of the atypical examples also has oblique blunting on its left side (illus 82: *2689*), but with opposed blunting at the tip making a bilateral point. The two other atypical examples are both bulbar bladelets with straight lateral blunting.

The only absolutely complete microlith is one of the obliquely blunted points (4556), which measures 22.0mm by 12.4mm by 2.2mm. However, seven of the scalene triangles are intact enough to suggest the length range is between 19–30mm, with a mean at the lower end of this range, a breadth range between 5mm and 7mm, and the maximum thickness between 1.9mm and 2.8mm. The crescent, with only a slight break at its base, is 19.8mm by 4.8mm by 2.3mm. The obliquely blunted examples, as the complete example indicates, have a shorter and squatter range, the length between 15mm and 22mm, and they are made on broader blades, up to 7mm to 12mm in breadth.

Insofar as it is possible to ascertain, all the microliths are on blades from platform cores. At least two of the unclassifiable fragments (eg illus 82: *4557*) are probably parts of scalene triangles, while one tiny fragment with a microburin-like facet (illus 82: *980*) is probably an example of a so-called 'Krukowski microburin' (Brézillon 1983, fig 27e), indicating a microlith which has broken during manufacture.

The three microburins, which are waste products created during the manufacture of blanks for microliths by specialized notch-and-snap technique, comprise two butt types (illus 82: *916*; *4038*), notched on the left-hand side, and one tip type (illus 82: *1441*), notched on the right-hand side. Two are from silver sand contexts, one from a midden context. The two butt types are clearly on blanks struck from platform cores.

Rejoining pieces 5132/5133 (illus 82) from test-pit Z2, layer 6, appear to be an instance of failed microlith production by microburin technique. After notching the broad blade on the right-hand side it has broken in two with a simple snap rather than a typical microburin facet. These two pieces are included in the totals for the miscellaneous retouched category.

The only microlith from a refitting sequence is the proximal fragment of an atypical unclassifiable fragment, with an intact bulb and blunting down one lateral edge (illus 85: *4510*). The other refitting pieces in this sequence and the core itself demonstrate very clearly the type of blank being exploited for microlith production.

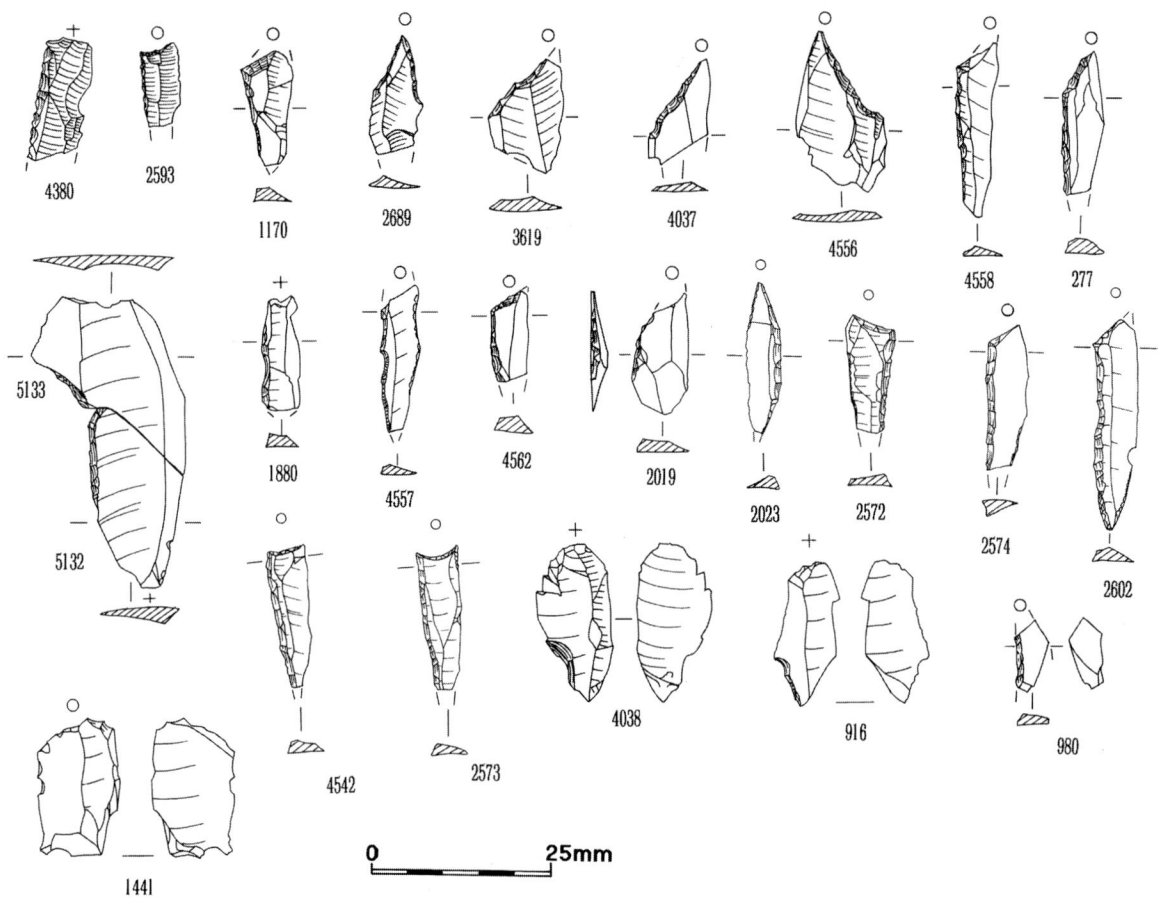

82 Microliths, microburins and related pieces (see text and Table 35 for details).

KNIVES (ILLUS 81 & 83)

The 18 pieces in this category comprise flakes with substantial edge modification, usually in the form of extensive and elaborate invasive retouch, which establishes one or more sharp edges. The problem of typological separation between certain scrapers and knives has already been mentioned, but normally the knife will have shallower retouch and the edge will not exhibit the marked arris blunting common on scrapers. Two of the 'knives' (illus 83: *1919*; *2555*) fall into a separate category, where the blank is prismatic and the retouch bilateral and steep. These are sometimes described as 'slug knives' (cf Clark 1932) though, despite their label, these implements may not functionally speaking be knives at all. One of these (illus 83: *1919*) was incorrectly described by Burgess (1976, 204 & pl 10.III.g) as a 'missile head'; it has an apparently close parallel in the 'beaked flake' implement from Camster Long (Wickham-Jones 1997, 162 & illus 25:*369*). The other sub-type present is the scale-flaked plano-convex knife (Clark 1932), represented most definitively by one bilaterally retouched example (illus 83: *3417*), even though it is not wholly flaked over the dorsal surface, which retains cortex. Another example (illus 81: *1486*) with unilateral retouch could be regarded as a plano-convex knife *sensu lato*, but the remaining pieces, while including some elaborately retouched pieces, are more amorphous in character and not assignable to specific types.

Sixteen are complete or near complete, though not all of these retain a bulb and platform. The ten which do are flakes with a plain platform, while there are two knives which appear to be on anvil-struck flakes (illus 81: *1991*; illus 83: *1860*). The size range demonstrates a preference for larger, robust flakes: length range 33.6mm to 78mm, mean 46.5mm; breadth 21.6mm to 47.6mm, mean 31.2mm; thickness 6.4mm to 17.6mm, mean 10.1mm; weight 6.4g to 32.5g, mean 14.4g. The retouched sharp edges are mostly convex and in all cases except one (illus 81: *4885*) are on the dorsal face. Ancillary retouch on opposed edges is present in some cases (eg illus 81: *4885*; illus 83: *1727*; *3167*; *3418*) and is usually blunting.

The provenance of the knives (table 29) can be summarized as two from the topsoil; one from between topsoil and the midden; nine from the midden; one from the silver sand; one from basal peat; and four unstratified. The silver sand example is a fragment (2144), which on grounds of condition, type of retouch and character of the blank would not appear to be Mesolithic. This is also the case with the example from basal peat (2700), which has ventral flaking to remove and thin the butt. There are, however, two knives which appear intrinsically probable Mesolithic types, and which are both unstratified finds (illus 83: *846*; *3167*). The characteristically late Neolithic/Early Bronze Age plano-convex knives (illus 81: *1486*; illus 83: *3417*) are both from the midden, while the similarly datable 'slug knives' are from the midden (illus 83: *1919*) or unstratified (illus 83: *2555*). Other examples which would normally be identified as post-Mesolithic come from the midden (4886; illus 81: *4885*; 5020; illus 83: *1727*; *1860*; *3418*) or just above it (illus 81: *1991*).

PIERCERS (ILLUS 83)

The 11 piercers range in type from the fairly elaborately retouched and robust to the minimally retouched and ad hoc. The two most elaborate are on thick split-pebble flakes with bilaterally formed points (illus 83: *1519*; *2586*), in one case after initial core-like removals (illus 83: *2586*). One piercer (2319) is on an anvil-struck core fragment with retouch enhancing a naturally pointed corner, another is on a substantial core rejuvenation tablet (illus 83: *649*) with retouch at the proximal end removing the platform and bulb to create a point, now damaged. All the other points are on less robust flakes and blades (eg illus 83: *2143*; *2561*), with varying amounts of retouch enhancing a distal pointed termination.

Two of the piercers are from the topsoil, one from sand between the topsoil and the silver sand, three from the midden, four from the silver sand, and one unstratified (table 29). The silver sand examples include one small fragment (2660) from the tip of a piercer of unknown overall form. While that fragment is undatable typologically, two of the others are on the distal end of Mesolithic blades (2619; illus 83: *2143*),

TABLE 30
Typology and distribution of microliths, and distribution of microburins and truncated blade.

Year/Trench	Layer or feature	Scalene triangle	Crescent	Obliquely blunted point	Atypical	Unclassified	Microburin	Truncated blade	Total
73/A1	7	–	–	–	1	–	–	–	1
73/A2	5	–	1	1	–	–	–	–	2
73/B1	6	–	–	1	–	–	–	–	1
73/B2	7	–	–	–	–	1	1	1	3
73/E1	4	3	–	1	1	5	–	–	10
76/G1	8	–	–	–	–	1	–	–	1
76/G1	8b	1	–	–	–	–	–	–	1
76/G2	131	–	–	–	–	1	1	–	2
76/G2	132	1	–	–	–	–	–	–	1
76/G3	4	–	–	–	–	–	1	–	1
76/H1	7	1	–	–	–	–	–	–	1
76/H1	7a	3	–	–	–	–	–	–	3
76/H1	7b	1	–	–	–	–	–	–	1
76/H2	7	–	–	–	1	–	–	–	1
Totals		10	1	3	3	8	3	1	29

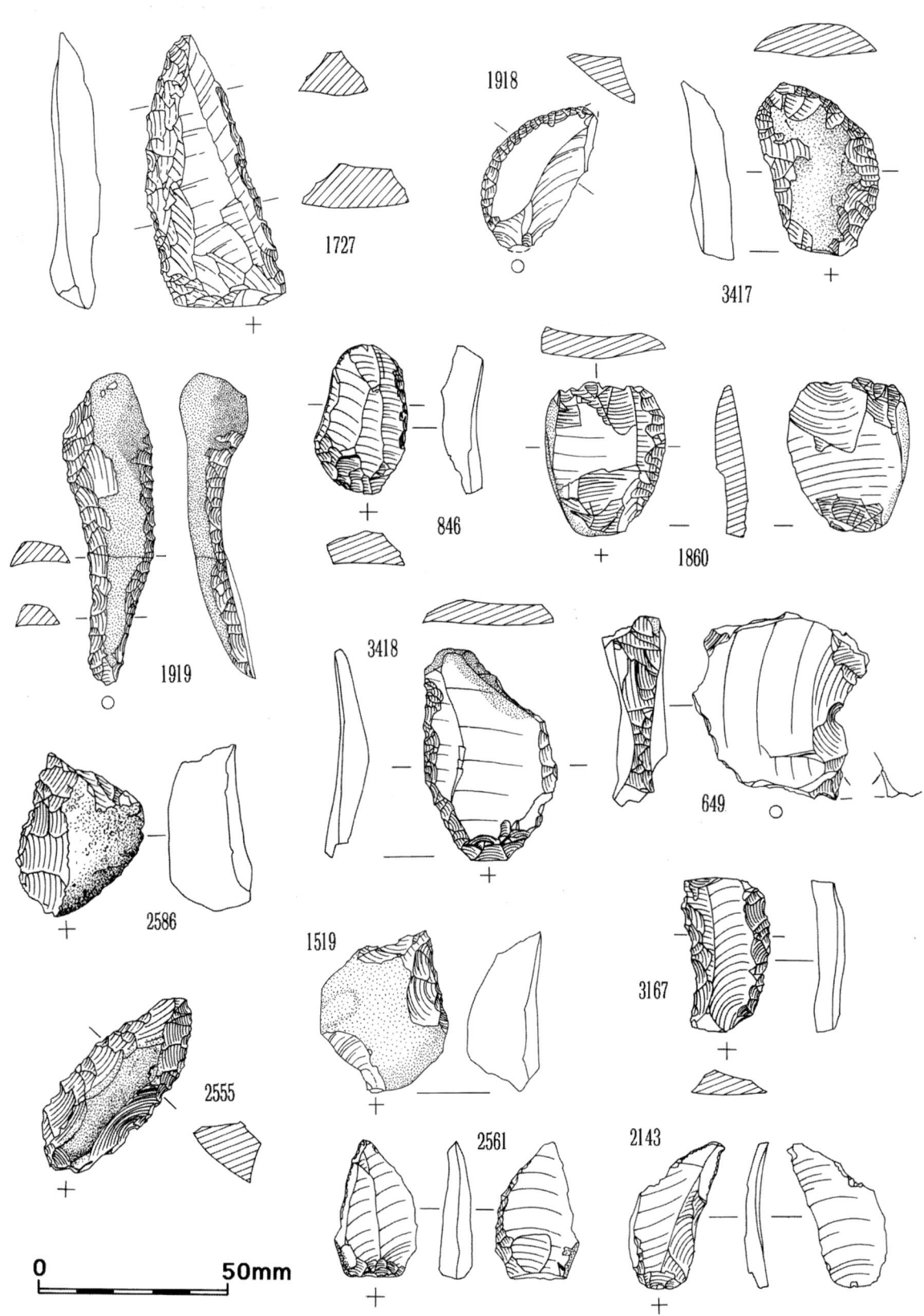

83 Knives and piercers (see text and Table 35 for details).

and one of the robust points is on an extensively flaked split pebble (illus 83: *2586*) of Mesolithic character. The other piercer of this latter type (illus 83: *1519*) is from the topsoil, but is also likely to be a Mesolithic example. Equally Mesolithic in character is the piercer on a large core rejuvenation tablet (illus 83: *649*), even though this comes from the midden. The piercer (illus 83: *2561*) from between topsoil and silver sand is also very Mesolithic in character, condition, and nature of its retouch. None of the other piercers have any traits particularly suggestive of being either Mesolithic or post-Mesolithic, except that on an anvil-struck core fragment from topsoil, which is probably post-Mesolithic.

ARROWHEADS (ILLUS 84)

The seven arrowheads (table 31) comprise four leaf-shaped examples, one fragment which is probably from a leaf-shaped arrowhead (1976), and two barbed-and-tanged arrowheads. Apart from one leaf-shaped arrowhead (illus 84: *3248*), found on the surface in 1959, which has no location, the distribution is all from within the main excavation area. One of the leaf-shaped arrowheads (illus 84: *2965*) is a Class B type with only marginal trimming of a suitable flake, and in this case the original flake may possibly have been struck from an anvil core.

Of the three stratified leaf-shaped arrowheads, one is from the silver sand (illus 84: *4036*), one from the midden (illus 84: *3537*), and the fragment (1976) is from the grey-brown sand immediately below the topsoil. The single stratified barbed-and-tanged arrowhead (illus 84: *264*) is from the old turf line between midden and silver sand.

In addition to the arrowheads proper, there is a broad flake in the miscellaneous retouched category (see below) which may represent a failed or abandoned attempt at manufacturing a barbed-and-tanged arrowhead (illus 84: *4029*). Burgess (1976, 204) mentions a further barbed-and-tanged arrrowhead from the site which was in the possession of the former farmer at Kilellan.

TRUNCATED FLAKE (ILLUS 79)

Apart from the microliths and the microburin, the most diagnostically Mesolithic retouched piece is this tertiary flake, with a plain platform and struck from a platform core, which has oblique blunting retouch at its distal end (illus 79: *4124*). It is from the silver sand in trench B2, cream in colour, and measures 29.9mm by 17.9mm by 4.3mm.

SERRATED FLAKE (ILLUS 80)

This piece (illus 80: *2846*) is a blade-like flake with rather coarse micro-denticulation on a 12mm long medial segment of the left edge. The removals forming the denticulation are from the dorsal surface across the ventral face. There is no indication of silica edge-gloss. The flake has a plain platform and has come from a platform core; it is complete except for minor damage at the distal tip and measures 27.2mm by 14.5mm by 3.2mm. This implement

TABLE 31
Typology and distribution of arrowheads (n = 7).

Catalogue number	Year/ Trench	Layer	Type	Dimensions in mm (weight in grams)	Classification (Green 1984)
264	76/G1	7b	Barbed-and-tanged	25 × 17 × 4 (1.1)	Sutton B
1976	73/A2	2	Leaf-shaped	Max 23 (0.9)	Fragment
2965	59/F1	X	Leaf-shaped	25 × 15 × 5 (1.7)	4A
3166	59/G4	Surface	Barbed-and-tanged	28 × 22 × 4 (1.8)	Sutton B
3248	59/?	X	Leaf-shaped	40 × 16 × 4 (2.1)	3C
3537	61/3	6	Leaf-shaped	31 × 15 × 3 (1.2)	3B ogival
4036	73/B2	7	Leaf-shaped	31 × 18 × 4 (1.6)	3A

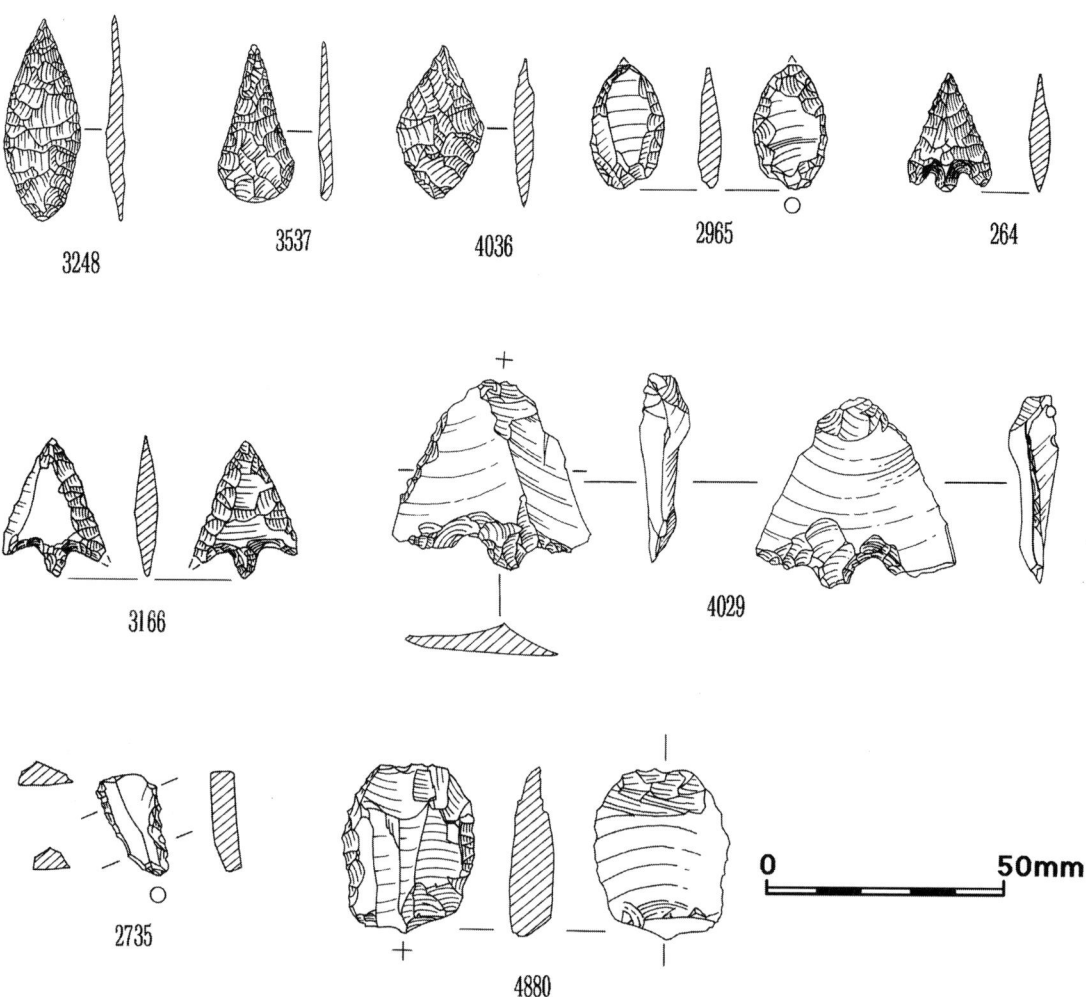

84 Arrowheads and miscellaneous retouched pieces (see text and Table 35 for details).

comes from the ginger sand overlying the silver sand in trench L2. Serrated-edge flakes and blades are more commonly a Neolithic type, but in this instance the overall character of the piece suggests it is part of the Mesolithic assemblage.

MISCELLANEOUS RETOUCHED PIECES (ILLUS 84 & 86)

As usual in any assemblage, there are a number of pieces with retouch which cannot be classified further into distinct types, either because they are fragmentary and retain insufficient diagnostic traits, or because of their idiosyncratic or amorphous character. In many cases the amount of retouch is very small, perhaps because they were abandoned before being finished or they were utilized in a largely unmodified form, and in some cases the retouch is no doubt fortuitous. The distribution of these pieces is ubiquitous and they were not analysed in any detail. Only four pieces are illustrated. One is an undoubtedly Mesolithic example, albeit from a superficial horizon, of a stubby, hinged-out tertiary flake with blunting retouch on both edges (illus 84: *2735*). The others are probably Early Bronze Age. One of these (illus 84: *4880*) is a substantial tertiary, plain platform flake with retouch on both lateral edges. The retouch is scraper-like but the edges are sharp, and the inverse distal splintering appears to post-date the retouch. It could be a damaged extended-end scraper, but this is uncertain. This piece is from the midden and

TABLE 32
Distribution of burnt pieces (only contexts with five or more burnt pieces are included).

Year/ Trench	Layer or feature	Unclassified burnt pieces	Burnt unretouched flakes	Other burnt artefacts	Totals
73/A1	2	7	4	1	12
73/A2	5	14	18	–	32
73/A3	1	3	5	–	8
73/B1	6	9	2	1	12
73/B2	6	5	–	1	6
73/E1	4	18	8	1	27
73/F1	6	13	1	2	16
76/G1	6	14	6	–	20
76/G2	6	5	4	2	11
76/G2	132	78	1	–	79
76/H1	7	8	6	–	14
76/K3	110	5	–	–	5
	Totals	179	55	8	242

is virtually undiscoloured. Another (illus 86: *3032*), unstratified, is a refitting anvil-struck flake, classified as miscellaneous retouched, since it has inverse retouch on its left-side.

The final illustrated piece (illus 84: *4029*) from this category is a curiosity from the midden in trench 73/B2. It appears to be an abandoned roughout for a barbed-and-tanged arrowhead. A broad flake with a central, longitudinal dorsal ridge has begun to be retouched both proximally, to reduce the thickness of the bulb, and distally on both faces to initiate by double-notching the appearance of a central barb and two lateral tangs. If indeed this was the purpose of the initial secondary work, it seems to have been realized at this point that the blank was unsuited for some reason and then rejected. The dimensions are 36.7mm by 40.2mm by 8.5mm, and the weight 8.3g.

UNCLASSIFIED BURNT PIECES

This category comprises all the burnt pieces of flint which are not otherwise classifiable into particular artefact or implement categories. Nevertheless most of the pieces are probably struck, mainly comprising fragments of unretouched flakes and spalls, which have subsequently become burnt, rather than being burnt pieces of unmodified flint or chips created by burning. Despite the inclusion of some substantial flake fragments and chunks, seven of which each weigh more than 10g, the overall mean weight of 1.4g reflects the presence of numerous spalls weighing 0.1g or less.

The unclassified burnt pieces are of no typological significance, but their distribution (table 32) is of interest in suggesting the probable existence of a Mesolithic hearth or hearths at silver sand level in trench G2 (context 132), and possibly the hints of former hearths also at silver sand level in trenches E1 and H1. Unsurprisingly the midden also contained burnt flints, but, unless they were not assiduously collected or retained during excavation, these are insufficiently numerous to suggest any *in situ* hearths.

REFITTING (ILLUS 85 & 86)

In total 115 pieces (weighing 1051.7g) were found to refit, confirming the suggestion made in the interim report that refitting flakes were present (Burgess 1976, 204). This total represents a relatively small proportion of the collection (2% by number; 6% by weight), but it must be remembered that there was

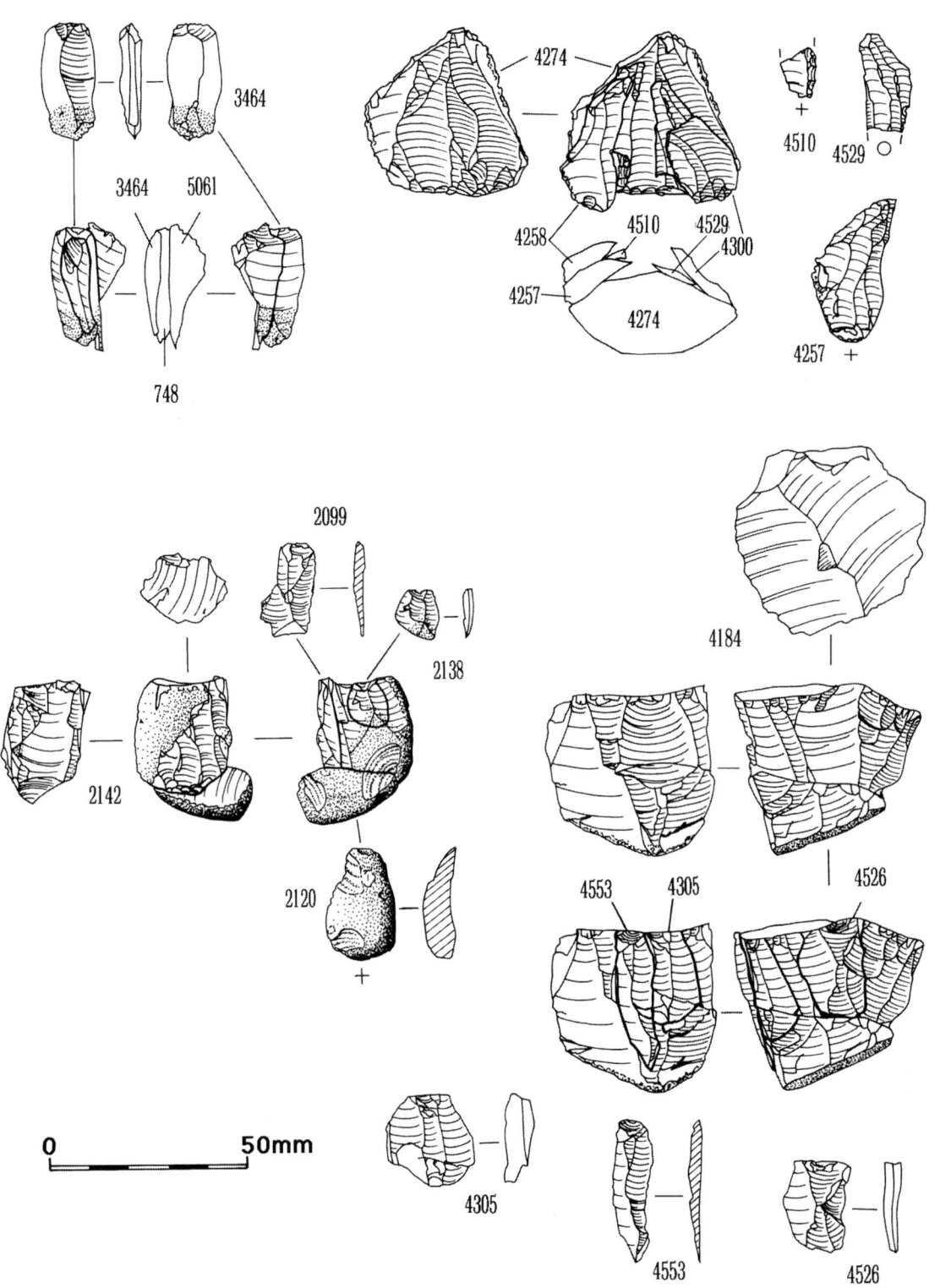

85 Refitting pieces (see text and Table 35 for details).

STRUCK LITHIC ARTEFACTS

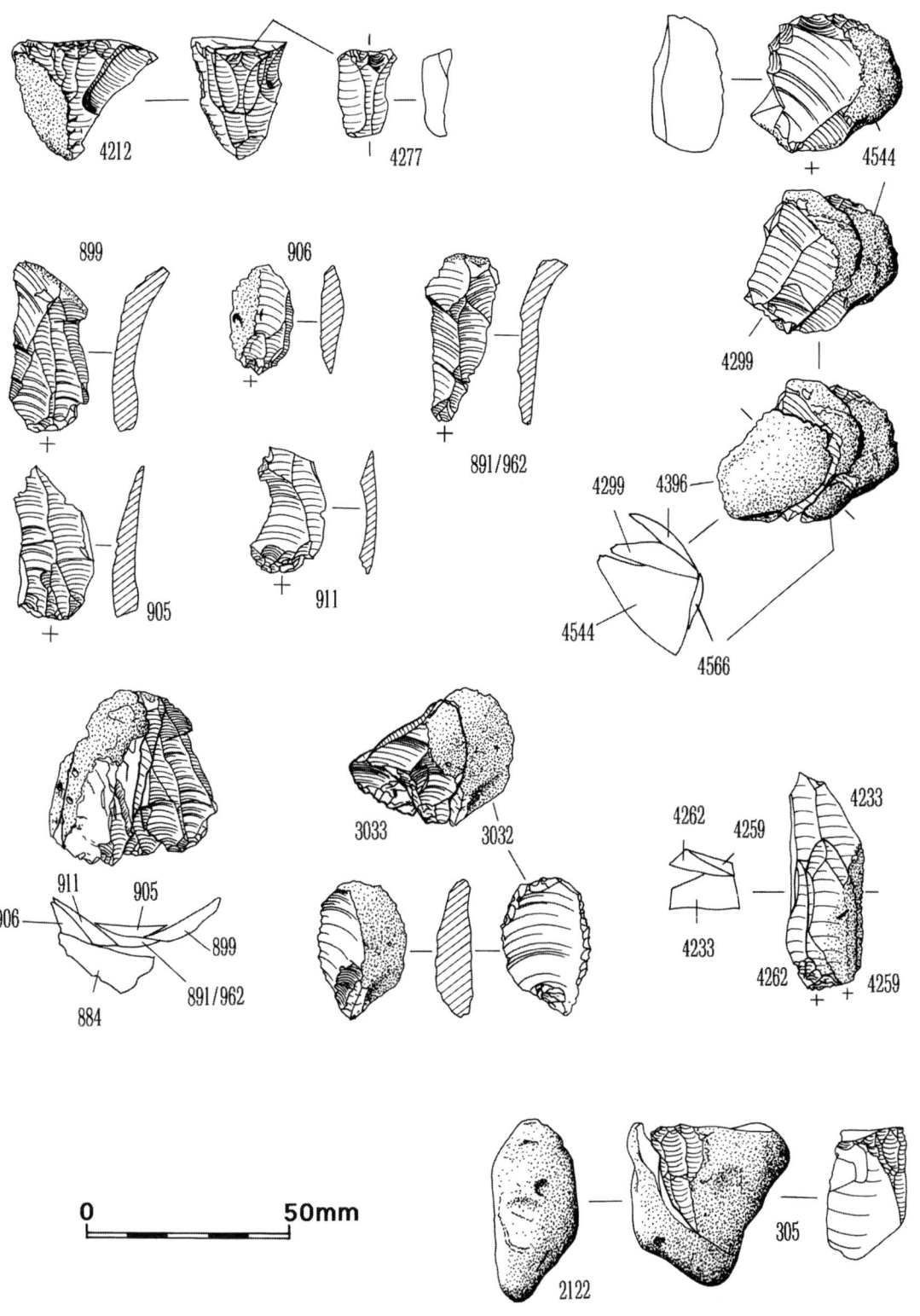

86 Refitting pieces (see text and Table 35 for details).

incomplete excavation of any of the flint-bearing contexts and that there was probably well below full recovery of flints from the areas which were excavated. Even so, the potential for refitting within this collection has almost certainly not been fully achieved, in part because of the complex system of small excavation trenches and the resulting divisive recording and bagging of the artefacts, and in part because of inadequate laboratory space in which to lay out all the artefacts at the same time during analysis. This has especially hampered the search for cross-refitting between trenches and layers.

The 115 refitting pieces resolve into 44 separate, relatively simple refit groupings of various types, of which the maximum number of pieces involved in any one grouping is seven, and by far the majority involve only two pieces:

single artefacts found as two separate segments, refitting at old transverse breaks: 10 instances;

rejoining pairs of what were probably single artefacts which have split longitudinally (Siret fractures) at the time of initial detachment: 3 instances;

core and single refitting flake: 10 instances;

core fragment and single refitting flake: 1 instance;

core and two refitting flakes: 1 instance;

core and three refitting flakes: 2 instances;

core and five refitting flakes: 1 instance;

two sequential flakes: 11 instances;

three sequential flakes: 2 instances;

four sequential flakes: 2 instances;

six sequential flakes: 1 instance;

implement/retouched piece with one refitting flake: 2 instances;

implement with three refitting flakes: 1 instance;

two core fragments refitting to form a complete core: 1 instance; and

two core fragments refitting to form a still incomplete core: 1 instance.

(Note that these instances total 49, not 44, because six of the single refitting artefacts are involved in five further refits.)

Nevertheless, despite the absence of lengthy sequences, these refit groupings do document with greater clarity some of the technological aspects of the assemblage. The reduction strategy involving the opening of a pebble by removing a primary flake from one or more ends of the pebble to create a platform, which is then utilized for flake removals without further preparation, is shown by two of the groupings (illus 85: *2099/2120/2138/2142*; illus 86: *305/2122*). It is of interest to note that in one of these cases (illus 86: *305/2122*), because of its configuration, the core was classified as a core fragment until the refit demonstrated this was not so.

The progressive detachment of blades, or blade-like flakes, some of which were suitable blanks for tools, is shown by several groupings (eg illus 85: *4257/4258/4529/4274/4300/4510*; *4184/4305/4526/4553*; illus 86: *884/891–962/899/905/906/911*). In one of these cases (illus 85: *4510*) a detached blade has received blunting retouch prior to a break, and is categorized as an unclassified microlith fragment (see above).

Eleven of the groupings include a platform core, and the high quality of production possible from them is shown by several (eg illus 82: *5132/5133*; illus 79: *2592/2620*; illus 86: *4233/4259/4262*). Only four of the refit groupings involve anvil-flaked cores (eg illus 85: *748/3464/5061*), but a further six groupings were thought to involve anvil-struck flakes (eg illus 86: *3032/3033*).

The other aspect to the refitting exercise is the production of distributional information relevant to site formation processes. The majority of refits, involving 83 of the total 115 pieces, are between pieces from the silver sand horizon. Almost all of these are from within single trench units (73/A1: two pieces in one group; 73/E1: 42 pieces in 14 groups; 73/E2: six pieces in three groups; 73/Z2: two pieces in one group; 76/G2: 27 pieces in nine groups; 76/H1: two pieces in one group), the exception being one group of two refitting pieces from the adjacent trenches 73/A2 and 76/G1 respectively. This confirms the *in situ* and relatively undisturbed nature of the Mesolithic deposits in the silver sand. The only refit between a piece from the silver sand and another horizon involved a grouping of four pieces from trench 73/A2 (illus 85: *2099/2120/2138/2142*), of which three were from the silver sand and one (illus 85: *2099*) from the midden.

From wholly within the midden horizon there are 10 refitting pieces from single trenches, representing five groups of two pieces (trenches 61/I; 73/A2; 73/B3; 73/F1; 76/G1), and a single group of two refitting pieces from trenches 61/III and 73/B1 respectively. There is also a group of three refitting pieces, two from the midden in trenches 73/F2 and 76/G2 respectively, and the third from the topsoil in trench 61/II, and a further group of three refitting pieces, one from the midden in tench 76/G2 and two from the topsoil in trench 73/A4. Since the midden horizon, by its very nature, implies redeposition, even this limited number of refits, only one of which involves two segments of a single flake, is perhaps surprising.

The remaining refits involve pieces from wholly within the topsoil (two groupings of two pieces each) and two groupings of two pieces each, with in each case one piece from the topsoil and one piece unstratified. The absence of any 'long-distance' refits among the flints from Kilellan is noteworthy, but may reflect the constraints mentioned at the beginning of this section, since the pottery assemblage included many more between-trench conjoining sherds.

DISCUSSION

In order to effect a comparison between the Mesolithic and later elements of the Kilellan assemblage, those artefacts from silver sand and midden contexts were compared (table 33). It is recognized that the midden does contain residual Mesolithic material and that the silver sand could have intrusive later material, so the comparison is not between Mesolithic and later without qualification. Nevertheless, the silver sand artefacts appear on the whole sufficiently homogenous (in terms of technology, typology, condition and refitting) to constitute a viable Mesolithic sample. That accepted, the key contrasts in terms of retouched pieces are the relative absence of scrapers, edge-trimmed flakes and knives in the silver sand, and of microliths in the midden.

TABLE 33
Comparison between the total assemblages from the silver sand and the midden.

Artefact type	Midden Number	Midden Weight in grams	Silver sand Number	Silver sand Weight in grams
Unretouched flakes	2011	5152.4	1035	2183.8
Cores	104	1629.9	45	967.0
Core fragments	117	1050.5	14	158.2
Flaked lumps	5	106.8	5	333.4
Scrapers	40	391.8	5	112.5
Edge-trimmed flakes	16	71.9	3	4.7
Microliths	3	0.7	22	3.9
Knives	9	137.3	1	7.0
Piercers	3	31.8	4	30.0
Arrowheads	1	1.2	1	1.6
Microburins	1	0.7	2	0.8
Truncated flake	–	–	1	1.7
Miscellaneous retouched pieces	59	402.5	20	115.3
Unclassified burnt pieces	87	153.9	117	85.0
Totals	2456	9131.4	1275	4004.9

Key: Midden trenches (and contexts) with flints: 59/FI(4); 59/FI(5); 60/FII(5); 60/FII(6); 61/I(6); 61/II(6); 61/III(6); 73/A1(2); 73/A1(6); 73/A1-3(2); 73/A2(5); 73/A3(2); 73/A4(6); 73/B1(6); 73/B2(6); 73/B3(6); 73/E2(6); 73/F1(6); 73/F2(6); 76/G1(6); 76/G1(102); 76/G1(106); 76/G1(109); 76/G2(6); 76/G2(100); 76/G2(103); 76/G2(104); 76/G2(106); 76/G2(107); 76/G2(108); 76/G2(109); 76/G2(133); 76/G2(138); 76/G3(3); 76/G3(4); 76/G4(3); 76/J1(5); 76/J2(19); 76/J2(30); 76/J2(32); 76/K3(5).
Silver sand trenches (and contexts) with flints: 73/A1(7); 73/A2(6); 73/B1(7);73/B2(7); 73/B3(7); 73/E1(4); 73/E2(7); 76/G1(8); 76/G1(110); 76/G2(8); 76/G2(126); 76/G2 (131); 76/G2(132); 76/G3(7); 76/H1(7); 76/H2(7); 76/K1(8); 76/L2(12).

Otherwise, the two sub-assemblages are quite similar at this broad level of analysis, except for the large number of core fragments in the midden, which may be related to the higher incidence of anvil-knapping after the Mesolithic.

External comparisons from elsewhere on Islay for the Mesolithic element of the Kilellan assemblage are plentiful in view of recent work by Mithen (2000a) and his team on the Southern Hebrides Mesolithic Project (SHMP), together with the previous Mesolithic material from excavations at Newton (Clarke 1989), but are much less so for Neolithic and Early Bronze Age flintwork.

The structure of the Kilellan assemblage cannot be compared in close detail with the SHMP assemblages, because the latter were recovered by fine sieving. Nevertheless, it is clear from the preceding analyses that, as at the SHMP sites, knapping was an on-site activity, involving the reduction process from initial opening of selected pebbles to implement production and then tool use on site. The surveys undertaken in conjunction with the SHMP (Marshall 2000b, 77) suggest that the shore of Loch Gruinart was not a source of raw material for knapping, although fieldwalking close to Kilellan produced, as did Kilellan itself, numerous unworked pebbles as well as knapped material (Mithen et al 2000a: field GRU13). However, proximity to very good raw material supplies on the west coast of the Rinns means that acquisition of pebbles would not have been a logistical problem.

The attribution to period of the anvil-flaked material at Kilellan is problematic. On the one hand there seems little doubt that anvil-flaking was fully part of the Mesolithic reduction strategy, while on the other it appears more prevalent in post-Mesolithic contexts. This does not mean that all post-Mesolithic flaking was of anvil character, since, for example, the knives demonstrate the importance of flakes struck from platform cores. Nor, although platform-core production of blades and blade-like flakes was the regular way in which to provide blanks for microliths, was it impossible to produce blades by anvil technique.

Mesolithic anvil-cores were not, it would appear, present at Newton (Clarke 1989, 32), but they do feature in many of the SHMP assemblages from Islay (Finlay et al 2000, 557) particularly at Gleann Mor (Mithen & Finlayson 2000, 195), where bipolar technology is described as a normal part of the technological repertoire. Description and illustration of the SHMP cores, however, concentrated on the platform examples and no bipolar cores were illustrated. The present report intentionally restores the balance somewhat by giving anvil-struck cores a fuller treatment.

Variability within the retouched component from the silver sand follows approximately the pattern to be anticipated from previous work, with microliths dominant, but this assemblage is too small to be compared closely with the SHMP retouched inventories (Finlay et al 2000, 572). In terms of basic typology there are of course general parallels, as well as more distinct ones, for example, a similar dominance of scalene triangles among the microliths (Finlay et al 2000, 576). There is an even more specific parallel with the Newton assemblage in this regard. Clarke (1989, 33–4) drew attention to the scalene triangle type with a concave short edge at Newton, a type which is actually more common at Kilellan than those with a convex edge. There is a danger in over-interpreting small differences in microlith typology, but this could be a pointer to a specific link between these two sites, only 11 kilometres apart as the crow flies.

The date of the Mesolithic activity at Kilellan must be assumed, on the basis of the radiocarbon dates from Newton and the SHMP sites, to be within the bracket 8000–6500 BP (approximately 7000–5500 cal BC). No finer resolution is possible, but it might be argued that the low density of the Kilellan material is more likely to represent short-lived occupation than the large assemblages from what are probably multi-phase occupations of the SHMP sites. It could be interpreted as a temporary camp used by one of the groups of mobile hunter-gatherers which favoured the Rinns area of Islay (Mithen 2000b, 619).

In many respects it is the post-Mesolithic flintwork at Kilellan which is the more interesting and potentially significant, and thus it is all the more disappointing that it is not possible to isolate a homogenous sample from the Neolithic or the Early Bronze Age. It does seem possible, however, that many of the scrapers and most of the knives are to be associated with the Early Bronze Age activity, together with the barbed-and-tanged arrowheads and extensive use of anvil-core technology. This would be the most parsimonious explanation, but caution is necessary, particularly in view of the evidence for knife forms in the Neolithic rather than the Early Bronze Age. This applies in Scotland both generally (Henshall 1972, 185–6; Piggott 1972, 44) and specifically on Islay at the Port Charlotte tomb (Pierpoint 1980, 126), which produced four knives, two of them with pressure-flaking. The Port Charlotte knives (Pierpoint 1980, fig 5.1), which are said to predate the Neolithic pottery from the tomb, offer reasonably close parallels for some of the Kilellan knives, which must make their attribution to the Early Bronze Age at Kilellan less reliable.

Finally, in view of the continuing debate concerning the use of flint technology in the later Bronze Age and Iron Age (Humphrey 2003), it can be noted that the very small numbers of flint artefacts from the area of Late Bronze Age and Middle Iron Age activity in trenches L and J/K are best regarded as residual elements from the Mesolithic and Early Bronze Age occupation.

The complete catalogue of struck lithic artefacts is deposited with the excavation archive.

TABLE 34
Flint totals by trench and year.

Year	Trench	Number	Weight in grams
1959	C5	26	56.8
1959	C6	4	3.6
1959	D5	11	25.6
1959	D6	25	21.7
1959	E5	12	25.6
1959	E6	9	8.8
1959	E7	7	40.2
1959	F1	32	73.4
1959	F2	16	36.7
1959	F3	7	7.2
1959	F4	14	18.0
1959	F5	10	14.5
1959	F6	14	31.7
1959	G1	22	28.5
1959	G2	32	56.2
1959	G3	13	7.9
1959	G4	59	106.1
1959	G5	31	81.9
1959	unknown	47	400.7
1960	F2	83	323.4
1960	L23	1	3.3
1960	unknown	13	80.9
1961	1	118	556.1
1961	2	73	309.3
1961	3	70	230.4
1961	unknown	1	14.8
1973	A1 & A1/A3	453	1751.0
1973	A2	206	606.7
1973	A3	189	558.3
1973	A4	37	182.4
1973	B1	147	467.3
1973	B2	369	1368.3
1973	B3	48	172.8
1973	C1	18	62.7
1973	E1	403	1704.3
1973	E2	146	781.1
1973	F1	309	1119.9
1973	F2	88	433.3
1973	Z1	1	6.8
1973	Z2	16	107.6
1973	unknown	183	758.1
1976	G1	380	1195.6
1976	G2	1026	2582.8
1976	G3	47	196.0
1976	G4	36	383.2

TABLE 34
Flint totals by trench and year (*cont*).

Year	Trench	Number	Weight in grams
1976	H1	114	359.1
1976	H2	24	45.5
1976	J1	3	21.1
1976	J2	4	78.1
1976	K1	8	74.9
1976	K2	13	62.6
1976	K3	14	41.1
1976	K1/K2/K3	5	0.9
1976	L1	6	15.6
1976	L2	65	387.1
1976	L2a	14	50.5
1976	M1	7	20.3
1976	unknown	3	95.2
1977	unknown	1	32.5
	Totals	5133	18.286 kg

TABLE 35
Catalogue of illustrated flints.
Illus 78. Cores.

Illustration/ catalogue number	Type	Year/Trench code	Layer/Square or Feature no
1370	Core – anvil, bipolar, bifacial	76/G2	100/08
1914	Core – anvil, bipolar, bifacial	73/A1–3	1
2374	Core – anvil, unipolar, unifacial	73/–	–
4083	Core – anvil, bipolar, bifacial	73/B2	7
353	Core – platform (A2)	76/G1	109
4720	Core – anvil, bipolar, bifacial	73/F1	1
632	Core – anvil, bipolar, unifacial	76/G2	6/42b
4115	Core – anvil, bipolar, bifacial	73/B2	7
1427	Core – anvil, tripolar, bifacial	76/G3	3
4388	Core – platform (A2)	73/E1	4
433	Core – anvil, bipolar, bifacial	76/G2	6/05a

TABLE 35 (*cont*)
Illus 79. Cores, hammerstone, unretouched blades, and truncated flake.

Illustration/ catalogue number	Type	Year/Trench code	Layer/Square or Feature no
1487	Core – anvil, bipolar, bifacial	76/G4	3
2265	Core – anvil, bipolar, bifacial	73/A3	1
5082	Core – anvil, bipolar, bifacial	73/F2	6
1586	Core – platform (A2)	73/A1	1
4543	Core – platform (B2)	73/E1	4
4639	Core – platform (A2)	73/E2	7
3930	Core – platform (A2)	73/B2	6
3200	Hammerstone	59/G5	–
2884	Unretouched blade	59/C6	–
2600	Unretouched blade	76/H1	7a
3460	Unretouched blade	61/1	6
4231	Unretouched blade	73/E1	4
2592/2620: refit group 40	Unretouched blade	76/H1	7 & 7b
4124	Truncated flake, oblique	73/B2	7

Illus 80. Serrated flake and scrapers.

Illustration/ catalogue number	Type	Year/Trench code	Layer/Square or Feature no
2846	Serrated flake	76/L2	118/02
425	Scraper – side	76/G2	6/05a
650	Scraper – extended end	76/G2	6/58
1946	Scraper – end	73/A2	1
3297	Scraper – end	60/F2	6
260	Scraper – extended end	76/G1	7a
619	Scraper – side	76/G2	6/27b
755	Scraper – extended end	76/G2	6/72e
3421	Scraper – end	61/1	6
3929	Scraper – end	73/B2	6
259	Scraper – end	76/G1	7a
423	Scraper – end	76/G2	6
1540	Scraper – side	73/A1	1
4545	Scraper – extended end	73/E1	4
4547	Scraper – end and side	73/E1	4
1535	Scraper – side	73/A1	1
3419	Scraper – end, 'nosed'	61/1	6
261	Scraper – side	76/G1	7b

TABLE 35 (*cont*)
Illus 81. Scrapers, edge-trimmed flakes and knives.

Illustration/ catalogue number	Type	Year/Trench code	Layer/Square or Feature no
1408	Scraper – end	76/G3	2
3420	Scraper – extended end	61/1	6
4548	Scraper – end, denticulate	73/E1	4
1453	Scraper – end	76/G4	3/17
2411	Scraper – end	73/–	–
1776	Edge-trimmed flake	73/A1	2
1542	Edge-trimmed flake	73/A1	1
3259	Edge-trimmed flake	60/–	–
4229	Edge-trimmed flake	73/E1	4
3007	Edge-trimmed flake	59/F4	–
1674	Edge-trimmed flake	73/A1	2
1486	Knife	76/G4	3
5020	Knife	73/F1	6
1991	Knife	73/A2	3/4
4885	Knife	73/–	6

Illus 82. Microliths, microburins and related pieces.

Illustration/ catalogue number	Type	Year/Trench code	Layer/Square or Feature no
4380	Microlith – atypical, edge-blunted bladelet	73/E1	4
2593	Microlith – scalene triangle	76/H1	7
1170	Microlith – scalene triangle	76/G2	132
2689	Microlith – atypical	76/H2	7
3619	Microlith – obliquely blunted point	73/B1	6
4037	Microlith – unclassified	73/B2	7
4556	Microlith – obliquely blunted point	73/E1	4
4558	Microlith – scalene triangle	73/E1	4
277	Microlith – scalene triangle	76/G1	8b
5132/5133	Miscellaneous retouched piece – ?failed microlith/microburin (refit group 19)	73/Z2	6
1880	Microlith – atypical, edge-blunted bladelet	73/A1	7
4557	Microlith – unclassified	73/E1	4
4562	Microlith – scalene triangle	73/E1	4
2019	Microlith – obliquely blunted point	73/A2	5
2023	Microlith – crescent	73/A2	5
2572	Microlith – scalene triangle	76/H1	7a
2574	Microlith – scalene triangle	76/H1	7b
2602	Microlith – scalene triangle	76/H1	7a
4542	Microlith – scalene triangle	73/E1	4
2573	Microlith – scalene triangle	76/H1	7a
4038	Microburin	73/B2	7
916	Microburin	76/G2	131
980	Microlith – unclassified	76/G2	131
1441	Microburin	76/G3	4

TABLE 35 (*cont*)
Illus 83. Knives and piercers.

Illustration/ catalogue number	Type	Year/Trench code	Layer/Square or Feature no
1727	Knife	73/A1	2
1918	Knife	73/A1–3	1
3417	Knife	61/1	6
1919	Knife	73/A1–3	2
846	Knife	76/G2	–
1860	Knife	73/A1	6
2586	Piercer	76/H1	7
3418	Knife	61/1	6
649	Piercer	76/G2	6/57d
2555	Knife	73/–	–
1519	Piercer	73/A1	1
3167	Knife	59/G4	–
2561	Piercer	76/H1	4
2143	Piercer	73/A2	6

Illus 84. Arrowheads and miscellaneous retouched pieces.

Illustration/ catalogue number	Type	Year/Trench code	Layer/Square or Feature no
3248	Leaf-shaped arrowhead	59/–	–
3537	Leaf-shaped arrowhead	61/3	6
4036	Leaf-shaped arrowhead	73/B2	7
2965	Leaf-shaped arrowhead	59/F1	–
264	Barbed-and-tanged arrowhead	76/G1	7b
3166	Barbed-and-tanged arrowhead	59/G4	–
4029	Miscellaneous retouched piece	73/B2	6
2735	Miscellaneous retouched piece	76/K1	103
4880	Miscellaneous retouched piece	73/F1	6

TABLE 35 (*cont*)
Illus 85. Refitting pieces.

Illustration/ catalogue number	Type	Year/Trench code	Layer/Square or Feature no
Refit group 20			
748	Unretouched flake	76/G2	6/70c
3464	Core – anvil, bipolar, unifacial	61/2	1
5061	Unretouched flake	73/F2	6
Refit group 1			
4257	Unretouched flake	73/E1	4
4258	Unretouched flake	73/E1	4
4274	Core – platform (A2)	73/E1	4
4300	Unretouched flake	73/E1	4
4510	Microlith – unclassified	73/E1	4
4529	Unretouched flake	73/E1	4
Refit group 33			
2099	Unretouched flake	73/A2	5
2120	Unretouched flake	73/A2	6
2138	Unretouched flake	73/A2	6
2142	Core – platform (B2)	73/A2	6
Refit group 13			
4184	Core – platform (A1)	73/E1	4
4305	Unretouched flake	73/E1	4
4526	Unretouched flake	73/E1	4
4553	Unretouched flake	73/E1	4

TABLE 35 (*cont*)
Illus 86. Refitting pieces.

Illustration/ catalogue number	Type	Year/Trench code	Layer/Square or Feature no
Refit group 10			
4212	Core – platform (A2)	73/E1	4
4277	Unretouched flake	73/E1	4
Refit group 12			
4299	Unretouched flake	73/E1	4
4396	Unretouched flake	73/E1	4
4544	Scraper – end	73/E1	4
4566	Unretouched flake	73/E1	5
Refit group 27			
884	Unretouched flake	76/G2	131
891/962	Unretouched flake	76/G2	131
899	Unretouched flake	76/G2	131
905	Unretouched flake	76/G2	131
906	Unretouched flake	76/G2	131
911	Unretouched flake	76/G2	131
Refit group 41			
3032	Miscellaneous retouched piece	59/F6	–
3033	Unretouched flake	59/F6	–
Refit group 6			
4233	Unretouched flake	73/E1	4
4259	Unretouched flake	73/E1	4
4262	Unretouched flake	73/E1	4
Refit group 35			
0305	Core fragment	76/G1	8c
2122	Unretouched flake	73/A2	6

Chapter 5

Coarse stone artefacts

ANN CLARKE

The assemblage comprises 84 objects of coarse stone and is composed mainly of a variety of cobble tool types. In addition there are a few stone flakes and grinders and a number of miscellaneous pieces (see table 36). All of the tools have been made on rounded cobbles of the locally available rock with greywacke, quartzites, sandstone and granite being the most common raw materials.

The cobble tools include faceted hammerstones, bevelled pebbles, a few stones with pecking on the face and a number of plain hammerstones. The modification of the cobble tools is through use-wear alone, for none of the pieces has been shaped prior to use. The faceted hammerstones exhibit pecked or ground facets sometimes with flaking from the outer edge of the facet depending on the extent of wear. Greywacke and quartzite were selected for these tools in preference to the other raw materials available. The original cobbles are varied in size and shape and in most cases only single facets have been formed, usually on one end. However, on five of the complete pieces double facets have been worn on one end to form a ridge (illus 87, 1: no 22). In addition, six of these tools exhibit pecking on the flat face of the cobble which is most often localized and in one case forms a discrete linear pattern (illus 87, 3: no 26). A further seven cobbles exhibit facial pecking as the sole form of wear. The functions of these faceted tools are most probably quite varied given the mix of shapes and sizes of the cobbles and the resultant patterns of wear. Certainly none of them resembles the classic pounder/grinders that can occur in the Bronze Age as the tools from Kilellan tend to exhibit much smaller facets. Many of these tools were likely to have been involved in flint knapping with the facets being produced through

TABLE 36
Coarse stone artefacts by period.

Type	MESO	EBA	EIA	MIA	?	Total
Faceted hammerstones	–	24	3	–	1	28
Plain hammerstones	4	15	–	2	1	22
Bevelled pebbles	–	5	–	1	1	7
Facially pecked cobbles	1	5	–	1	–	7
Stone flakes	–	4	–	–	2	6
Grinders	–	4	2	–	–	6
?Saddle querns	–	1	1	–	–	2
Perforated objects	–	1	–	2	–	3
Socketed stone	–	–	–	1	–	1
Polisher	–	–	–	1	–	1
Pebble hammer	–	1	–	–	–	1
Total	5	60	6	8	5	84

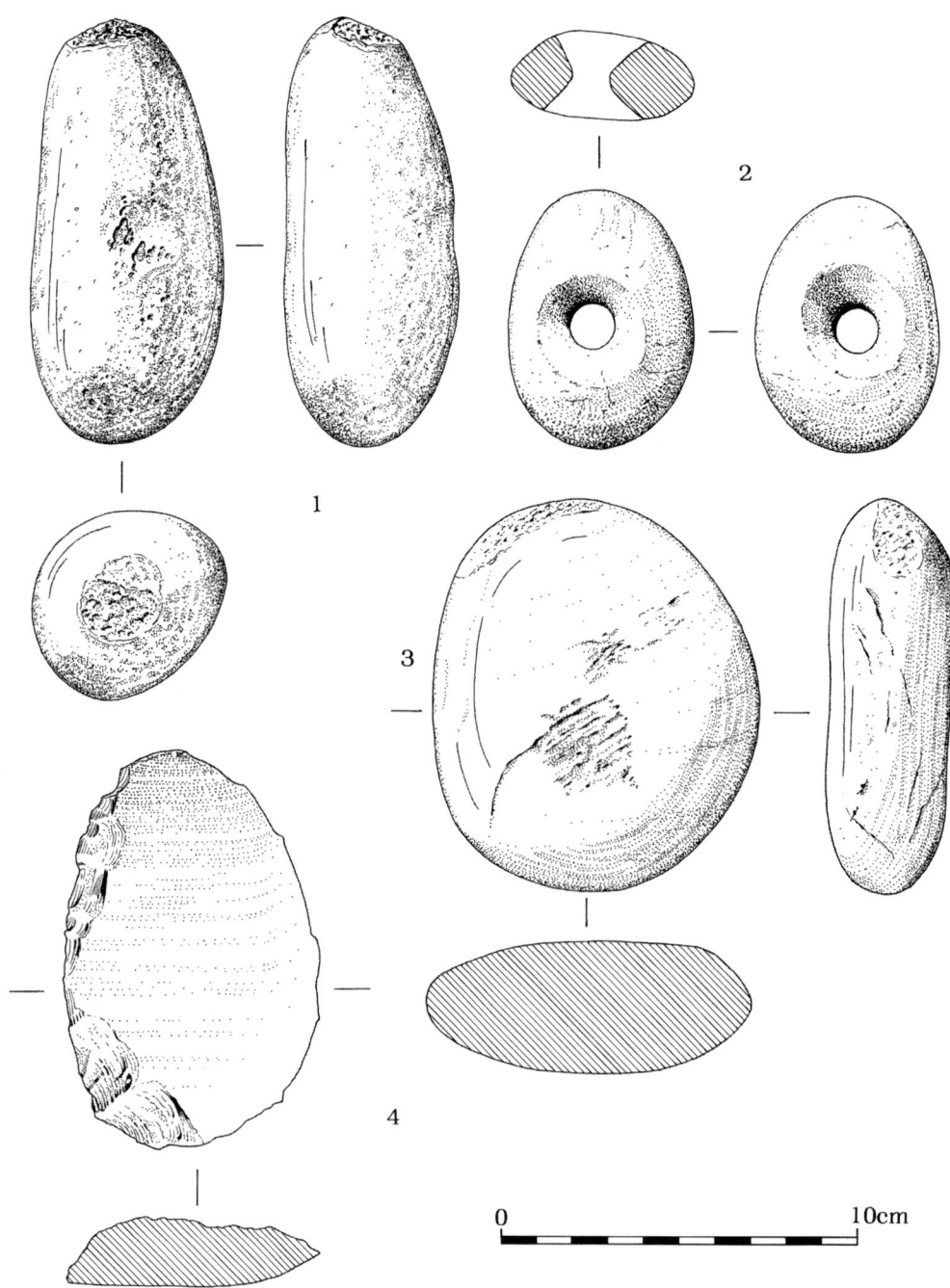

87 Coarse stone artefacts: 1, no 22; 2, no 84; 3, no 26; 4, no 77.

striking flakes from parent nodules. Facial pecking, with or without additional wear, is also common on such hammerstones and where the pecking forms a depression or linear pattern this may be indicative of the use of the cobble as an anvil in bipolar knapping (Clarke 1990, 123).

The bevelled pieces have normally been worn on pebbles with a flat cross-section and schists, greywacke and sandstones have been selected. The ends of these tools have been worn bifacially by pecking and flaking to form a characteristic rounded or bevelled profile (illus 88, 2: no 35). The precise

COARSE STONE ARTEFACTS

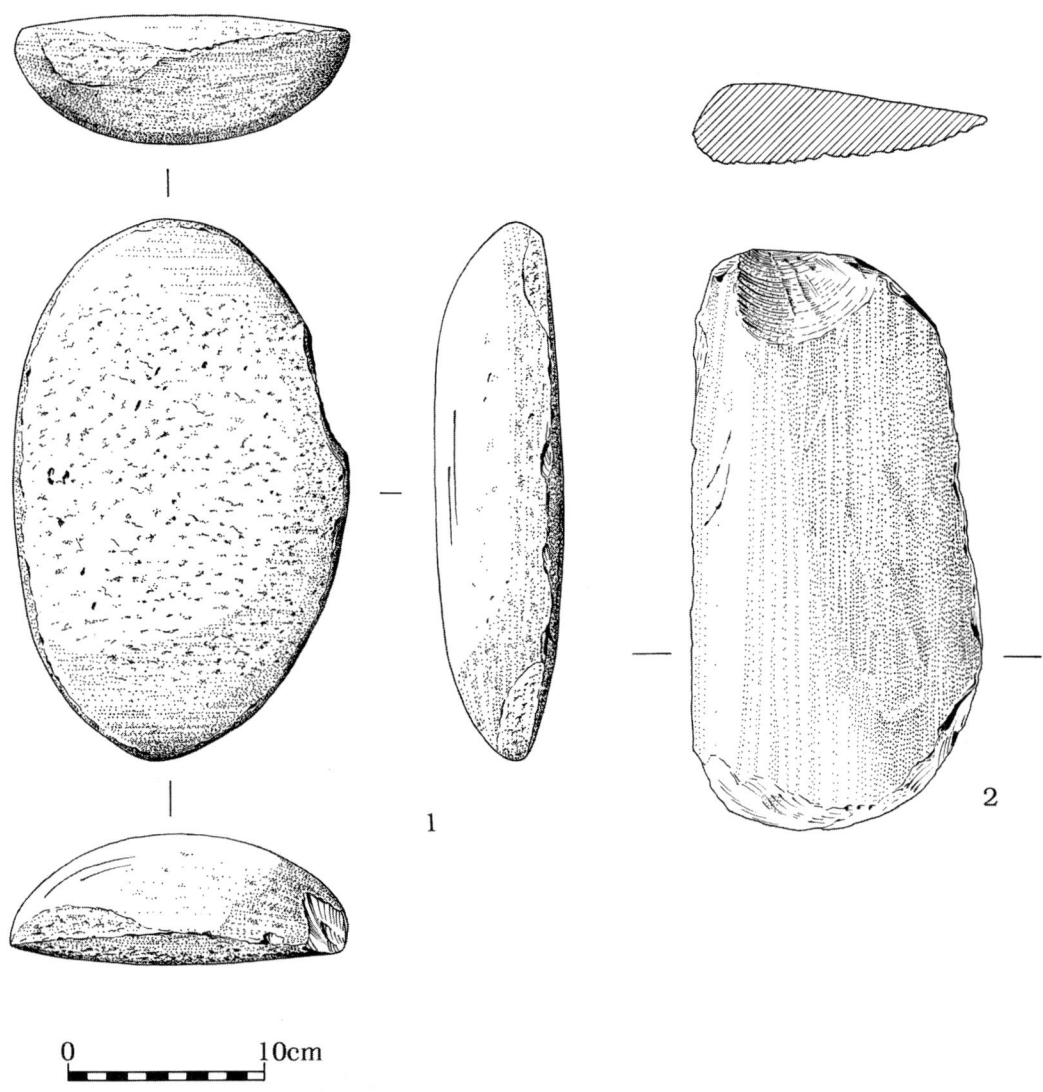

88 Coarse stone artefacts: 1, no 68; 2, no 35.

function for these tools is not known but they are often referred to in the literature as limpet hammers despite the seemingly wide range of size, shape and wear patterns that this term encompasses. Research into the use and wear patterns of such tools may prove fruitful given the common occurrence of bevelled pebbles on Scottish West Coast sites of both Mesolithic and Bronze Age dates.

A large number of plain hammerstones are present and these are cobbles which tend to have more randomly placed or lighter wear patterns than the above. None of them exhibits faceting or bevelling but some of the pieces may represent the early stages of wear in the use of such tools.

The six grinders are made on flat oval boulders of greywacke or granite and all are of a similar size. They have been pecked over the whole of one face in preparation for use and this face has subsequently been worn by grinding to form a longitudinal convex surface. On two of the pieces there are finely ground facets at either end continuous with the ground face (illus 88, 1: no 68). No 65 appears to be unfinished as it exhibits a partially pecked face with no grinding; this piece may have been abandoned prior to use because of breakage. Two of the grinders, nos 69 and 70, have had secondary use as an anvil and their association with worked serpentine suggests that this re-use was in modern times (Chapter 6, no 18).

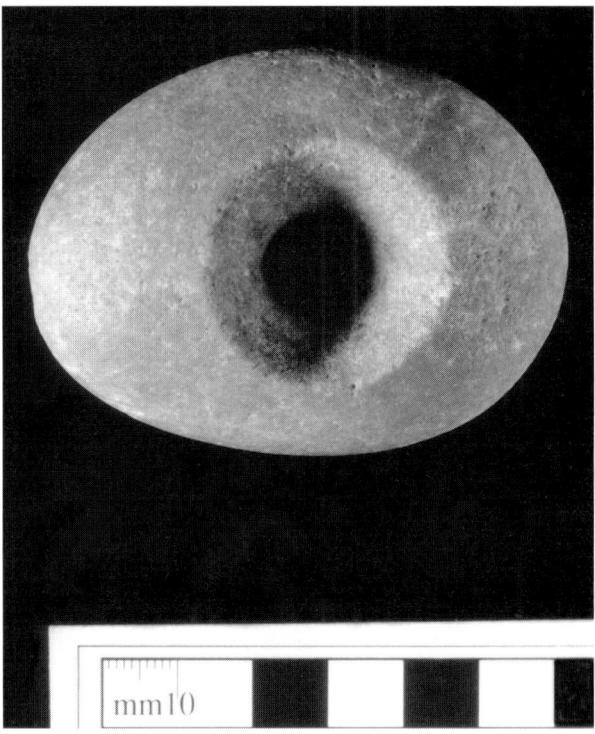

89 Pebble hammer no 84.

A few stone flakes from greywacke and quartzite cobbles are present and at least one of the flakes has been detached accidentally as the result of hammerstone use. It is likely though that other flakes were made deliberately for use; one piece exhibits wear in the form of chipping around the distal edge whilst another (illus 87, 4: no 77) has been modified, prior to use, around the distal end with bifacial flaking. Deliberately made flakes of coarse stone are a common feature of Neolithic and later sites in Orkney and Shetland where they often occur in large quantities with most flakes being unretouched. Elsewhere in Scotland the presence of such flakes has not been noted and although this may be a factor of non-recognition of such simple artefacts during excavation, it is likely that they did not form a significant component of the tool assemblage from the sites.

The remaining object of note is a pebble hammer (illus 87, 2: no 84; illus 89), which conforms to others of this type: an unshaped pebble, often of quartzite, with a central hour-glass perforation that is worn smooth in the centre. The ends of these hammers are often worn in a manner similar to that from Kilellan (Roe 1979, 36).

Only five objects of coarse stone were recovered from Mesolithic contexts and these are all cobble tools with simple wear traces. The majority of the pieces are from Early Bronze Age contexts, including four of the grinders, one perforated object and the pebble hammer. The cobble tools from this period, in particular the faceted hammerstones and bevelled pebbles, are similar in nature to those from the nearby Bronze Age site at Ardnave 2 (Ritchie & Welfare 1983). The later phases have a few cobble tools similar to those from the Early Bronze Age as well as two of the grinders, the two large perforated pieces, the socketed stone and the pebble polisher.

CATALOGUE

The entries are ordered by artefact type and then by trench number, layer number and site find number, or, in the case of stray finds and finds from Whittaker's excavations, by the National Museums of Scotland accessions number; note that there may be more than one artefact with the same finds number. 'Gruinart midden' refers to finds made in 1930 'in kitchen deposit near Gruinart' (NMS accessions book), and it is uncertain whether this may be identified with Kilellan.

Measurements are in millimetres: ML maximum length; MW maximum width; MTh maximum thickness. Weight is in grams.

FACETED HAMMERSTONES

1. HR 1179 (Whittaker 1956)
Oval greywacke pebble. Coarse facet with some flaking at narrower end, burnt.
ML 138mm; MW 81mm; MTh 54m; 871g.

2. L2 119 A
Oval quartzite pebble, small pecked facet at narrower end.
ML 88mm; MW 50mm; MTh 45mm; 283g.

3. A1 1 SF971
Flat oval quartzite pebble with two ground facets on one long edge. ML106mm; MW 62mm; MTh 31mm; 300g.

4. HR 1178 (Whittaker 1956)
Flat oval quartzite pebble, two ground facets at one end form ridge, light area of pecking in centre of one face.
ML 106mm; MW 94mm; MTh 43mm; 624g.

5. HR 1175 (Whittaker 1954 site B)
Flat oval quartzite pebble, two ground facets at one end form ridge.
ML 87mm; MW 73mm; MTh 46mm; 416g.

6. A1 6 SF838
Flat oval ?greywacke pebble with black deposit on surface. Narrow pecked facet at both ends.
ML 70mm; MW49mm; MTh 21mm; 122g.

7. KN 76 unstratified, near G
Flat triangular quartzite pebble, single ground facet on two corners, one with additional flaking. Localized spread of pecking on one face.
ML 111mm; MW 92mm; MTh 54mm; 779g.

8. L2 119 B
Flat round quartzite pebble, narrow ground facet on one end.
ML 90mm; MW 84mm; MTh 37mm; 409g.

9. F1 6 SF587
Greywacke spall from faceted hammerstone, part of ground facet.
ML 52mm; MW 35mm; MTh 15mm; 27g.

10. HR 838 (Gruinart midden), 1930–553
Oval greywacke pebble, abraded, broken laterally, single broad rounded pecked facet at intact end with some flaking, two flat faces show twin areas of heavy localized pecking.
ML 124mm; MW 99mm; MTh 67mm; 1239g.

11. G2 605 SF163
Flat oval quartzite pebble, narrow pecked facet worked at one end, some light pecking down side.
ML 107mm; MW 91mm; MTh 39mm; 228g.

12. G2 surface
Flat oval quartzite pebble, narrow pecked facets at four points along narrow edge and flake removed from one end.
ML 116mm; MW 81mm; MTh 45mm; 548g.

13. G2 658 SF402
Spall from greywacke pebble, three pecked facets.
ML 116mm; MW 81mm; MTh 45mm; 548g.

14. G3 2 SF21
Spall from quartzite pebble, fire-reddened, pecked facet.
ML 58mm; MW 47mm MTh 36mm; 277g.

15. G2 661 SF352
Spall from quartz pebble, pecked facet.
ML 52mm; MW 47mm; MTh 31mm; 77g.

16. G2 672
Spall from greywacke pebble, burnt, pecked facet.
ML 102mm; MW 63mm; MTh 51mm; 382g.

17. G3 2 SF21
Quartz pebble, broken laterally, tiny pecked facet on one corner.
ML 86mm; MW 53mm; MTh 50mm; 277g.

18. G3 2 SF21
Spall from greywacke pebble, part of ground facet.
ML 48m; MW 48mm; MTh 14mm; 33g.

19. G3 2 SF21
Spall from ?granite pebble, part of pecked facet.
ML 48mm; MW 48mm; MTh 14mm; 33g.

20. G2 623 SF97
Elongated greywacke pebble, pecked facet at narrow end, localized light pecking on flat face.
ML 121mm; MW 80mm; MTh 55mm; 665g.

21. KN 59 G4
Elongated greywacke pebble, ground facet at narrower end.
ML 107mm; MW 40mm; MTh 32mm; 196g.

22. HR 1177 (Whittaker 1954, site A hearth)
Elongated greywacke pebble, two small facets at narrow end form a ridge.
ML 113mm; MW 55mm; MTh 50mm; 437g. (illus 87, 1)

23. L2 10 SF16
Elongated greywacke pebble, broken laterally, burnt, ground facet on one end.
ML 54mm; MW 50mm; MTh 47mm; 173g.

24. G2 676e
Elongated quartzite pebble, two facets on one end form ridge.
ML 128mm; MW 56mm; MTh 53mm; 471g.

25. G2 672 ?
Elongated greywacke pebble, rounded pecked facet at narrower end.
ML 130mm; MW 70mm; MTh 62mm; 885g.

26. A1 1
Flat oval quartzite pebble, ground facet on one end, localized heavy pecking on one face forms a linear pattern.
ML 105mm; MW 90mm; MTh 37mm; 536g. (illus 87, 3)

27. G1 6 SF24
Oval quartzite pebble, small ground facet at one end, localized areas of pecking on both flat faces.
ML 115mm; MW 80mm; MTh 54mm; 672g.

28. HR 1181 (Whittaker 1954 site C, from U-shaped setting)
Elongated greywacke pebble, two facets at narrow end form a ridge.
ML 155mm; MW 38mm; MTh 33mm; 323g.

BEVELLED PEBBLES

29. G2 605 SF115
Elongated flat greywacke pebble, bevelled on broad end with some additional flaking.
ML 108mm; MW 47mm; MTh 18mm; 139g.

30. G2 602/604 SF409
Elongated flat greywacke pebble, bevelled at one end with some additional flaking.
ML 125mm; MW 51mm; MTh 17mm; 177g.

31. K3 5 SF71
Flat elongated schist pebble, bevelled at both ends with additional rough flaking.
ML 133mm; MW 40mm; MTh 15mm; 149g.

32. H1 2 SF7
Flat elongated schist pebble, abraded, bevelled at one end.
ML 118mm; MW 35mm; MTh 15mm; 98g.

33. F1 6 SF908
Flat elongated sandstone pebble, abraded, broken laterally, bevelled at broad end.
ML 112mm; MW 41mm; MTh 11mm; 80g.

34. HR 1182 (Whittaker 1954, near hearth A)
Elongated greywacke pebble, bevelled on broad end.
ML 127mm; MW 38mm; MTh 19mm; 116g.

35. HR 837 (Gruinart midden)
Primary sandstone flake, bevelled at either end with heavy flaking at narrower end.
ML 138mm; MW 74mm; MTh 26mm; 300g. (illus 88, 2)

FACIALLY PECKED COBBLES

36. G2 surface
Flat round greywacke pebble, single areas of localized pecking on both flat faces.
ML 85mm; MW 40mm; MTh 498mm; 7g.

37. G2 surface
Greywacke pebble, broken, burnt, localized pecking on one flat face.
ML 113mm; MW 57mm; MTh 53mm; 404g.

38. G2 108.02 SF396
Oval quartz pebble, broken, localized areas of pecking on both flat faces, some pecking on edge.
ML 92mm; MW 62mm; MTh 46mm; 386g.

39. G2 636 SF282
Elongate greywacke pebble, localized pecking and some polishing on both flat faces.
ML 108mm; MW 38mm; MTh 29mm; 274g.

40. G2 624 SF134
Oval greywacke pebble, localized areas of pecking on three flat faces.
ML 86mm; MW 74mm; MTh 47mm; 409g.

41. E1 7 SF980
Oval greywacke pebble, small area of localized pecking on one face and possibly on opposite face.
ML 230mm; MW 124mm; MTh 105mm; 4315g.

42. J2 110 SF50
Oval flat cobble, heavy pecking on both flat faces.
ML 304mm; MW 268mm; MTh 110mm; 13500g.

PLAIN HAMMERSTONES

43. K3 210 SF35
Oval quartzite pebble, light pecking on flatter face.
ML 86mm; MW 64mm; MTh 55mm; 415g.

44. HR 1176 (Whittaker 1954 site A)
Oval sandstone pebble, pecked and flaked at narrow end.
ML 84mm; MW 46mm; MTh 26mm.

45. A ?2 ?SF711
Flat oval sandstone pebble, pecked and flaked at one end.
ML 123mm; MW 79mm; MTh 27mm; 401g.

46. HR 1180 (Whittaker 1956)
Flat oval greywacke pebble, broken laterally, pecked and flaked at one end.
ML 157mm; MW 82mm; MTh 35mm; 690g.

47. H1 7 SF32
Irregular oval ?greywacke pebble, localized pecking at one end.
ML 88mm; MW 58mm; MTh 49mm; 374g.

48. E1 7 SF272
Oval quartzite pebble, pecking at both ends.
ML 59mm; MW 47mm; MTh 44mm; 167g.

49. G2 624 SF134
Flat oval quartzite pebble, burnt, pecking at one end and on both faces.
ML 90mm; MW 62mm; MTh 35mm; 263g.

50. G2 623 SF97
Oval limestone pebble, abraded, light pecking at both ends.
ML 60mm; MW 38mm; MTh 22mm; 70g.

51. G2 618 SF170
Oval quartzite pebble, burnt, light pecking at one end.
ML 64mm; MW 35mm; MTh 24mm; 76g.

52. G2 659 SF163
Oval ?greywacke pebble, light pecking on one end.
ML 60mm; MW 36mm; MTh 22mm; 66g.

53. G2 605 SF337
Oval limestone pebble, pecking at both ends.
ML 82m; MW 46mm; MTh 41mm; 200g.

54. G2 642 SF129
Spall from greywacke pebble, pecking at apex.
ML 63mm; MW 51mm; MTh 31mm; 87g.

55. G2 605 SF337
Flat oval greywacke pebble, pecked and flaked at both ends.
ML 108mm; MW 67mm; MTh 25mm; 260g.

56. G1 604 SF79
Triangular greywacke pebble, narrow band of pecking along two adjoining edges, linear pecking on one flat face.
ML 162mm; MW 117mm; MTh 75mm; 1826g.

57. K3 201 SF24
Elongated oval sandstone pebble, light pecking on both ends.
ML 134mm; MW 37mm; MTh 34mm; 282g.

58. KN 59?
Elongated greywacke pebble, flaked at both ends, localized pecking at end of one face.
ML 88mm; MW 37mm; MTh 26mm; 117g.

59. F4
Elongated greywacke pebble, pecking at narrower end.
ML 86mm; MW 43mm; MTh 25mm; 128g.

60. E6
Oval greywacke pebble, pecking at one end.
ML 61mm; MW 30mm; MTh 20mm; 52g.

61. F2 5
Oval quartzite pebble, light pecking at one end.
ML 72mm; MW 33mm; MTh 29mm; 101g.

62. H1 7
Elongated sandstone pebble, abraded, pecking at one end.
ML 135mm; MW 29mm; MTh 25mm; 104g.

63. B2 6 ?SF622
Elongated greywacke pebble, pecked at wider end, one face possibly ground flat.
ML 63mm; MW 18mm; MTh 13mm; 22g.

64. E1 7 SF980.
Oval greywacke cobble, localized pecking on two sides.
ML 230mm; MW 123mm; MTh 116mm; 4315g.

GRINDERS

65. G2 108 SF300
Oval greywacke boulder, broken longitudinally, one face pecked overall to edge of stone forming a convex face, no sign of grinding or smoothing, opposite face pecked in central area.
ML 265mm; MW 132mm; MTh 88mm; 5055g.

66. G2 317
Oval flat granite boulder, most of one face pecked overall and ground longitudinally to convex surface, opposite face has localized central pecked area.
ML 108mm; MW 156mm; MTh 63mm; 3443g.

67. L2 126
Oval flat granite boulder, one face pecked and ground overall to a shallow convex face.
ML 231mm; MW 140mm; MTh 46mm; 2245g.

68. L2 10.101 SF57
Oval greywacke boulder, one face pecked overall and ground longitudinally to a convex surface, single finely-ground facets at either end contiguous with convex face.
ML 268mm; MW 168mm; MTh 64mm; 4194g. (illus 88, 1)

69. HR 1185 (Whittaker 1954 hearth A)
Oval flat granite boulder, one end broken, one face pecked and ground overall to a longitudinal convex surface, secondary use as an anvil shown by pecking through ground face, this pecked surface blackened.
ML 234mm; MW 182mm; MTh 48mm; 3749g.

70. HR 1186 (Whittaker 1954 hearth A)
Oval flat granite boulder, one face pecked and ground overall to a longitudinal convex surface, single finely-ground facets at either end contiguous with convex face, secondary use as an anvil similar to above.
ML 288mm; MW 169mm; MTh 69mm; 6602g.

SADDLE QUERNS

71. G2 674
Oval flat sandstone boulder, one face partially weathered away, worn surface looks natural, putative quern.
ML 296mm; MW 225mm; MTh 56mm; 5244g.

72. L2 114
Rectangular sandstone boulder, slightly concave face possibly worn by use as quern.
ML 460mm; MW 256mm; MTh 78mm; c 18000g.

PEBBLE FLAKES

73. G2 6.05 SF76
Primary ?quartzite flake.
ML 95mm; MW 90mm; MTh 13mm.

74. B1 6 SF468
Primary greywacke flake, roughly chipped around edge.
ML 96mm; MW 65mm; MTh 15mm.

75. G2 6.12 SF83
Primary greywacke flake. The crushed distal end indicates that the flake is probably detached from a hammerstone.
ML 60mm; MW 53mm; MTh 12mm.

76. KN 71 LR
Primary greywacke flake.
ML 82mm; MW 62mm; MTh 19mm.

77. KN ?73
Primary quartzite flake, retouched bifacially around distal end to form denticulate outline and steep edge.
ML 108mm; MW 74mm; MTh 20mm. (illus 87, 4)

78. A2 6 SF481
Primary greywacke flake.
ML 97mm; MW 92mm; MTh 15mm.

PERFORATED OBJECTS

79. HR 1183 (Whittaker 1954 site B)
Flat oval ?sandstone pebble, broken, abraded, hour-glass perforation truncated by breakage.
ML 131mm; MW 65mm; MTh 29mm; 380g.

80. K3 107 (amongst tumble from 102)
Fragment of large flat perforated stone, hour-glass perforation c 60mm diam, irregular faces. ?Anchor.
ML 254mm; MW 246mm; MTh 60mm; 6013g.

81. J2 110 SF25
Fragment of large flat perforated stone, hour-glass perforation c 68mm diam, irregular faces. ?Anchor.
ML 370mm; MW 220mm; MTh 76mm; weight unknown (*in situ* in souterrain wall).

MISCELLANEOUS

82. K3 106
Socketed stone. Irregular flat boulder, abraded.
ML 213mm; MW 152mm; MTh 74mm; 3335g; circular dished hollow on one face, 56mm diam, 12mm deep.

83. J1 25 SF84
Polisher. Flat round ferruginous sandstone pebble, polished on one flat face.
ML 45mm; MW 42mm; MTh 18mm; 116g.

84. G2 643 SF108
Pebble hammer. Flat oval ?quartzite pebble, almost central hour-glass perforation, 12–30mm diam, with narrow section of perforation polished by wear, light pecking at either end.
ML 69mm; MW 51mm; MTh 26mm; 114g. (illus 87, 2; illus 89)

POSTSCRIPT

In 1999, the author reported on the coarse stone assemblage from Dun Aonghasa, Co Clare, Ireland, as part of the Western Hill Forts Project for the Discovery Programme (unpublished). The assemblage includes sixteen grinding slabs that are similar in size and shape to the six grinders from Kilellan. On the Irish examples the working face is flat and very smooth and often bears polish towards the outer edge of the face, which is in contrast to the convex cross-section and ground face of the Kilellan examples. On three of the Irish grinding slabs smoothed facets were worn down the side or sides contiguous to the worked face, and these are comparable to the worn edges of the Kilellan grinders. Other examples of Irish grinding slabs come from the hill fort at Dun Eoghanachta and Clonfinlough. The dating of these grinding slabs is uncertain, but at Dun Aonghasa they were most probably associated with occupation of the substantial Late Bronze Age fort of 1100–500 BC.

The similarity of the Irish grinding slabs with those from Kilellan is noteworthy, especially since there are, as yet, no known examples of such artefacts from mainland Britain. Though the wear traces are slightly different, the similarity between the Scottish and Irish grinders in size, shape, raw material and worn edges is considered to be significant, and to indicate communications between Ireland and the west coast of Scotland during the Bronze Age, based on shared technology.

Chapter 6

Metal, bone, glass, clay and fine stone artefacts

ANNA RITCHIE

All the artefacts catalogued here belong to the Middle Iron Age settlement or to the Early Historic period or later and are discussed individually.

SILVER

1. Dress-pin, cast in debased silver, 47mm long, with a disc-shaped head, 7mm diam and 5mm thick, set with two convex garnets, one on either side; side of head decorated with incised lines, and silver edges hammered over garnets to keep them in place; swollen shank 4.5mm max diam, upper part circular in section with two incised lines below the head and a single line just above the point of maximum swelling, lower part faceted and octagonal in section with vertical lines of ?stamped? open circles between each facet. K3 201 SF98. (illus 90)

This silver pin set with garnets is an unusual discovery in Scotland, where amber or glass insets are more common on jewellery of the 7th and 8th centuries AD. A garnet mount, 4mm square and 1.1mm thick, was found in the Pictish horizon on the Brough of Birsay, Orkney (Curle 1982, 122, no 648), and is likely to have come from, or, since there is evidence of fine metalworking on site, to have been destined for the embellishment of a penannular brooch. Garnets are readily available in Scotland, and the preference for amber or red glass may reflect a local fashion for prestigious exotic or imported materials. Both garnet jewels were identified as almandine garnets with a significant pyrope proportion, and the silver proved to be heavily debased with copper and to have traces of zinc, gold and lead (Appendix 3).

Disc-headed pins of copper-alloy have been found in northern Scotland in Orkney and Shetland, and moulds for this type of pin are known from western Scotland. An unprovenanced copper-alloy pin from Orkney (Laing 1973, 56–8, fig 1, a), and one of iron from Howe, Orkney (Ballin Smith 1994, 217, illus 130, 284) have decorated discs, whereas copper-alloy examples from East Broch of Burray, Orkney (Stevenson 1955, 284, fig A, 17) and Upper Scalloway, Shetland (Campbell 1998, 169–70, fig 109, 15) have plain discs. It is conceivable that jewels of some sort might have been stuck to one or both sides of the heads of these pins, for the plain discs are otherwise at variance with the decoration on the shank or, in the case of the East Broch of Burray pin, on the side of the head. Moulds for disc-headed pins have been found at Dunadd, Argyll (eg Craw 1930, 122, fig 7, 2) and at Mote of Mark,

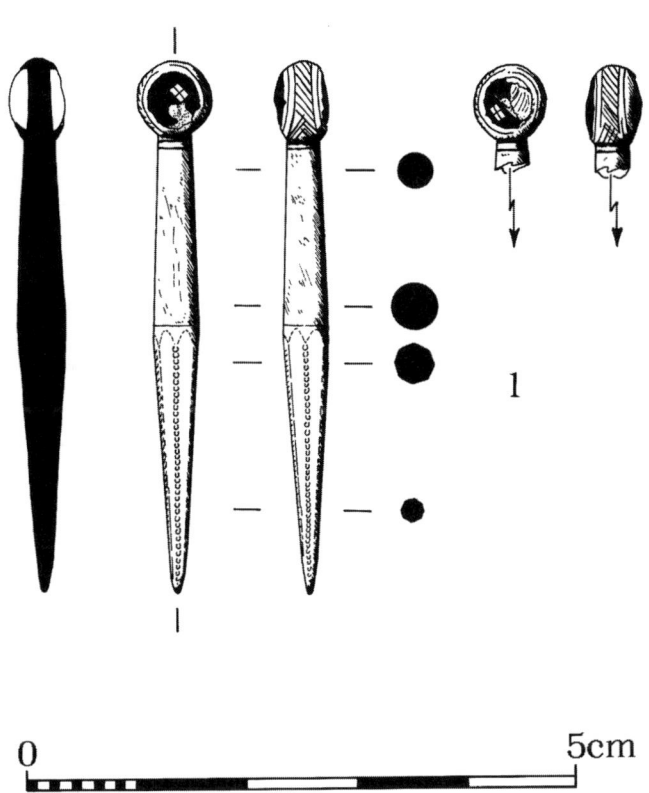

90   Silver pin no 1.

143

Kirkcudbrightshire (Laing 1973, 68), and Laing suggested that the pin produced in the latter mould may have had an inlay on the head. Oblique incised hatching similar to the Kilellan pin occurs on the top of the fan-shaped head of the copper-alloy pin from Machrihanish, Kintyre (Batey 1990). Faceted shanks like the Kilellan pin are rare, but the Upper Scalloway pin has a lower shank of hexagonal section. Campbell has argued for a 7th- or 8th-century date for the unprovenanced Orkney pin and the Upper Scalloway pin (Campbell 1998, 170).

An example of a variant of this type of pin, the disc-headed pin with small lappets at the base of the head, was discovered as a stray find near Ardnave Point, north of Kilellan (Ritchie & Welfare 1983, 341–3, fig 18 no 65). This class of pin has a distribution in western and northern Scotland similar to that of plain disc-headed pins, and is thought to date from the 9th and 10th centuries (Laing 1973, 70).

There are no close parallels to the Kilellan pin from Scotland, but a copper-alloy disc-headed pin with an amber stud inlaid on one side is recorded from Lagore, Co Meath, Ireland (Hencken 1951, 75, fig 16, no 226).

In general, the Kilellan pin conforms best in its raw materials and jewelled disc-headed form to a well-known group of Anglo-Saxon pins, and Dr Seamus Ross has confirmed that this group includes pins with either garnet or glass studs, with either hipped or tapering shanks normally decorated with horizontal linear ornament, and dating to the early 7th century (pers comm; Ross 1991). There are a number of Anglo-Saxon jewellery imports into Early Historic Scotland, including the Dumfries mounts, the Burghead blast-horn mount, and the Talnotrie silver disc-headed pins, all belonging to the 8th and 9th centuries (Webster & Backhouse 1991, nos 135, 247, 248), and the gold and garnet sword-harness mount from Dalmeny, West Lothian, belonging to the 7th century (Alcock 1993, fig 15, right). The Kilellan pin could fit quite easily into this pattern of imports from Anglo-Saxon England, but there are aspects that suggest local manufacture.

The proportions of all these metal pins, Celtic and Anglo-Saxon, are very different from those of the Kilellan pin, which, in comparison, looks short, thick and stubby. The extra silver required may in itself have been a prestigious feature. The length of the pin is comparable to that of the small bone pins common in northern and western Scotland in the late Iron Age, as is its swollen shank (Foster 1990, 150–1). Dr Euan Campbell suggests that the garnets may have been re-used from an item of Anglo-Saxon jewellery (pers comm), citing such re-use at Dunadd (Lane & Campbell 2000, 150–1).

The raw materials were available locally. There are the remains of extensive lead-workings on Islay (RCAHMS 1984, no 436), including shallow opencast workings, the history of which may well go back considerably beyond the documented later Middle Ages. At Mulreesh near Finlaggan, 'The old adventurers worked by trenching, which is apparent everywhere: the trenches are not above six feet deep' (Pennant 1772, 249). Veins of silver and copper were found in the lead ore, and use of this source could account for the debased silver of the Kilellan pin. Garnetiferous rocks occur in Argyll, but it is not possible to attribute with any certainty the Kilellan stones to that source.

IRON

2. Iron knife-blade and part of tang, 91mm long with blade 56mm long and max 22mm wide; single-sided concave blade with convex back. K3 2 SF8. (illus 91)

This is a common type of knife found on Early Historic sites, eg Buiston crannog in Ayrshire (Crone 2000, fig 119, no 230), Machrins in Colonsay (Ritchie, J N G 1981, fig 3, nos 1–3).

3. Iron sickle blade, incomplete, 127mm long, blade 19mm wide. K3 5 SF47. (illus 91)

A similarly small sickle blade was found at Dun Cuier, Barra (Young 1956, 316, pl XXI, 2).

4. Iron tanged disc, 19mm diam, 1–3mm thick, 33mm long with incomplete tang. A4 1 SF803. This was a topsoil find and may be relatively modern. (illus 91)

COPPER ALLOY

5. Loop-headed dress-pin, cast in copper alloy, 82mm long; shank bent and circular in section, 3mm max diam; head hammered flat, decorated with three incised grooves, and folded over to form circle 3–4mm diam. 1961 I 4, a stray loss in the sand-dunes. (illus 91)

This pin was probably designed to have a loose ring through the head. A very similar pin, still with its spiral ring, was found at Dunadd in Lorn, Argyll, and a 6th- to 8th-century date was suggested (Lane 2000, 155–8, no 44). The looped head of the Dunadd

METAL, BONE, GLASS, CLAY AND FINE STONE ARTEFACTS

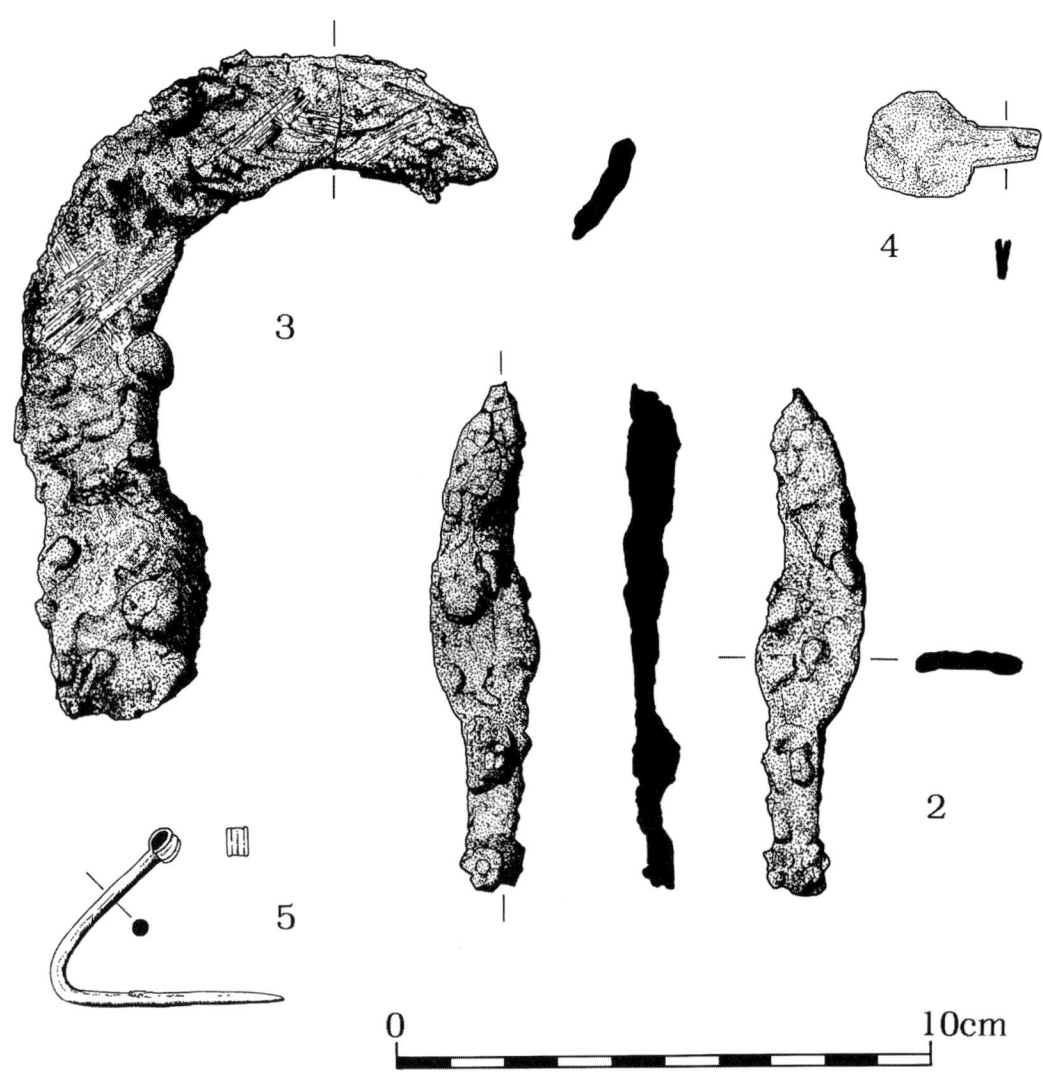

91 Iron, copper alloy artefacts nos 2–5.

example is decorated with two grooves. If the Kilellan pin had a spiral ring, it would be the second example in Scotland of an essentially Irish type of dress-pin. The pin from a burial at Machrins, Colonsay, has a solid ring and no decoration on the rolled-over head (Ritchie, J N G 1981, fig 5, no 32).

BONE

6. Dress-pin, two conjoining fragments of shank and head and two conjoining fragments of lower shank, overall incomplete length 63mm; shank circular in section, max 5mm diam; flattened ball-head, 9.5mm diam, roughly faceted and burnt on one side. K3 5 SF99. (illus 92)

7. Tip of shank of dress-pin, 24mm long, circular in section, 4mm max diam; probably belongs to no 6. K3 201 SF26. (illus 92)

These fragments of pin (nos 6 & 7) are black in colour and resemble jet, but analysis has shown that they are made of bone and have been deliberately blackened by fire, presumably to emulate jet (Appendix 2). Fraser Hunter suggests that the pin may be a skeuomorph of a Roman jet pin.

145

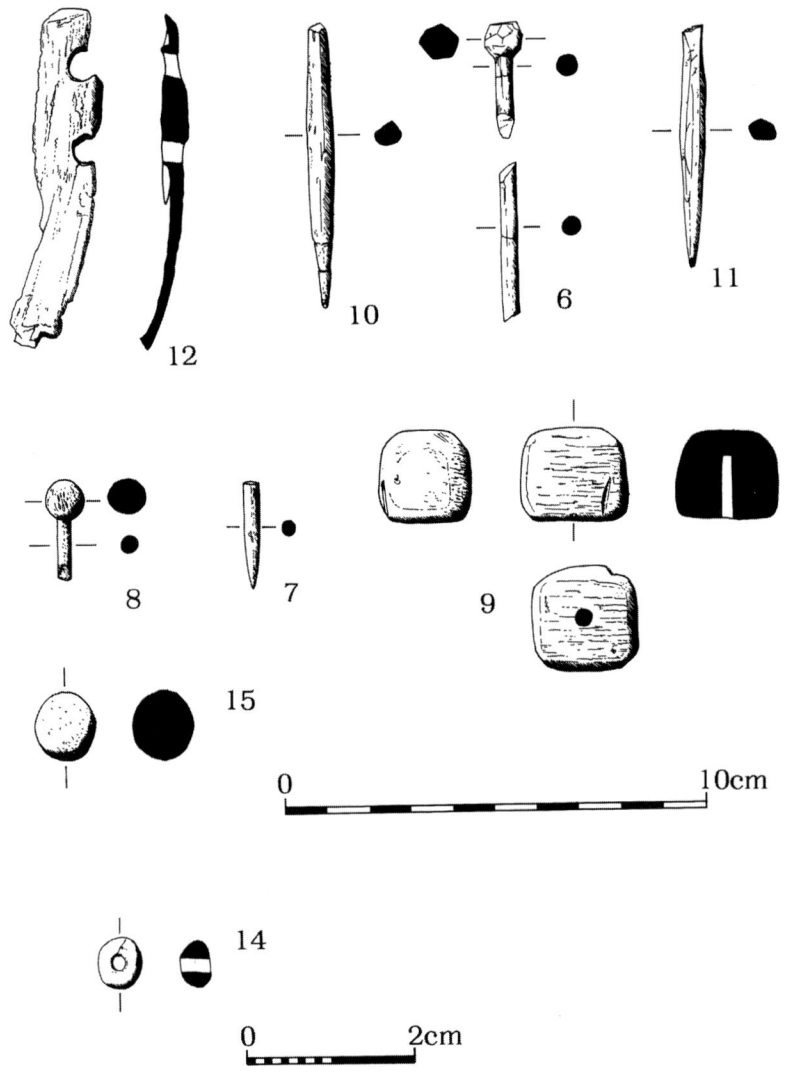

92 Bone, glass and clay artefacts, nos 2–12 and 14–15.

in fact pegged playing pieces (1986, 166). A circular pegged gaming piece of bone was found on the Brough of Birsay (Curle 1982, ill 38, no 271), and the same site produced part of the type of gaming board with holes for which such pegged pieces were designed (eg Curle 1982, illus 50, no 274). An alternative function might be as a handle for a small awl.

10. Bone peg with wear rings, roughly finished, 65mm long, 6.5mm max diam. J1 26 SF89, lower midden. (illus 92)

A possible function for this peg is in stretching skins on a wooden frame during the curing process.

11. Bone peg, roughly finished, 56mm long, 7mm max diam. J1 unstrat SF86. (illus 92)

12. Bone mount, incomplete, slightly curved, 78mm long, 8mm wide, 6mm max thickness, with two perforations 3–4mm diam. J1 7 SF17, upper midden. (illus 92)

Perforated bone mounts have been found on sites of the mid to later first millennium AD in northern Scotland, for example, Broch of Burrian, North Ronaldsay (MacGregor 1974, fig 9, nos 130–1), Buckquoy, mainland Orkney (Ritchie, A 1977, fig 5, nos 45–6). A variety of functions is possible for these mounts, but none has been found with more than its bone pegs in place.

8. Head and upper part of shank of dress-pin, 22mm long; shank circular in section, 3mm in diam; ball-head 8mm in diam. K3 201 SF27. (illus 92)

9. Square solid cetacean bone playing piece, max 25mm × 24mm × 20mm, circular socket for missing peg, 4mm diam, 14mm deep. K3 201 SF25. (illus 92)

The provenance of this artefact in the Early Historic horizon suggests that it should be interpreted as a playing piece rather than as a pin-head of the type identified by Stevenson as a 'native' type of pin with an iron shank (1955, 292–3). Joanna Close-Brooks has argued that most of the so-called pin-heads were

13. Bone point, roughly finished, polished by wear, partially burnt, broken at both ends, 43mm long, 12mm max diam. K3 5 SF87.

14. Bone point made from flat sliver, 63mm long, 18mm max width. J1 26, lower midden.

GLASS

14. Globular bead of dark blue translucent glass, 5.5mm max diam, 3.5mm max width, perforation 1.5mm diam. G2 5a SF8. (illus 92)

METAL, BONE, GLASS, CLAY AND FINE STONE ARTEFACTS

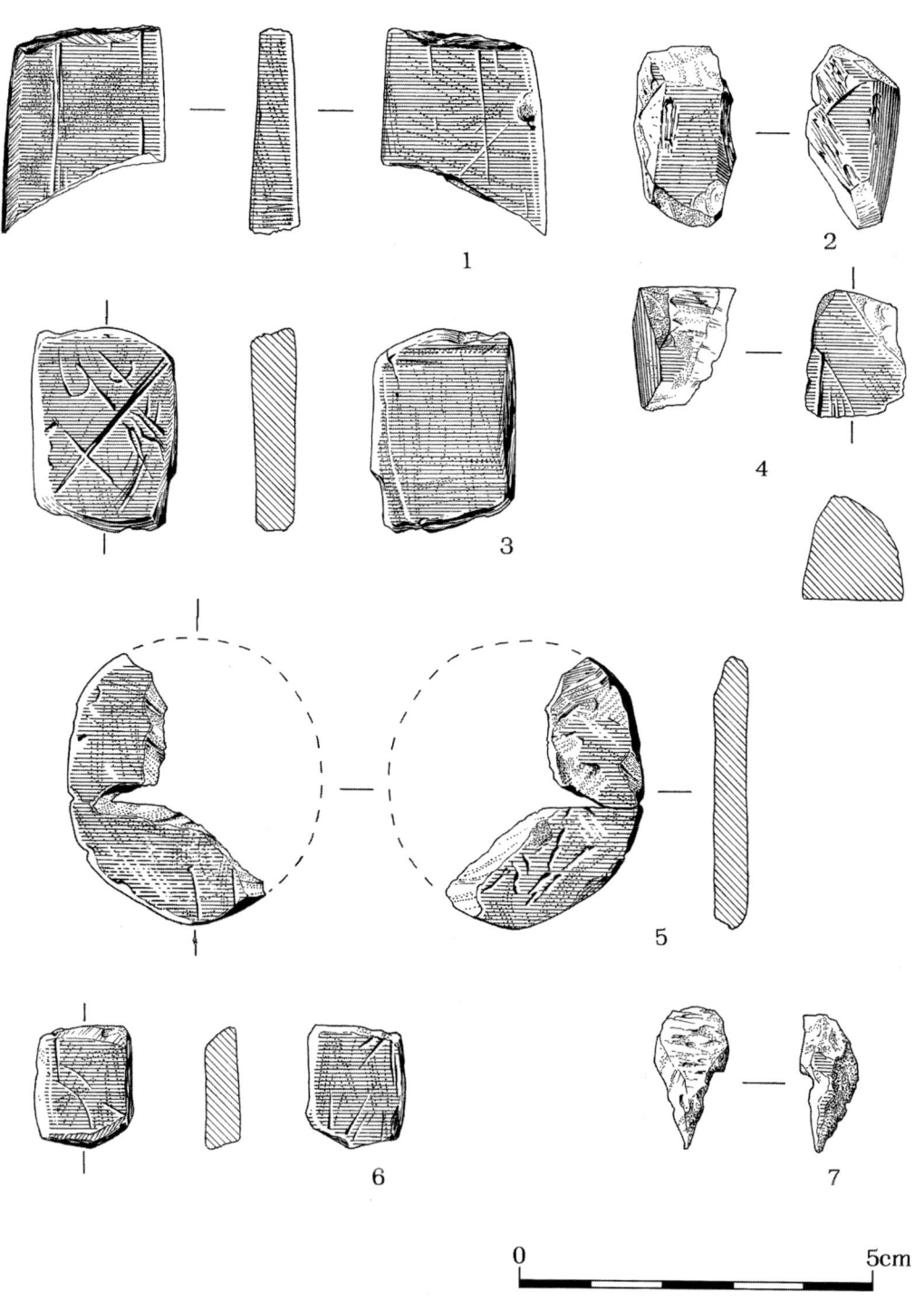

93 Serpentine artefacts (no 18), 1–7.

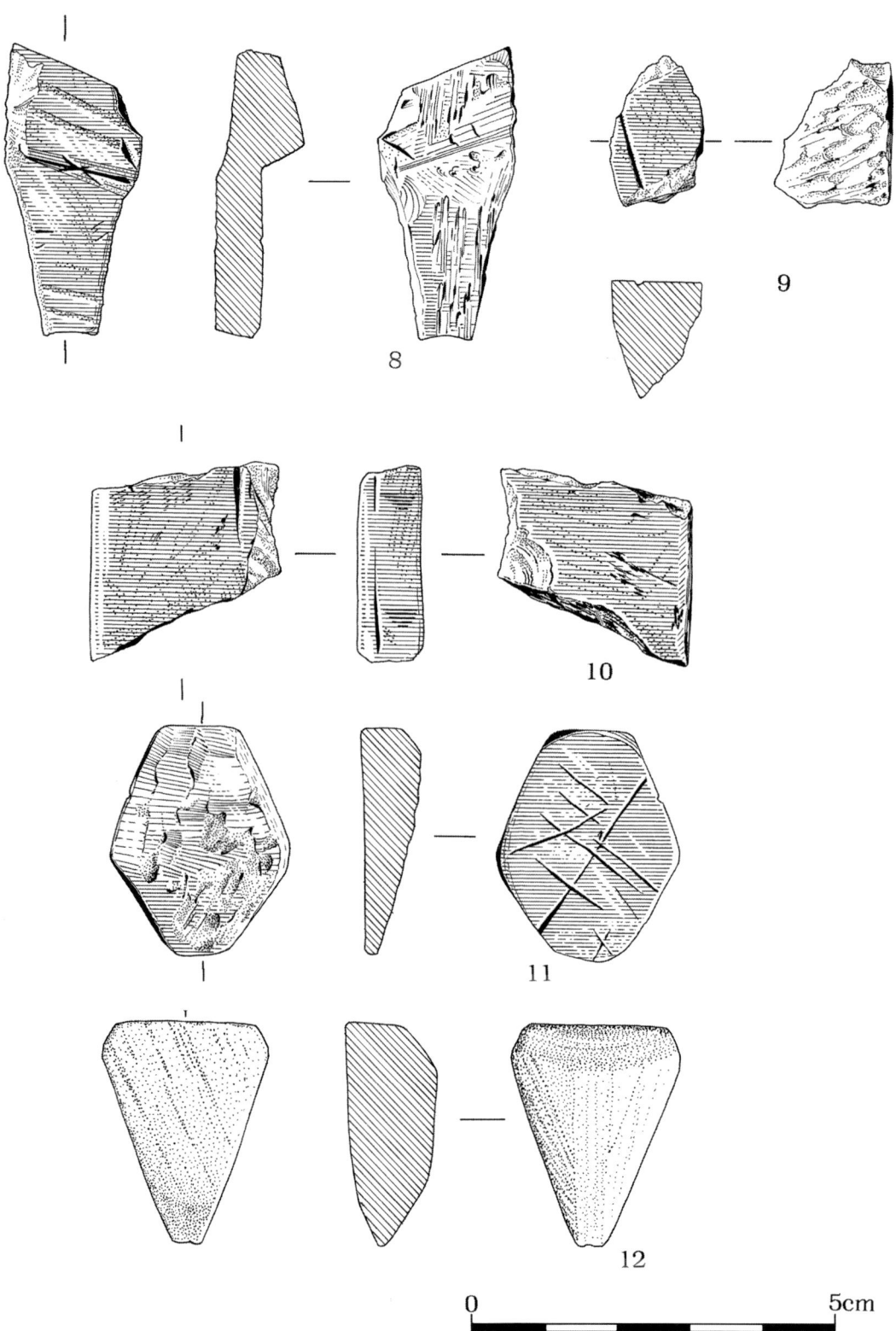

94 Serpentine artefacts (no 18), 8–11, and bevelled polisher (no 19), 12.

Simple small blue beads such as this are not closely datable but are likely on Irish evidence to belong to the period 7th–10th centuries AD (Guido 1978, 67–8). Both globular and annular examples were found at Dunadd (Guido 2000).

CLAY

15. Ball of fired clay, damaged, 12mm diam, 1.8g. G2 677e. (illus 92)

STONE

16. Pale grey quartzite ball, natural, 16mm diam, 4.4g. L2 10 SF23.

17. Chip of copper-rich ferruginous quartz or chalcedony, 30mm × 23mm × 14mm, 9.5g; from slab near Hearth A, Whittaker 1954. HR 1188.

18. Eleven fragments of green serpentine and one of green ozocerite (no 18.7), some blackened by heat, partially hand-cut and polished, some fragments grooved, largest 33mm × 23mm × 8mm, smallest 19mm × 9mm × 8mm; from slab near Hearth A, Whittaker 1954. Most appear to be fragments of larger objects, including two that join to form part of a disc *c* 38mm in diameter (no 18.5). One (no 18.11) may be a finished object, but its purpose is unclear. James Whittaker regarded them all as amulets, but R B K Stevenson suggested that some might be industrial polishers. Nearby were two stone grinders re-used as anvils (Chapter 5, nos 69 & 70). HR 1187. (illus 93–94, 1–11)

Both serpentine and ozocerite are easily cut by flint or metal tools. Serpentine is available in Iona (Iona marble), Skye and the Western Isles. Ozocerite occurs in beds of coal or with bituminous deposits and could be local to Islay.

19. Triangular bevelled polisher of metamorphic mica schist, 30mm × 23mm × 12mm, 9.6g; from Hearth A, Whittaker 1954. HR 1174. (illus 94, 12)

Chapter 7

Animal husbandry and the environmental context

DALE SERJEANTSON, V SMITHSON and T WALDRON

The animal bones from Kilellan are from the two main periods of occupation: the Early Bronze Age (535 bones) and the Middle Iron Age (2070). There are also 14 bones from the Mesolithic contexts (table 37). An additional 26 identified bones from the Iron Age are from layers which could not be distinguished between the upper and lower midden, and 48 are from the topsoil and contexts which could not be phased. Some bones from the excavations of 1960 and 1961 were examined by George Hodgson (Burgess 1976, 195); the listed identifications, now in the site archive, suggest that finds were similar to those described below. In this report the environment of the site is first considered. This is followed by a description of the bones from the two periods of occupation from which animal bones survived: the Early Bronze Age and the Middle Iron Age assemblages. Three aspects of the findings are selected for discussion: the high proportion of calf bones, the conflicting evidence for pig, and the red deer. The analysis of the bones and the environmental study was carried out between 1983 and 1987. The report was written in 1993 and does not take account of some important studies that have subsequently been published.

ENVIRONS OF THE SITE

Interpretation of the role of the animals kept, captured, used and eaten at the settlement can only be discussed in the light of the immediate environment of the site and its capability for agriculture and exploitation of wild animals. The interim account of the Bronze Age phase at Kilellan concluded that 'these people were essentially pastoralists herding cattle and to a lesser extent sheep' (Burgess 1976, 206), but the 1976 season produced carbonized barley (Chapter 2, Phase 2.4) and work at the Udal (Crawford & Switsur 1977), Rosinish (Shepherd & Tuckwell 1977) and Ardnave 2 (Ritchie & Welfare 1983) has shown that cereal cultivation was part of the life of contemporary settlements in similar locations.

For this reason a field study of the environs of the site was undertaken and the past vegetation and topography have been considered. In 1983 the present day soils were mapped using the technique

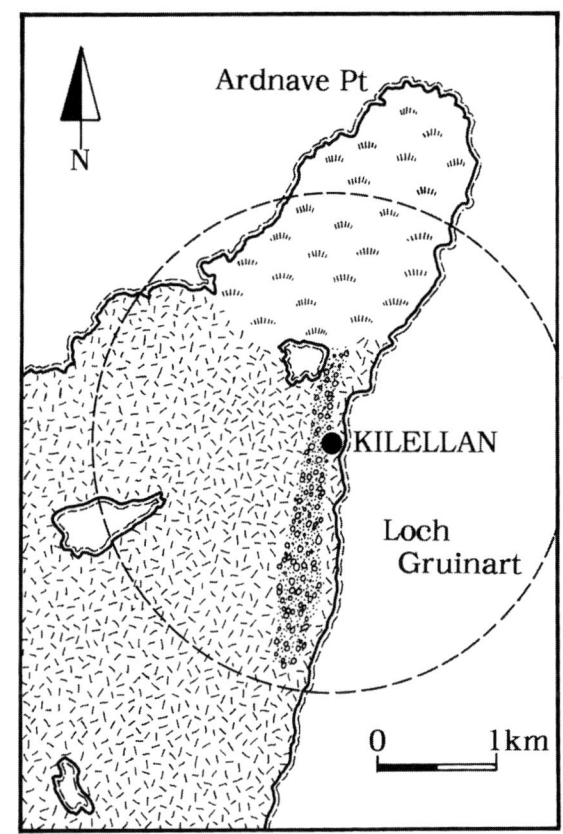

95 Environs of the site at Kilellan.

TABLE 37
Kilellan: animal bones from the Mesolithic, Early Bronze Age and Middle Iron Age deposits.

	Identified	Identified to element	Unidentified	Total
Mesolithic	0	0	14	14
Early Bronze Age	111	148	276	535
Middle Iron Age: lower midden	443	717	351	1511
Middle Iron Age: upper midden	187	253	119	559

of site catchment analysis (Higgs & Vita-Finzi 1975) and by reference to modern soil surveys made available by the Macauley Institute, Oban. The bed rock is Torridonian grits and slates interrupted by basalt dykes. In the interior of the peninsula the bedrock is overlain by boulder clay, which is now a peaty podsol or is covered with blanket peat. In a band along the shore the bedrock is covered by raised beach and, towards the end of the peninsula, by a light calcareous shell sand, the machair (illus 95). Within 2km of the settlement the proportions are approximately 60% bedrock, peat and peaty podsols, 30% raised beach, and 10% machair. Of these, the most productive for cereal cultivation in the past was the raised beach, which was fertile and well drained, and the machair. The raised beach was still in cultivation in 1983 but today is used only for grazing. The machair is a light calcareous blown shell-sand. Two samples taken at the site in 1983 had a pH of 7.6 and a second an anomalously high 9.4. When dressed with seaweed, the machair could be cultivated repeatedly to produce barley and primitive wheats, but not bread wheat. It was cultivated until the present century, and traces of the 'rigs' survive on the Ardnave peninsula, but today it is used only as pasture. There is evidence from elsewhere on the island at An Sithean (Barber & Brown 1985) that the boulder clays were cultivated before they became podsolized, and before the blanket peat developed. The Ardnave peninsula has few trees today, and the

TABLE 38
Stages of eruption and wear of cattle and sheep teeth, as discussed in the text.

Stage	Definition	Approximate Age
Cattle		
1	deciduous teeth unworn or enamel wear only	0–4 weeks
2	deciduous teeth in wear; M1 not in wear	1–5 months
3	M1 and M2 in wear	5 months–*c* 2 years
4	M3 in early wear	2–3 years
5	M3 in full wear	over 3 years
Sheep		
1	deciduous teeth unworn	newborn to 3 weeks
2	slight wear on deciduous teeth; M1 unworn	3 weeks to 3 months
3	DPMs in full wear; M1 and M2 in wear	3 months to 18 months
4	M3 in early wear; PMs erupting	18–30 months
5	M3 in full wear; PMs in wear	over 30 months

TABLE 39
Early Bronze Age (EBA): species present and number of identified fragments (NISP).

Species	NISP	% ID
Cattle *Bos taurus*	49	44.1
Sheep *Ovis aries*	45	40.5
Red deer *Cervus elaphus*	13	11.7
Pig *Sus scrofa*	1	0.9
Hare *Lepus sp.*	1	0.9
Shag *Phalacrocorax aristotelis*	1	0.9
Razorbill *Alca torda*	1	0.9
Rabbit *Oryctolagus cuniculus*	(14)	–
		% Total
Subtotal identified	111	20.7
Unidentified fish	2	0.4
Unidentified bird	2	0.4
Cattle-size fragments	73	13.6
Sheep-size fragments	71	13.3
Unidentified mammal	276	51.6
Total	535	100

unrestricted grazing combined with impoverished soils impede re-establishment of trees, but the soils could have supported scrub woodland in the past (Chapter 8).

These two processes, podsolization and peat formation, have been shown to start in the later Bronze Age at many sites in western Scotland, though some episodes of peat formation have been dated earlier. The location of the site on a patch of the best agricultural soils of the island strongly suggests that cereal cultivation was important both in the Early Bronze Age and the later period. If the date of peat formation at An Sithean can be extrapolated to the Ardnave peninsula, it is likely that by the Middle Iron Age cultivation would have been restricted to the raised beach and machair.

As the site is on a sea loch, sea fishing was one of the options of the inhabitants, both of the estuarine species and those of deeper waters. The loch also provides an excellent seasonal habitat for geese and ducks. The nearest seabird nesting colonies are about 5km distant at Sanaigmore. The range of mammals on Islay today is restricted compared to the mainland (Arnold 1978), though the number is greater than on other less favoured Hebridean islands, and the only wild mammal found is the red deer.

THE ANIMAL BONES

The sediments were mainly sandy, and organic only where middens had formed. In such sediments hand recovery of bone is good, as bones are easily visible. Many of the deposits were sieved, and the results combine those recovered by hand and those recovered in the sieves. Small bones such as phalanges and carpals, which are readily overlooked on excavations on more stony sediments, are relatively numerous, partly because they are easily recognized in the sandy soil, and partly because deposits were sieved. The rodent and amphibian bones are from samples.

The bones were identified at the London University Centre for Extra-Mural Studies, Birkbeck College, by students of the class in Animal Bones in Archaeology in 1982 and 1983, under the supervision of the first author, using the reference collection there. The identification of bird bones was confirmed at the British Museum, Natural History, where necessary. Records for each bone were entered on cards in coded form, and subsequently transferred to Dbase files for analysis. After responsibility for publication was taken on by Anna Ritchie and final information on phasing was received, the data were analysed by the authors in 1992. The bones are stored in the National

Museums of Scotland. A hard copy of the database records and a key to the codes used is with the site archives and the first author.

In identification and recording certain problems were encountered which were tackled as follows. All caprovine bones were coded as sheep or goat, and, in order to establish whether goats as well as sheep were present, horn cores and metapodials were examined carefully. None is from goat, so in the absence of any positive evidence for goat, in this report all are referred to as sheep. The cattle and red deer bones are similar in size, so these were carefully distinguished, and where there was any doubt, fragments were recorded as cattle-size. Vertebral fragments, undiagnostic limb-bone splinters and ribs were identified only to cattle-size or sheep-size. The former will include red deer and, in the Iron Age, horse, and the latter, sheep and pig. All fragments were counted, which has enhanced the number of unidentified bones. Loose deciduous premolars and the third molar have been included in the totals. Loose M1s and M2s could not always be distinguished, and have only been included if they belong to a stage for which there is otherwise no evidence. Jaws and teeth have been assigned to five stages of eruption and wear for cattle and sheep (table 38), and the stages correlated with approximate age, using the work of the 19th-century veterinarian Simonds (1854). His work, as Legge (1992) has shown, provides the most reliable guide to early dental eruption at present available, and supersedes the listings compiled by Silver (1969), which have now been demonstrated to be based on early sources which were largely erroneous. The first stage defined for cattle, in which the deciduous premolars have erupted through the bone and are unworn or have some enamel wear

TABLE 40
EBA: sheep, cattle and red deer: number of identified fragments (NISP) and minimum number of bone elements (MNE).

	Sheep		Cattle		Red deer	
	NISP	MNE	NISP	MNE	NISP	MNE
Mandible	15	8	15	8	3	2
Maxilla	11	5	11	–	3	2
ID skull	1	1	5	–	–	–
Horn core	2	1	–	–	–	–
Hyoid	1	1	–	–	–	–
Atlas	1	1	1	1	–	–
Th vert	1	1	2	2	–	–
Scapula	–	–	–	–	1	1
Humerus	–	–	1	1	–	–
Radius	2	–	–	–	–	–
Ulna	1	1	1	1	–	–
Carpals	1	1	1	1	–	–
Metacarpal	2	1	2	1	2	1
Pelvis	1	1	1	1	–	–
Femur	2	1	2	1	–	–
Tibia	1	1	1	1	1	1
Astragalus	–	–	1	1	1	1
Calcaneum	1	1	–	–	1	1
Metatarsal	2	1	2	1	1	1
Phalanx 1	–	–	1	1	–	–
Phalanx 2	–	–	2	2	–	–
Total	45		49		13	

TABLE 41
EBA: eruption and wear of cattle and sheep teeth, after Grant (1982).

Stage	DPM4	M1/M2
Cattle		
1	a	–
1	b	–
1	b	–
1	c	–
1	c	–
2	f	b
2	–	c
3	–	–
4/5	–	k
Sheep		
1	a	–
1	b	–
2	–	a
3	g	b
3	–	c
3	–	e
4/5	–	g
4/5	–	g
4/5	–	g
4/5	–	g

only, is found in calves from birth to three weeks of age: this was established from a sample of modern jaws collected by J Baker and the author, now in the Laboratory for Zooarchaeological Research, University of Southampton. Where data are very sparse, stages have been amalgamated.

MESOLITHIC

The 14 bones from the Mesolithic layers are eroded scraps of mammal bone that could not be identified more closely.

EARLY BRONZE AGE

The Bronze Age bones are from midden sediments. They are few (table 39), very fragmented, and most are severely eroded. The erosion and much of the fragmentation is no doubt the result of chemical degradation from water percolation in the sandy sediments. The damage was not the result of dog gnawing, as evidence for this was not seen on any bones from this period. A consequence of the post-depositional damage is that there is a high proportion of loose teeth among the identified bones: >40% for cattle (table 40) and >50% for sheep. There is also a low proportion (21%) of identified bones. A small number (3% of all bone fragments) are charred or calcined from contact with fire.

The bones of all the main species, including the red deer, were disarticulated and from all parts of the carcass. Both the number of identified specimens (NISP) is shown and a calculation of the minimum number of elements (MNE). The part present, whether proximal or distal end, and whether that part was complete, over half present, or an identifiable fragment was recorded and the MNE calculated from whichever part of the bone was most common. Despite the poor surface preservation, five were seen to have traces of chops or smashes and three have cut marks.

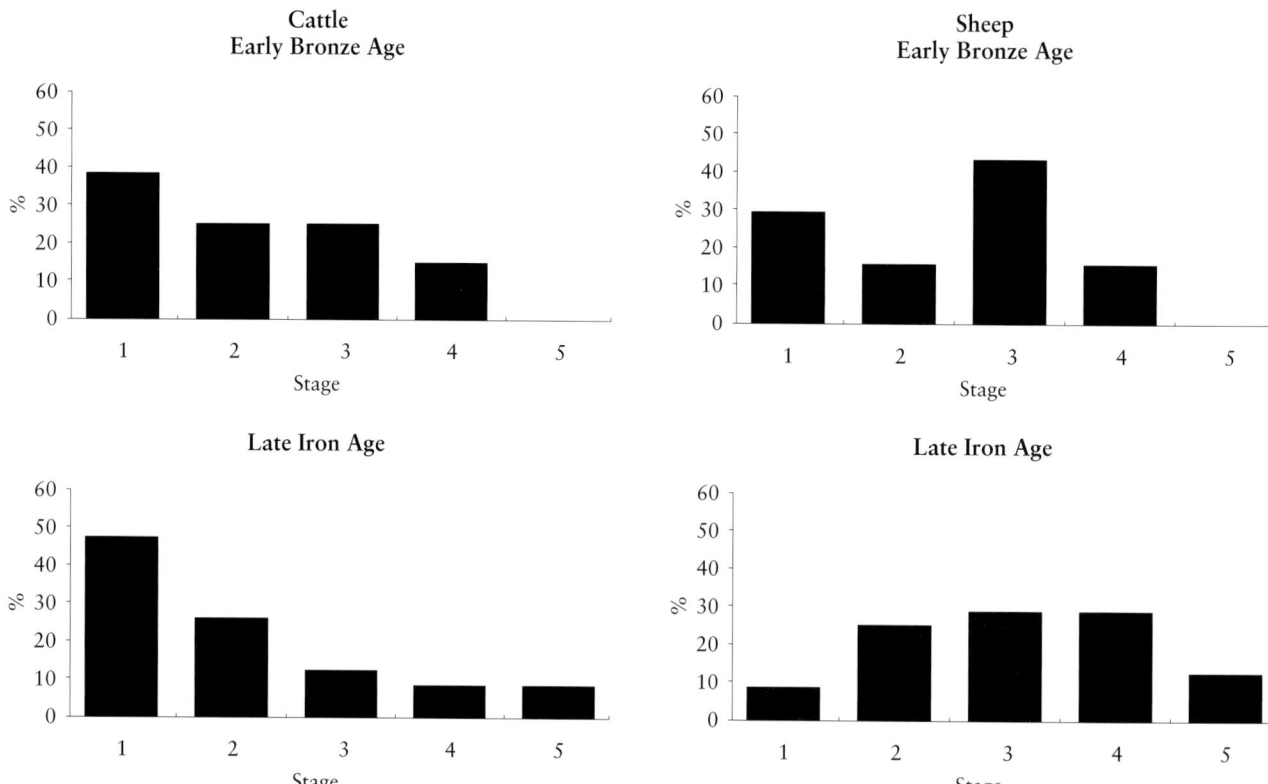

96 Age at death of cattle and sheep in the Early Bronze Age (top) and Iron Age (below). Age stages defined in Table 38.

Domestic mammals

Cattle and sheep bones are present in almost equal numbers, whether calculated from NISP (44% and 41%) or from MNI, which for both species is based on the MNE of the jaws and teeth, six from each species. The only bone tentatively identified as from pig is a juvenile humerus shaft. Hodgson too, found only two possible pig bones among those he examined. There are none from dogs, and no bones were certainly gnawed in this period, and it is possible that dogs were not kept. One of the main uses of the domestic dogs of the early farmers was to protect flocks from wolves, and Islay, like the other offshore islands of Britain, has had no attested wolf population since the sea level rise which separated it from Ireland.

The peak ages of slaughter of the cattle and sheep at Kilellan are best assessed from the jaws and loose teeth (table 41). Though both young and old cattle are present, five of the eight countable jaws are from very young calves, three from calves in the first weeks of life (illus 96). The maxillary teeth confirm the ages indicated by the lower teeth, with five of seven teeth being at Grant stage b. Though absolute numbers at Kilellan are small, a high proportion of very young calves is also found in the Middle Iron Age levels at Kilellan and at other Hebridean sites. Interpretations of this mortality pattern are discussed below. The age classes are different for sheep: of the eight jaws that could be aged, three are from young lambs. The post-cranial bones are so fragmentary that they provide little additional evidence for the age at death. Three cattle limb bones are juvenile or unfused, and one, a second phalanx, is fused. Among the sheep bones are at least three from newborn or young lambs, but otherwise no bones preserve fusion evidence.

Wild animals

There are 13 bones and teeth of red deer *Cervus elaphus*, one of hare, four of birds, two of fish and 14 of rabbit *Oryctolagus cuniculus*. The rabbit bones (from G1, layer 6) are a part skeleton: two scapulas, six limb bones and seven vertebrae from the same animal. Rabbits were introduced to the Hebrides in late medieval times, and they burrow extensively

ANIMAL HUSBANDRY AND THE ENVIRONMENTAL CONTEXT

TABLE 42
Measurements of red deer, after Driesch (1976). UM = upper midden, LM = lower midden.

	Specimen No			\multicolumn{4}{c}{Early Bronze Age}			
				GL	Bd	Dd	BFd			
	705	Calcaneum	R	1004	–	–	–			
	706	Tibia	R	–	426	337	–			
	707	Astragalus	R	449	–	–	300			

				\multicolumn{7}{c}{Middle Iron Age}
				GLP	BG	LG	SLC			
UM	154	Scapula	R	485	332	–	325			
LM	919	Scapula	L	429	291	343	–			
LM	559	Scapula	L	–	351	–	322			
				GL	Dp	Bp	BFp	SD	Bd	Dd	BFd
LM	842	Humerus	R	–	–	–	–	–	513	–	498
LM	921	Radius	L	–	–	485	450	–	–	–	–
UM	689	Ulna	L	–	–	455	500	–	–	–	–
LM	328	Femur	R	–	–	–	–	–	716	–	–
LM	163	Tibia	L	–	–	–	–	–	430	355	–
LM	562	Metacarpal	R	–	256	360	–	–	–	–	–
LM	560	Metatarsal	R	–	–	–	–	–	386	–	–
LM	187	Metatarsal	R	–	–	–	–	–	318	–	–
LM	604	Astragalus	R	489	–	–	–	–	–	–	317
LM	267	Calcaneum	R	968	–	253	–	–	–	–	–
LM	924	1st Phalanx	L	–	132	113	–	85	–	–	92

on the site today, and thus the rabbit bones are best explained as intrusive. When evidence for wild animals on an island is found it is always of interest to consider the means by which the species concerned reached the island. In the case of Islay, during the last glaciation there was a land bridge between Islay and Ireland, and submarine contours suggest that this persisted longer than the land bridge between Ireland

TABLE 43
Hebridean assemblages of the 2nd millennium BC: cattle, sheep, pig and red deer.

	Cattle		Sheep		Pig		Red Deer		Total
	NISP	%	NISP	%	NISP	%	NISP	%	
Northton (Neo)	170	28.0	414	68.1	1	0.2	23	3.8	608
Rosinish	188	37.3	266	52.8	0	0.0	50	9.9	504
Kilellan	49	45.4	45	41.7	1	0.9	13	12.0	108
Northton (BA)	268	36.8	248	34.1	3	0.4	209	28.7	728
Ardnave 2	60	24.6	128	52.5	42	17.2	14	5.7	244

TABLE 44
Middle Iron Age (MIA): lower and upper middens: species present and number of identified fragments.

Species	Lower Midden		Upper Midden	
	NISP	% ID	NISP	% ID
Cattle *Bos taurus*	153	34.5	90	48.1
Sheep *Ovis aries*	161	36.3	62	33.2
Red deer *Cervus elaphus*	86	19.4	14	7.5
Pig *Sus scrofa*	33	7.4	16	8.6
Horse *Equus* sp.	3	0.7	4	2.1
Canid n.f.i.	2	0.5	–	–
Mallard *Anas platyrhynchos*	1	0.2	–	–
Gannet *Sula bassana*	1	0.2	–	–
Petrel *Pterodroma* cf *feae*	1	0.2	–	–
Corvid *Corvidae*	1	0.2	–	–
Wader ?redshank *Tringa* sp.	1	0.2	–	–
Peregrine *Falco peregrinus*	–	–	1	0.5
		% Total		% Total
Subtotal identified	443	29.3	187	33.5
Unidentified rodent	6	0.4	–	–
Unidentified amphibian	13	0.9	–	–
Unidentified fish	5	0.3	–	–
Unidentified bird	3	0.2	–	–
Cattle-size fragments	402	26.6	166	29.7
Sheep-size fragments	288	19.1	87	15.6
Unidentified mammal	351	23.2	119	21.3
Total	1511		559	

and Mainland Britain. At the end of the last glaciation, therefore, Ireland and Islay shared a land mammal fauna, and the red deer and hare may be part of that shared fauna. The hare is represented only by an atlas vertebra, which could not be distinguished between the common hare *Lepus capensis* and the mountain hare *Lepus timidus*, both of which are found on Islay today (Arnold 1978). The measurements (following von den Driesch 1976) are:

BFcr   10.7mm   BFcd   13.9mm

The mountain hare is thought to be a component of the original mammal fauna, and the common hare introduced by humans some time in the past, but this find cannot establish which species was present by the Early Bronze Age.

The red deer from both the Bronze Age and the Middle Iron Age are small (measurements in table 42) compared with prehistoric red deer from the mainland. The possibility that some of the bones are from fallow deer can be ruled out, because of the early date of the deposits, though some fragments are similar in size to modern fallow deer. If red deer did not reach Islay via Ireland early in the post-glacial, they could have reached the island via Jura, since distances between Jura and Islay, and the mainland and Jura, are within their swimming capabilities. A third possible origin of the population is that deer were carried to the islands by human settlers, as has been proposed for Colonsay (Grigson & Mellars 1987) and Uist (Serjeantson 1990). The small size of the Islay red deer in the Bronze Age suggests that they are an island population which has already undergone some dwarfing in size, so are unlikely to be a recent introduction at that time.

The four bird bones include the radius of a razorbill *Alca torda* and the carpometacarpus of a shag *Phalacrocorax aristotelis*, both species which breed near Kilellan today. Only two fish bones were recovered, both of which were broken and were not identified. As the settlement was on the coast, the lack of evidence for seabirds, and especially fish, is surprising. Several samples were taken from the Bronze Age levels, so if fish remains had survived it is likely that they would have been recovered. The evidence suggests that exploitation of the wild resources other than red deer was scant, but in view of the poor preservation of the Bronze Age assemblage this cannot be demonstrated with certainty.

COMPARISON WITH OTHER SECOND MILLENNIUM SITES

Comparisons can be made with Ardnave 2, the Bronze Age settlement close to Kilellan (Harman 1983), the Beaker midden at Rosinish, Benbecula (Serjeantson nd a), and Northton, Harris (Finlay 1983), where there are both Late Neolithic and Bronze Age levels (table 43). All are coastal sites, on machair soils with a local potential for cereal cultivation to complement stock raising. There is evidence for cultivation at Ardnave and Rosinish. Like Kilellan, Northton and Rosinish have a high proportion of red deer. At Rosinish pig bones are absent or rare, and a high proportion of the cattle teeth are from young calves. At Rosinish as at Kilellan, there is little evidence for dog gnawing.

The pattern of animal husbandry in the second millennium BC in the Western Isles includes sheep in relatively higher numbers than on contemporary mainland sites together with cattle, but few pigs. By this period the sheep's woolly coat had developed; there is unlikely to have been a delay in introducing breeding stock with such an improvement into the island herds. Wool was plucked rather than shorn, just as it was until the 19th century in the Hebrides (MacDonald 1811), and as it still is today on the Soay breed. The main wild resource is red deer, but neither fish nor seabirds were part of the normal diet. In the absence of any satisfactory means of comparing the relative importance of cereals and plant foods in the diet with that of animal foods, we can only infer that cereals must have been important from the location of the sites on or close to the best agricultural soils.

MIDDLE IRON AGE

The bones from the Middle Iron Age are from two main phases, mainly from midden accumulations. Of the *c* 2000 bones, 1511 are from the lower midden and 559 from the upper midden. Those from the Middle Iron Age middens are rather better preserved than those from the Early Bronze Age deposits, especially where they have been protected by surrounding organic sediments. The surface of those from the heart of the midden is uneroded, but the bones are denatured and friable, and, despite care in retrieval, suffered excavation damage. The proportion identified to species, a function of bone condition where recovery methods are the same between phases, is rather higher than for the Early Bronze Age group: 29% in the lower midden and 34% in the upper midden, compared with only 21% in the Early Bronze Age (table 44).

Butchery traces, both chops and cut marks, are clearly evident on 51 (11.5%) of the identified bones from the lower midden and 13 (7%) from the upper midden (table 45). A higher proportion of bone from the lower midden was burnt (8.4%) than from the upper midden (3.2%). In spite of the later fragmentation it was clear that much of the bone breakage was deliberate chopping not just for carcass

TABLE 45
MIA: bones with evidence of carnivore gnawing, butchery and burning.

	Lower midden gnawed	Upper midden gnawed	Lower midden butchery	Upper midden butchery	Lower midden burnt	Upper midden burnt
N	9	1	51	13	37	6
Total	443	187	443	187	443	187
Per cent	2.0%	0.5%	11.5%	7.0%	8.4%	3.2%

TABLE 46
MIA: cattle: number of identified fragments (NISP) and minimum number of bone elements (MNE).

	Lower Midden		Upper Midden	
	NISP	MNE	NISP	MNE
Mandible	35	11	26	13
Maxilla	26	9	14	6
Horn core	4	2	–	–
Other skull	5	1	4	2
Hyoid	1	1	–	–
Atlas	–	–	1	1
Axis	1	1	1	1
Thor vert	2	2	5	–
Caud vert	1	1	–	–
Scapula	5	3	1	1
Humerus	3	3	2	1
Radius	5	3	1	1
Ulna	5	3	2	1
Carpals	3	3	5	4
Metacarpal	4	4	4	3
Pelvis	9	6	2	2
Femur	3	1	1	1
Patella	–	–	1	1
Tibia	3	3	4	3
Lat mall	–	–	2	2
Astragalus	6	4	1	1
Calcaneum	–	–	1	1
Nav.-cub.	1	1	2	2
Other tars	1	1	2	2
Metatarsal	9	7	3	2
Phalanx 1	7	7	–	–
Phalanx 2	11	10	3	3
Phalanx 3	3	3	2	2
Total	153		90	

dismemberment, but also for marrow extraction. Even allowing for the fact that other breaks may have masked evidence of carnivore gnawing, the proportion (2% and <1%) is smaller than would be expected on a contemporaneous mainland site, and could be taken to indicate that dogs were less ubiquitous than on mainland sites.

Domestic mammals

The most common domestic species in the lower midden are cattle (35% of NISP) and sheep (36%); there are also 33 pig bones (7%) and three of horse. The MNI, based on the MNE calculated as described above, is 11 cattle (table 46), 15 sheep (table 47), four pigs (table 48) and one horse. The distribution of elements reflects their relative density and suggests that whole animals are represented (illus 97). Two shaft fragments found in the lower midden, a femur and a tibia, were identified as from a small canid; these are compatible with either a small domestic dog or a fox. Bones of the latter species were identified at Ardnave.

In the upper midden, from which the sample is smaller, the proportion of identified cattle bones

TABLE 47
MIA: sheep: number of identified fragments (NISP) and minimum number of elements (MNE).

	Lower Midden		Upper Midden	
	NISP	MNE	NISP	MNE
Mandible	44	15	24	8
Maxilla	27	11	8	2
Horn core	1	1	–	–
Other skull	2	1	3	1
Axis	1	1	–	–
Scapula	6	2	2	2
Humerus	5	3	–	–
Radius	4	3	5	5
Ulna	8	4	3	2
Carpal	–	–	1	1
Metacarpal	4	2	1	1
Pelvis	6	4	–	–
Femur	9	5	1	1
Tibia	10	7	2	2
Astragalus	7	7	3	2
Calcaneum	7	6	1	1
Nav.-cub.	–	–	1	1
Metatarsal	11	9	2	2
Phalanx 1	7	6	4	4
Phalanx 2	2	2	1	1
Total	161		62	

(48%) is higher than in other periods; sheep are 33% and pig 9%. The estimated MNI of cattle is 13, of sheep, eight, and of pig, two. There are four bones of horse. In view of the small sample it would be unsafe to place too much reliance on any interpretation in the rise in the percentage of cattle in the upper midden, particularly as the sediments closer to ground level were more damaged, and in this case bones of larger animals survive better than of smaller ones.

In cattle the largest age class represented in both the lower and upper middens is again calves in the first weeks of life (table 49). Five DPM4s are from neonatal or very young calves, one is from a young animal less than one year, while three M3s are from mature or old animals. The proportion of young calves is even higher in the upper midden, with seven DPM4s from calves less than one month and only two M3s from older animals (illus 96). From each group some loose molars were present from intermediate age groups. Of the 83 post-cranial bones from the lower midden, 14 (17%) are from very young calves, as are five (11%) of 46 from the upper midden. The discrepancy between the percentage of jaws and the percentage of teeth of young calves is not surprising; it was also seen in the assemblages from the rather later site of Grimes Graves (Legge 1992). The explanation offered there was that the carcass other than the head was fed to the dogs. It is equally if not more likely that here the carcass was food for the human population. Calf bones are very porous, and if not rapidly buried they stand a poorer chance of survival in all conditions than bones of older animals.

A proximal cattle phalanx has evidence of severe osteoarthritis affecting the distal joint. The lesion has the three major diagnostic criteria of this condition, eburnation and grooving of the joint surface and new bone growth around the joint. It is a not uncommon finding in cattle bones from archaeological sites.

TABLE 48
MIA: pig: NISP and MNE.

	Lower Midden		Upper Midden	
	NISP	MNE	NISP	MNE
Mandible	8	4	6	2
Maxilla	3	2	3	1
ID skull	4	1	–	–
Atlas	1	1	–	–
Scapula	1	1	–	–
Humerus	–	–	1	1
Carpals	–	–	1	1
Metacarpal	3	2	1	1
Pelvis	2	1	1	1
Femur	2	2	–	–
Tibia	1	1	2	2
Astragalus	1	1	–	–
Tarsal	1	1	–	–
Metatarsal	2	1	–	–
Lat metapodials	3	2	–	–
Phalanx 1	–	–	–	–
Phalanx 2	–	–	1	1
Lat Phal	1	1	–	–
Total	**33**		**16**	

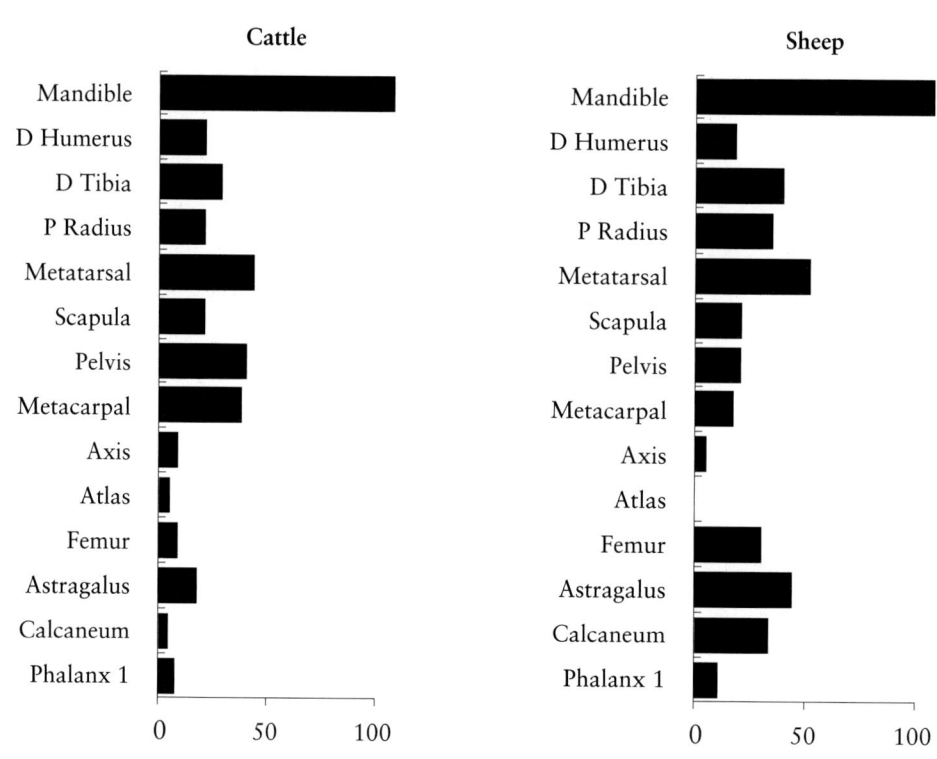

97 Iron Age cattle and sheep (upper and lower midden combined); per cent survival of parts of the body, based on MNE. Mandibles, the most frequent part, shown as 100%.

TABLE 49
MIA: eruption and wear of teeth of cattle (top) and sheep (below), according to Grant (1982).

Cattle

Lower midden				Upper midden			
Stage	DPM4/ P4	M1/M2	M3	Stage	DPM4/ P4	M1/M2	M3
1	a	V	–	1	b	–	–
1	b	V	–	1	b	–	–
1	b	–	–	1	b	–	–
1	b	–	–	1	b	–	–
1	b	–	–	1	b	–	–
2	f	a	–	1	b	–	–
3	–	d	–	2/3	c	b	–
3	–	e	–	2/3	–	b	–
4	–	j	b	2/3	–	b	–
5	h	k	j	2/3	–	b	–
5	–	o	j	2/3	–	c	–
				4	–	j	a
				5	–	–	j

Sheep

Lower midden				Upper midden			
Stage	DPM4/ P4	M1/M2	M3	Stage	DPM4/ P4	M1/M2	M3
2	b	–	–	1	a	–	–
2	c	c	–	1	a	–	–
2	d	a	–	3	–	c	–
2	e	a	–	3	–	d	–
2	e	a	–	3	–	e	–
2	e	a	–	3	–	f	–
3	g	b	–	4/5	–	g	b
3	g	c	–	4/5	–	g	d
3	–	d	–	4/5	–	g	–
4/5	–	g	b	4/5	–	g	–
4/5	–	g	c	4/5	–	g	–
4/5	–	g	e	4/5	–	g	–
4/5	–	g	–	4/5	–	h	–
4/5	–	g	–	4/5	–	j	–
4/5	–	g	–	–	–	–	–
4/5	–	g	–	–	–	–	–
4/5	–	g	–	–	–	–	–
4/5	–	g	–	–	–	–	–
5	–	h	g	–	–	–	–
5	–	–	h	–	–	–	–
5	–	–	j	–	–	–	–

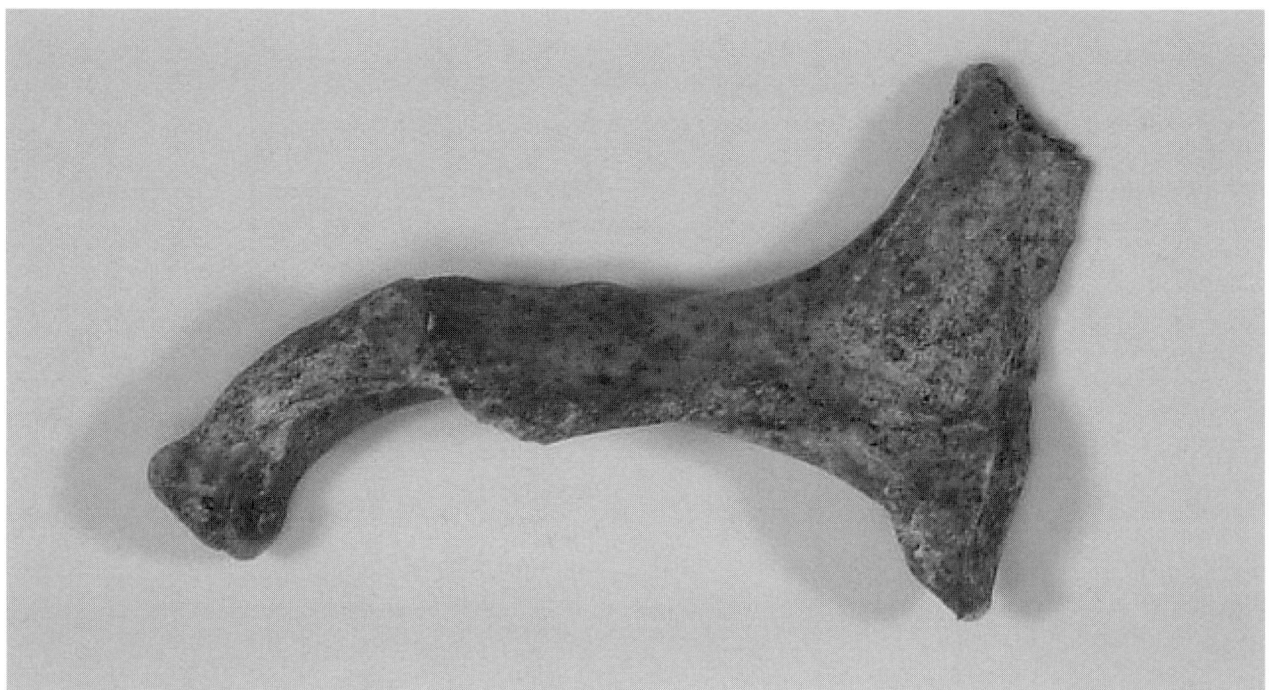

98 Coracoid of a medium-sized gadfly petrel.

The age at death of the sheep is more evenly spread over the five stages identified (table 49). The proportion of neonatal and very young lambs is fewer: only one jaw from the lower midden and two from the upper midden are from this age class. In contrast with the cattle, three of 15 in the lower midden and four of eight in the upper midden were slaughtered or died between three and 18 months, an age at which the animals are chosen for meat (illus 96). The pig bones and teeth are from animals of all ages, including juvenile and old animals.

Horses were used for riding and for carrying packs, and at least from Viking times there is written evidence that they, rather than cattle, were used for ploughing the sandy machair soils. The carcasses were used after death here, as one phalanx has been chopped through, the method usually employed for marrow extraction.

Wild species

Red deer again are common: in the lower midden they are 19% of the identified bones. They are less common (8%) in the upper midden. The decline in the upper levels cannot be ascribed to survival as the bones are more robust and almost as large as the cattle bones. As with the other main species, all parts of the carcass are found (table 50). Post-cranial bones, jaws and teeth substantially outnumber antler fragments, showing that the remains are from animals killed and eaten, and not merely encouraged because they could provide antler. Antler was used in the production of artefacts, as the presence of three worked fragments shows. Only eight bird bones were found in the Iron Age middens, indicating that there was apparently no systematic exploitation of birds, either wild or domestic at this time. No bones of domestic fowl were found. Of the wild birds, single bones were found of gannet and mallard and an immature tarsometatarsus from a small corvid. Most enigmatic is the coracoid of a medium-sized gadfly petrel (illus 98). Today there is no petrel species which breeds around the coasts of Western Europe with which it compares, though the bone matches one or two other small to medium petrels from other parts of the world. Other bones from what seem to be the same species have been found at the Udal, North Uist. The bone is a close match with Fea's petrel (*Pterodroma feae*), which today breeds only on one small island off Madeira and in the Azores. The finds suggest that this species had a wider breeding range in the past; alternatively the bones from the Hebrides are from a species that is now extinct (Serjeantson 2005).

TABLE 50
MIA: red deer: NISP and MNE.

	Lower Midden		Upper Midden	
	NISP	MNE	NISP	MNE
Mandible	13	4	5	3
Maxilla	8	4	1	1
Antler	9	2	2	1
Scapula	4	2	1	1
Humerus	1	1	–	–
Radius	6	4	–	–
Ulna	2	2	1	1
Carpals	2	1	–	–
Metacarpal	6	3	–	–
Pelvis	5	2	–	–
Femur	2	1	–	–
Tibia	3	1	–	–
Astragalus	4	4	–	–
Calcaneum	3	2	–	–
Nav.-cub.	1	1	1	1
Metatarsal	8	3	–	–
Phalanx 1	2	1	3	1
Phalanx 2	2	2	–	–
Phalanx 3	3	3	–	–
Cerv vert	1	1	–	–
Lumb vert	1	1	–	–
Total	86		14	

TABLE 51
Percentages of cattle, sheep, pig and red deer on Hebridean Iron Age sites.

	Cattle		Sheep		Pig		Red Deer		Total
	NISP	%	NISP	%	NISP	%	NISP	%	
Iron Age									
Dun Cul Bhuirg	80	44.4	34	18.9	36	20.0	30	16.7	180
Dun Mor Vaul	348	28.2	574	46.6	54	4.4	256	20.8	1232
Dun Ardtreck	666	51.1	107	8.2	166	12.7	364	27.9	1303
Northton (IA)	74	18.8	92	23.4	2	0.5	225	57.3	393
Kilellan LM	145	33.4	160	36.9	32	7.4	97	22.4	434
Kilellan UM	83	48.0	61	35.3	16	9.2	13	7.5	173
The Udal	2607	38.9	3961	59.1	106	1.6	24	0.4	6698
Iona Ditch 1	170	82.5	12	5.8	5	2.4	19	9.2	206
Iona midden	438	47.2	81	8.7	83	8.9	326	35.1	928

More surprising than the paucity of evidence for seabird exploitation is the scant evidence of fish. Only five fragments were found of which two are probably from the skate or ray family. While it is not impossible that fish bones have failed to survive in the site sediments, it is more likely that this absence reflects a genuine lack of dependence on fishing. Though marine shells were found in the midden, these too are considered to have been collected as a casual rather than systematic resource (Chapter 9). The implication of this is that the range of agricultural products available, plus the red deer, was sufficient for the needs of the community in the Middle Iron Age.

DISCUSSION

Three aspects of the assemblages are discussed in more detail here. These are 1) the high proportion of calves in both the Early Bronze Age and Middle Iron Age deposits; 2) the role of pigs at each period, and 3) the high percentage of red deer in both periods.

HIGH PROPORTION OF CALVES

The presence of skeletal remains from neonatal and young cattle and sheep on a settlement demonstrates that the stock were being raised there, undoubtedly the case at Kilellan. There are opposing interpretations of whether these are from calves that were deliberately slaughtered or from animals that died. A high proportion of young calves, together with mature animals but few between one and four years, in archaeological assemblages has been interpreted (Legge 1981; 1992) as evidence that the cattle husbandry at the settlement was focused heavily on dairying, with the milk, butter, cheese and other milk products taking precedence over the other products which cattle can provide meat, traction, hides and horn. If the benefit in food to be gained from rearing the calf for months or years for eventual consumption is less than the yield of milk from the cow, which would otherwise be drunk by the calf, there is no advantage in keeping the calf on and it can be slaughtered as soon after birth as lactation in the cow has been established. Intensive dairying is a particularly attractive option for Hebridean sites like Kilellan, where there is good quality grazing for most of the year, but where until recently there was no market or other centre to which calves could be exported for rearing elsewhere. Raising cattle for milk was one of the mainstays of the agricultural economy of the Hebrides, if not the most important element (Martin 1716; McDonald 1811), until it was superseded in historical times by raising calves for sale in the mainland markets.

This interpretation of early cattle husbandry has been contested by some authors. The opposing view is best summarized by McCormick (1992), who reiterates the argument that primitive cattle did not let down their milk unless the calf was present at the time the cow was milked, and cites as evidence a passage concerning milch cows in the Irish Law Tracts (quoted by Lucas 1989) which states that the calves 'shall not be disturbed until they run dry'. If, McCormick argues, cattle required the presence of the calf to let down their milk in the 5th century AD, then they must also have done so in prehistoric times. The cattle remains from the early sites in Ireland which he has studied lack evidence for animals slaughtered soon after birth, and this is cited to confirm his argument. He interprets the high proportion of young animals found on sites in the west of Scotland as the result of high natural mortality in calves.

These opposing views cannot be resolved from the small samples here, but it is of interest that the finds from Kilellan add to the consistent picture that is now seen at other Hebridean sites. Even if the degree of intensity of cattle exploitation is in doubt, the evidence points to the importance of milk as the major cattle product.

CONFLICTING EVIDENCE OF PIG

The proportion of pigs on Hebridean sites is very variable. The number and proportion of identified bones of the four main mammals, cattle, sheep, pig and red deer from Kilellan can be compared with nearby Ardnave 2 and ten other groups from seven sites (table 51). At the second millennium sites of Rosinish and Northton, as at Early Bronze Age Kilellan, pig remains are fewer than 1%, though Ardnave, a few centuries later, has over 17%. The Iron Age and Early Historic sites include four, Dun Mor Vaul on Tiree (Noddle 1980), Ditch 1, Iona, (McCormick 1981) and the Udal (Serjeantson nd b) and Northton (Finlay 1983) with <5% pig, but also three others, Dun Cul Bhuirg (Noddle ibid) and the midden (Noddle 1981) on Iona and Dun Ardtreck, Skye (Noddle ibid) where, like Kilellan, proportions of pig approach or exceed 10%. Thus while most sites have scarce evidence for pigs, some have distinctively high proportions, including Ardnave and to a lesser degree Iron Age Kilellan. Elsewhere in Britain pigs are common in features associated with Grooved Ware

(Grigson 1981), in different settings, an association which appears to owe more to cultural than environmental pressures. The Hebridean sites with very high proportions of pig remains, Ardnave and Dun Ardtreck, are not linked by similar environments, at least so far as these can be reconstructed today, as Ardnave is sited on fertile machair soils while Dun Ardtreck stands on a rocky knoll above a sea cliff.

Swine herding is undesirable where soils are fragile, as they are in many environments in Scotland (Ross 1983). The machair, if not the raised beaches, in the vicinity of Kilellan, would have been vulnerable to damage from rooting pigs, which destroy the cover and expose light unconsolidated soils to the strong winds characteristic of the Hebrides. According to a survey of the island carried out in 1764 (Walker 1812), the domestic swine 'graze on the hill like sheep; their sole food is herbage and roots'. They were acknowledged then to cause damage. The possibility has already been raised (Ritchie & Welfare 1983, 320) that 'pigs contributed to its [the machair's] instability' at the end of the occupation at Ardnave.

It therefore appears that there must have been powerful social reasons for keeping pigs, which prevailed against the unsuitability of the terrain. Consumption of pigs in the Celtic world is associated with feasting and status, and their presence in high numbers has to be considered a social phenomenon. When the fine detail of the timing and nature of the environmental degradation which has taken place in the west of Scotland and the islands is better understood, it will be interesting to see if there is any correlation with episodes of pig keeping.

RED DEER

The proportion of red deer at Kilellan in both the Early Bronze Age and the Middle Iron Age is higher than is usually found on early sites in mainland Britain. On mainland sites, while antler fragments may be common, other parts of the skeleton rarely make up more than a small percentage of the total finds. Kilellan is not unique, however, as other sites in the Scottish islands also have high numbers of red deer. They are over 20% of identified bones at Northton, the midden at Iona, Dun Ardtreck and Dun Mor Vaul. While high proportions on Skye might be expected, and bones from Iona sites may be from herds on Mull, the finds identified from Dun Mhor Vaul are very enigmatic. Tiree, which has a high proportion of the machair soils favoured for cultivation and lacks extensive grazing areas, is a most unlikely habitat for substantial herds of deer.

The reasons for this contrast with mainland sites are not satisfactorily resolved. If deer were introduced originally either as a supplementary food supply which could be called on in times of hardship or as a source of antler for craft use (Serjeantson 1990), numbers would need to be kept in check, as the wolf, their only natural predator other than man, is absent. The deer, like the cattle, sheep and pigs when present, would need to be kept off growing crops. There is a good material reason for controlling the population and consuming the surplus, but this does not explain the contrast with mainland sites. Unlike the pigs, it is hard to invoke a social reason for high proportions of red deer, as high numbers are found in all periods, and at times when the material culture suggest links rather than contrasts with mainland Britain.

CONCLUSION

The pattern of animal husbandry attested in historical times, in which cattle were raised for milk, while sheep were the main meat animals, and pigs rare or kept in small numbers compared to the other two domesticates, has been shown here and at other sites to have roots which go back at least to the second millennium BC. Pigs were kept in considerably smaller numbers than cattle and sheep during the later first millennium BC and the early first millennium AD, and were even rarer earlier. The numbers and anatomical parts of red deer show that in both periods they provided a fair proportion of the meat consumed. At Kilellan evidence for fish and birds is scant in both periods, suggesting a surprisingly small reliance on wild food resources other than red deer. This, together with the intensive pattern of cattle husbandry, shows that in both periods the community at Kilellan was able to provide for its needs by cultivation and animal husbandry with little recourse to the more casual food supplies of fish and seabirds. With the exception of the apparent change in pig keeping, the continuity of subsistence from the Early Bronze Age into the Middle Iron Age is powerful evidence of how here the environment and resources and available technology constrained the possible economic strategies, which were nevertheless an effective and appropriate mix for the locality.

Chapter 8

The charcoal

SHEILA BOARDMAN

Charcoal from 40 samples collected in 1973 and 1976 was submitted for identification. The tree species are listed by context group and by sample in the site archive. The results are summarized below.

SPECIES REPRESENTED
(IN ORDER OF ABUNDANCE)

Mesolithic: silver sand (H1 7.02, H1 7.03)

Alnus (alder), *Salix* (willow), *Corylus* (hazel), *Betula* (birch), *Quercus* (oak), Pomoideae [latter incorporates *Crataegus* (hawthorn), *Malus* (crab apple) and *Sorbus* (rowan/service/whitebeam)].

Third or fourth millennia BC

Turf line (G2 7, K1 7)
Quercus, Corylus, Betula.

Early Bronze Age midden (A1 2, A2 6, B1 6, B2 6, ?B3 6, F1 6, G2 6.07, G2 6.31, G2 6.55, G2 100.57, G4 100)
Salix, Quercus, Pomoideae (including *Sorbus*), *Alnus, Betula, Corylus, Prunus avium/padus* type (wild cherry/bird cherry type).

First millennium BC

Occupation floor (L2 10, L2 10.101, L2 10.2)
Quercus, Corylus, Alnus, Betula, Pomoideae, *Prunus avium/padus* type.

Pit fill (L2 113)
Betula, Quercus.

Pit fill (L2 117)
Betula, Quercus, Corylus, Salix.

Souterrain (L2 118)
Corylus, Prunus avium/padus type, *Quercus, Prunus spinosa* type (sloe type), *Prunus,* Pomoideae (including *Sorbus*).

Stone-lined pit (L2 126)
Corylus, Betula.

Middle Iron Age

Hearth (K3 110)
Betula, Prunus avium/padus type.

Midden (J1 20, J1 24, J1 25, J1 26, J1 28)
Betula, Pomoideae (including *Sorbus*), *Quercus.*

Midden (J2 19, J2 30, J2 113)
Betula, Salix.

Contexts contemporary with the souterrain (K3 201, K3 202, K3 108)
Betula, Fraxinus (ash), *Quercus, Salix, Alnus.*

Midden (K3 5)
Betula, Salix, Alnus, Corylus, Quercus.

DISCUSSION

The tree species represented by charcoal at Kilellan are all found on modern Islay (Morton 1959). Non-native species such as *Picea* (spruce) were not recovered and thus the role of driftwood cannot be assessed. *Fraxinus* (ash) was present in only one sample, from a Middle to Late Iron Age context (K3 201). Isochrone maps derived from pollen data suggest that *Fraxinus excelsior* L. reached Islay between 4000 and 3000 BP. The other species would appear to be present throughout the prehistoric periods (Birks 1989). *Fraxinus* is intolerant of shade and probably grew in light secondary woodland or in isolated stands.

The Mesolithic samples produced very little charcoal, among which *Alnus* (alder) was the most abundant. *Salix* (willow), *Corylus* (hazel), *Betula* (birch), *Quercus* (oak) and Pomoideae [including *Sorbus* (rowan/whitebeam)] were also present. Other early prehistoric contexts produced the same range of taxa, plus *Prunus avium/padus* type (wild cherry/bird cherry type) charcoal and much *Quercus*. Some samples from the Early Bronze Age midden were dominated by *Salix* (eg G2 6, G2 100). *Quercus* and *Corylus* were important components of the later prehistoric samples, with *Betula* and *Prunus* charcoal frequent in some features. *Prunus spinosa* (sloe) type charcoal was present in one sample from the souterrain (L2 118.01). Most of the early historic samples were heavily dominated by *Betula* charcoal, much of this apparently derived from roundwood.

At Ardnave 2, close to Kilellan, deposits dating to the second millennium BC and the early first millennium AD produced a similar range of charcoal taxa. *Picea* (spruce) charcoal was also present and almost certainly arrived as driftwood (Dickson, in Ritchie & Welfare 1983, 358–60).

Both pollen and charcoal evidence are available from Newton, central Islay (McCullagh 1989). Mesolithic and Neolithic deposits produced charcoal identified as *Alnus*, *Corylus*, *Prunus avium* type, Pomoideae (*Crataegus/Sorbus*), *Quercus* and *Salix*. Some Mesolithic layers contained large numbers of *Corylus* nutshells. The later ring ditches, of possible early Christian date, produced much *Calluna* (heather, ling) charcoal, plus some *Corylus* and Pomoideae roundwood (McCullagh 1989, 42). A range of tree taxa are indicated by the pollen diagram from Newton, including *Ulmus* (elm), *Pinus* (pine) and *Tilia* (lime). The latter two species probably reflect long distance pollen transport. The pollen spectra from Newton suggest an early prehistoric tree cover which was dominated by *Corylus*, *Betula*, *Quercus* and *Ulmus*. Major disturbances occurred around 5000 BC, and were followed by an increase in Coryloid pollen, possibly reflecting clearances by fire. This is followed by a period of open woodland. A decrease in the contribution of *Ulmus* pollen occurred around 3150 BC and woodland was cleared. There are suggestions of agricultural activity. Pit fill layers, pre- and post-dating 2930±60 BC, also produced small amounts of Ericaceae pollen. These suggest the onset of acidification at an earlier date to that indicated by the pollen diagram. This process, commencing shortly after large-scale exploitation of the soils, may have been accelerated by overgrazing (Andrews, in McCullagh 1989, 38–42).

With the exception of the Mesolithic deposits, there were significant quantities of burnt organic material throughout the samples, including probable burnt peat. On the basis of the presence of this material, peat seems to have been burnt as fuel from at least the fourth millennium BP. Within this context it is perhaps surprising that no clear evidence for collected driftwood was found at the site.

SEED IMPRESSION ON POT

G2 121, Chapter 3 no 111
Cereal: *Hordeum* sp. (barley)

The impression is *c* 6mm in length and 3mm in width but, due to a slight blurring effect towards its edges in the coarse texture of the sherd, this initially appeared larger and a little too circular for a cereal impression. The sherd was first observed by eye, then under a low power (×8) binocular microscope. The interior of the impression contained a charred, fairly amorphous residue. This was first thought to have been left by a larger seed or pip which had partially disintegrated on firing of the pot. Higher power magnification (up to ×95) combined with very gentle brushing (using an ultra-fine paint brush) to remove some of the loose sooty particles, revealed some surviving fragments of an impression beneath, that of the dorsal side (without groove) of a cereal grain. The shape of the impression clearly resembles barley. There were no characteristic hulls and the very slight wrinkling of the dorsal surface also suggests naked barley. The grain appears to be slightly asymmetric (most noticeable at embryo end) so may represent *H. vulgare* L. var. *nudum* (naked six row barley). The latter is the commonest cereal found on archaeological sites of Neolithic and Bronze Age date in Scotland.

Chapter 9

Marine mollusca

JOHN G EVANS

The site was not visited by the author and context information is taken from the 'Draft excavation report 1992' and correspondence from Anna Ritchie. The relation of the shell assemblages to layers and structures are in site notes, drawings and photographs.

FIELD OBSERVATIONS

The general distribution, abundance and nature of occurrence of shells is not described other than that shells 'seem to have been fairly evenly distributed within the layers' and an occasional comment such as 'midden seems to be layered, with sterile grey and brown band between shell layers'. There is some indication of the distribution and abundance of shells in specific instances. Thus there were some rich layers, eg for the Early Bronze Age, trench G4 ?306 (or immediately above it), and for the Middle Iron Age, upper midden, trench J2 layer 19, the souterrain fill. Concentrations of shells comprised fairly low spreads. For the Early Bronze Age these are (for numbers 1 to 13 in brackets, see below): 3) B2 layer 6, 'shells … in tight little heaps'; 5) F1 layer 6, 'different shells [species] in different piles … limpets, mussels, winkles', with an irregular pile of winkles c 1.4m by 1.4m; 7) G2 0632b, limpet pile; G2 0672e, limpet heap in shelly layer; 7) G2 101b, 136d and 137, limpet piles in layer 6; 7) G2 138, shells in fill of 'shallow scoop' in layer 6; and 7) G3 layer 3, 'large quantity of shell including shells stacked one into another'. For the Middle Iron Age, lower midden, they are: 8) J1 layers 25–8, 'extremely rich in shells', mainly limpets and cockles. For the same period, upper midden, they are: 10) J2 layer 19 pile 114, c 1.0m by 0.75m; 11) J2 layer 19 pile 107, 'winkle heap contained well-sorted groups of winkles and limpets', the heap being c 0.5m by 0.5m; 12) J1 layer 9 pile 103, winkle pile in upper-midden; and 13) K3 layer 5 pile 109, 'a very large heap of winkles'.

SHELL COLLECTIONS: PROCEDURE

Shells in paper bags, labelled by year, trench and layer/context, were submitted by Colin Burgess and studied in Cardiff. The significance of the individual bags of shells, many from the same context, is unknown. The mode of collection whether total or a sample and how it was done in relation to the site lithostratigraphy and archaeological contexts are generally unclear, although some specific features and shell dumps were treated individually. In 1973 all shells were collected, except that mussels were very fragile and likely to be under-represented. In 1976 prolific layers were sampled, which accounts for the very low numbers of shells in piles 101b, 136d and 137 from G2, layer 6. Only pile 107 in layer 19 trench J2 11) was totally collected.

Overall, shells were collected from the area of Early Bronze Age midden in trenches A1, B2, F1, F2, G2 and G3, the Middle Iron Age occupation in trenches J1, J2, K1, K2 and K3, and some Mesolithic contexts in A2, G2 and G3. No shells were found in trenches G4 (Early Bronze Age), L2 (Late Bronze Age/Early Iron Age), C1, H1 and H2. The shells indicated as being Mesolithic may derive from overlying layers since the Mesolithic sand is acidic, lacking the shell content of later sandblows, and there was contamination of the sand by Early Bronze Age midden, but they are considered here at their face value.

The shells from each collection were identified and the results amalgamated into 13 groups on the basis of context, excavation area and archaeological age:

1. Mesolithic: A2 6; G2 128d; G3 5, 607 and 7
2. Early Bronze Age midden: I 6, II 6 and III 6; A1 2; A2 5
3. Early Bronze Age midden: B1 6 and B2 6
4. Early Bronze Age midden, excluding winkle patch: F1 6 and F2 6
5. Early Bronze Age midden, winkle patch: F1 6
6. Early Bronze Age midden: G1 6 and 102

TABLE 52
Marine mollusca.

	1	2	3	4	5	6	7	8	9	10	11	12	13
Cancer pagurus	1	–	2	–	–	–	23	–	5	–	–	–	–
Patella sp.	401	645	8903	2117	89	688	10729	1535	298	529	125	3	118
Gibbula sp.	–	–	–	–	–	–	–	–	–	–	1	–	–
Calliostoma zizyphinum (L.)	–	–	–	–	–	–	–	–	1	–	–	–	–
Littorina obtusata (L.)	–	1	13	6	–	1	12	2	2	1	1	1	2
Littorina littorea (L.)	154	268	690	773	2895	220	1641	264	220	–	313	3305	915
Nucella lapillus (L.)	–	–	1	–	–	–	–	–	–	–	–	–	–
Buccinum undatum (L.)	–	–	5	1	–	–	6	1	–	–	–	–	–
Mytilus edulis L.	4	1	69	10	–	6	110	20	11	–	–	1	3
Ostrea edulis L.	–	1	2	1	–	1	7	1	1	–	1	–	–
Pecten maximus (L.)	1	11	24	2	–	4	31	3	2	–	–	–	1
Cerastoderma edule (L.)	51	52	663	106	1	234	479	1443	58	2	1	17	9
Arctica islandica (L.)	6	20	51	34	2	27	126	33	4	–	3	–	5
Veneridae	–	–	3	3	–	–	3	–	–	–	1	–	1
Mya truncata (L.)	–	1	2	1	–	–	8	–	1	–	–	–	–

7. Early Bronze Age midden: G2 6, 100, 107, 108d, 108d, 133, 106b; G3 3 and 4; shell piles in 6 101b, 136d, 137; shallow scoop 138, 138d and 1380
8. Middle Iron Age site, lower midden: J1 layers 21, 23, 25, 26, 27 and 28
9. Middle Iron Age site, upper midden: J1 layers 5, 6, 7, 10, 11 and 14; J2 layers 19, 29, 30, 31, 32, 106 and 113; K3 layer 5
10. Middle Iron Age site, upper midden, limpet pile, J2 19 114
11. Middle Iron Age site, upper midden, winkle and limpet pile, J2 19 107
12. Middle Iron Age site site, upper midden, winkle pile, J1 9 103
13. Middle Iron Age site, upper midden, winkle pile, K3 5 109

The numbers on the left of this list are specific to this report and refer to table 52, where 41,707 shells are identified. The original identifications by paper bag collection, including a few from unstratified or poorly provenanced contexts and some sparse collections from blown sand layers not presented here, are in the site archive.

SHELL COLLECTIONS: RESULTS

There are three main species, *Patella* spp. (limpets), *Littorina littorea* (the edible winkle) and *Cerastoderma edule* (the edible cockle). All others are in very low numbers. There are no general changes in species proportions through time except for the abundance of cockles in the lower midden of the Middle Iron Age occupation (8). Otherwise the predominance of limpets, then winkles and then cockles is present from the Mesolithic, through the Early Bronze Age, on into the lower and upper middens of the Middle Iron Age layers. There is some spatial variation, as seen also in the field, with dumps of winkles and limpets, but the small size of these indicates individual collections rather than trends towards specialization at particular stages.

Measurements (all in millimetres) were made of limpet height and length from individual (paper bag) collections covering all groups except 6, 12 and 13, and of cockle length and breadth from all groups except 6, 10, 11, 12 and 13. The data are in the site archive. There is no significant difference between the measurements for each parameter from the different groups. The means for limpets, based on a total of 695 measurements in 27 collections, are: length, $x = 35.84$,

SD ± 2.21; height, x = 13.48, SD = ±1.49. The means for cockles, based on a total of 588 measurements in 26 collections are: length, x = 37.13, SD = ±1.44; breadth, x = 33.76, SD = ±1.00.

DISCUSSION

Judging from present day habitats, with limpets and winkles living on rocky shores more or less exclusively and cockles inhabiting substrata like sand and mud, the most likely environmental scenario is a sandy shore with ambient rocky areas. Limpet shape indicates that this was neither very exposed nor sheltered and that the limpets were from the mid-tide zone. All three species were presumably being collected by humans for food or bait, and if the latter then for crabs rather than fish in view of the virtual absence of fish bone. The small dumps of limpets and winkles indicate the collection and use of single species, probably no more than a reflection of their patchiness on the shore. The only outstanding variation of a general nature is the abundance of cockles in the lower midden of the Middle Iron Age occupation (8) and this may reflect a shift in preference of collecting area and/or shellfish species at this time.

The discrete dumps also indicate primary disposal immediately after use, as is hinted at, too, by limpets stacked into each other and tight little dumps. The more uniform dispersal of the majority of the shells in the midden layers, however, suggests some reworking after primary deposition.

The minority species represent incidental use for a variety of purposes and incorporation into the deposits by a variety of means. *Littorina obtusata* (formerly *L. littoralis*) (the flat-topped winkle) lives closely attached to fucoid seaweeds and is often incorporated incidentally when seaweed is gathered for fertilizer, although the low numbers of this species and the domestic nature of the site suggest that this may not have been their origin here. *Pecten maximus* (the great scallop) and *Cyprina islandica*, may have been collected dead for use as containers, and the usually fragmentary nature of the tough shells of the latter suggests that they may have been heated on a fire. *Mytilus edulis* (the edible mussel) and *Cancer pagurus* (the edible crab) may have been formerly present in greater numbers but become largely destroyed owing to the fragility of their shells, as noted for the former by Colin Burgess. The very occasional shells of *Ostrea edulis* (the edible oyster) and *Buccinum/Neptunea* (whelks) may have been collected dead as curios.

By comparison with the adjacent site of Ardnave 2 (Ritchie & Welfare 1983) where limpets were the predominant species, with few winkles and no cockles, the assemblages from Kilellan are diverse. However, there were only three main collections from Ardnave in comparison with eleven from Kilellan so the former may be unrepresentative. Limpet length mean, at 35.84mm, is smaller than at Ardnave (38.1–39.4mm) (Ritchie & Welfare 1983), but the significance of this is unclear, and too much should not be made of it since two or three species may be involved.

More generally, however, the assemblages are of low diversity. Other rocky shore species that might be expected in abundance and that occur in coastal middens are topshells, whelks like *Buccinum* and *Neptunea*, mussels (although perhaps under-represented because of their fragility) and, most especially, *Nucella lapillus*. These are all readily collectable in the intertidal zone, so their paucity suggests an environmental effect. Shelter allows seaweeds to colonize rocky shores and to out-compete mussels, so this supports the limpet-shape evidence for a sheltered locale. The fact that whelks prey on mussels may be a further point of relevance. Likewise with regard to sandy and muddy shore species, there are several which occur in middens, like razor shells and carpet shells, which are totally or virtually absent. Razor shells require more skill in collecting than other groups since they have to be dug for deeply and quickly before they escape below spade's reach, so in this case human laziness rather than availability may be involved. Species of the low-tide and sub-tidal zones such as oysters and *Cyprina* are also probably rare because they required more effort to collect.

These considerations suggest that shellfish were collected on a casual and not especially purposeful basis. Like many coastal sites of the agricultural economies, shellfish collecting was probably an adventitious activity, a minor supplement to a conventional meat, dairy products and cereal based diet (cf Benson *et al* 1990). The virtual absence of fish bones supports the lack of emphasis on the coast.

Chapter 10

Discussion

ANNA RITCHIE

The original academic objective of the excavations at Kilellan was to explore the little-known domestic dimension of Early Bronze Age settlement in the southern Hebrides, and it was allied to the clear need to rescue the vestiges of a rich Early Bronze Age midden from destruction by erosion. The results presented above show this objective to have been achieved as far as was possible. In the course of tracing the surviving extent of the midden, the chronological and structural component of the site was expanded to include palynological data associated with a raised beach, Mesolithic deposits and evidence of intermittent later settlement from Late Bronze Age/Early Iron Age to recent times, all of which has an importance in terms of understanding social development and changes in land-use in the area. There is substantial archaeological evidence for human activity at Kilellan during four main periods of prehistory: Mesolithic, Early Bronze Age, Late Bronze Age/Early Iron Age and Middle Iron Age. The quantity of decorated Early Bronze Age pottery ensures that it is this aspect of the site that will dominate future discussion, but there are also very useful contributions to be made to Mesolithic and Iron Age studies.

PHASE 1
THE MESOLITHIC HORIZON
(*with* ALAN SAVILLE)

Islay is one of several islands in the Inner Hebrides where excavations over the last twenty-five years have located traces of Mesolithic activity. The work of John Mercer on Jura (1980, with earlier references), of Paul Mellars on Oronsay (1987), of Caroline Wickham-Jones on Rum (1990), of Rod McCullagh on Islay (1989) and of Steven Mithen and the Southern Hebrides Mesolithic Project on Colonsay and Islay (2000a) has emphasized the richness of this area for information about Mesolithic settlement. At present, evidence for Mesolithic activity in the southern Hebrides first appears around 7000 cal BC, some 1000 years later than at Kinloch on Rum in the northern Hebrides (Mithen 2000b, 600), and at Kilellan is likely to fall within the bracket 7000–5500 cal BC (Chapter 4).

Until recently, Mesolithic presence in Islay appeared to have been concentrated in the Rinns, the western part of the island, but the site at Newton, near Bridgend, discovered by air photography (McCullagh 1989), implied that the known distribution of Mesolithic settlement was too restricted. This has been confirmed by fieldwork undertaken during the Southern Hebrides Mesolithic Project (Mithen *et al* 2000a), which has added another 12 sites east of Lochs Gruinart and Indaal, as well as more sites within the Rinns, and by Mesolithic finds from excavations at Finlaggan (David Caldwell pers comm). Work on sedimentary evidence from Loch Gruinart by Dawson and Dawson (2000) has refined understanding of sea level changes in this area and has demonstrated that the tidal strait between the Rinns and the rest of Islay was open between about 9000 and 2000 BP (*c* 8500–200 cal BC). Thereafter the level of the sea dropped, creating the present topography of low-lying ground between the sea-lochs of Gruinart and Indaal. The strait between the Rinns and eastern Islay would have presented no barrier to movement by boat, indeed it may have been possible to cross it on foot at low tide (Mithen *et al* 2000b, 239), and Alan Saville has indicated a possible link between the assemblages at Kilellan and Newton on the basis of similarities in microlith typology (Chapter 6). The beaches along the west coast of Islay are likely to have been the main source of flint pebbles for Mesolithic communities throughout the archipelago (Marshall 2000). The SHMP survey identified another Mesolithic and later prehistoric site on the western shore of Loch Gruinart (GRU 13), about 1.8km south of Kilellan and in a similar topographical location (Mithen *et al* 2000a, Fig 4.2.4, 179).

In many respects, the Mesolithic horizon at Kilellan fits in well with the evidence from other sites in the Inner Hebrides, although the relatively small size of the flint assemblage and the apparent absence of contemporary midden soils suggest that the nature of the occupation at Kilellan may have been ephemeral by comparison. The main concentration of excavated flints lay on the relatively flat and well-drained land behind the raised beach of the Main Postglacial Shoreline, a typical location for Mesolithic settlement. At this point on the Ardnave peninsula the raised beach was the bed of a marshy pond that had formed behind a line of sand-dunes above the contemporary shore, and the Mesolithic activity was thus sited upslope from a freshwater marsh that may have attracted birdlife. The small amount of charcoal (4.8g) from the Mesolithic horizon suggests mixed scrub in the vicinity, including alder, willow, hazel, birch, oak and rowan or whitebeam (Chapter 8), a type of environment that is likely to have been highly productive for game, fowl and vegetable resources (Hirons 1990, 142–3). The bone fragments recovered were too eroded to be identified other than as mammal, and nothing is known about the activities that took place on the site apart from flintworking and the limited structural evidence. There is virtually no flint on the adjacent beach today, and only 85 small unworked pebbles were retrieved from the Kilellan excavations overall, but beach flint was readily available elsewhere in the Rinns, along the west coast and on the shores of Loch Indaal.

No definite hearths or post-holes were found, though the burnt flint from trench G2 suggested a hearth or hearths nearby. The pebble patches and shallow pit are common features on Mesolithic sites elsewhere (Wickham-Jones 2004). In particular, the patch of flat stones in B3 layer 7 is similar to a paved patch some 1.25m across at Lussa Wood on Jura (Mercer 1980, 7). In the sand at Kilellan, the paved and cobbled patches would create relatively stable working-surfaces, but there was no hint of their purpose. One striking contrast with other Mesolithic sites is the absence from Kilellan of carbonized hazelnut shells. The geographical extent of Mesolithic activity is likely to have been wider than the excavated area, for flints were found in the equivalent sand layer on the higher ground to the west in trenches L and K, and it is possible that the main focus of settlement was not revealed by the excavations.

In character the flint assemblage equates with the general pattern to be expected at Later Mesolithic sites in Scotland (Saville 2004). One of its chief interests is that anvil-knapped as well as platform cores are part of the basic lithic technology, while the refitting exercise demonstrates the *in situ* nature of much of the assemblage and the enormous potential of this technique for Mesolithic research when similarly well-preserved horizons are located and excavated in the future.

Mithen has argued for an essentially localized pattern of Mesolithic settlement in the southern Hebrides (2000b, 603). Kilellan in Mesolithic times may not have been more than a temporary stopping-place on hunting expeditions, where tools were repaired or replaced, but its locational advantages would probably have favoured repeated re-use during this period. The few flint artefacts of Neolithic type suggest an even more ephemeral presence on the site, particularly in the absence of pottery or other evidence of domestic activity, although it is possible that wind erosion truncated any layer of Neolithic date (Chapter 2).

PHASE 2
THE EARLY BRONZE AGE OCCUPATION

The immediate topography of Kilellan around 2000 BC appears to have been much the same as in earlier Mesolithic times, and the only addition to the woodland species was wild cherry. The lack of species likely to represent driftwood is in contrast to Ardnave 2, where spruce was found (Dickson 1983), and may reflect very localized collection of wood. Driftwood is more likely to have been washed up on the west shore of the peninsula, where Ardnave 2 lies, than on the east deep within the Gruinart–Indaal tidal strait. The freshwater marshy area behind the dunes was still in existence, and domestic refuse was dumped immediately inland from it. The settlement itself may have been located somewhere upslope or along the slope, although there was certainly structural activity within the area of the midden. Colin Burgess suggested that the two concentric palisades of Phase 2.2 represented the remains of 'a small, double stockaded farmstead' (Burgess 1980, 219), and he has also suggested that an alternative interpretation might be as revetments against wind-blown sand (pers comm). Another possibility is that they were windbreaks to shelter a working area of the midden. At a late stage in the build-up of the midden there was a house or working floor very close to the perimeter of the dumping area (Phase 2.5). It may be that domestic activities and refuse dumping were not entirely separate. Some of the small pits in the midden may have been dug to extract material for use elsewhere, perhaps as token deposits buried for symbolic purposes (Gibson

DISCUSSION

2003, 141; Needham & Sørensen 1988, 125). The fact that sherds of the same vessel could be widely distributed both vertically and horizontally indicates that the midden was far from static. It is noticeable, however, that the one area of the midden to retain traces of a domestic house (trench G4, Phase 2.6) also was the one area to display selectivity in vessel form, for most of the pottery represents decorated jars. The overall composition of the midden was very similar to that at Ardnave 2 (Ritchie & Welfare 1983), with intermittent dumping and build-up of sand, but Ardnave lacked the dense black shell-rich deposits found at Kilellan. Discrete piles of shells, sometimes composed of just one species of shellfish, indicate primary dumping from specialized activities, normally on a small scale apart from the great pile of winkles in F1. The excavated extent of the midden was about 650 sq m but its original extent was considerably larger, and its surface may have been used for cultivation. The survival of carbonized barley in Phase 2.4 indicates that cereal cultivation may have taken place locally, at least in the later phases of the settlement.

The houses at Ardnave 1 and 2 demonstrate the variety of house-plan and building techniques that were in use locally during the Bronze Age, from the circular plan and post-and-panel stone wall-face of Ardnave 1 (RCAHMS 1984, no 241) (illus 98) to the more linear plans and simple stone facings of Ardnave 2 (Ritchie & Welfare 1983). The later structures at Ardnave 2 appeared to be subrectangular and about 4.5m by 3.3m (ibid, Period 2, 307, and a detached floor nearby, 313), and the Phase 2.5 floor excavated at Kilellan (G4, 100) may have been of similar size and shape. In all cases at the Ardnave sites, the basal walls of the buildings were simply stone revetments against sand, and the same arrangement is likely at Kilellan. The Kilellan floor was bounded on one side by a cut in the sand, which may indicate where a stone revetment stood before the house was dismantled. The upright stones used at the base of the house wall at Ardnave 1 were very similar in size and shape to

99 The Bronze Age house at Ardnave 1, Islay.

177

those used at Kilellan to line a pit dug into the early midden in F1 (illus 29). Roof support was provided by timber posts.

Cattle and sheep were kept in almost equal numbers, but pig appears to have been far more rare at Kilellan (Chapter 7) than at Ardnave 2 (Harman 1983). The high proportion of calves among the surviving cattle bones suggests that milk was the major cattle product (Chapter 7). Exploitation of wild resources appears to have been restricted to hunting red deer and gathering shellfish, and the absence of fishbones at both Kilellan and Ardnave 2 is puzzling in view of their coastal locations. The shellfish collected by the inhabitants of Kilellan were more diverse than at Ardnave 2 (Chapter 9), with limpets supplemented by winkles and cockles as well as by small numbers of other species, but the numbers of shells indicate that this resource was of minor importance to the community. Unless there was some taboo against the consumption of fish, the products from cattle and sheep seem to have satisfied the milk and meat requirements of Early Bronze Age Kilellan. Impressions made with the shells of both *mytilus edulis* and *cardium edule* have been identified on the pottery (Chapter 3), but *cardium edule* is noticeably absent from the marine mollusca assemblages both at Kilellan and Ardnave 2. Shells of *cardium edule* were presumably collected from elsewhere for the specific purpose of pottery decoration.

The chief interest of Kilellan at this period is the pottery. The midden yielded a very large assemblage of pottery, both forms known already from funereal contexts and forms apparently purely domestic. As Rosemary Cowie points out in Chapter 3, 'Kilellan is the first domestic site to validate the clear relationship that exists between vases, vase urns and encrusted urns', and in general the assemblage will act as a yardstick for other sites in western Scotland and the Irish Sea area. In form the vessels comprise cups, bowls, vases and jars, used probably to serve or store food. Decoration is rich and varied, and techniques include impression, incision, grooving, applied, cordoned, white inlay and false relief. Chapter 3 also re-assesses some of the interpretations that have appeared in the literature since the interim report published in 1976 by Colin Burgess, for the final season in 1976 produced more pottery and more precise contexts. In particular, the presence of a round-based Neolithic element and a Beaker element is now seen to be unlikely.

Apart from the pottery, the artefact assemblage from the Early Bronze Age levels is neither extensive nor unusual, and in this aspect too the site reflects the situation at Ardnave 2. There are, however, flint arrowheads and a perforated pebble hammer, neither of which were types found at Ardnave, and the relative numbers of artefacts suggest either that the Kilellan settlement was larger than that at Ardnave, or that its occupation spanned a longer period. Unfortunately the single radiocarbon date from this period at Kilellan cannot usefully be compared with the series of dates from Ardnave, other than noting that it falls easily within Ardnave's span of 2500–1700 cal BC. Despite the soil conditions at Kilellan that allowed the survival of animal bones, albeit in a poor state, there were no bone artefacts.

PHASE 3
THE LATE BRONZE AGE/EARLY IRON AGE OCCUPATION

A millennium or so later, the shrubland around Kilellan provided oak, hazel, birch, willow and wild cherry as before, and the only new wood to appear was sloe. The character of the site revealed in trench L2 is difficult to assess, but it appears to have been domestic, either a house or a working floor, occupied during the period 828–412 cal BC. The large number of pits is more likely to reflect the inevitably short life of a pit dug into sand than a long period of activity on the site, and the fact that they were allowed to infill gradually rather than being deliberately filled may suggest that the site was an open-air working floor rather than a house. Some of the pits may have been dug to hold skin water bags, particularly if bronze-working was taking place. Despite the evidence in some features for heavy burning, the quantity of charcoal present (a total of 99g) did not indicate metalworking on any scale. Minute quantities of metallurgical debris indicated that a high-lead bronze was being worked, but there were no moulds, crucibles or scrap metal, and the pieces of fired clay were not burnt. Fires appeared to have been lit in pits 113, 115, 117 and 119, as well as in the clay- and pottery-lined pit 128, but there was no evidence to indicate their individual purpose. The souterrain and stone-lined pit indicate considerable need for cool but not watertight storage, a need that had become redundant by the time that the occupation layer 10 began to accumulate. Thus the character of the activities carried out on this site may not have remained the same throughout its occupation. It seems likely that the site was kept clean, and that debris was deposited elsewhere, although there were no associated midden deposits immediately surrounding the site and no comparable pottery was recovered from the excavated areas downslope to the east. The pottery was plain and too fragmentary to allow any estimate of its form, but most of it was heavily burnt.

Whereas Kilellan site L displayed plenty of structural evidence and a dearth of artefactual evidence, Jarlshof in Shetland, which may have been contemporary, produced quantities of artefacts and very little physical structure. Some 200 fragments of clay moulds, 44 fragments of mould gates, and more than 20 pieces of clay outer casings were recovered, but the only structural traces were a small heavily burnt hearth and a 'cavity filled with sand', which was interpreted as a device to hold the moulds upright while casting (Hamilton 1956, 23, 29). The debris had been dumped in a small cell adjacent to the working area. There is likely to have been a considerable element of ritual surrounding the practice of bronze-working, and removal of debris may have been one aspect of the behaviour considered appropriate.

PHASE 4
THE MIDDLE IRON AGE SETTLEMENT

At the margin of the stable cultivable land on the plateau a stone-walled round house was built sometime before the turn of the first millennium AD. There were no diagnostic finds and the house cannot be dated securely, but the stratigraphy suggests that it was not significantly earlier than the adjacent souterrain and midden. Only a segment of the house survived, but enough to show that its floor was markedly dished, a feature noted at An Sithean, Islay, where it was interpreted as evidence that the floor had been scoured for hygienic purposes (Barber & Brown 1984, 185). A number of sites of hut-circles, some associated with field-systems, have been identified around the Loch Gruinart area (RCAHMS 1984, 12–14), and it is likely that this Kilellan house represented a similar, though later, social unit. As well as for hygiene, house floors are likely to have been scoured in order to add their enriching contents to arable fields, a practice that has been documented from Neolithic times (Simpson 1998). A second inner wall-face may suggest that the house was contracted in internal area at some point in its occupation, as was the case at Cùl a'Bhaile in Jura (Stevenson 1984). The eastern side of the house was demolished probably at the time that the souterrain was constructed, and no trace was found in the excavated area of the house served by the souterrain. The midden that accumulated around and over the souterrain is likely to have been broadly contemporary with its use and was radiocarbon dated to the period 183 cal BC to cal AD 224.

The economy of this farmstead was based primarily upon breeding cattle, sheep and pigs, and deer were hunted, but, as in earlier times, the food resources of the nearby sea were largely ignored (apart from one large pile of winkle shells in the midden) (Chapters 7 and 9). As Dale Serjeantson concludes in Chapter 7, the pattern of animal husbandry in Islay in prehistoric as in historic times was one in which cattle were raised for milk, while sheep were the main meat animals and pigs were kept only in small numbers. The high proportion of red deer in both the Early Bronze Age and Middle Iron Age assemblages is difficult to explain in an island context (Chapter 7). Three fragments of worked antler were found, but there were no finished antler artefacts. Birch dominated the charcoal samples (Chapter 8), which suggests that the formerly diverse scrub had diminished over centuries of cultivation of the peninsula. Pottery was scarce, undecorated and crudely made (Chapter 3).

The cultivation traces in trench L2 were unfortunately not closely datable, other than being later than the Late Bronze Age/Early Iron Age occupation below, but it is possible that they represent cultivation associated with the house of Phase 4.1. The spade-dug furrows may be compared with those found at the Ardnave 2 site (Ritchie & Welfare 1983, 315–16), where the last phase of cultivation was thought likely to have taken place in the 4th or early 5th centuries AD. One individual spade-mark was recognized at Ardnave, which indicated a blade up to 250mm in width and was therefore comparable to the Kilellan evidence for a blade about 200mm wide. Ard-marks at Cùl a'Bhaile, Jura, preceded a farmstead of the late second/early first millennia BC (Stevenson 1984, 137–8), and cultivation and field banks at An Sithean, Islay, were broadly contemporary (Barber & Brown 1984). The ard-marks and spade-marks at Kilellan are unlikely to date much later than the occupation layer into which they penetrated, and the phase of cultivation that they represent was probably closer in date to those at An Sithean and Cùl a'Bhaile than to that at Ardnave 2.

The discovery of two souterrains at Kilellan suggests that this class of structure may be more common in Argyll than the current archaeological record indicates. One is known in the island of Coll and two in Tiree (RCAHMS 1980, nos 231–3), and there is a possible site in Kintyre (RCAHMS 1971, no 378). In Islay, a possible souterrain has been excavated at Finlaggan (David Caldwell pers comm). These are outliers of a western group of souterrains that is concentrated in Skye and the Western Isles (Miket 2002). Apart from the very large souterrains of Angus and Perthshire, which are likely to have had a special function in helping to feed the Roman army (Macinnes 1984, 245; Armit 1999, 593), Scottish souterrains tend to be small and were probably used for multiple purposes that included food storage (Pollock 1992, 158; Miket 2002, 82–5). The overall length of the Kilellan souterrains is uncertain: that in trench L2 was more than 5m long, while that in trenches J1–2 and K3 may have been up to 15m long. The earlier of the two, 118 in L2, was 0.6m to 1.0m wide and 1.0m deep, whereas the later souterrain, 110 in J/K, was 1.0m wide and 0.8m deep, and both were lined with stone. In comparison, the souterrains of Coll and Tiree to the north-west of Islay appear to have been somewhat larger (up to 1.6m wide and 1.7m deep and 15m long) and to have had passages leading to slightly wider chambers, all built in stone and predominantly with stone lintels forming the roofs. Dating evidence is scarce, but excavation of the souterrain at Arnabost, Coll, in 1896 yielded a bronze dress-pin, and previously two blue glass beads had been found (RCAHMS 1980, no 231), all of which suggest activity on the site in the period 7th–10th centuries AD.

The occupation to which the souterrain in trench L2 belonged has been radiocarbon dated to the period 828–412 cal BC, thereby extending backwards the known scientific chronology for Scottish souterrains (Miket 2002, 81–2). Souterrains and crannogs are common both in Scotland and, even more plentifully, in Ireland. In both cases, the radiocarbon and conventional dates for the Scottish examples show that they were in use in Scotland considerably earlier than in Ireland (Crone 1993; Warner 1979).

PHASE 5
EARLY HISTORIC ACTIVITY

The finds of Early Historic date from Kilellan (Chapter 6, nos 1, 2, 5 and 15) fit well with the evidence for an Early Christian presence in the area (Chapter 1). In particular, worshippers walking or riding northwards from Kilnave, where a prayer cross was set up in the 8th century AD and where there may have been a contemporary church (probably beneath the extant ruins of the late medieval chapel), would have passed by the Kilellan site. They would have been on their way to Ardnave Point, whence a boat could be taken across to Nave Island. A fragment survives of another 8th-century cross on Nave Island, associated with an ovoid enclosure of early appearance (Fisher 2001, 4, 10, 16, 140). It is likely that there was settlement in the Ardnave area at this period, and it may be noted that the fall of the burn draining from Ardnave Loch to Loch Gruinart is such that the water could have powered a small horizontal mill of the type known to have been in use at this period. The fact that most of the artefacts of Early Historic date from Kilellan were found within one small part of trench K3 suggests that there may have been a settlement here, of which hearth 110 is the only structural trace surviving within the excavated area. The silver pin set with garnets (no 1) appears to show cultural links with Anglo-Saxon England, although its manufacture is likely to have been relatively local, and it is a prestigious and costly item of personal adornment. Its presence at Kilellan suggests that there may have been a settlement of high social status close by.

PHASE 6
LATER ACTIVITIES

The grid of U-shaped slots found in trenches K1–2 may have been associated with the fishing industry of recent centuries. The remains of a 19th-century fishing station exist to the north of Kilellan at Sgeir Liath, and the station is marked on the second edition Ordnance Survey 25-inch map of 1899, but nothing was recorded at Kilellan other than the farm itself on either the second edition or the first edition of 1880. The latter records saltings at Tayvallin, close to Kilellan, which suggests fishing and salting fish on a commercial scale, and dry-curing on wooden racks may also have been carried out. A grid can be seen on air-photographs of Kilellan taken in April 1956, which seems to correlate with the bedding trenches excavated (copies of these photographs are in the excavation archive).

Appendix 1

History of excavations at Kilellan Farm, Islay

STEPHEN SPEAK

Hints of a prehistoric settlement site in the general area of Kilellan Farm were forthcoming from casual finds recovered over the years, some definitely from Kilellan (*Proc Soc Antiq Scot*, 86 (1951–2), 210; 80 (1958–9), 120), others with a more general provenance somewhere in the Loch Gruinart area (*Proc Soc Antiq Scot*, 85 (1950–1), 9; 92 (1945–6), 151). Individual attention to Kilellan was first initiated by Robert B K Stevenson of the National Museum of Antiquities of Scotland, who urged an amateur enthusiast, James Whittaker, to investigate the area around Tobar Neill Neonaich ('the well of Neil the Curious'), the area around which most of the casual finds had been reported.

Whittaker was a singular and determined character, intensely proud of his childhood on Islay. Although he owned five publishing houses he was never financially well off, but he returned to Islay whenever his limited resources allowed. He was always immeasurably impressed with the archaeological potential of Islay and equally appalled at the lack of interest displayed in the island by the archaeologists of his day, particularly as Islay has always been one of the easiest of the Inner Hebrides to reach. He pursued relentlessly the task set him by Stevenson of investigating the Kilellan area, and the list of people he contacted or consulted over the site and its finds reads as a veritable who's who of archaeologists: Sir Mortimer Wheeler, Sir Leonard Woolley, Sir Ian Richmond, Stuart Piggott, V Gordon Childe and A D Lacaille are amongst the notables, with several lesser lights involved as well.

Aside from his surface collections at Kilellan, Whittaker excavated two small trial trenches at the site in 1954 and 1956, from which he derived a reasonably accurate overall stratigraphy, and recovered sufficient decorated and plain sherds and flintwork to identify the site tentatively as belonging to the Early Bronze Age. Whittaker was never a trained excavator, but he pursued his digging not only with his personal brand of enthusiasm but also with a diligent regard for his recording. He also persuaded the farmer, Sandy Maclellan, to desist from his occasional 'treasure-hunting' activities on the site and to part with a number of finds he had made over the years which, with the typical canniness of the native Ileachs, he had hidden behind stones in field-walls or within barns. He also managed to dissuade him (temporarily) from burying his dead stock within the confines of the site.

Upon his sudden if not altogether unexpected death in 1957 at the age of 51, the site became one of the projects of the newly-formed Thames Basin Archaeological Observers Group (a number of whom formed the Islay Archaeological Survey Group), who published in 1959 the *Preliminary Handbook to the Archaeology of Islay*. Work on the site involved surface collection and the preparation of a plan of the now seriously eroded sand-bunker area containing the site. In the late 1950s small trial trenches were excavated under the direction of Francis Celoria (1959, 1960), supervised by Susannah Pearce. After her departure to South Africa in 1961, Colin Burgess continued excavation of the site during that year. These three seasons of excavation indicated that Whittaker's assessment of the area was fully justified, and that despite the attention the site had received almost non-stop from the early 1950s a major excavation was clearly needed. This was not possible until 1973 when Burgess returned to the site with a large team (up to 40 members), mostly from another organization, the Northumberland Archaeological Group. Excavation and survey during the 1973 season revealed two aspects of the site, whilst confirming its Early Bronze Age character: that the machair sands over the site covered a far larger settlement than had previously been envisaged, and that the site was now very seriously threatened by intensive corridor erosion. In fact only half of the area protected by machair in 1961 still survived in 1975, and with this in mind a final season of excavation was mounted in 1976, again under the auspices of the Northumberland Archaeological Group. This had been formed specially for funding and carrying out the excavations for Colin Burgess's extra-mural students at the University of Newcastle. Subsequent to the 1976 season further erosion over the Kilellan site has taken place, and eventually it will disappear, leaving only scattered stones and spreads of pottery as a poignant reminder of its existence – other sites investigated in the Ardnave peninsula during 1976 had already reached this unhappy state (Ritchie & Welfare 1983) and many others must have been totally lost before being recorded.

Appendix 2

Analysis of unusual bone pins from Kilellan Farm, Islay, and MacArthur Cave, Oban

FRASER HUNTER

During the course of various projects underway in the Artefact Research Unit, questions arose concerning the identification of some unusual pin fragments. The problem stemmed from the identification of the material used, since it was deep black and jet-like in appearance. Given that there are no known examples of pins of jet-like material in Scotland, non-destructive surface analysis by X-ray fluorescence was vital to establish their true nature.

METHOD

The objects examined were: a highly-polished point from MacArthur Cave, Oban (NMS HL 28) and fragments of a pin with a rectangular faceted head from Kilellan Farm, Islay (Chapter 6, no 6). The area to be analysed was swabbed in industrial methylated spirits to remove any surface contamination. Spectra were collected in air for 200 live seconds, at an accelerating voltage of 46kV to a rhodium target and a tube current of 30mA. The spectra were collected by a multi-channel analyser and analysed on an IBM-compatible computer. A single spectrum was run for the MacArthur Cave point, while all the Kilellan fragments were analysed, with some replicate analyses.

RESULTS

All spectra showed a similar pattern of very high calcium levels, high strontium and a range of minor elements such as manganese, iron and zinc. This is consistent with the objects being of skeletal origin rather than any known jet-like material.

DISCUSSION

The black colour must derive from charring or burning the bone. The evenness of the finish is noteworthy: although an area of the head of the Kilellan pin is white, the regularity of colour is otherwise remarkable. Given the normal variation in colour of partially cremated bone, the even colour of these artefacts suggests that the blackening was a deliberate decorative effect. NMS collections include a single further example of blackened bone, from cave 1 at Archerfield, East Lothian (NMS HM 11; Cree 1909, 254, fig 5.2).

In date these objects seem to be Iron Age. The datable material from Archerfield is Roman Iron Age, while recent work has shown the multi-period nature of the Oban Cave deposits and revealed an Iron Age phase in at least some of them, including MacArthur Cave (Saville & Hallén 1994). The Kilellan example is the most intact specimen, and its rectangular faceted head is unusual for the native Scottish Iron Age but is well-known in Roman jet and shale pins (eg Allason-Jones & Miket 1984, nos 7.199, 7.201; Crummy 1983, fig 24). It is possible that at least some of these blackened bone pins are not simple decorative variants but are deliberate skeuomorphs of Roman jet pins.

Appendix 3

Analysis of a silver and garnet pin from Kilellan Farm, Islay

PAUL WILTHEW

The pin (Chapter 6, no 1; illus 90) was originally identified as copper alloy, and it was submitted for analysis because during conservation by Tom Bryce it became clear that the alloy was almost certainly a white metal. The alloy was identified by energy dispersive X-ray fluorescence (XRF) and the microstructure of the metal examined using scanning electron microscopy (SEM). The two hemispherical stones mounted in the head of the pin were analysed using SEM based energy dispersive microanalysis (SEM–EDX) and were identified by Brian Jackson of the Department of Geology.

ANALYTICAL METHODS

No preparation of the surface of the object was carried out prior to any of the analyses or examinations. All results were therefore qualitative, but they allowed the principal questions to be answered.

Energy dispersive X-ray fluorescence

The analysed areas were irradiated with a primary X-ray beam produced by a Rhodium target X-ray tube run at 46KV with an anode current of 0.30mA.

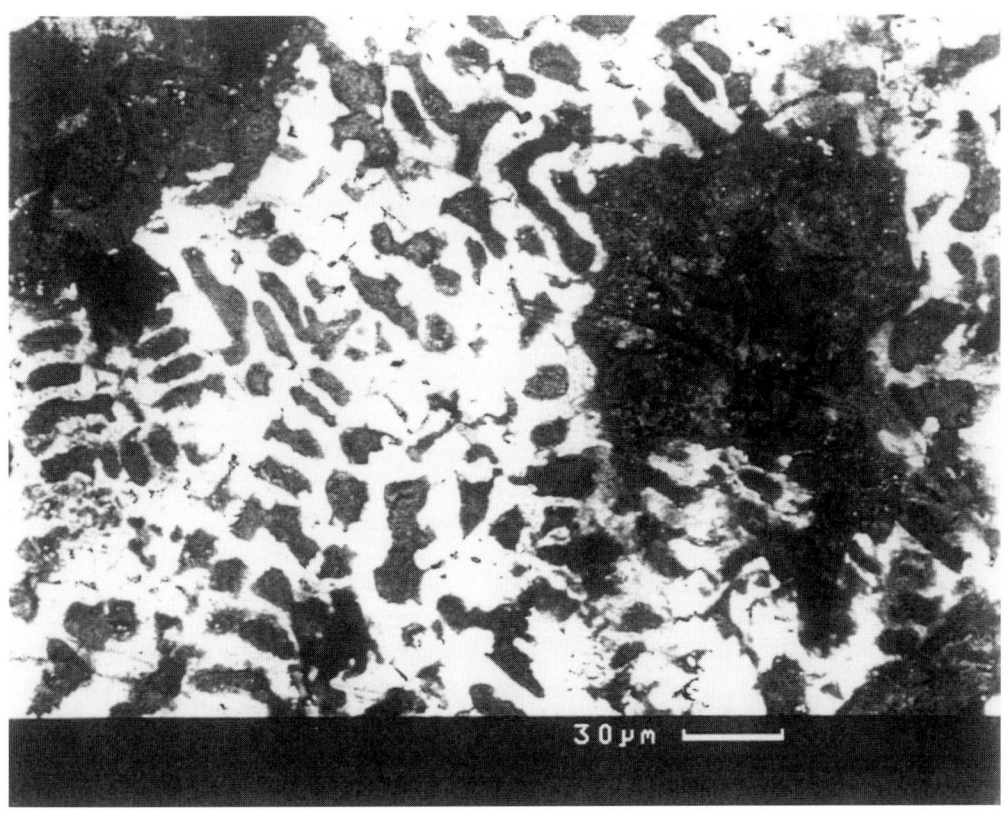

100 Back scattered electron image of the surface of the silver pin no 1, showing grey copper dendrites in lighter silver-copper eutectic matrix. The large irregular grey areas are corrosion products.

The primary beam was collimated to give an elliptical irradiated area about 1.5mm × 1mm. Secondary X-rays were detected using a silicon (lithium) solid state detector.

The path between the sample and detector is through air which limits the range of detectable elements to those of atomic number 20 or above. The detection limit varies for different elements and according to the matrix composition but is typically between about 0.05 and 0.2.

SEM-EDX

A Link Systems AN10000 system attached to a Camscan Series 4 scanning electron microscope was used to carry out the analyses. The microscope was operated at an accelerating voltage of 20kV with the object at the optimum working distance of 30mm giving a take-off angle to the silicon (lithium) detector of 30 degrees, assuming that the surface being analysed was horizontal. The detector was used with the beryllium window in place.

Examination of the microstructure was carried out using back scattered electron (BSD) imaging on the SEM. This gives an image in which contrast is principally due to variations in mean atomic number in different areas.

RESULTS AND DISCUSSION

1 Metal

XRF analysis showed the metal to be silver and copper rich, with zinc, gold and lead also present (spectrum F4504B). This confirmed that the pin was (debased) silver rather than a copper alloy. BSD examination showed that the microstructure consisted of copper dendrites in a silver-copper eutectic matrix (illus 99). For copper dendrites to be produced the concentration of copper (assuming a simple binary silver-copper alloy) must exceed 28%. The observed microstructure suggests that the copper concentration was in fact considerably greater than 28%, although an accurate quantitative analysis could not be carried out non-destructively. The silver was certainly heavily debased. The microstructure did not appear to be significantly distorted, which suggests that the pin was cast.

2 Stones

The more complete stone was analysed by SEM-EDX and the major elements present were found to be silicon, aluminium, iron and magnesium with minor amounts of other elements such as calcium and copper. The stones were submitted to Brian Jackson for identification:

Less complete stone

The stone exhibited an absorption spectrum characteristic of almandine garnet, namely a broad absorption band at the blue/green boundary, a second broad absorption band in the near green and a third absorption band in the yellow. This stone contained natural 'silk' inclusions, which are often seen in garnets. I would have expected these inclusions to be less planar, thereby indicating their alignment to the dodecahedral faces of the common crystallographic form for garnet.

More complete stone

This stone contained natural inclusions namely tubes (probably liquid filled) and opaque black coloured crystals. No absorption spectrum was seen. The chemistry is however consistent with that of a garnet in the pyralspite series. The magnesium content suggests a significant pyrope proportion though it is likely that the major proportion is that of almandine garnet despite the lack of a confirmatory spectrum.

Following this identification, the chemistry of the less complete stone was checked by SEM-EDX and found to be similar to that of the other stone.

CONCLUSION

The pin was found to consist of silver heavily debased with copper (zinc, gold and lead were also detected), rather than copper alloy as originally identified. SEM examination of the as-received surface revealed a microstructure consisting of copper dendrites in a silver-copper eutectic matrix. The structure was not significantly distorted and it is concluded that the pin was cast. The two jewels mounted in the head of the pin were identified as garnet, principally almandine but including a significant pyrope proportion. The chemistry of the garnet is consistent with that of garnets from metamorphic terrains. Although garnetiferous metamorphic rocks occur in Argyll, it is not possible, without extensive analyses for comparison, to say whether or not Argyll is the source of the Kilellan garnet.

Appendix 4

Plant remains from the peat deposit on the raised beach at Kilellan Farm, Islay

ROBERT LORD, ELAINE MATHESON and NICOLA WILLIAMS

The deposit (H1, 8) is dark brown in colour, highly compacted and without free water, although deposits, both organic and inorganic, commonly have a high initial water content. The deposit shelved gently with the pebbles of the raised beach and at its thickest in this excavation contained what is best described as a main vegetation layer 0.25–0.50m in thickness, in which the proportion of organic material to matrix silt is high and silica content fairly low. Towards the base of this layer stratification was present in wide bands (approx 30mm thick), but they were neither continuous nor easily discernible. There was no distinct layering as such, and any colour change was very gradual. Also towards the base of this layer the organic material to matrix silt ratio decreased and siliceous material in the form of sand grains proportionally increased. Below the main vegetation layer, a wet orange-brown deposit was present but again was not continuous up the beach, where the whole deposit was at its thinnest. Here the main vegetation layer was replaced by a faintly layered clay/sand mix.

A large sample of the material (25kg) has been examined and because of its highly compact nature caused considerable problems in the extraction of remains. The material was soaked in water, boiled in a commercial water softener, washed, warmed in 10% potassium hydroxide, washed, sieved and the products sorted. The remains are only fragmentary. No whole specimens of flowers or leaves have been found and only small pieces of woody stem have come out, the largest measuring approximately 25mm in diameter and 150mm in length, none showing any sign of having been cut or worked. Thin sections revealed *Betula* sp. (tree birch), *Alnus glutinosa* (alder) and *Salix* sp. (willow). The deposit is not wholly fibrous although a large amount of root material is mixed, with the subaerial woody remains. From the main vegetation layer has come a variety of identifiable higher plant remains including seeds, fruits, flower parts and, buds, mostly in a poor state of preservation, together with the heads, limbs, thoracic and abdominal segments of insects. The lower plant remains present include the stems, rhizomes and resting bodies of *Equisetum* sp. (horsetails), pinnules and sporangia of *Pteridium aquilinum* (bracken), various mosses and the black, dense and variably sized spores (or resting bodies) of the fungus type *Cenococcua*, of which neither the function status nor distribution are well known but such objects are present in most similar deposits.

List of plants from the main vegetation layer. Unless stated all identification is from seeds.

Viola palustris, L.	Marsh violet
Hypericum pulchrum, L.	Beautiful St John's wort
Lychnis flos-cuculi, L.	Ragged robin
Cerastium vulgatum, L.	Common Mouse-ear Chickweed
Rubus sp. (cf *fruticosus*, L.)	Bramble, blackberry
Potentilla erecta (L.) Raüschel	Common tormentil
P. palustris (L.) Scop.	Marsh cinquefoil
Hippuris vulgaris, L.	Mare's-tail
Hydrocotyle vulgaris, L.	Pennywort, white-rot
Betula sp.	Tree birch (wood)
Alnus glutinosa (L.) Gaertner	Alder (wood)
Ajuga reptans, L.	Bugle
Urtica dioica, L.	Stinging nettle
Cirsium sp. (cf *palustre* (L.) Scop.)	Marsh thistle
Potamogeton polygonifolius, Pourret	Bog pondweed
Juncus sp.	Rushes
Carex paniculata agg.	Sedge
Carex sp.	Sedge
Sparganium sp.	Bur-reed
Scirpus sp.	Club rush
Phragmites australis, (Cav.) Steudel	Common reed
Graminae	Grasses (seeds, culms and leaves)
Equisetum sp.	Horsetails (rhizomes and stems)

Pteridium aquilinum	Bracken (pinnae)
Sphagnum tenellum	Bog moss (stems, leaves)
Sphagnum sp.	Bog moss (stems, leaves)
Bryum sp.	Bog moss (stems, leaves)
Other mosses	(stems, leaves)
Cenococcum	(spores/resting bodies)

From the layer below the main vegetation layer extremely humified remains of *Sphagnum* sp. (von Post V/VI) have been found, along with *Cenococcum*. This layer is proportionally high in silt and fine silica grains constitute about 40% by volume.

The deposit appears to be a fen peat and all the species, with the exception of *Hypericun pulchrum*, *Rubus* sp. and *Urtica dioica*, are indicators of fresh water or fen conditions. The three exceptions are more commonly found in woodland clearings and margins or where, in the case of the latter, habitation has existed. The presence of *Hippuris vulgaris* and *Potamogeton* sp. suggests that standing fresh water was present for at least part of the year, but the number of seeds of these two species is very low and like the above may have been derived. The commonest seeds found were those of *Viola palustris*, *Ajuga reptans*, *Rubus* sp. and assorted grasses. The remains of *Pteridium aquilinum* were scattered throughout but the rhizomes and stems of *Equisetum* sp. were found *in situ* with swollen inter-nodes (resting bodies) on side branches. All the species are well distributed in Britain today.

References

Alcock, L 1993 *The neighbours of the Picts: Angles, Britons and Scots at war and at home*. Rosemarkie: Groam House Museum.

Alcock, L & Alcock, E 1980 'Scandinavian settlement in the Inner Hebrides: recent research on place-names and in the field', *Scot Archaeol Forum*, 10 (1978), 61–73.

Alexander, D 2002 'The oblong fort at Finavon, Angus: an example of the over-reliance on the appliance of science?', *in* Ballin Smith, B and Banks, I (eds) *In the Shadow of the Brochs. The Iron Age in Scotland*, 45–54. Stroud: Tempus.

Allason-Jones, L & Miket, R 1984 *The catalogue of small finds from South Shields Roman fort*. Newcastle: Society of Antiquaries of Newcastle.

Armit, I 1999 'The abandonment of souterrains: evolution, catastrophe or dislocation?', *Proc Soc Antiq Scot*, 129 (1999), 577–96.

Arnold, H R 1978 *Provisional Atlas of the Mammals of the British Isles*. Abbots Ripon: National Environment Research Council.

Ashmore, P 1997 'Radiocarbon dates from archaeological sites in Argyll and Arran', *in* Ritchie 1997, 236–83.

Ballin Smith, B 1994 *Howe: four millennia of Orkney prehistory*. (Soc Antiq Scot Monograph, no 9) Edinburgh.

Barber, J 1981 'Excavations on Iona, 1979', *Proc Soc Antiq Scot*, 111 (1981), 282–380.

Barber, J & Brown, M M 1985 'An Sithean, Islay', *Proc Soc Antiq Scot*, 114 (1984), 161–88.

Barrett, J 1991 'Bronze Age pottery and the problem of classification', *in* Barrett, J, Bradley, R & Hall, M (eds), *Papers on the Prehistoric Archaeology of Cranborne Chase*, 201–30. (Oxbow Monograph, no 11) Oxford.

Batey, C 1990 'A Pictish pin from Machrihanish, Kintyre', *Glasgow Archaeol J*, 16 (1989–90), 86–7.

Benson, D G, Evans, J G, Williams, G H, Darvill, T and David, A 1990 'Excavations at Stackpole Warren, Dyfed', *Proc Prehist Soc*, 56 (1990), 179–245.

Birks, H J B 1989 'Holocene isochrone maps and patterns of tree-spreading in the British Isles', *Journal of Biogeography*, 16 (1989), 503–40.

Bonsall, C 1988 'Morton and Lussa Wood, the case for early Flandrian settlement of Scotland: comment on Myers', *Scot Archaeol Rev*, 5 (1988), 30–3.

Brézillon, M 1983 *La Dénomination des Objets de Pierre Taillée*. Paris: Centre National de la Recherche Scientifique.

Burgess, C 1976 'An early bronze age settlement at Kilellan Farm, Islay, Argyll', *in* Burgess & Miket 1976, 181–207.

Burgess, C 1980 *The Age of Stonehenge*. London: J M Dent & Sons Ltd.

Burgess, C & Miket, R F (eds) 1976 *Settlement and Economy in the Third and Second Millennia B.C.* (Brit Archaeol Rep, Brit Ser, no 33) Oxford.

Campbell, E 1998 'Metal pins', *in* Sharples, N *Scalloway: a broch, Late Iron Age settlement and medieval cemetery in Shetland*, 168–71. (Oxbow Monograph, no 82) Oxford.

Childe, V G 1935 'Excavation of the vitrified fort of Finavon, Angus', *Proc Soc Antiq Scot*, 69 (1934–5), 49–80.

Clark, J G D 1932 'The date of the plano-convex flint knife in England and Wales', *Antiq J*, 12 (1932), 158–62.

Clarke, A 1989 'The flaked lithics', *in* McCullagh 1989, 32–7.

Clarke, A 1990 'Coarse stone tools', *in* Wickham-Jones 1990, 117–26.

Close-Brooks, J 1986 'Excavations at Clatchard Craig, Fife', *Proc Soc Antiq Scot*, 116 (1986), 117–64.

Cool, H E M 1982 'The artefact record: some possibilities', *in* Harding, D (ed) *Later Prehistoric Settlement in South-East Scotland*, 92–100 (Univ Edinburgh Dept Archaeol Occas Paper, no 8) Edinburgh.

Cowie, T G 1978 *Bronze Age food vessel urns*. (Brit Archaeol Rep, Brit Ser, no 55) Oxford.

Cowie, T G 1983 'Pottery: discussion', *in* Ritchie & Welfare 1983, 328–31.

Crawford, I A & Switsur, R 1977 'Sandscaping and C14: the Udal, North Uist', *Antiquity*, 51 (1977), 124–36.

Cree, J E 1909 'Notice of the excavation of two caves, with remains of Early Iron Age occupation, on the Estate of Archerfield, Dirleton', *Proc Soc Antiq Scot*, 43 (1908–9), 243–68.

Crone, B A 1993 'Crannogs and chronologies', *Proc Soc Antiq Scot*, 123 (1993), 245–54.

Crone, A 2000 *The history of a Scottish Lowland crannog: excavations at Buiston, Ayrshire 1989–90*. (Scottish Trust for Archaeological Research, Monograph, no 4) Edinburgh.

Crummy, N 1983 *The Roman small finds from excavations in Colchester 1971–9*. Colchester: Colchester Archaeological Trust.

Dawson, A G 1984 'Quaternary sea-level changes in western Scotland', *Quat Sci Rev*, 3 (1984), 345–68.

Dawson, S & Dawson, A 2000 'Late Pleistocene and Holocene relative sea-level changes in Gruinart, Isle of Islay', *in* Mithen 2000a, 99–114.

Dickson, C 1983 'Fruits, seeds and charcoal from Ardnave, Islay', *in* Ritchie & Welfare 1983, 358–60.

Finlay, J I 1983 *Faunal evidence for prehistoric economy and settlement in the Outer Hebrides to c 400AD*. Unpublished PhD dissertation, University of Edinburgh.

Finlay, N, Finlayson, B & Mithen, S 2000 'The secondary technology: its character and inter-site variability', *in* Mithen 2000a, 571–87.

Fisher, I 2001 *Early Medieval Sculpture in the West Highlands and Islands*. Edinburgh: Society of Antiquaries of Scotland/Royal Commission on the Ancient and Historical Monuments of Scotland.

Gibson, A 1982 *Beaker Domestic Sites*. (Brit Archael Rep, Brit Ser, no 107) Oxford.

Gibson, A & Woods, A 1990 *Prehistoric Pottery for the Archaeologist*. Leicester.

Gibson, A 1995 'The Neolithic pottery from Allt Chrisal', *in* Branigan, K & Foster, P (eds), *Barra: Archaeological Research on Ben Tangaval*, 100–15. Sheffield: Sheffield Academic Press.

Gibson, A 2003 'What do we mean by Neolithic Settlement? Some approaches, 10 years on', *in* Armit, I, Nelis, E M E & Simpson, D (eds) *Neolithic settlement in Ireland and Western Britain*, 136–45. Oxford: Oxbow Books.

Grant, A 1982. 'The use of tooth wear as a guide to the age of domestic ungulates', *in* Wilson, B, Grigson, C & Payne, S *Ageing and Sexing Animal Bones from Archaeological Sites*, 91–108. (Brit Archaeol Rep, Brit Ser, no 109) Oxford.

Green, S 1984 'Flint arrowheads: typology and interpretation', *Lithics* 5 (1984), 19–39.

Grigson, C 1981 'Mammals and man on Oronsay', *in* Brothwell, D & Dimbleby, G (eds) *Environmental Aspects of Coasts & Islands*, 163–90. (Brit Archaeol Rep, Int Ser, no 94) Oxford.

Grigson, C & Mellars, P A 1987 'The mammalian remains from the middens', *in* Mellars 1987, 243–89.

Guido, M 1978 *The glass beads of the prehistoric and Roman periods in Britain and Ireland*. (Report of the Research Committee Society of Antiquaries of London, no 35) London.

Guido, M 2000 'Beads', *in* Lane & Campbell 2000, 175–7.

Hamilton, J R C 1956 *Excavations at Jarlshof, Shetland*. Edinburgh: HMSO.

Harman, M 1983 'Animal remains from Ardnave, Islay', *in* Ritchie & Welfare 1983, 343–50.

Hawkes, C 1981 'Alcoholic food vessels', *Current Archaeol*, 79 (1981), 255.

Hencken, H 1951 'Lagore crannog: an Irish royal residence of the 7th to 10th centuries AD', *Proc Royal Irish Acad*, C, 53 (1950–1), 1–247.

Henshall, A S 1972 *The Chambered Tombs of Scotland, vol. 2*. Edinburgh.

Higgs, E H & Vita-Finzi, C 1975 'Site catchment analysis: a concise guide to field methods', *in* Higgs, E S (ed), *Palaeoeconomy*. Cambridge.

Hirons, K 1990 'The postglacial environment', *in* Wickham-Jones 1990, 137–43.

Humphrey, J 2003 'The utilization and technology of flint in the British Iron Age', *in* Humphrey, J (ed) *Researching the Iron Age*, 17–23. Leicester: University of Leicester, School of Archaeology and History (Leicester Archaeology Monograph 11).

Hunter, F J, McDonnell, J G, Pollard, A M, Morris, C R & Rowlands, C C 1993 'The scientific identification of archaeological jet-like artefacts', *Archaeometry*, 35 (1993), 69–89.

Inizan, M-L, Reduron-Ballinger, M, Roche, H & Tixier, J 1999 *Technology and Terminology of Knapped Stone*. Nanterre: Cercle de Recherches et d'Etudes Préhistoriques.

Islay Archaeological Survey Group 1960 *Preliminary handbook to the archaeology of Islay*.

Jardine, W G 1987 'The mesolithic coastal setting', *in* Mellars 1987, 25–51.

Kavanagh, R M 1973 'The encrusted urn in Ireland', *Proc Royal Irish Acad*, C, 73 (1973), 507–617.

Kavanagh, R M 1977 'Pygmy cups in Ireland', *J Royal Soc Antiq Ireland*, 107 (1977), 61–95.

Kinnes, I, Gibson, A, Ambers, J, Bowman, S, Leese, M & Boast, R 1991 'Radiocarbon dating and British beakers: the British Museum programme', *Scot Archaeol Rev*, 8 (1991), 35–68.

Kitson Clark, M 1937 'The Yorkshire Food-Vessel', *Archaeol J*, 94 (1937), 43–63.

Lane, A 1990 'Hebridean pottery: problems of definition, chronology, presence and absence' *in* Armit, I (ed), *Beyond the Brochs: Changing Perspectives on the Later Iron Age in Atlantic Scotland*, 108–30. Edinburgh: Edinburgh University Press.

Lane, A & Campbell, E 2000 *Dunadd: an early Dalriadic capital*. Oxford: Oxbow Books.

Legge, A J 1981 'The Agricultural Economy', *in* Mercer, R J *Grimes Graves, Norfolk. Excavations 1971–2*, 79–103. (Dept Environment Archaeol Report, no 11) London.

Legge, A J 1992 *Excavations at Grimes Graves, Norfolk 1972–1976: the Bronze Age, Fascicule 4: Animals, Environment and the Bronze Age economy*. London: British Museum Press.

Leitch, R 1990 ' "Here chapman billies tak their stand": a pilot study of Scottish chapmen, packmen and pedlars', *Proc Soc Antiq Scot*, 120 (1990), 173–88.

Liversage, G D 1968 'Excavations at Dalkey Island, Co. Dublin, 1956–59', *Proc Royal Irish Acad, C*, 66 (1968), 53–233.

Longworth, I H 1967 'Further discoveries at Brackmont Mill, Brackmont Farm and Tentsmuir, Fife', *Proc Soc Antiq Scot*, 99 (1966–7), 60–92.

Lucas, A T 1989 *Cattle in Ancient Ireland*. Kilkenny.

McCormick, F 1981 'The animal bones from ditch 1', *in* Barber 1981, 313–18.

McCormick, F 1992 'Early faunal evidence for dairying', *Oxford J Archaeol*, 11, 2 (1992), 201–9.

McCullagh, R 1989 'Excavation at Newton, Islay', *Glasgow Archaeol J*, 15 (1988–89), 23–51.

MacDonald, J 1811 *General View of the Agriculture of the Hebrides*.

MacGregor, A 1974 'The Broch of Burrian, North Ronaldsay, Orkney', *Proc Soc Antiq Scot*, 105 (1973–4), 63–118.

MacKie, E W 1969 'Radiocarbon dates and the Scottish Iron Age', *Antiquity*, 43 (1969), 15–26.

MacKie, E W 1974 *Dun Mor Vaul, an Iron Age Broch on Tiree*. Glasgow: University of Glasgow Press.

Maltman, A, Elliott, R, Muir, R & Fitches, B 1990 *A guide to the geology of Islay*. Aberystwyth: Institute of Earth Studies, University College of Wales.

Marshall, G 2000a 'The distribution and character of flint beach pebbles on Islay as a source for Mesolithic chipped stone artefact production', *in* Mithen 2000a, 79–90.

Marshall, G 2000b 'The distribution of beach pebble flint in western Scotland with reference to raw material use during the Mesolithic', *in* Mithen 2000a, 75–7.

Martin, M 1716 *A Description of the Western Isles of Scotland*. Facsimile 1970, Edinburgh.

Meaney, A L & Hawkes, S C 1970 *Two Anglo-Saxon cemeteries at Winnall*, London. (Soc Medieval Archaeol Monograph, no 4) London.

Mellars, P A (ed) 1987 *Excavations on Oronsay: prehistoric human ecology on a small island*. Edinburgh: Edinburgh University Press.

Mercer, J 1980 'Lussa Wood I: the late glacial and early post-glacial occupation of Jura', *Proc Soc Antiq Scot*, 110 (1979–80), 1–31.

Miket, R 2002 'The souterrains of Skye', *in* Ballin Smith, B & Banks, I (eds) *In the Shadow of the Brochs: the Iron Age in Scotland*, 77–110. Stroud: Tempus Publishing Ltd.

Mithen, S (ed) 2000a *Hunter-gatherer Landscape Archaeology: the Southern Hebrides Mesolithic Project 1988–98*. Cambridge: McDonald Institute Monographs.

Mithen, S 2000b 'The Mesolithic in the Southern Hebrides: issues of colonization, settlement and the transitions to the Neolithic and farming', *in* Mithen 2000a, 597–626.

Mithen, S & Finlayson, B 2000 'Gleann Mor, Islay: test-pit survey and trial excavation', *in* Mithen 2000a, 187–205.

Mithen, S, Finlayson, B, Mathews, M & Woodman, P E 2000a 'The Islay survey', *in* Mithen 2000a, 153–86.

Mithen, S, Woodman, P E, Finlay, N & Finlayson, B 2000b 'Aoradh, Islay: test-pit survey and trial excavation', *in* Mithen 2000a, 231–40.

Moore, H & Wilson, G 2003 *Report on a Coastal Zone Assessment Survey of Islay*. Historic Scotland archive report, Edinburgh.

Morrison, A 1968 'Cinerary Urns and Pygmy Vessels in South-West Scotland', *Trans Dumfriesshire Galloway Natur Hist Antiq Soc*, 45 (1968), 80–140.

Morton, J K 1959 'The Flora of Islay and Jura,' *Supplement to the Botanical Society of the British Isles Proceedings*, 3 (1959), Part 3, 1–59.

Needham, S P & Sørensen, M L S 1988 'Runnymede refuse tip: a consideration of midden deposits and their formation', *in* Barrett, J C & Kinnes, I A (eds) *The archaeology of context in the neolithic and bronze age: recent trends*, 113–26. Sheffield: Department of Archaeology, University of Sheffield.

Needham, S and Spence, T 1996 *Refuse and disposal at Area 16 East, Runnymede. (Runnymede Bridge Research Excavations, vol. 2)*. London: British Museum Press.

Noddle, B A 1980 'Animal bone from Dun Cul Bhuirg', *in* Ritchie & Lane 1980, 225–7.

Noddle, B A 1981 'A comparison of mammalian bones found in the "Midden Deposit" with others from the Iron Age site of Dun Bhuirg', *in* Reece, R *Excavations in Iona 1964–1974*, 38–50. (Inst Archaeol Occas Publ, no 5) London.

O'Riordain, B & Waddell, J 1993 *The Funerary Bowls and Vases of the Irish Bronze Age*. Galway: Galway University Press for the National Museum of Ireland.

Orton, C, Tyers, P & Vince, A (eds) 1993 *Pottery in Archaeology*. Cambridge: Cambridge University Press (*Cambridge manuals in archaeology*).

PCRG 1992 Prehistoric Ceramics Research Group *The study of later prehistoric pottery: guidelines for analysis and publication*. (PCRG Occas Paper, no 2) Oxford.

Peltenburg, E J 1982 'Excavations at Balloch Hill, Argyll', *Proc Soc Antiq Scot*, 112 (1982), 142–214.

Pierpoint, S 1980 *Social Patterns in Yorkshire Prehistory 3500–750 B.C.* (Brit Archaeol Rep, Brit Ser, no 74) Oxford.

Piggott, S 1972 'Excavation of the Dalladies long barrow, Fettercairn, Kincardineshire', *Proc Soc Antiq Scot* 104 (1971–2), 23–47.

Pollock, R 1992 'The excavation of a souterrain and roundhouse at Cyderhall, Sutherland', *Proc Soc Antiq Scot*, 122 (1992), 149–60.

Rice, P M 1987 *Pottery Analysis*. Chicago and London: University of Chicago Press.

Ritchie, A 1977 'Excavations of Pictish and Viking farmsteads at Buckquoy, Orkney', *Proc Soc Antiq Scot*, 108 (1976–7), 174–227.

Ritchie, G & Crawford, J 1978 'Recent work on Coll and Skye: (i) Excavations at Sorisdale and Killunaig, Coll', *Proc Soc Antiq Scot*, 109 (1977–8), 75–84.

Ritchie, G & Welfare, H 1983 'Excavations at Ardnave, Islay', *Proc Soc Antiq Scot*, 113 (1983), 302–66.

Ritchie, J N G 1981 'Excavations at Machrins, Colonsay', *Proc Soc Antiq Scot*, 111 (1981), 263–81.

Ritchie, J N G & Lane, A M 1980 'Dun Cul Bhuirg, Iona', *Proc Soc Antiq Scot*, 110 (1978–80), 209–29.

Roe, F E S 1979 'Typology of stone implements with shaftholes', *in* Clough, T H McK & Cummins, W A (eds) *Stone Axe Studies*, 23–48. (CBA Research Report, no 3) London.

Ross, E B 1983 'The Riddle of the Scottish Pig', *BioScience*, 33 (2) (1983), 99–106.

Royal Commission on the Ancient and Historical Monuments of Scotland 1983 *Argyll: an inventory of the ancient monuments, vol. 5, Islay, Jura, Colonsay and Oronsay*. Edinburgh: HMSO.

Rye, O S 1981 *Pottery Technology, Principles and Reconstruction*. Washington.

Saville, A & Hallén, Y 1994 'The "Obanian Iron Age": human remains from the Oban cave sites, Argyll, Scotland', *Antiquity*, 68 (1994), 715–23.

Saville, A 2004 'The material culture of Mesolithic Scotland', *in* Saville (ed) 2004, 183–218.

Saville, A (ed) 2004 *Mesolithic Scotland and its Neighbours*. Edinburgh: Society of Antiquaries of Scotland.

Schiffer, M B 1990 'The influence of surface treatment on heating effectiveness of ceramic vessels', *J Archaeol Sci*, 17 (4) (1990), 373–82.

Serjeantson, D 1990 'The introduction of mammals to the Outer Hebrides and the role of boats in stock management', *Anthropozoologica* 13 (1990), 7–18.

Serjeantson, D 2005 'Archaeological records of a gadfly petrel *Pterodroma* sp. from Scotland in the first millennium AD', *Documenta Archaeobiologiae*: Yearbook of the State Collection of Anthropology and Palaeoanatomy, Munich, 2.

Serjeantson, D nd 1 'The mammal, bird and fish remains from Rosinish', *in* Shepherd, I A G, *Excavations at Rosinish, Benbecula*. Unpublished MS.

Serjeantson, D nd 2 *Mammal, bird and fish remains from the Udal (North), N Uist: interim report*. Unpublished MS.

Shepard, A O 1956 *Ceramics for the Archaeologist*. Washington DC.

Shepherd, I A G 1976 'Preliminary results from the Beaker settlement at Rosinish, Benbecula', *in* Burgess & Miket 1976, 209–19.

Shepherd, I A G & Tuckwell, A 1977 'Traces of Beaker period cultivation at Rosinish, Benbecula', *Proc Soc Antiq Scot*, 108 (1976–7), 108–13.

Shepherd, I A G 1986 *Powerful pots: beakers in northeast prehistory*. Aberdeen: Anthropological Museum University of Aberdeen.

Sheridan, A 1993 'The Manufacture, Production and Use of Irish Bowls and Vases', *in* O'Riordain, B & Waddell, J *The Funerary Bowls and Vases of the Irish Bronze Age*, 45–75. Galway: Galway University Press.

Sheridan, A 2003 'New dates for Scottish Bronze Age cinerary urns: results from the National Museums of Scotland Dating Cremated Bones Project', *in* Gibson, A, *Prehistoric Pottery. People, pattern and purpose*, 201–26. (Brit Archaeol Rep, Inter Ser, no 1156/ Prehistoric Ceramics Research Group: Occas Paper, no 4) Oxford.

Silver, I A 1969 'The ageing of domestic animals', *in* Brothwell, D & Higgs, E (eds) *Science in Archaeology*, 283–302. London.

Simonds, J B 1854 *The Age of the Ox, Sheep and Pig*. London: W S Orr.

Simpson, D D A 1976 'The later Neolithic and Beaker settlement at Northton, Isle of Harris', *in* Burgess & Miket 1976, 221–31.

Simpson, I A 1998 'Early land management at Tofts Ness, Sanday, Orkney: the evidence of thin section micromorphology', *in* Mills, C M & Coles, G (eds) *Life on the edge: Human settlement and marginality*, 90–8. (Oxbow Monograph, no 100) Oxford.

Stevenson, J B 1984 'The excavation of a hut-circle at Cùl a'Bhaile, Jura', *Proc Soc Antiq Scot*, 114 (1984), 127–60.

Stevenson, R B K 1953 'Prehistoric pot-building in Europe', *Man*, 97 (1953), 65–8.

Stevenson, R B K 1955 'Pins and the chronology of brochs', *Proc Prehist Soc*, 21 (1955), 282–94.

Tolan-Smith, C 2001 *The Caves of Mid Argyll: an archaeology of human use*. (Soc Antiq Scot Monograph, no 20) Edinburgh.

Tomalin, D J 1983 *British Biconical Urns: Their Character and Chronology and their Relationship with Indigenous Early Bronze Age Ceramics*. Unpublished PhD thesis, University of Southampton.

Topping, P G 1987 'Typology and chronology in the later prehistoric pottery assemblages of the Western Isles', *Proc Soc Antiq Scot*, 117 (1987), 67–84.

Waddell, J 1990 *The Bronze Age Burials of Ireland*. Galway: Galway University Press.

Walker, J 1812 *An Economic History of the Hebrides and Highlands of Scotland*. Edinburgh.

Wardle, P 1992 *Earlier Prehistoric Pottery Production and Ceramic Petrology in Britain*. (Brit Archaeol Rep, Brit Ser, no 225). Oxford.

Warner, R 1979 'The Irish souterrains and their background', *in* Crawford, H (ed) *Subterranean Britain: aspects of underground archaeology*, 100–44. London: John Baker.

Webster, L & Backhouse, J (eds) 1991 *The Making of England: Anglo-Saxon Art and Culture AD 600–900*. London: British Museum Press.

Wickham-Jones, C R 1990 *Rhum: mesolithic and later sites at Kinloch, excavations 1984–86*. (Soc Antiq Scot Monograph, no 7) Edinburgh.

Wickham-Jones, C R 1997 'The flaked stone', *in* Masters, L 'The excavation and restoration of the Camster Long chambered cairn, Caithness, Highland, 1967–80', *Proc Soc Antiq Scot*, 127 (1997), 160–71.

Wickham-Jones, C R 2004 'Structural evidence in the Scottish Mesolithic', *in* Saville (ed) 2004, 227–40.

Young, A 1951 'A Tripartite Bowl from Kintyre', *Proc Soc Antiq Scot*, 85 (1950–1), 38–51.

Young, A 1956 'Excavations at Dun Cuier, Isle of Barra', *Proc Soc Antiq Scot*, 89 (1955–6), 290–328.

Index

Page references in *italics* denote page numbers of illustrations.

Aberlemno, pottery from 77
agricultural activities, Kilellan Farm (*see also* animal bones, cereal etc) 37-8, 39, 41, *42*, 179
Allt Christal, Barra, vessel from 74
An Sithean 152, 179
Anglo-Saxon jewellery and Finlaggan disc-headed pin 144
Angus and Perth 180
animal bones, Kilellan Farm 45, 151-67, 178
   bird 158, 159, 164,
      petrel (*Pterodroma feae*) 158, 164
   cattle, 151-63, *165*, 166, 167, 178, 179
   fish 158, 166, 178
   hare 156, 158
   horse 158, 164
   pig 151, 153, 154, 158, 159, 160, 161-2, 164, 165, 166-7
   rabbit 156-7
   red deer 151, 153-9, 164-7, 179
   sheep 151-66, 178, 179
animal husbandry and environmental context, Kilellan Farm 151-67
antler 86, 179
   working 179
Archer, John xvi
Archerfield, East Lothian, bone from 183
ard marks, ploughmarks, spade marks and furrows, Kilellan Farm 37-8, 39, 41, *42* , 179
Ardnave peninsula and sites (excluding Kilellan Farm) xviii, 1, 3, 5, 178, 179, 180
   cereal cultivation 151, 159, 182
   charcoal from 170
   crannog, Ardnave Loch 3
   houses 177-8
   Iron Age pottery from 86
   disc-head pin from 144
   occupation deposits 177-8
   pottery from 74-6
   work by RCAHMS 3, 5, 177, 179
Arnabost, Coll, beads from 180
arrowheads
   barbed and tanged 13, 98, 117, *118*, 119, 123, 130
   leafshaped 13, 98, 117, *118*, 123, 130
Ashmore Patrick, xv, xvi, 5, 20,
Atkinson, James xv
Atkinson, Mona xv

balls, clay *146*, 149
   stone 149
Balloch Hill, Kintyre, pottery 85

Barrett, John xv, 77
Barrett, Kath xv
beads, glass 48, 146-7, 180
beaker pottery and Kilellan (*see also* pottery, Early Bronze Age) 74, 76, 178
bird remains, Kilellan Farm 158, 159, 164
   petrel (*Pterodroma feae*) 158, 164
blades, flint (*see also* flakes, edge trimmed and struck lithic artefacts) 97, 112, *116*, 123, 128
Boardman, Sheila xiii
   on the charcoal from Kilellan Farm 169-70
bone artefacts
   cetacean bone playing piece 146
   dress pin, Kilellan Farm 145-6
   mount 146
   peg 146
   pins, analysis of 183
   points 146
Bonsall, Clive xv
Booth, Gordon xv
Bowmore Distillery xv
Braby, Alan R xiii, xvi
Bracegirdle, Mark xvi
Bronze Age period *see under* Early Bronze Age and Late Bronze Age
bronze artefacts: dress-pin, loopheaded 47-8, 144, *145*
bronzeworking
   Jarlshof 179
   Kilellan Farm 36, 37, 178-9
   moulds 143-4, 178, 179
brooches: bow 3
Brough of Birsay, Orkney, disc-headed pin from 143
Broxmouth, pottery 85
Burgess, Colin, acknowledgements by xv
   and work at Kilellan Farm 3-5, 7, 9, 11, 47, 181-2
   on cattle and sheep 151
   on Early Bronze Age occupation 176
   on Early Bronze Age midden 17, *19*
   on flint flakes 105
   on Mesolithic activity 16
   on midden material 28
   on Middle Iron Age settlement 39
   on pottery 51, 55, 67, 70, 71, 73-4, 77, 85
Burghead, Moray, blast-horn mount 144
Butler, Jan xvi

Caldwell, David 175
Campbell, Euan, on Kilellan Farm disc-headed pin 144

cattle, Kilellan Farm 151–63, 165, 166, 167, 178, 179
cereal
   barley 151
   cultivation 151–3
   impression on pot 170
Celoria, Frances, work at Kilellan 3, 181
cetacean bone, playing piece, Kilellan Farm 146
chalcedony 48
Chapman, Colin xv
charcoal, Kilellan Farm 29, 39, 44, 169–70, 178, 179
Childe, VG and Kilellan Farm 181
   on Finavon 85
cists, Ardnave Peninsula 3
Clark, Ann xiii
   on coarse stone artefacts, Kilellan Farm 133–41
Clarke, David V xv
clay
   ball *146*, 149
   daub 49, 71
   floor 29–30
Close-Brooks, Joanna xv
coarse stone artefacts 133–41
   cobbles 133–6, 138
   grinders/grinding slabs 133, 135, 139–40, 141
   hammerstones, faceted 133, 135, 136–8
   pebble hammers 133, 134, *136*, 138–9, 141
   pebbles, bevelled 133, 134–5, 138
      pecked, Mesolithic 16
   polishers 133
   querns, saddle 140
cobbles 133–6, 138
Cockburn, H xv
Cohen, Alan xvi
Cohen, Bernice xvi
Coll, Isle of, pottery from 77
   souterrains 179, 180
Cook, Gordon xvi, 20
copper alloy artefacts
   dress-pin, loopheaded, Kilellan Farm 47, 144, *145*
cores, flint, and core fragments 16, 97, 99, 100–5, *106*, 112, 123, 124, 127–8, 131, 132
Cowie, Rosemary xiii, xvi
   on the pottery from Kilellan Farm 49–96
Cowie, Trevor xv
   on Ardnave pottery 76
crannogs 3, 180
Crawford, T xv
crosses, high xvii, 3, 180
Cruach Mhor, Islay, pottery from 77
Cul a'Bhaile, Jura 179
cultivation, *see also* agricultural activities, ard marks etc 179
   of cereal, Kilellan Farm 151–3

Dalkey Island, Co Dublin, pottery from 76
daub 49, 71
deer, red 151, 153–9, 164–7, 179
disc, iron, Kilellan Farm 144, *145*
disc-headed pins 143
dogs, evidence for at Kilellan 156, 159, 160, 161
dress-pin, loop-headed, bronze 47, 144, *145*
dry-curing, of fish xvii, 180
Dun Aonghasa, Co Clare 141

Dun Ardtreck, animal bones from 165, 167
   animal bones from 165
Dun Cul Bhuirg, Iona 85
Dun Mhor Vaul, Tiree, animal bones from 165, 167
   pottery from 85, 86
Dunadd, Argyll, disc-headed pin moulds from 143, 144
Dunagoil, pottery 85–6
Dunbeath, pottery 77

Early Bronze Age period
   Kilellan Farm xvii, 13, 98, 105, 110, 117, 118, 124–5, 175, 176–8
      animal bones 152
      coarse stone artefacts, 133, 134–6
      marine mollusca 171–2
      midden 3, 17–30
      occupation 176–8
      pottery xvii 17, 18, 23, 49–78, 86–95
      structural remains *21, 22, 23, 24, 25*–7, *28*
Early Historic Period
   activity at Kilellan Farm 47–8, 180
   crannog 3
   disc-headed pins 143–4
Early Iron Age/Late Bronze Age period
   Kilellan Farm 11, 30–9, 175, 178–9
   pottery 36–7, 82–6
   East Broch of Burray, disc-headed pin from 143
environmental context and animal husbandry, Kilellan Farm 151–67
Esslemont, David xv
Esslemont, Barbara xv
Evans, John G xiii
   marine mollusca from Kilellan 171–3

Finavon, Angus 85
Finlaggan, Islay, Mesolithic finds from 175
   souterrains 180
fish, Kilellan Farm 158, 166, 167, 178
   drying xvii, 180
flakes, flint 97, 123
   edge-trimmed 110–13, 123, 129
   refitting 113, *119*–23, 131
   serrated 97, *109*, 112, 117–18, 128
   truncated *106*, 117, 123, 128
   unretouched 97, 105–8, 123, 128, 131, 132
flint artefacts
   arrowheads 97, 98, 117, *118*, 119, 123, 130
      barbed and tanged 98, 117, *118*, 119, 123, 130
      leafshaped 98, 117, *118*, 123, 130
   blades (*see also* edge trimmed flakes) 97, 112, *116*, 123
   cores and core fragments 97, 99, 100–5, *106*, 112, 123, 124, 127–8, 176
   flakes 97, 123
      edge-trimmed 110–13, 123, 129
      refitting 113, *119*–23, 131
      serrated 97, *109*, 112, 117–18, 128
      truncated *106*, 117, 123, 128
      unretouched 97, 105–8, 123, 128, 131, 132
   hammerstones 97, 102, 128
   knives 97, *111*, 112, 114–15, *116*, 123, 130
   microburins 97, 113–14, 123, 129
   microliths 97, 98, 113–14, 123, 124, 129, 131
   piercers 97, 112, 115–17, 123, 130

INDEX

flint artefacts (*cont*)
    refitting flakes 113, *119*–23, 131
    scrapers 97, 108-10, 112, 123, 128–9
flint sources and raw material 99, 124, 175
flint technology 100–13, 176
food vessels and Kilellan pottery 51, 67, 74, 77
freshwater sources and Kilellan Farm 1, 66, 181

garnet
    and silver pin, Kilellan Farm xvii, 39, 47–8, 143–4, 180
        X-ray fluorescence analysis of 185–6
    sources of in Argyll 186
Gibson, Alex xv
    on Kilellan pottery 73, 74, 76
glass artefacts, bead 48, 146–7, 180
Gleann Mor 124
Goring, Marion xvi
grain
    carbonized 28–9
    barley 151
    cereal impression on pot 170
Grimes Graves, animal bones from 161
grinders/grinding slabs 133, 135, 139–40, 141

Halliday, Strat xv
    on clay floor at Kilellan Farm 29
hammerstones 97, 102, 128
    faceted 133, 136–8
    flint Mesolithic 16
hare, Kilellan Farm 156, 158
Harland, Frank xv
hazelnut shells, lack of at Kilellan Farm 176
'hearths', Kilellan Farm 33, 35, 36–7, 44
high cross, Kilnave xvii, 3, 180
Hill of Foulzie, Aberdeenshire, pottery from 77
Hill, Peter xv
Historic Scotland, and Kilellan Farm xvi, 5
Hodgson, George xv
houses/house structures
    Bronze Age
        Ardnave 177–8
        Kilellan Farm 21, 22–30, 176–8
    Iron Age
        Kilellan Farm 30–3, 39–41, 44, 179
horse, Kilellan Farm 158, 164
Howe, Orkney, disc-headed pin 143
Hunter, Alex xv
Hunter, Fraser xiii
    analysis of unusual bone pins from Kilellan Farm and
        MacArthur Cave, Oban 183
    pins from Kilellan Farm 145

Iona, animal bones from 165, 167
Ireland, crannogs 180
Irish Vase tradition and Kilellan 76, 77
Iron Age/Late Bronze Age Period, Kilellan Farm (*see also* Early
    Iron Age period)
    discussion of at Kilellan 175, 178–9
    occupation, Kilellan Farm 30–9
    pottery 82–6
    sequences at Kilellan Farm 11
iron artefacts
    disc, Kilellan Farm 144, *145*

iron artefacts (*cont*)
    knife 144, *145*
    sickle 44, 144, *145*
Islay Archaeological Survey Group 3, 181
Islay Archaeological Trust xv
Islay, souterrains 179–80

Jackson, Brian xv
Jarshof, Shetland 179
jet, Kilellan bone pins as imitation of 183
jewellery, *see under* artefact type or material
Johns, CM xv
Jura, work by Mercer 175

Kidd, Dorothy xvi
Kilchoman Cave, Islay 3, 48
Kilellan Farm excavations, by period (*see also* contents list v–vi
    and topic entries)
    Mesolithic Period xvii, 7, 10, 13–17, 44, 175–6
        animal bones 152, 155, 176
        coarse stone tools 133, 134–6
        charcoal 169–70, 176
        marine mollusca 171–2
        struck lithic artefacts (*see* struck lithic artefacts for detailed
            entry) 13–14, 16, 97–125
        structural traces 13–16
    Neolithic period
        cereal 170
        lithic artefacts 13, 98, 117, 118, 124–5, 176
        pottery 178
    Early Bronze Age xvii, 13, 17–39, 98, 105, 110, 117, 118,
        124–5, 175, 176–8
        animal bones 152
        coarse stone artefacts 133, 134–6
        marine mollusca 171–2
        midden 3, 17–30, 176–7, 178
        occupation 176–8
        pottery (*see under* pottery for details) xvii, 17, 18, 23,
            49–78, 86–95
        structural remains *21–4*, 25–7, 28
    Late Bronze Age/ Early Iron Age 11, 175, 178–9
        occupation 30–9
        pottery 36–7, 82–6
    Middle Iron Age 39–47
        animal bones 152
        marine mollusca 172
        midden 45, 175, 179–80
    Early Historic 47–8, 180
        crannog 3
        disc-headed pins 143–4
Kilellan Farm, history of excavations at 181–2
Kilnave, Islay, High Cross from xvii, 3, 180
knapping techniques, flint, and technology 100–13, 176
knives, Kilellan Farm
    flint 97, *111*, 112, 114–15, *116*, 123, 130
    iron 144, *145*

Lacaille, AD, and Kilellan Farm 181
Lagore, Co Meath, disc-headed pin from 144
Lane, A on Hebridean pottery 85
Late Bronze Age/Early Iron Age period
    discussion of at Kilellan 175, 178–9
    occupation, Kilellan Farm 30–9

197

Late Bronze Age (*cont*)
   pottery 82–6
      as pit lining 36–7
      sequences at Kilellan Farm 11
Legge, AJ xvi
Leitch, Roger xvi, 48
Leuchar Brae, pottery from 77
lithic artefacts (*see under* coarse stone artefacts, struck lithic artefacts and individual artefact types)
Loch Gruinart xvii, 1, 3, 175, 176, 179, 180
Lord, Robert xv
   et al on plant remains from peat depost on raised beach, Kilellan Farm 187–8
Lussa Wood, Jura 176

MacArthur Cave, Oban, analysis of bone pins from 183
McCullagh, Rod, work on Islay xvi, 175
Machrihanish, Argyll, pin from 144
MacKie, Euan 85
MacLellan, Sandy 3, 181
marine mollusca, Kilellan 45, 57, 74, 75, 171–3, 177, 178
   and pottery decoration 57, 74, 75
Matheson, Elaine xv
   et al on plant remains from peat deposit on raised beach, Kilellan Farm 187–8
Mellars, Paul, work on Oronsay 175
Mercer, John, work on Jura 175
Mesolithic Period, Kilellan Farm xvii, 7, 10, 13–17, 44, 175–6
   animal bones 152, 155, 176
   coarse stone tools 133, 134–6
   charcoal 169–70, 176
   marine mollusca 171–2
   struck lithic artefacts (*see* struck lithic artefacts for detailed entry) 13–14, 16, 97–125, 129, 131
      structural traces, Kilellan 13–16, 176
metalworking
   Jarlshof 179
   Kilellan Farm 36, 37, 178–9
   moulds 143–4, 178, 179
microburins 16, 97, 98, 113–14, 123, 124, 129
microliths 14, 97, 98, 113–14, 123, 124, 129, 131
middens
   deposition 67, 71, 73
   Early Bronze Age, Kilellan Farm 17–30, 176–7, 178
   Middle Iron Age, Kilellan Farm 45, 175, 179–80
Middle Iron Age period, Kilellan Farm
   animal bones 152
   marine mollusca 172
   midden 45, 175, 179–80
   settlement 39–47
Mithen, Steven 124, 175, 176
Moir, Gordon xv
mollusca, marine from Kilellan 45, 57, 74, 75, 171–3, 177, 178
   and pottery decoration 57, 74, 75
Moss, Ron xv
Mote of Mark, disc-headed pin moulds from 143–4
moulds, metalworking 143–4, 178, 179
mount, bone 146
Mulreesh, Finlaggan, leadworking 144
Munroe, The Rev xv

Nave Island xvii, 3, 180
Needham, Stuart 67, 71, 73

Neolithic period, Kilellan Farm
   cereal 170
   lithic artefacts 13, 98, 117, 118, 124–5, 176
   pottery 178
Newton, Islay 170, 175
   radiocarbon date 124
National Monuments Record for Scotland (NMRS) xvi
National Museums of Scotland (NMS) xvi, 175
Northton, Harris
   animal bones 159, 165, 167
   pottery 76
Northumberland Archaeological Group 3, 181–2

Oronsay, work by Mellars 175
ozocerite, polisher 48, *147*, 149

Palmer, Stephen xv, *4*
Pearce, Susannah 3, 181
peat deposit, raised beach, Kilellan Farm, plant remains from 187–8
pebble hammers 133, 134, *136*, 141
pebbles, bevelled 133, 134–5, 138
   flint 99
peg, bone 146
Pettit, Zillah xv
piercers, flint 97, 112, 115–17, 123, 130
Piggott, Stuart, and Kilellan Farm 181
pigs and Kilellan Farm 151, 153, 154, 158, 159, 160, 161–2, 164, 165, 166–7
pins
   bone, analyses of 183
   bow 3
   silver with garnets xvii, 39, 47–8, 143–4, 180
      X-ray fluorescence analysis of 185–6
   bronze, loop-headed, dress 47–8
   disc-headed 3, 143
   dress, bone 145–6, 183
      copper alloy 144, *145*
   ring headed 3
   rosette 3
plant remains, Kilellan Farm
   barley 151
   cereal cultivation 151–3
      impression on pot 170
   charcoal 29, 39, 44, 169–70, 178, 179
   grain, carbonised 28–9
   peat deposit on raised beach, Kilellan Farm 187–8
   tree species 169–70, 178, 179
ploughmarks, ard marks, spade marks and furrows, Kilellan Farm 37–8, 39, 41, *42*
points, bone 146
polishers
   bevelled, mica schist *148*, 149
   ozocerite 48, *147*, 149
   serpentine 48, 135, *147*–8, 149
Port Charlotte, Islay 124
pottery
   beaker and Kilellan Farm 76, 78, 174
   Bronze Age period, Kilellan Farm, from raised beach deposits 78
   Early Bronze Age period, Kilellan Farm xvii, 17, 23, 49–78, 86–95
      discussion of assemblage 70–8, 178

pottery (cont)
    decoration and surface treatment of vessels 55–62, 63, 65, 66, 67, 69, 73, 76, 77, 78
    distribution and phasing of vessels 67–70
    firing of vessels 65–6
    form and fabric of vessels 50–5, 70
    function and capacity of vessels 55, 66–7, 70
    manufacture of vessels 55
    summary of vessels 56–65
    food vessels and Kilellan pottery 51, 67, 74, 77
  grass-marked 81, 82, 85
  Irish Vase tradition and Kilellan 76, 77
  Late Bronze Age/Early Iron Age, Kilellan 39
  as pit lining 36–7
  Iron Age and later, Kilellan Farm 82–6
  Neolithic, Kilellan 178
  Trenches J and K 81–6
  Trench L2 Kilellan Farm 78–81

querns, saddle 140

rabbits, Kilellan Farm 156–7
radiocarbon dates 45
  Kilellan Farm xvii, 20, 25, 29, 39, 74, 79, 85, 178, 179, 180
  Ardnave, Islay 74, 86, 178
  Balloch Hill 85
  Finavon 85
  Leuchar Brae 77
  Newton 124
raised beach deposits, Kilellan Farm 11–12, 13
  analysis of plant remains from peat deposit 187–8
Royal Commission on the Ancient and Historical Monuments of Scotland (RCAHMS) 3, 5, 177, 179
red deer 151, 153–9, 164–7, 179
Reekie, Robert xv
refitting, flint flakes 113, *119–23*, 131
Richmond, Sir Ian, and Kilellan Farm 181
Rickards, Lucy xv
Ritchie, Anna xiii
  on excavations at Kilellan Farm 1–48
    acknowledgments by xv–xvi
    on metal, bone, glass, clay and fine stone artefacts 143–9
    discussion of excavations at Kilellan 175–80
Ritchie, Matthew xvi
Ritchie, Roy xv
Rosinish, Benbecula 77, 151, 159
  cereal cultivation and animal bones 151, 159
  pottery 77
Ross, Seamus xv
  on disc-headed pins 144
roundhouse, Kilellan Farm 39–43
Rum, work by Caroline Wickham-Jones 175
Runnymede, midden 71

Saville, Alan, work on Kilellan Farm xii, 5
  on struck lithic artefacts 97–132
  on Mesolithic horizon 175–6
scrapers, flint 97, 108–10, 123, 128–9
Sellins, Val xvi
Serjeantson, Dale xiii, xvi
  et al on animal husbandry and the environmental context, Kilellan Farm 151–67
  on animal husbandry, Kilellan 179

serpentine polishers 48, 135, *147–8*, 149
sheep, Kilellan Farm 151–66, 178, 179
shells/shellfish, marine mollusca from Kilellan 44, 171–3
Sheridan, Alison xvi, 66
sickle, iron, Kilellan Farm 44, 144, *145*
silver, sources of in Argyll 144
silver artefacts, Kilellan Farm
  pin with garnets xvii, 39, 47–8, 143–4, 180
    analysis of 185–6
Smithson, V xvi
  et al on animal husbandry and the environmental context, Kilellan Farm 151–67
Society of Antiquaries of Scotland xv, 3
socketed stones 133
soil survey, Kilellan Farm 151–2
Sørensen, Stig 67, 71, 73
souterrains
  Argyll 179
  Kilellan Farm xvii, 3, *31, 32*, 33, 35, 39, *40*, 43–5, *46*, 178, 179
  Skye and Western Isles 180
Southern Hebrides Research Project (SHMP) 124, 175
spade marks, ploughmarks and ard marks, Kilellan Farm 37–8, 39, 41, *42*, 179
Speak, Stephen xiii
  on history of excavations at Kilellan Farm 181–2
  on raised beach and peat deposits at Kilellan Farm 11–12, *13*
  work at Kilellan Farm 5
springs and water sources, Kilellan Farm 1, 66, 181
Stevenson, Robert BK xv, 48, 181
  on Kilellan 181
struck lithic artefacts Kilellan Farm
  arrowheads, flint 97, 98, *117, 118*, 119, 123, 130
    barbed and tanged 98, *117, 118*, 119, 123, 130
    leafshaped 98, *117, 118*, 123, 130
  blades (see also flakes, edge trimmed) 97, 112, *116*, 123
  cores and core fragments 97, 99, 100–5, *106*, 112, 123, 124, 127–8, 176
  flakes 97, 123
    edge-trimmed 110–13, 123, 129
    refitting 113, *119–23*, 131
    serrated 97, *109*, 112, 117–18, 128
    truncated *106*, 117, 123, 128
    unretouched 97, 105–8, 123, 128, 131, 132
  hammerstones 97, 102, 128
  knives 97, *111*, 112, 114–15, *116*, 123, 130
  microburins 97, 113–14, 123, 129
  microliths 97, 98, 113–14, 123, 124, 129, 131
  piercers 97, 112, 115–17, 123, 130
  refitting flakes 113, *119–23*, 131
  scrapers 97, 108–10, 112, 123, 128–9
  sources and raw material 99, 124, 175
  technology 100–13, 176

Talnotrie, disc-headed pins from 144
Tayvallin, saltworks 180
Tentsmuir, Fife, pottery from 77
Thames Basin Archaeological Observers Group 181
timber structures, Kilellan Farm 21–23, 25–7
Tiree, souterrains 179, 180
Tobar Neill Neonaich, as water source 1, 66, 181
Tomalin, DJ on pottery 67, 77

Topping, Peter xv
   on Dunagoil Ware 86
Townshend, Angie xv
tree species, Kilellan Farm 169–70, 176, 178, 179

Udal, the, animal bones from 164, 165
   cereal cultivation 151
University of Newcastle xv
Upper Scalloway, Shetland, disc-headed pin from 143
urns, and Kilellan Farm pottery 77

Waldron, G xvi
Waldron, T xvi
   et al on animal husbandry and the environmental context, Kilellan Farm 151–67
Walton, Margaret xv
water sources, Kilellan Farm 1, 66, 181

Welfare, Adam xv
well, Tobar Neill Neonaich 1, 66, 181
Wheeler, Sir Mortimer, and Kilellan Farm 181
Whittaker, James and work at Kilellan 3, 13, 22, 48, 181
Wickham-Jones, Caroline, work on Rum xv, 175
Williams, Nicola xv
   et al on plant remains from peat deposit on raised beach, Kilellan Farm 187–8
Wilthew, Paul xiii
   on x-ray fluorescence analysis of silver and garnet pin from Kilellan Farm 185–6
Woodroe, Mr xv
Woolley, Sir Leonard, and Kilellan Farm 181

X-ray fluorescence analysis
   of bone pins 183
   of silver and garnet pin from Kilellan 185–6